Campus Crusade for Christ Library

THE MODERN STUDENT'S LIFE
OF CHRIST

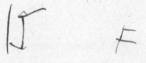

BY PHILIP VOLLMER, Ph.D.

NEW TESTAMENT SOCIOLOGY.
Cloth, $2.25.

THE MODERN STUDENT'S LIFE
OF CHRIST.   Cloth, $2.00.

THE MODERN STUDENT'S LIFE OF CHRIST

A Textbook

FOI

Higher Institutions of Learning
and Advanced Bible Classes

BY

PHILIP VOLLMER, Ph.D., D.D.

*Professor of the New Testament in the
Eden Theological Seminary,
St. Louis, Mo.*

NEW YORK   CHICAGO   TORONTO

Fleming H. Revell Company

LONDON AND EDINBURGH

Copyright 1912
BY THE
HEIDELBURG PRESS
AND
FLEMING H. REVELL COMPANY

840

BT
302
V924
1912

FOREWORD.

The object, method and spirit of this book may be stated in a single sentence. It is a textbook of the Life of Christ, for advanced students following modern methods, but strictly evangelical in spirit and view point, based on the exact words of the gospels and having for its chief object the nurture of Christian character.

1. Being a *text book* for study and not a book for easy reading, it aims at conciseness, sometimes at the expense of elegance of diction, because verboseness is the foe of accuracy and of the student's time; it follows the analytical method, separating introductory matter, narrative, explanations and practical lessons, for this promotes clearness of teaching and thoroughness of study; the type also has been selected with a view to making the text as plain as possible.

2. The *Life of Christ* being of fundamental importance and therefore the chief target of attack, no student's education should be considered complete without a thorough course in it, and no congregation should allow a year to pass without having one or more groups of members studying this great subject, especially in those years when the Sunday School lessons are not selected from the gospels. (See "Directions for Study.")

3. This book is intended for *advanced Bible study* in the higher institutions of learning, where our future ministers, physicians, lawyers, statesmen, leaders of thought and teachers of both sexes are being trained. Here this great subject should be a required course, and not simply offered as an elective or treated merely as a "devotional" study for which little preparation is expected. The book is also adapted to that happily increasing class of old and young people in our churches who, though they may not have enjoyed a higher education, have, in various ways, ac-

quired a taste for more thorough, comprehensive and systematic Bible study.

4. Having these classes of Bible students in mind, the book follows *modern scientific methods.* It is comprehensive in scope as a glance over the table of contents will show; it follows the grammatical-historical method of exegesis; in its apologetic discussions it aims to be fair. Special features of it are the copious references to the literature on the subject. Besides the larger works on the Life of Christ and the great number of elementary guides, a textbook of this character has therefore a place.

5. In point of view, spirit and specific teaching, this book is *uncompromisingly evangelical.* The discussions of the various problems are conducted in such a way as not to obscure its positive teaching that Christ is the Son of God, and his gospel the power of God to save both the individual and society. We cannot prevent our educated classes from imbibing error, for current literature is saturated with it, but the church must sow into men's minds, more thoroughly than hitherto, the good seed before the enemy sows the tares, and should at all times be ready to provide the antidote to the poison.

6. The narrative part is given as much as possible in the *exact words of the gospels.* Mere references to the Bible lead to superficiality. A minimum knowledge of the facts must be required, and that minimum should be printed in full, as in textbooks of secular history. In addition to this minimum the notes insist on a thorough inductive study of the entire text of the gospels.

7. The ultimate object of this book is not merely to acquire accurate knowledge of the Life of Christ, though this in itself is in the deepest sense of the word devotional, but to *produce* and *develop Christian character.* Therefore, every opportunity is seized upon to apply the truth to the heart and conscience of the student.

The author owes much to the researches of others, especially of German and French scholars. The chapters will show the amount of his indebtedness.

PHILIP VOLLMER.

Central Theological Seminary, Dayton, O.

DIRECTIONS FOR STUDY

I. For Whom This Book is Intended.

1. *For Colleges, Seminaries, Academies,* Preparatory Schools, and similar higher institutions of learning. The teacher in these schools will have no difficulty in making selections from the material according to the time at his disposal and the capacity of the students.

2. *For advanced Bible classes in the Sunday School.* When it is planned to study the entire subject in one year, the work should start with chapter 10 and end with chapter 49, referring to the introductory matter and the "General Aspects" (ch. 50-54) as these points come up. If more time is available, the class may start with chapter 1 and study the entire book in a thorough manner.

3. *For entire Sunday Schools.* In this case the lower classes should be assigned selected narratives while the higher classes may choose material from the notes according to the grade of each.

4. *For S. S. teachers* in preparing for class work.

5. *For the various young people's societies,* brotherhoods, Y. M. C. A.'s, normal classes, W. C. A's and similar organizations. These may study the entire subject in one year; yet it pays not to hurry but to devote to each of the three "Parts" of the book enough time for thorough preparation, discussion, side reading and papers.

6. *For catechetical and pastor's classes* on weekdays, in connection with, or in place of the denominational catechism.

7. *For religious vacation and week-day parochial* schools.

8. *For weekday prayer meetings* in place of the address, or after the meeting. All that may be present are treated as a class.

9. *For home study,* in connection with the S. S. Home Department; also for inquirers or skeptics.

10. *As a "desk copy" for ministers* and Christian workers, for quick reference or for suggestions for addresses.

11. *For Correspondence Courses and Courses of Study for Ministers.*

II. How the Book Should be Used.

(a) By the Students.

1. Master the facts of the narrative; for the first duty of an historian is to know his sources.

2. To this end make extensive use of the Bible or a good Harmony of the Gospels. Read the whole Scripture sections from which the narrative is drawn; name and compare sources; look up and read all other Bible references in the book. Memorize the suggested Bible texts. Remember that Bible study is study of the Bible, with emphasis on both words.

3. Draw at least three different maps at different periods, one of Palestine, a plan of the Temple, and a map of Jerusalem and surroundings.

4. Trace on the map the events of the Life of Christ in their chronological sequence and in their organic connection. This is fundamental in any historical study.

5. Begin each lesson with a brief review of the previous lesson, and at the end of larger periods take a general review. "Not what I can remember but what I can never forget constitutes knowledge. Therefore drill! drill!! drill!!! Review! review!! review!!!" (Moninger). Prepare, mentally or in writing, your answers to the review questions.

(b) By the Teacher.

1. Discourage indifferent work. The consciousness of mastering the work is inspiring, and holds the class together. Do not assign work beyond the capacity of the class but then insist on thoroughness.

2. Encourage questions; if possible, occasionally conduct a round table discussion, but do not allow the class to "discuss" the subject before they have prepared the assigned material, for this leads to superficiality and self-sufficiency.

3. If time and other things are favorable brief papers and talks may be brought into the class.

CONTENTS

PART I.

Introduction to the Life of Christ.

The World in which Jesus Lived.

CHAPTER 1.

The Importance of the Historical Background.
General Aspects of Palestine; Names; Antiquity; Location, Extent, Roads, Fertility, Climate.
Physical Divisions, Mountains and Waters.
Political Divisions and Chief Places.

CHAPTER 2.

Jewish History: Babylonian, Persian, Greek, Egyptian, Syrian, Maccabean, Roman rule.
Rule of Herod the Great and his Family, later History of the Jews.
Government, Sanhedrin, Taxation, Divisions, Names and Languages.
History of the Roman Empire.

CHAPTER 3.

Jewish Culture and Literature: Apocrypha, Apocalyptic books, Philo and Josephus.
Greek Philosophy and Roman Culture.

CHAPTER 4.

Religious Condition among the Jews: Messianic Hope, Pharisees, Sadducees, Essenes, Scribes, Lawyers, Zealots, Proselytes, Great Synagog, Mission of the Jews.

Sacred Buildings: Temple at Jerusalem, the Synagogs, Temple at Heliopolis, Sacred Year.
Samaritan, Greek and Roman Religions.

Chapter 5.

Corruption in the ⌐reek-Roman World. Paul's Testimony, Pompeii's Excavations, Emperors, Enormous Wealth, Slaves, Labor Degraded, Luxury.
Family Life: Woman, Divorce, Children.
Fivefold Preparation for Christ's Coming.

Chapter 6.

Pagan, Jewish and Christian Sources.
The Three Synoptic Gospels. Authorship, Aim and Character of each. Outline of the Synoptic Problem.
John's Gospel. Authorship and Credibility.

Chapter 7.

General Divisions.
Date of Christ's Birth, Opening and Length of Public Ministry, Date of Death.
Relative Chronology.

Chapter 8.

Books on the "historical background." Best Dictionaries of the Bible. Principal Lives of Christ. Books on Paintings and Views.

Chapter 9.

PART II.

The Events of the Life of Christ.*

Division I.

The Thirty Years of Preparation.

From the Birth of Jesus to His Baptism, Dec. 25, B. C. 5—Jaⁱ.., A. D. 27.

---

*To avoid unnecessary repetition this table of contents has been so arranged as to serve at the same time as a " Chronological Chart " of the Life of Christ.

Division II.

The Year of Obscurity.

From Christ's Baptism to the Beginning of the Galilean Ministry. Jan., A. D. 27-Dec. A. D. 27.

First Subdivision.

The Opening Events of Christ's Ministry.

Christ's Baptism to the Passover, Jan., A. D. 27-April 11, A. D. 27

Second Subdivision.

The Early Judean Ministry.

From Passover to the Opening of the Galilean Ministry. April
11-Dec., A. D. 27.

Division III.

The Year of Popularity.

From the Opening of the Galilean Ministry to the Crisis at Capernaum. Dec., A. D. 27-April, A. D. 29—about 16 months.

First Subdivision.

First Period of the Galilean Ministry.

From the Opening of the Galilean Ministry to the Choosing of the
Twelve. Dec., A. D. 27-early summer A. D. 28—about 6 months.

CHAPTER 19.

CHAPTER 20.

CHAPTER 21.

CHAPTER 22.

Second Subdivision.

The Second Period of the Galilean Ministry.

From the Choosing of the Twelve to the Crisis at Capernaum.
Early Summer. A. D. 28-April 18, A. D. 29—about 10 months.

Division IV.

The Year of Opposition.

From the Crisis at Capernaum to the Triumphal Entry into Jerusalem. Passover, April 18, A. D. 29-Palm Sunday, April 2, A. D. 30, about one year.

First Subdivision.

The Third Period of the Galilean Ministry.

From the Crisis at Capernaum until the Final Departure for Jerusalem. April 18th, A. D.-Nov., A. D. 29, about seven months.

CHAPTER 29.

CHAPTER 30.

CHAPTER 31.

Second Subdivision.

The Perean Ministry.

From the final Departure for Jerusalem until the Triumphal Entry into Jerusalem, Nov. A. D. 29, to Palm Sunday, April 2, A. D. 30; about 5 months.

Contents.

Division V.

The Week of Passion.

From the Triumphal Entry into Jerusalem to the Resurrection
Palm Sunday, April 2nd—Easter Sunday, April 9, A. D. 30.

Contents.

CHAPTER 49.

PART III.

General Aspects of the Life of Christ.

CHAPTER 50.

    1. *Physical Characteristics.*—Inferences from Bible Passages; ancient descriptions of Christ's appearance; legendary and real portraits; modern conception of Jesus' picture.

    2. *Christ's Intellectual Powers.*—Four mental characteristics; penetration, keenness, breadth, originality.

    3. *Emotional Life of Jesus.*—(1) Love to God expressed in his trust, communion, reverence, submission; (2) love to man, manifested in his appreciation of man, his sympathy, generosity, accessibility, simplicity, self-surrender, friendship, humility, obedience, candor, graciousness; (3) His love for nature, and his humor; (4) effect of these feelings: he was happy, optimistic, enthusiastic.

    4. *Christ's Will Power.*—(1) Outgoing manifestations: self-assertion, energy, self-limitation, indignation; (2) the inholding powers: patience and caution.

    5. *The Harmony of Christ's Character.*—(1) He participated in each of the four temperaments, he was (2) sinless, (3) a strong, and (4) a great man.

CHAPTER 51.

    1. Did Christ have a conscious Plan of work, and what was it?

    2. The Execution of his Plan.

        (1) Christ as a Preacher: substance, method, aim.

        (2) Christ as a Teacher of the Twelve.

        (3) Christ as a Controversialist.

THE MODERN STUDENT'S
LIFE OF CHRIST

PART I.

Introduction to the Life of Christ

The World in Which Jesus Lived

CHAPTER I.

The Physical World in Which Jesus Lived.

1. The life of Christ cannot be adequately understood without some knowledge of his surroundings. Therefore we shall study first the physical, political, intellectual, religious, moral and social conditions of the world in which Jesus lived. This will furnish the historical background and a proper setting or frame for our portrait of Christ.

2. **General Aspects of Palestine.** The physical world in which Jesus lived was Palestine. (1) *Names:* (a) *Canaan,* before it became the home of Israel. (Gen. 16:3; 17:8). (b) *Israel,* from the Conquest till the Babylonian Captivity (2 Kings 5:2). (c) *Judea,* after the Babylonian Captivity (Neh. 5:14; Mark 1:5). (d) *Palestine* (from Philistia), since the days of Christ. The name was first used to designate the country of the Philistines. Josephus applied it to the whole land.—(e) Other designations: "The Land of Promise" (Heb. 11:9), "The Holy Land" (Zech. 2:12). (2) *Antiquity.* It is older than Greece and Rome. Abraham dwelt at Sychar 2,000 years before Christ rested at its well. Joshua conquered it 200 years before Troy fell. Solomon was dead 200 years before Romulus founded Rome in 754 B. C. Gideon and Achilles, Elijah and Homer were contemporaries. (3) *Location:* In West-

ern Asia, bounded by Syria, Arabia, Egypt and the Mediterranean Sea. (4) *Extent:* In shape and size it is much like the state of New Hampshire. Including Perea it contains 12,000 square miles; without it, about 9,000. Its sea-coast from Tyre to Gaza is 140 miles long; its Jordan line, from Mt. Hermon to the south end of the Dead Sea is 156 miles. It is from 25 to 70 miles wide. (5) *Roads:* Four great highways, linking Asia, Europe and Africa, cross it. Up and down these coast roads the great armies of the Old World passed. Sennacherib, the Assyrian, Alexander of Macedon, Pompey, Titus, Saladin, Napoleon, all led their armies over this highway. (6) *Fertility:* It was a land "flowing with milk and honey," and was cultivated like a garden to the very tops of the mountains. No modern land has been made to support so dense a population. Wheat, barley, the vine and the olive grew luxuriantly. (7) *Climate:* Palestine is semi-tropical, the heat being tempered by its mountains. Snow is rare and the winters are short.

3. **Physical Divisions.** (1) Along the Mediterranean lies the *sea coast plain* two or three miles wide at the north, but widening as it goes southward, to nearly 20 miles at Gaza. (2) Crossing this are the *Shephelah* or foot hills; a terrace of low hills from 300 to 500 feet high. (3) Ascending these, we reach the *mountain region,* a range of mountains broken by ravines, varying from 2,500 to 3,000 feet in height. This region was the home of the Israelites in all their history. The plains and valleys were mainly foreign and heathen in their population. (4) Crossing the mountain we descend to the *Jordan Valley,* lower than the sea level, and from 5 to 20 miles wide. (5) Beyond the valley rises the *Eastern Table-land* with higher mountains but more level summits, and broken by fewer valleys. The mountains gradually decline to the great Syrian desert on the east.

4. **Sacred Mountains.** (1) *Quarantania,* the traditional mount of temptation, in the wilderness between Jerusalem and the Dead Sea. (2) *Mount of Beatitudes* (Horns of Hattin), the scene of the Sermon on the Mount, just

west of the Sea of Galilee. (3) *Mount Tabor,* the traditional Mount of Transfiguration. (4) *Mount Hermon,*
probably the real Mount of Transfiguration, 30 miles north
of the Sea of Galilee. (5) *Mount Calvary,* the place of the
crucifixion, "without the gate," on the north of ancient
Jerusalem, but now within the modern city. The gospels
simply call it "a place," not a mount.

5. **Sacred Waters.** (1) The *Jordan,* rising in Mt. Hermon, flowing south 130 miles through Lake Merom, and
the Sea of Galilee to the Dead Sea, narrow, swift, with occasional fords. (2) The *Sea of Galilee,* 13 miles long and
8 wide, encircled by a dense population. The only navi-
gable water in Palestine. Other names: Lu. 5:1—Sea of
Genesaret; John 6:1—Sea of Tiberias. (3) The *Brook
Kedron,* flowing between the Temple and the Mount of
Olives, now dry most of the year. (4) The *Pools of Siloam*
and *Bethesda,* on the south and east of Jerusalem. (5) The
Great Sea, or *Mediterranean,* bounding Palestine on the
west, the outpost of ancient commerce and travel. (6) The
Dead Sea, 20 miles southeast of Jerusalem, 46 miles long,
10 wide, and 1,200 feet below the Mediterranean.

6. **Political Divisions.** Five Provinces: (1) *Galilee,*
on the north, west of the Jordan. (From the Hebrew
Galil, "circle" or district), divided into Lower and Upper
Galilee, inhabited by a brave, simple-hearted people, mainly
Jews, but with many gentiles among them. Hence called
"Galilee of the Gentiles." (Isa. 9:1-2; Matt. 4:15, 16),
hence also the contempt in which it was held at Jerusalem.
(John 7:41, 52). (2) *Samaria,* in the center. It was
not a province with a political organization, but only a district around the cities of Shechem and Samaria; extending
neither to the Jordan nor to the Mediterranean, and of uncertain limits; governed from Judea, and inhabited by a
composite people, partly Israelites, partly heathen in their
origin. (3) *Judea,* the southernmost province. As the
largest and special home of the Jewish people it often gave
its name to the whole land, as in Mark 1:5, Lu. 7:17, Acts

10:37. The southern part of it was *Idumea,* a narrow belt of rugged highlands, 100 miles long by 20 wide, stretching from the southeast of the Dead Sea, to the eastern arm of the Red Sea; the land of the Edomites, descendants of Esau. (4) *Perea,* on the east of the Jordan and the Dead Sea. The Word means "beyond." In the N. Testament the region is called, "the borders of Judea, beyond the Jordan" (Matt. 19:1; Mark 10:1). (5) *Philip's Tetrarchy,* in the northeast embracing five sections; Gaulanitis, Auranitis, Trachonitis, Iturea, Batanea. Scattered throughout this province was *Decapolis* (Mark 7:31), a league of ten Greek cities which was probably formed at the time of Pompey's invasion of Palestine (64-63 B. C.). The cities were perhaps first settled by Greek soldiers from the armies of Alexander the Great. By these cities Pompey was hailed as a deliverer from the Jewish yoke. According to Pliny, their names were Scythopolis, Hippos, Gadara, Pella, Philadelphia, Gerasa, Dion, Canatha, Damascus, and Raphana. The formation of a confederation of Greek cities in the midst of a Semitic population was necessary for the preservation of Hellenic civilization and culture. In the Roman period all the cities of Decapolis had the right of coinage and asylum, and were allowed to maintain a league for defense against their common foes. The ruins of temples, theatres and baths at Gerasa, Philadelphia and Gadara impress one with the glories of the Grecian life in Palestine during the period of our Lord's earthly ministry and for some centuries afterward.

7. **Places in Galilee and Samaria Mentioned in the Gospels.** (1) *Bethsaida.* The evidence seems to point to two places by this name, one east and the other west of the Jordan. The former, Bethsaida of Gaulanitis, was rebuilt and beautified by Herod Philip and named B. Julias, the Latin genitive being added in honor of Augustus' abandoned daughter. The western B. seems to have been situated near Capernaum and to have been distinguished from the other by being called Bethsaida of Galilee (John 12:1).

It was the early home of Andrew, Peter and Philip (John 1:44). (2) *Capernaum.* An important city on the north-western shore of the Sea of Galilee; its exact site is much disputed. Scholarly opinion which for some time inclined to locate it at Khan Minyeh nearly eight miles southwest of the entrance of the Jordan, is now leaning toward *Tel Hum,* about half way between these points where extensive ruins point to a place once of great importance. It was a station for a Roman garrison and a custom-house. It had at least one public synagogue. *Tel Hum* shows the remains of a splendid structure of this kind. (3) *Cana of Galilee.* A town probably about 4 miles east of Nazareth. (4) *Chorazin.* A city mentioned in Matt. 11:21; Luke 10:13. Its location was probably two or three miles north of *Khan Minyeh,* the supposed site of Capernaum. (5) *Dalman-utha.* A city on the western shore of the Sea of Galilee; location is unknown. (6) *Magdala.* (A. V. Matt. 15:39 where the R. V. reads Magadan, although some think that the two were not identical). A miserable little Moslem village on the west shore of the Sea of Galilee, the reputed home of Mary Magdalene. (7) *Nazareth.* A town in southern Galilee, where Jesus passed the first thirty years of his life. The region is beautiful. The hill above the town gives an extensive view. It is not mentioned in the O. T., but exists to-day as *En-Nasira,* with a population of 11,000. (8) *Nain.* A town six miles southeast of Nazareth, at one time a place of considerable importance but now a collection of miserable mud hovels. It seems never to have been surrounded by a wall, "the gate of the city" mentioned in Luke 7:12 seems to have been merely the point where the main road enters the town. The situation affords one of the finest views in Palestine. In Samaria are: (9) *Sychar.* (Shechem), a little village at Mt. Ebal, probably where the modern village of Askar now stands. It is about half a mile north of Jacob's Well. (10) *Ænon,* propably a group of springs about four miles north of Salim. (11 \ *Salim,* probably a town about four miles east of Shechem, and two and a half miles east of Jacob's Well.

8. **Places in Judæa.** (1) *Jerusalem: Shape.* An irregular quadrilateral, covering five mountains, Acra, Bezetha, Moriah, Ophel, Zion. *Districts.* (1) "Zion" or the "Upper City" on the south, upon Mt. Zion and Ophel; (2) the "Lower City" on Acra, including the Temple on Moriah. (3) Bezetha, Herod's "New City," farthest north. *Buildings.* An ancient writer called it "A city of marble and gold." The most famous in Christ's day were (1) Herod's Temple, covering 20 acres; (2) Herod's Palace; (3) The Tower of Antonia; (4) the net work of pools and subterranean aqueducts. *Walls.* (1) David's, around Zion and Ophel, enclosing the Old Jebusite city. (2) Hezekiah's, encircling Acra and Moriah. (3) Herod Agrippa's, built after Christ, sweeping northward around Bezetha. (4) The present wall was built by the Turks, about 400 years ago. *Gates.* The ancient city had eight outside gates, chief of which were (1) "Damascus Gate" on the north, opening toward Samaria and Galilee; (2) "Valley" or "Joppa" gate on the west, leading to Joppa and Bethlehem; (3) "Fountain Gate" on the south, opening on the Pool of Siloam; (4) "Shushan" or the "Lily Gate" of the Temple, on the east, leading across Kedron to Bethany and Jericho *Valleys.* (1) Jehoshaphat or Kedron, running past the Temple on the east; (2) Hinnom, on the west and south; (3) Tyropœan, coming through the city from north to south. *Sacred Places.* The more noted were: (1) Sepulchres of David and the Prophets at the south. (2) Gethsemane, and Bethesda on the east; (3) Calvary and the tombs of kings and judges on the north. (2) *Bethlehem.* An ancient town six miles south of Jerusalem, the birthplace of David and of Christ. (3) *Bethany.* A village less than two miles from Jerusalem, situated on the southeastern slope of the Mount of Olives, and on the road that leads to Jericho. The present village El-Azariyeh, "the place of Lazarus" contains about 200 inhabitants, who show several places

which they connect with the history of Lazarus, but which are of much later date. (4) *Ephraim,* fourteen miles north from Jerusalem. It was situated on a lofty hill overlooking the Jordan. (5) *Hebron.* Ancient capital of Juda, a priest city, and probably birthplace of John. (6) *Jericho,* city next to Jerusalem, the most important in Palestine, situated five miles west of the Jordan, and seventeen northeast from Jerusalem. It was the favorite residence of Herod the Great, the center of an extensive commerce, and the abode of many Jerusalem priests.

9. **Places in Perea and Philip's Tetrarchy.** (1) *Bethany beyond Jordan.* (A. V. Bethabara), the traditional site is at the fords of the Jordan, east of Jericho. Many modern authorities favor a place thirteen miles south of the Sea of Galilee. (2) *Fortress Machaerus,* east of the Dead Sea, where the Baptist was imprisoned. (3) *Caesarea Philippi,* situated at the foot of Mt. Hermon, greatly enlarged and beautified by Philip the Tetrarch. He changed its name Paneas to Cæsarea, in honor of Augustus Cæsar, and added the Latin genitive "Philippi," ("Of Philip") to distinguish it from Cæsarea on the sea coast. From a cavern in a limestone cliff flows one of the main sources of the Jordan. The cavern was sacred to the god Pan, to whom Herod the Great erected a marble temple. The entire region is one of the most charming in all Palestine. (4) *Gerasa,* or Gersa, the modern Khersa, an obscure village on the eastern shore of the Sea of Galilee. (5) *Bethsaida Julias,* north of the Sea of Galilee and east of the Jordan. (See Western Bethsaida in Galilee.)

10. **Reference Literature.** Farrar, Ch. 12; Hastings D. of C. on Golgatha I, 655; Jerusalem I, 849; Trade and Commerce II, 738; Palestine II, p. 309; Hast. D. of Bible, Roads and Travels V, 375; Galilee I, 98. Stanley, Sinai and Palestine, p. 175-274. Smith, Hist. Geog. 3-90 is unsurpassed. Breed, Preparation of the World, Ch. 1. Fullerlove and Kelman, The Holy Land. Walker, Jesus and his Surroundings. Anthony, A. W., "Introduction to the Life of Jesus."

CHAPTER 2.

The Political World in Which Jesus Lived.

11.   **Jewish History.**   The last period of Jewish history extends from the Babylonian Captivity, in 588 B. C. to the destruction of Jerusalem, A. D. 70.   It is a period of foreign rule and may be divided into seven parts: (1) The *Babylonian Rule,* about 50 years (588-536 B. C.), from the Babylonian Captivity to the Fall of Babylon through Cyrus.   Jerusalem lay in ruins, and the godly Jews were homesick (Ps. 137).   (2) The *Persian Rule,* about 200 years (B. C. 536 to 330).   Cyrus, the Persian, overthrew the Babylonian Empire and in 536 B. C. allowed the Jews to return and rebuild the Temple in Jerusalem.   Only 42,360 Jews returned under Zerubbabel and Joshua, and laid the foundations of the Temple (Ezra 1:64; 3:10-13).   The Samaritans offered to help, but were refused.   Thereupon they accused the Jews of treason at the Persian court, which led to a cessation of the work for twelve years.   In 516 the Temple was finally completed.   In 458 Ezra was sent from Persia to Jerusalem, and in 445 came Nehemiah.   Both men reorganized the national life (See their books in the O. T.).   (3) *Greek Rule.*   Nine years, 330-321 B. C.   Alexander the Great destroyed the Persian Empire and ruled Palestine about nine years.   He sent from Tyre to Jerusalem and demanded submission.   When the Jews refused he marched against the city, but was pacified by a procession of priests coming to greet him.   He entered the Temple, and had the prophecies of Daniel concerning himself read to him.   He treated the Jews with great kindness, and when he founded his Egyptian capital, Alexandria, he offered them the most liberal inducements which very many accepted.   After Alexander's death, Palestine became the bone of contention between Syria and Egypt.   (4) *Egyptian Rule,* 120 years (B. C. 321-198).   Alexandria became the centre of Jewish influence.   In 285 occurred the translation

of the O. T. into Greek, called the Septuagint (LXX). (5) *Syrian Rule,* about 40 years (198-166 B. C.). King Antiochus Epiphanes ("The Illustrious," some called him, Epimanes—"The Madman") oppressed the Jews most cruelly. His object was to extirpate the Jewish religion and force upon them Greek religion and culture. Jerusalem was twice captured and sacked, the Temple desecrated by sacrificing swine on its altars, and finally closed. This treatment drove the Jews to revolt (168). After a two years struggle, led by the priest Mattathias and his five sons, especially Judas Maccabæus ("hammer"), they gained their independence in B. C. 166. (6) *Maccabean Independence,* 126 years (B. C. 166-40). Civil war, treachery, bloodshed and anarchy characterized this period of Asmonean rule (from "Hashman" the ancestor of Maccabæus). John Hyrcanus (135-105 B. C.) destroyed the Samaritan temple and forced the Idumeans to become Jews. (7) *Roman Rule.* (40 B. C.-70 A. D.). This came on gradually and was at first indirect. Antipater, an Idumean officer of wealth, influence and ability, acquired complete control over the feeble Hyrcanus II. When the latter and his brother Aristobulus could not agree on the succession they appealed to the Roman general Pompey, who had just completed his victory over Syria and Pontus. In 63 B. C. Pompey came to Jerusalem and to the horror of the Jews entered the Holy of Holies which he found empty (Tac. Hist. v.). He decided for Hyrcanus. After the death of Pompey, Antipater saw that his advantage lay in supporting Julius Cæsar (Pompey's enemy) in his eastern campaign. In consequence, the latter, out of gratitude, conferred upon Antipater Roman citizenship and confirmed Hyrcanus in the high priesthood. Soon after this Antipater made his son Herod governor of Galilee. In 43 B. C. Antipater was poisoned. In order to ally himself with the reigning Asmonean House, Herod married the beautiful Mariamne, the granddaughter of Hyrcanus. In 40 B. C. the Roman senate appointed Herod king of Palestine. The Jews resisted desperately and it took Herod three years to capture Jerusalem. He was the first foreigner to rule directly over the Jews.

12. **Rule of Herod the Great.** (37-4 B. C.). After the conquest of Jerusalem, Herod killed Antigonus, the last of the Maccabean priest-kings, 45 of his most prominent opponents, and every member of the Sanhedrin but two. He was an exceedingly bad man but a ruler highly talented, having met with great success. On this account he is called "the Great." He built a harbor and called it Cæsarea, in honor of the Roman Emperor. This city became the political capital of Palestine under the procurators. He introduced foreign customs, erected a theatre within, and an ampitheatre without the walls of Jerusalem, instituted games, and even gladiatorial combats with wild animals. In 20 B. C. he proposed to rebuild the Temple. The people on the contrary believed he intended to destroy it. To assure them of his sincerity, he agreed to prepare the materials before a stone of the old building should be removed. In 18 B. C. the building began and was completed in 65 A. D., only five years before its final destruction. He was bitterly hated by the people for his cruelty and constant annoyance. Among other things he placed a large golden eagle, the emblem of Roman power, over the principal gate of the Temple. This enraged the Jews. Instigated by two rabbis some young men removed it and were burned alive. At another time ten men formed a plot to kill Herod. They were betrayed and tortured to death. Herod died after excruciating pains in March B. C. 4 (A. U. C. 750), after a reign of 34 years.

13. **Rule of Herod's Family.** (4 B. C.-101 A. D.). In his will Herod the Great divided Palestine among three of his sons: (1) *Archelaus* to be tetrarch of Judea and Samaria (Matt. 2 "king") ; (2) Herod *Antipas* (4 B. C.-39 A. D.), tetrarch of Galilee and Perea (tetrarch was the name of a ruler of the fourth part of a territory, but loosely used of any tributary prince inferior in rank to a king). His capital was Tiberias; he lived in open sin with Herodias

and was of a crafty nature ("Fox," Luke 13:32). (3) *Philip,* tetrarch of Iturea (4 B. C.-33 A. D.), was the best of the three. (4) A Jewish deputation (Luke 19:14), joined by 8,000 Jews living in Rome, met Augustus in the temple of Apollo requesting him not to confirm the will of Herod, but rather incorporate Judea into the province of Syria.   But Herod's will was confirmed.   In 6 A. D. Archelaus was accused by the Jews of cruelty and deposed by Augustus.   Henceforth Judea and Samaria were ruled by a Roman procurator who stood under the Roman legatus of the imperial province of Syria.   The fifth man to hold this office was Pontius Pilate 26-36 A. D.   In 37 A. D. the Roman emperor Caligula (37-41) gave to a grandson of Herod the Great, Agrippa I (37-44) the tetrarchy of Philip (who had died in 33), also the title "king."   In 39, after Antipas was banished, Caligula added to it Galilee and Perea.   In 41, Claudius (41-54) gave him also Judea and Samaria, so that all Palestine became once more united under an Herodian prince.   In order to please the Jews, Agrippa persecuted the Christians, killed James and imprisoned Peter (Acts 12).   When, in 44 A. D., he died, his son was only 17 years old.   Claudius therefore annexed all Palestine to Syria and had it again governed by procurators, two of whom were Felix and Festus (Acts 23:24; 24:27).   In 53 Claudius gave Agrippa a part of Philip's tetrarchy and the title "king," and later also parts of Galilee and Perea.   Over this territory he reigned as Agrippa II, from 53-101, undisturbed by the Jewish war and its dire results.

14. Genealogy of the Herodian House:

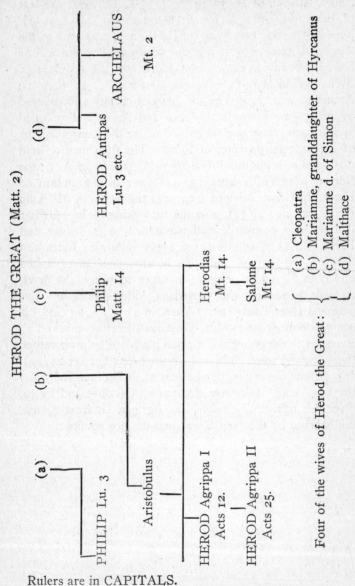

HEROD THE GREAT (Matt. 2)

(a) PHILIP Lu. 3

(b) Aristobulus — HEROD Agrippa I Acts 12. — HEROD Agrippa II Acts 25.

Herodias Mt. 14.

Salome Mt. 14.

(c) Philip Matt. 14

(d) HEROD Antipas Lu. 3 etc. — ARCHELAUS Mt. 2

Four of the wives of Herod the Great:

(a) Cleopatra
(b) Mariamne, granddaughter of Hyrcanus
(c) Mariamne, d. of Simon
(d) Malthace

Rulers are in CAPITALS.

15. **Later History of the Jews.** (1) *The Jewish War* (66-70). In A. D. 66, after a period of general anarchy and violence, open war with Rome broke out. It took the Roman legions four years to suppress it. By the spring of A. D. 70, Vespasian had conquered the whole country, except Jerusalem, which he turned over to his son Titus as he had been proclaimed emperor. The following September, after a siege in which the frantic defenders endured unparalleled horrors, the city was captured, razed to the ground, the Temple destroyed, the wretched survivors slain or sold into slavery, and the ruins occupied by a Roman garrison. (2) *Last Revolt*. Another rebellion occured in 132-135 A. D., the cause being Emperor Hadrian's determination to build a heathen city on the site of Jerusalem, and to erect a temple to Jupiter on the ruins of Jehovah's Temple. Bar-Cochbar ("son of a star"), one of the many false Messiahs, led the revolt, supported by the great Rabbi Akiba; 580,000 men fell in battle. "All Judea was well nigh a desert," writes Dio Cassius. (3) *Later History*. When the Roman Empire was divided in the fourth century, Palestine fell to the share of the Eastern Emperor at Constantinople, and remained under the government of Constantinople until 637 A. D., when it was overrun and conquered by the Arabian Saracens. It has since then, with little interruption, been under Mohammedan power. The Seljukian Turks seized the country in 1073, and by their barbarous treatment of Christian pilgrims brought on the Crusades. The Latin kingdom, with its nine successive sovereigns, established in 1099, held Jerusalem until 1187 and stayed in Acre till 1291. In 1517, the Ottomans came in and made the country a part of the Turkish Empire. It was snatched from the Sultan Mohammed Ali in 1832, but Europe intervened, and in 1841 it was given back again. At present a movement is on foot among the Jews called "Zionism," the object of which is to buy Palestine from Turkey and colonize it with Jews.

16. **Mode of Government and Taxation.** (1) The

Roman rule was harsh and unfeeling, but the Jews, under their high priests and the Sanhedrin, enjoyed a large measure of home rule. (2) The Sanhedrin ("Presbytery," Lu. 22:66, "senate," Acts 5:21), was the supreme governing council of the Jews having judicial and within certain limitations, executive authority. Its decrees were of binding force even among the Jews of the diaspora (Acts 9:2). (3) Its *origin* was traced back by the Jews to Moses (Deut. 16:27, 8), but it is almost certain that it came into being only after the Babylonian captivity, and its name ("Synedrion") indicates that it originated under Greek rule. (4) Its membership was composed of 70 men, called elders and rulers, with the high priest as president ex-officio. In the time of Christ the members came from two leading classes: chief priests (heads of the 24 orders), who appear to have been for the most part Sadducees, and Scribes, representing the Pharisees who at this time had the greater influence among the people. Those not included in these two classes are designated elders, i. e., heads of families. In Christ's time, the Pharisees had the majority, but the Sadducees the presidency. The members of this council were probably chosen for life by the Sanhedrin itself, or upon nomination of the latter were appointed by the king or Roman procurator. (5) The qualifications for membership were that a man must be good looking, of blameless life and morals, the father of a family, and learned in the law, in science and language. (6) There may have been a small Sanhedrin, composed of 24 members— a bare quorum (night trial of Jesus). (7) Its regular place of meeting was in Jerusalem, in the hall or Chamber Gazith within the Temple enclosure. (8) In course of time its jurisdiction was much curtailed: first by Herod and afterwards by the Romans. It could, e. g., not execute a sentence of death until the case had been reviewed by the Roman governor (Jno. 18:31; 19:6; Jos. Ant. XX, 9:1). (9) Ordinary cases came before the Lesser Sanhedrin, of which there were two in Jerusalem, and one in every town with more than 121 inhabitants. (10) *Taxation.*

Usually the Romans farmed out the revenues of a district or on a certain article to a local collector for a lump sum, who with his employees collected as much as they could. Zachaeus was such a "chief of publicans." Extortion was the rule, and only limited by the victim's ability to pay. A Jew who held such a position became a social outcast, first, on principle, because paying any kind of taxes to a heathen power was considered treason to Jehovah, their invisible King (hence the offerings of publicans were not accepted at the synagogue) ; second, because most of them were personally dishonest (Lu. 15 : 1-2).

17. **Divisions, Names and Language.** (1) The Jewish nation was divided into two sections : The Jews in Palestine, and the Jews of the Dispersion. The latter were more numerous than the former and were found in all countries (John 7 : 35 ; Acts 2 : 10 ; Jas. 1 : 1 ; 1 Peter 1 : 1). There were four sections of the Dispersion : (1) the original Dispersion in Babylon, (2) in Syria and Asia Minor (Antioch) ; (3) in Egypt (Alexandria) ; (4) in the West (Rome). (2) *Names.* In the N. T. the Jews are known by three names : (a) *Jew (contracted from Judean).* Originally the name of the people of Judah, but after the exile including all the children of Israel. In the Fourth Gospel it is almost uniformly used in a hostile sense to denote the enemies of Jesus. This name denotes the nationality in opposition to "Greek," or "Gentile" (Jos. Ant. II, 5, 7 and 8). (b) *"Hebrew,"* a Jew in respect to his language and education, in opposition to a "Hellenist," a Jew speaking Greek. The Jews in Palestine and the East were called "Hebrews" because they used the Aramaic, and the rest "Hellenists" or "Grecians" because they used the Greek language. (c) "Israelite," a Jew in respect to his religious privileges. (Trench N. T. Synonyms). (3) In the New Testament we find traces of *four languages*—1. *Old Hebrew,* lost in Babylon, but still read in Christ's time in the synagogue, yet not well understood, needing interpretation through the 'Aramaic paraphrases. (Targums). After the return from Babylon it became the

language of worship and revelation, and with the aroma of old associations, it was kept for holy uses. (2) *Aramaic*, cognate to Hebrew and therefore easily adopted by the Jews in Babylon and retained after their return to Palestine. It is the "Syrian language," mentioned in 2 Kings 18:26; Isa. 36:11; Dan. 2:4. As this was the language of the Jews in the time of Christ, it was undoubtedly the mother tongue of our Lord. See instances in Mark 7:34; 15:34. This is the language referred to in John 19:20, 21 and Acts 22:2, as "Hebrew." (3) *Greek*. The language of polite literature in all countries, strongly opposed by the Pharisees, but employed by the Jews of the Dispersion, and used in the court of Herod and Pilate (Acts 21:37). (4) *Latin*, the official language of the Roman government, was not used by the Jews, and not generally understood by them. It was thought necessary to write the inscription over the cross in all three languages.

18. **History of the Roman Empire.** (1) Though the name appears only twice in the gospels (John 11:48; 19:20), Rome and the Romans formed a strong background to the action of the leading figures in the life of Christ as is shown by numerous references to the emperor (Matt. 22:17; Mark 12:14; Lu. 2:1; 3:1; 20:22; 23:2; Jno. 19:12), to governor Pilate, the centurions and the soldiers. A brief sketch of Roman conditions will therefore aid us in our study of the life of Christ. (2) The Roman republic which had lasted 500 years (509 to 31 B. C.) was finally destroyed and the Roman empire established by the double battle at Philippi, B. C. 42, and the naval battle at Actium, west of Greece, in September, B. C. 31, in all three of which Augustus commanded the imperial forces and defeated those of the republic. (3) The emperors of the first Christian century were: (a) *Augustus,* 31 B. C. to 14 A. D. (Lu. 2:1). The Temple of Janus was closed, which was an indication that universal peace reigned throughout the world, when Jesus the "Prince of Peace" was born. The defeat of the Roman legions by Hermann, 9 A. D. in the

Teutoburg Forest, was the last serious attempt of the Romans to subjugate the Germans beyond the Rhine. He rebuilt and beautified Rome. (b) *Tiberius,* 14-37 (Lu. 3:1), a great military commander and at first an able ruler. By degrees, owing to dissention with his wife, he became gloomy and suspicious and ended his life as a cruel and revengeful tyrant. He spent the last eight years of his life on Capri. Under his reign Jesus died, and it is said that Pilate sent him a report of the trial. Of the people he said "Let them hate me, provided they respect me." (c) *Caligula,* 37-41. His actions indicate insanity. He demanded divine honors, delighted in bloodshed, wished the Roman people might have only one neck which he might then cut off with a single stroke, had his favorite horse appointed a consul, built a bridge from the Capitoline hill to the Palatine in order to be nearer to the temple of Jupiter, whose equal he considered himself to be. His motto was "Let the people hate me, provided they fear me." (d) *Claudius,* 41-54, a man of learning, but weak and the slave of his two wicked wives, the second of which poisoned him. Under him Britain was conquered, the great aqueducts at Rome completed, and the Jews expelled from Rome (Acts 18:2). (e) *Nero,* 54-68, a knave beyond comparison, who killed his mother, wife, brother and his teacher Seneca. In 64 he set fire to Rome and put the blame on the Christians. This charge led to the first persecution of the Christians in 64-67, in which Peter was crucified and Paul beheaded. When a revolution in the armies of Gaul, Spain and Germany broke out against him, he committed suicide, his last words being, "What a great artist dies with me." (Read "Quo Vadis"). (f) *Galba, Otho and Vitellius,* three in the one year 68. (g) *Vespasian,* 69-79, the general in the war against the Jews (66-70), (which war his son Titus completed by capturing Jerusalem and destroying the temple in 70. Arch of Titus at Rome). He also built the Colosseum. (h) *Titus,* 79-81, won all hearts by his justice and humanity. "I have lost a day" he would say, when a day had passed without an act of kindness. The eruption of Mount Vesuvius destroyed Herculaneum and Pompeii on which occasion the elder Pliny, the author of a Natural History and a History of the Germans, perished. (i) *Domitian,* 81-96, the brother of Titus and a tyrant of the worst type. He banished the Apostle John to Patmos, and cited the relatives of Jesus to appear before him, because he had a suspicion that they might revive the claims of Jesus to the throne of David. (4) *The population* of the entire Roman empire was 120 millions: Of these, 40 millions were in Europe, 7 millions in Italy. Of the 120 millions, 60 millions were slaves, 40 millions tributaries and freedmen, and only 20 millions citizens. The army numbered 400,000, the navy 50,000.

19. **Reference Literature.** Read the O. T. books of Ezra, Nehemia and Esther; also I. and II. Maccabees in the Old Testament Apocrypha; Farrar, Excursus 13, on the Sanhedrin; consult dictionaries on the general topics, especially, Hastings D. C. on Augustus, Vol. I., 143; the Herods, I., 717; Romans II, 536; Dispersion I, 465; Pol Conditions II, 378; Pilate, 363; Newman's Church History I, 29, on Roman empire; p. 35 on Babylonian Captivity; p. 40 on Syrian rulers; p. 44 on Maccabees. Jos. Ant. XII and XIII, on the Greek and Maccabean Epochs; Schuerer, The Jewish People, Div. I, Vol. I, p. 186; Rigg's History, p. 260, Jewish Wars. On Antipas, Christoterpe 1909; Schuerer, Language, Div. II, Vol. I, pp. 8-10; Matthew's History of the N. T. Times; Rigg's History, After the War, p. 278; Grant, Between the Testaments, p. 6; Breed, Preparation of the World, Chapters 3-9; A. Meyer, Jesu Muttersprache; on the same subject an essay by Delitzsch in the "Daheim," translated for the "Chr. World," by Dr. A. Zerbe; Allan & Myers, Ancient History, Part 3; On the Jewish War, Farrar, Early Days of Christianity, Ch. 27, 29; Handel's Opera "The Maccabees;" Gess, Zukunft des Jued. Volkes, Christoterpe, 1882; Schmidt, Ramulda, Erzaehlung aus der Maccabaer Zeit, 310 pages; Seeley, The Hammer, a story of the Maccabean times.

CHAPTER 3.

The Intellectual World in Which Jesus Lived.

20. Christ lived in a highly developed intellectual age. Alexander the Great (336-323 B. C.) had diffused Greek civilization with its matchless language, literature, art, philosophy, and science over the whole civilized world, so that in his day Greek culture had reached its highest point. History shows plainly that while God used the Jews as His instrument to furnish the substance of Christianity (John 4: 22), Greek-Roman paganism, in the providence of God, contributed largely to its form. Without this co-operation Christianity would never have risen to the place of the universal world religion, but would have degenerated into a mere Jewish sect.

21. **Jewish Culture.** The Jews possessed, as the Talmud and the Old Testament show, a great mass of valid technical and general knowledge, but they lacked the power of logical abstraction. This showed itself in two ways; they could not frame definitions of objects but only gave descriptions, neither had they the right conception of law, but meant by law merely the precepts of a ruler. Consequently they had no real science and philosophy and very little art; the latter being discouraged by the 2nd commandment. They opposed the spread of Greek culture, and some Rabbis pronounced a ban on all who studied "Greek wisdom." At this period, however, the nation and individuals, especially the Hellenists were powerfully influenced by the general world-culture as is shown in their literature. Their writers were greatly aided by the translation of the Old Testament into Greek, the Septuagint (LXX).

22. **Jewish Literature.** The extra-canonical literature of the Jews falls into three classes: the Apocrypha, the Apocalyptic literature and a few later books. (1) The Apocrypha (hidden, or concealed, referring to suspected authorship or obscure teaching, but generally meaning only

extra-canonical) form a group of 17 books written in the Greek language between 200 B. C. and the time of Christ. They are the product of the Hellenistic Jews, incorporated into the LXX, but excluded from the Hebrew Canon. They were canonized by the Council of Trent 1546, and are recommended by many Protestants as "useful and good to read," yet not inspired. (2) Their titles are I & II Esdras, Tobit, Judith, Esther, Wisdom of Solomon, Ecclesiasticus, Baruch, Jeremy, Song of the Three Children, Susanna, Bel and the Dragon, Prayer of Manassas and I to IV Maccabees.

23. **Apocalyptic Literature.** (a) The term means to uncover or reveal. There are three classes of Apocalyptic literature: 1. the *early Jewish,* 200-100 B. C.; 2. the *Christian,* including John's Revelation, to Dante's Divine Comedia. 3. The *later Hebrew.* Only the first class need be noticed here. (b) List of Apocalyptic books before Christ: 1. Within the Old Testament Canon; Ezekiel, Daniel, Zechariah and Joel; 2. among the Apocrypha; II Esdras and Baruch; 3. otherwise extant; Book of Enoch, Secrets of Enoch, Book of Jubilees, Testament of the Twelve Patriarchs, Psalms of Solomon, Sibylline Oracles; Assumption of Moses; 4. Quoted by some early Fathers but not extant; Prayer of Joseph, Book of Eldad and Moldad, Apocalypse of Elijah, Apocalypse of Zephaniah; 5. Known only by name: Baruch, Habbakuk, Ezekiel, Daniel (See Bennett and Adeney, "A Biblical Introduction," page 268). (c) Common characteristics of the non-canonical Apocalyptic books. 1. The vision form. 2. The visions are expressed in symbolical figures; beasts and mystic numbers. 3. Highly developed angelology; 4. The Unknown as subject-matter. 5. Pseudonymity (False name of authors). 6. Optimism. 7. Theological ideas in common on sin, the Messiah, resurrection, judgment, punishment, reward, restoration of the world, predestination. (d) Reasons for the origin of this type of literature: As prophecy died out the Apocalyptists took its place. (e) Authorship: The Apocalyptic books

were either anonymous or pseudonymous (giving no name or a false name as author; the latter to secure authority to the book). (f) Importance: To a thorough study of the life of Christ some knowledge of the extra-canonical literature is necessary because a flood of light is shed by the form and contents of the Apocalyptic literature on Christ's life, his teaching, phraseology and works. (g) Its influence on the N. T. is shown: 1. In the *form* of whole N. T. books, (Rev.), or of parts (Matt. 24; II Thess. 2:2-12). 2. In prominent phrases, as "Son of Man," (Dan. 7:13), "day of judgment;" 3. In quotations (Jude 14, from Enoch; Jude 9, from Ass. of Moses). 4. Some of their subject-matter is freely adopted and spiritualized.

24. **Later Literature.** (1) In *Philo* (about 20 B. C.-53 A. D.), the type of philosophical thought known as the Jewish-Alexandrian reached its highest development. He applied to the Old Testament the allegorical method employed for centuries by the Greeks to the interpretation of Homer. By this method everything deemed unworthy of the gods was explained away. As Philo lacked the historical spirit, he was unable to appreciate the progressive character of revelation and to understand the relation of the human and divine in the Scripture. So in his anxiety to show the perfect harmony between Old Testament thought and Greek philosophy he used a method which enabled him to explain away whatever seemed to obstruct the attainment of his object. Whatever in the Old Testament seemed to him unworthy of God, or childish, or opposed to Greek philosophy, he spiritualized. Thus he came to the conclusion that everything that was wise and exalted in Greek philosophy lay concealed in the Old Testament. Philo also developed the Logos doctrine, and the relation between his teaching on the Logos and that of John is still a matter of dispute. (2) *Josephus* (37-103 A. D.), a Jewish priest, first a general of the Jewish rebels in Galilee, later a protegé of Titus. He wrote: 1. Antiquities, the History of the Jews, 2. Jewish War, 3. Against Apion and 4. An Autobiography. He

wrote in Greek and Aramaic. His works are highly interesting and should be consulted by Bible students who aim at thoroughness.

25. **Greek Culture.** Greek art, literature and philosophy ruled the world in which Christ lived absolutely, as they still do ours to a large extent. Of its great influence even the New Testament is witness. A sketch of the principal philosophical systems and schools is therefore helpful. (a) The *Epicureans* were skeptics and declared against all religion. The world arose from chance; there is no providence; soul is mortal; pleasure is the ultimate end of life (Paul at Athens). (b) The *Academics* were agnostics; and held it impossible to arrive at objective truth (Pilate). They questioned whether a god existed, whether the soul was immortal, also whether virtue was to be preferred to vice. (c) The *Aristotelians* were deists. God is a principle giving motion to the machine but is perfectly indifferent to the affairs of men. (d) The *Platonists* had a high idea of God but limited him in his perfections. Soul is immortal; (in Heb. 10: 1, we have an echo of Plato's "ideas"). (e) The *Stoics* were materialistic pantheists. Everything (our souls too) is part of the deity. Virtue is the chief end of life and should be practiced for its own sake. Mere pleasure should never be made an end. Freedom from passion is the mark of a perfect man. Stoicism defends suicide. It produced an elevated but sombre and morose type of character. On its ethical side it had much in common with Christianity (Paul at Athens). (f) The *Eclectics* held Plato in high esteem but selected from other systems whatever pleased them, as in all systems so many things seemed unreasonable and absurd. (g) The most *popular philosophies* in the time of Christ were the Epicurean and the various forms of skepticism. Their denial of the supernatural and the immortality of the soul, making pleasure the end of life, led to a frightful debasement of morals. Greek philosophy had exhausted the possibilities of the uninspired human mind, and the world was sadly in need of one who could say "I am the way and the truth and the life."

26. **Roman Culture.** Christ's time was the "golden age" of Roman literature, made illustrious by a large group of writers in prose and poetry. Its splendor and activity in art was such as had seldom existed in the history of the human race. (a) *Architectural works.* Cæsar Augustus himself built twelve temples, repaired 82 which had fallen into decay, laid out the new Forum Julium, completed the large Basilica Julia, constructed a mausoleum for himself. He could say "I have found Rome of brick and left it of marble." (b) *Roman art.* The arch was developed into the dome as employed in the Pantheon. Greek art, especially the Doric, Ionic and Corinthian style of architecture, was introduced. (c) *Literature.* 1. *Poets:* Virgil died in 19 B. C., wrote the Aeneid; Horace, died 8 A. D., is the model of lyric poetry. His odes, satires and epistles are models of wisdom. Ovid, died 17 A. D., wrote Metamorphoses. 2. *Prose writers:* Sallust, Livy, the greatest of Roman historians, Nepos, Julius Cæsar. Maecenes, a chosen counsellor of Augustus, was a munificent patron of literature, encouraging men like Horace an l Virgil. (3) *Statesmen and orators:* Cicero. (4) *Philosophers:* Seneca, Cicero, Epictetus. (5) Even in Rome the Greek was used as a literary medium and sign of higher culture.

27. **Reference Literature.** Consult D. B., especially Enclycl. by Stanford on Stoics, Talmud, Targum, N. T. Apocrypha, Seneca, Socrates, Egypt; Herzog and Schaff—Herzog on Hillel, Josephus, Midrash; Piercy on Jewish Language, Roman Empire, Rome, Hellenist. Hastings D. C. on Apocrypha and Apocal I, 79-94, 223; II, 577 on Jewish Science, Greek Influence in Palestine I, 691; Robert N. Wilson, M. D., Medical Men in Time of Christ; Snell, The Value of the Aprocrypha; Newmann's Church History I, ch. 2 on Graeco-Roman civilization; I, p. 21, Greek philosophy; p. 40 the LXX and Apocrypha; p. 59 on Philo. Breed, Preparation of the World, ch. 10; Koenig, Talmud and N. T.; Farrar, Life of Christ, Excur. 4, "Greek Learning," Excur. 7, Jewish Angelology, Excur. 12 on Talmud; Bennett and Adeney, Bibl. Introd. p. 268 on O. T. Apocrypha; Ueberweg and Schwegler, History of Philosophy; Sanders and Fowler, Bibl. Hist. and Lit., p. 117-168; On Philo, Farrar, Early

Days of Christianity, ch. 13 and 14; Grant, Between the Testaments, pp. 109-146; Bennet and Adeney, Bibl. Introd. pp. 268-274; Riggs' History of the Jewish People; Heinrici; Hellenismus und Christentum (Bib. Zeitfragen).

CHAPTER 4.

The Religious World in Which Jesus Lived.

28. **Religion among the Jews.** (1) The majority of the Jews in Christ's time, in Palestine and in the diaspora, were intensely religious, even to fanaticism. (2) There was a dark and bright side to Judaism in Christ's time. The dark side manifested itself in its deism, self-righteousness and licentiousness. The bright side was represented in characters like the family of Jesus, Zacharias, Elizabeth, Simeon, Anna, Nathanael, Nicodemus. Its literature, including the Talmud, contains many gems, some of which Jesus appropriated and spiritualized. The golden rule has been attributed to Hillel, and many features of his parables are also found in Jewish literature. There was a profound seriousness on the subject of religion and less professed atheism, indifference and levity than there has ever been in any society, ancient or modern. Even in Christ's time and afterwards, Judaism had the inner strength to produce martyrs (Zealots).

29. **Messianic Hope.** (1) The all-prevailing spirit of the Jewish religion was the expectation of the Messiah. This hope was inspired and strengthened by the "Messianic prophecies." (2) This term has two meanings: In its narrower sense it refers to all those specific predictions which connect the establishment of the kingdom of God with a definite, unique personality—the Messiah. (Greek, Christos; Latin, Christus; English, The Anointed; German, Der Gesalbte—in all languages from the verb to anoint). In its broader sense the term includes all the great institutions of the Hebrew nation, the prophetic order, the mon-

archy and the priesthood, which find their full meaning in
the Messiah and his kingdom, and which had meaning only
in so far as they pointed to a final and perfected salvation
in God's kingdom. (3) *Development.* The Messianic
predictions were at first vague, but became more definite as
they narrowed to a single family and to one person. The
Messiah was to be a man (Gen. 3 : 15), a Semite, an Israelite (Gen. 12 : 3), from the Tribe of Judah (Gen. 49 : 10),
from the House of David (Isa. 11 : 1) ; the place of birth
(Micah 5 :2) ; the time of appearance (Dan. 9 : 20, 25) ;
(Haggai 2 : 7 ; Mal. 3 : 1). (4) Fulfilment in Christ. It
was the great object of the gospels to vindicate the claim
of Jesus to the Messiahship by adducing proof that he was
the one to whom the finger of prophecy pointed. In the
spiritual sense, Christ fulfilled all the older types. He was
the prophet sent by God (Jno. 3 : 2 ; 17 : 8 ; Act. 3 : 22) ; a
Priest (Heb. 3 : 1, 2 ; 5 : 6 ; 7 : 23-28) ; a King (Matt. 2 : 2 ;
21 : 5, 11 ; Phil. 2 : 9, 11 ; Rev. 11 : 15 ; 17 : 14) ; the Servant
(Lu. 22 : 27) ; and the sacrificial offering (Heb. 9 : 13 ; 14 :
26). Even in respect to the material blessings proceeding
from him Christ fulfills with increasing measure, the dreams
of the seers of all the ages. (5) The rulers of Christ's
time rejected the claims of Jesus because they neither har-
monized with their perverted ideal of the Messiah, nor with
their notions as to the outward signs preceding his appearance. They expected a mere political deliverer who would
take revenge on their oppressors and erect a great Jewish
world empire. So when Jesus and his apostles emphasized
the spiritual meaning of the Messianic prophecies, the Jews
felt scandalized. They also believed that his appearance
would be preceded by a series of struggles and that these
would be announced by omens in the heavens. ("Swords
appear in heaven.") Elijah was to precede him.

30. **The Pharisees.** (1) There were *three religious
sects* among the Jews, the *Pharisees, Sadducees and Essenes,*
which may be generally characterized as the conservative
formalists, the advanced free thinkers and the mystical

pietists. (2) The name *Pharisee* is derived from the Hebrew parash, "separated," that is, people who by their superior holiness distinguished themselves from the multitude. (3) *Numbers:* There were about 6,000 in the time of Christ. (4) *Influence:* They were the popular party because they were orthodox, anti-foreign and had the majority in the Sanhedrin. (5) *Attitude toward the O. T.* Besides the written law they held to an "oral law" which was a digest of Jewish traditions. Some of it was later written down and was called the Mishna or Second Law, contained now in the first part of the Talmud. At Christ's time it was esteemed higher than the written law, but was condemned by him as a source of great error. (6) *Beliefs:* They believed in a future state, the resurrection of the dead, in a Divine providence acting side by side with the free will of man. (7) *Divisions.* In the time of Christ they were divided doctrinally into several schools, among which those of Hillel (liberal) and Shamai (conservative) are most noted. (8) *Morals.* As a class they represented the best morality; many were ascetics. Josephus compares them to the Stoics. Some individuals were good men (Nicodemus, Joseph of Arimathea, Gamaliel, Hillel, Shamai and St. Paul). Large numbers later joined the Christian church. (9) *Why opposed to Christ:* 1. Because of his humble origin and lack of higher education (Matt. 13: 55; Jno. 7: 15). 2. Because of the company he kept (Lu. 15: 2). 3. Because he opposed their ceremonialism and their wrong idea of the Sabbath. (10) *Reasons for Christ's opposing them:* Their perversion of the Messianic ideal, national narrowness, religious formalism and self-righteousness. (11) *Influence on the Apostolic Church:* The Judaizers who insisted on circumcision as a condition of salvation were no doubt former Pharisees and their followers. (12) *Survival:* They still exist as a party among eastern Jews and are called "Pharashim." So bad is their character that the bitterest form of reproach in Jerusalem is "You are a parish." How little they have changed from their character as Christ depicted it may be seen from the testimony of a Jewish writer, "They proudly separate themselves from the rest of their co-religionists, fanatical, bigoted, intolerant, quarrelsome, and in truth irreligious. With them the outward observance of the ceremonial law is everything; the moral law is little binding, morality itself is of no importance."

31. **The Sadducees and Essenes.** (1) The *Sadducees* derive their name from Zadoc. the priest who declared in favor of Solomon when Abiathar took the part of Adonijah (1 Kings 13: 32-45), or from the Hebrew word "tsadik," righteous. They constituted a kind of sacerdotal aristocracy, counting among their adherents the families of the governing class under Herod (Acts 5: 17). The Sadducees denied the leading beliefs of the Pharisees, and especially the authority of the oral law, the resurrection, future punishment and reward. Christ seldom came in contact with them. (2) The *Essenes* (probably meaning "seer" or the "silent," the "mysterious") were an ascetic sect, which aspired to ideal purity and divine communion. They were communists living in isolated settlements, the best known of which was on the northwest shore of the Dead Sea. They are not mentioned in the New Testament, and the probability is that the Lord never came in contact with any of them. Their ceremonial washings and the reverence paid to the sun, point to Persian influence, while their asceticism and the community of goods have a Pythagorean cast. They wore white garments.

32. **Professions and Factions.** (1) The *Scribes* were identical with the "lawyers." From the time of Jeremiah (Jer. 8: 8; Ezra 7: 6) they were copyists, custodians and interpreters of the Old Testament Scriptures. As formalists, worshipping the mere letter of the law, they called forth some of the sharpest rebukes of Jesus. (Matt. 5: 20; 23: 2, 3, etc.). As a class they belonged to the Pharisaic party. (2) The *Zealots* shared the sentiments of the Phar-

isees, but they were a party of action who insisted on war
against Rome.   Their agitation at last brought on the great
Jewish war (A. D. 66-70), with its terrible result.   (3) The
Herodians were a political party which supported the house
of Herod and the Romans.   (4) The *Proselytes* were Gentile worshippers of Jehovah.   The inability of paganism to
satisfy the deeper needs of humanity had long been felt by
the more thoughtful among the heathen themselves.   Large
numbers of these were attracted by the purer faith and
higher morality of the Jews.   Their number in Christ's
time is estimated as high as 700,000.   There were two
classes of them: (a) Proselytes of the Gate, which may
mean that they went as far as to the gate of full Judaism,
which is circumcision, or, that they were permitted to proceed only to a certain gate in the Temple beyond which the
uncircumcised were warned not to proceed under penalty
of death.   They bound themselves to avoid blasphemy,
idolatry, uncleanness, theft, etc.   They are also called,
"God-fearing men."   Most of the proselytes belonged to
this class.   (Cornelius).   (b) Proselytes of Righteousness,
those who fulfilled all righteousness, that is, they were circumcised, and kept the law.   (5) *Great Synagogue*.   Nehemiah (436 B. C.) is said to have formed what is called the
"Great Synagogue," supposedly composed of the eighty-
five priests, who pledged themselves to keep the law (Neh.
13:6-31)   Out of this grew a national organization, having for its object the promotion of the observance of the
law.   To this body is ascribed the formation of the Old
Testament Canon, the introduction of the new Hebrew
alphabet, the vowel points and accents, and the rabbinical schools for studying the Scriptures under professional
scribes.   (6) *Mission of the Jews*.   Belonging to the
Semitic race, the Jews were the people of religion, as the
Greeks were the people of art, and the Romans, the people
of law and order.   The great glory and mission of Israel
was, first, to perpetuate the knowledge of the one true God
in the world, and second, to receive and spread the final

revelation in Christ. To some extent they fulfilled this mission.

33. **Sacred Buildings.** (1) *The Temple in Jerusalem.* Three temples were built in succession. (a) Solomon's Temple, built 1000 B. C. and after standing 400 years, destroyed by Nebuchadnezzar. (b) The second Temple was built by Zerubbabel after the Captivity upon the original foundation and plan, though much inferior to the first Temple. (c) Herod the Great, a few years before Christ, greatly enlarged and enriched the second Temple, giving it

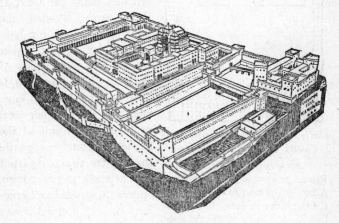

Dr. Schick's Model of the Temple.

his own name. In magnificence it exceeded Solomon's Temple, but it lacked its chief glory, the Arc of the Covenant. It was destroyed by the Romans, 70 A. D. (2) The *location* of the Temple was on Mt. Moriah, where Abraham was willing to offer up Isaac. (3) The *materials* were immense white stones, 40 to 60 feet long, pillars of Parian marble 40 feet in length; woodwork of cedar, fir and sandalwood, exquisitely carved and vast quantities of gold, silver and Corinthian brass. In the ceiling of the Most Holy Place alone thirty tons of gold were used. (4) The *Courts.* The Temple wall bounded the quadrangle and was entered by seven outer gates. Inside were three quadrangular "Courts," rising one above another, separated by walls of partition, and encircled by marble cloisters. The outer

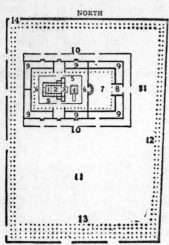

General Plan of Temple and Courts as Rebuilt by Herod.

1. Holy of Holies. 2. Holy Place. 3. Temple Porch. 4. Great Altar of Burnt Offerings. 5. Court of the Priests. 6. Court of Israel. 7. Court of the Women. 8. Beautiful Gate. 9. Priests' Chambers. 10. "Soreg" or Balustrade, within which Gentiles were not allowed to go. 11. Court of the Gentiles. 12. Solomon's Porch. 13. Royal Porch. 14. Entrance to Castle of Antonia.

was, "The *Court of Gentiles.*" Within and above this, entered through nine gates, 60 feet high, overlaid with gold and silver, was the *"Court of Israel"* for the Jews only, the eastern half being set apart as the *"Court of Women,"* the limit of approach for Jewish women. On a higher terrace was the "Court of the Priests." *The Temple Proper,* 120 feet long, stood on a yet higher level at the western end of the "Priests Court" opposite the Brazen Altar. Its front was a porch 180 feet high, covered with gold and precious stones. Behind it was the *Holy Place,* opening through the great veil into the *Holy of Holies.* (5) *Services.* 20,000 priests, assisted by twice as many Levites, in 24 courses, each serving one week in turn, were in charge. The Levites were guards, porters, musicians, etc. Only priests could sacrifice or burn incense. Two daily public services were held at 9 a. m. and 3 p. m. (6) *Temple near Heliopolis.* About 164 B. C. Onias, failing to secure the Jerusalem high-priesthood went to Egypt and transformed an old pagan temple into a Jewish Sanctuary in which services were held, until the Romans closed it in 73 A. D. While many Jews looked with disfavor on this movement, it marks a distinct stage in the liberalizing of Jewish religious thought, especially among the Hellenists.

34. **The Synagogue.** (1) *Origin.* During the Captivity where no Temple Service was possible. (2) *Universality.* Wherever ten heads of families could be found, there a Synagogue would be established, in and outside of Palestine. (Diaspora.) In Jerusalem were 460, and every nationality had its own (Acts 6:9). (3) *Arrangement:* It contained (a) An "arc"—a chest for the sacred rolls, placed in the end of the building toward Jerusalem. (b) Chief Seats, elevated, near and around the arc for the elders and leading men. (c) Platform and reading desk. (d) Places carefully graded according to rank. Gentile visitors were allowed near the door. (e) Lattice gallery where women could worship without being seen. (4) *Officers:* (a) 3 rulers of the Synagogue (one of whom was *the* ruler) who conducted the worship and possessed limited judicial authority. (b) The servant, (Luke 4:20) who united the functions of sexton, schoolmaster and constable, to pass judgment on offenders. (5) *Services:* Held on Saturday, Monday and Thursday. They consisted of prayer, reading and remarks. The selections were from the Law and the Prophets, according to an appointed order (Acts 15:21), called Parashim and Haphtharim, like our church pericopes.

35. **The Sacred Year.** The Jews of Christ's time observed seven solemnities, six of them feasts, and one a fast; only the first five were appointed by the Law of Moses. The six feasts may be divided into two groups: (a) the three great feasts (Passover, Pentecost and Tabernacles), and (b) the three lesser feasts (Trumpets, Dedication, Purim). Trumpets and Purim are not mentioned in the New Testament. Their order in the Jewish calendar is as follows:

Name.	Time.	Event Commemorated.
Passover	14 Nisan—April	Exodus.
Pentecost	Sivan—May	Harvest Home and Giving of the Law.
Trumpets	1 Tizri—September	New Year.
Atonement	10 Tizri—October	Repentance.
Tabernacles	15 Tizri—October	Life in the Desert.
Dedication	Chislev—December 25	Rededication of the Temple.
Purim	14 Adar—March	Plot of Haman.

36. **The Religion of the Samaritans.** This people was a mixed race which sprang up in Northern Israel after the fall of the Kingdom of Israel, in B. C. 722, as a result of the intermarriage of the heathen Assyrian colonists (II Kings 17:24-41) with the remnants of the Israelites left in the land. On account of this impurity of their descent and because of their opposition to the rebuilding of the Temple after the Captivity (Ezra, Chap. 4), they were hated by the Jews (John 4:9). There still remain between one and two hundred who live in Nablus, near the site of ancient Shechem. Under the teaching of a Jewish priest, sent by the King of Assyria, they gradually adopted a sort of Jehovah worship (II Kings 17:25). Of the Jewish canon they accepted only the Pentateuch. They observed the Passover and still do so. They expected the Messiah, not as a king, but to teach them all things. (Deut. 18:15; John 4:25).

37. **Pagan Religions.** Religion with the *Romans* was more a matter of form and ritualism than of feeling. A Pontifex Maximus at the head of minor pontiffs supervised all the religious affairs of the state. The Augurs were the official soothsayers, who by observing the flight of birds, determined the mind of the gods. At the time of Christ, disbelief in the current religion had become almost universal among the educated classes. Augustus strove in vain to restore religion to its former position, and even assumed

personally the office of Pontifex Maximus. The practice of deifying and worshipping the emperors exerted a most degrading influence on the religious life. Many Romans, to satisfy their religious cravings, embraced Judaism, others were imposed upon by Oriental priests, sorcerers, sooth-sayers and astrologers, like Apollonius of Tyana (3 B. C. to 96 A. D.). The upper classes treated current mythology as fables, but were the ready dupes of every quack, and foreign cult. Harlots, like Poppaea, Nero's wife, were deified, and sacrifices were offered for the preservation of Nero's "divine voice." There were a few who lived nobler lives like Seneca, Epictet, but their Stoicism was no remedy for the ills of the times.

38. **Reference Literature.** Farrar, Excursus 5 on Talmud and Oral Law; Exc. 14 on Phar. and Sad., Exc. 7 on Angels and Demons; Exc. 9, Hypocrisy of the Phar. Consult D. of B. especially, Hastings D. of C. on Feasts I, 584; Herodians I, 723; Messiah II, 171; Tradition II, 741; Samaritans II, 557; Hastings D. of B., Vol. III, 352, on Messiah; On the Essenes I, 767; on the bright side of Judaism II, 606. D. Smith's New Testament History, 164, on the sects of the Jews; In "Quo Vadis," ch. 13, the fake philosopher Chilon; Newman's Church History, Vol. I, p. 47, on Jewish sects; p. 36 on Persian Influence; p. 62 on Messianic Expectations; Matthews History of N. T. Times, Messianic Hope, p. 159; Rigg's History of Jewish People, pp. 105 and 215; Parties and Inner Life; Grant, Between the Testaments, p. 109, on literature; Breed, Preparation, Chaps. 12 and 15; Thompson, Books Which Influenced our Lord; Briggs, Messiah and the Gospels, pp. 1 to 40; Sellin, Die Israelitische Heilandserwartung; Caspari, Die Pharisaer (In "Biblische Zeitfragen"); Uhlhorn, Conflict, (on Religious Life); Orelli, Knecht Jahves; G. B. Smith, Modern Criticism and the Preaching of the O. T., Ch. 5; Kurtz's Church History, Vol. I, ¶7 to ¶12.

CHAPTER 5.

The Moral and Social World in Which Jesus Lived.

39. The moral degradation of the period when Jesus lived, has rarely been equalled and perhaps never exceeded in the annals of mankind. It may be judged from the following facts: (1) Paul's lurid picture of pagan wickedness in Rom. 1 : 18-32, which should not be regarded as a judgment from too lofty a moral standpoint, for all that he says is confirmed by pagan authors. (2) The excavated objects of *Pompeii* give us a faint glimpse of the horrible nature of the vice and crime at this period as a testimony to the fruit of heathenism. (3) The bare mention of the names of the *emperors* condemns a people which made them possible. (4) The enormous wealth and coarse luxury, created a sense of insecurity and terror. (5) Labor was considered a disgrace, and the middle class had disappeared. Among the 1,200,000 inhabitants of Rome at Christ's time (Cic. De Off. 11, 12), there were scarcely 2,000 proprietors. (6) The number of *slaves* increased with Roman conquests. In Italy there were 1,300,000, and in the whole empire, 6,-000,000. They were harshly treated, sometimes thrown into ponds to sweeten the meat of the fishes. A law was advocated that when a master was murdered all his slaves as being considered under suspicion should be put to death. (7) *Luxury* passed all bounds and was too horrible for description. Among the rich, the disgusting practice was in vogue to prepare for dinner by taking an emetic. Emperor Vitellius, in less than eight months, spent on feasts, several millions. Games on the most lavish scale continued for weeks and months. (8) The very *rites of religion* were used to satisfy unnatural lust. (9) *Family life* among the Romans had once been a sacred thing, and for 520 years divorce had been unknown. But under the Empire marriage was regarded with disfavor. Women, says Seneca, married in order to be divorced and were di-

vorced in order to marry. They counted the years, not by the Consuls, but by the number of their divorces. (10) *Children* were regarded as a burden, and their education handed over to slaves. The exposure of infants and the practice of abortions was the general custom. (11) Tacitus wrote his "Germania" as a "tendency book," intended for the purpose of holding up before his educated, but demoralized countrymen a people, uncivilized but possessing great virtues. In it he says of Rome: "Corrumpere et corrumpi saeculum est" (to corrupt and be corrupt is the spirit of the times).

40. **Preparation.** The preceding sketch of the world in which Christ lived emphasizes: 1. The *fivefold preparation* for His coming: (a) Universal Empire. The whole civilized world was welded into an organic whole in which law and order was enforced and through which excellent roads were constructed. By the extension of Roman citizenship throughout the Provinces, life was protected. (b) Universal language: the Greek, (c) Universal peace. (d) Universal need, and (e) Universal expectation. 2. It also emphasizes the superiority of Christ and his gospel over the culture and religion of the old world, for history shows that he gloriously succeeded in overcoming the political, intellectual, moral and religious errors of the world, and in appropriating and spiritualizing the better elements of ancient civilization. Thus has been confirmed Christ's saying: "Be of good cheer, I have overcome the world," and the words of John, "Our faith is the victory which hath overcome the world" (I Jno. 5:4).

41. **Reference Literature.** Consult Dict. and Encycl. by Hastings, Davis, Piercy, Herzog, Schaff-Herzog, Sanford on the various topics. Also Breed, Preparation, Chaps. 11, 13 and 14; Description of a Roman Banquet, in "Quo Vadis" I, Chap 7. For a fine description of pagan degradation with references to Roman authors, see Farrar, "Early Days of Christianity," Chap. 1; also 2, 3 and 4; Lecky, History of European Morals; Uhlhorn, Conflict of Christianity with Heathenism, p. 15 and Ch. 11, on Moral Conditions; Friedlander, Roman Society (the 2nd Chapt. on "Luxury").

CHAPTER 6.

Sources of our Knowledge of Jesus.

42.   **Pagan and Jewish Sources.**   We have pagan, Jewish and Christian sources for our knowledge of the Life of Christ.   Of these, the first two, as well as the Christian Apocrypha, are either very meagre, or very unreliable. Only the books of the New Testament are of decisive importance.   The *pagan* sources are as follows: (1) The Roman historian *Tacitus,* in his Annals, Chap. XV, 44, writes that the Christians "derived their name and origin from one Christ, who in the reign of Tiberius had suffered death by the sentence of the procurator, Pontius Pilate." (2) *Suetonius,* in his "Vita Claudii," c. 25, says that Emperor Claudius expelled the Jews from Rome "because of constant tumults under the leadership of Chrestus," which is generally taken as a reference to Christ, concerning whose Messiahship heated controversies arose in the Roman Synagogue.   (3) The younger *Pliny,* in his "Epistles" X, 96, speaks of the Christians in Bithynia as followers of one Christ who "bind themselves with an oath not to enter into any wickedness, or commit thefts, robberies, or adulteries, or falsify their word, or repudiate trusts committed to them."

Jewish Sources. (1) *Josephus* has very little to say. When speaking of the martyrdom of James, he calls him "the brother of Jesus who is called the Christ" (Ant. XX, 9, 1).   This is surprising, the more so, as he has in Ant. 18, 5, 2 a very appreciative notice of John the Baptist.   His reticence is usually explained by saying that he really approved of Jesus' life and teaching, but was too cowardly to say so.   The famous passage in Jos. Ant. 18, 3, 3 is an interpolation.   It reads, "At this time (Pilate's) appeared (a certain) Jesus, a wise man, if indeed he may be called a man; for he was a worker of miracles, a teacher of such men as receive the truth with joy and he drew to himself many Jews, and many also of the Hellenes.   This was the

Christ, and when at the instigation of our chief men, Pilate condemned him to the cross, those who at first loved him, did not fall away, for he appeared to them alive again on the third day, according as the holy Prophets had declared thus, and a thousand other wonderful things of him. To this day the sect of Christians called after him, still exists." No one but a Christian could have written thus (2) Indirectly the whole of the *Old Testament* literature, the Old Testament *Apocrypha,* the Apocalyptic books, and the *Talmud* contain valuable material, especially for our knowledge of the teaching of Christ. (3) The *Talmud* contains many notices of the parents and teachers of Christ but these are intentional, malicious slanders, and not sources.

43. **Christian Sources.** (1) *Outside of the New Testament:* (a) *The Apocryphal* Gospels contain chiefly legends connected with the birth and early days of Jesus, and with his death and resurrection. Most of them are crude and childish tales. Harnack has constructed a list of sixteen such gospels, the most important of which are: the Gospel of the Hebrews, of the Twelve Apostles, of Peter, of Thomas, of Matthias, of Philip, of Eve, of the Infancy, the Acts of Pilate, the Protevangelium of James, and of Marcion. (b) The *Agrapha,* i. e. sayings attributed to Christ and other information, not found in our gospels, but scattered through the writings of the post-apostolic age. They add but little to our knowledge of the life of Christ. *Justin* Martyr gives the descent of Mary from David, and depicts the outward appearance of Jesus. Clement of Alexandria gives the names of the seventy disciples; Clement of Rome says the excitement produced by Jesus reached as far as Rome. As sayings of Jesus are reported, "Be ye good moneychangers." (Clem. Homilies) and, "Wherein I seize you, therein I judge you." (2) *Within the New Testament:* (a) *Paul's Epistles* are the earliest existing records of the events in the life of Christ: e. g. On the Lord's Supper and on Christ's death, burial, resurrection and appear-

ance, (I Cor. 11:24; 15:3-8, written in 57); his descent
from Abraham and David, his life of obedience (Rom. 1:
3; 9:5; 5:19; 15:3, written in 58); his humility (Phil.
2:5-11, written in 63); his poverty (II Cor. 8:9, written in
57). In *Acts* 20:35, Paul quotes as a saying of Christ "It
is more blessed to give than to receive." (b) *Hebrews* 2:
17; 4:15; 5:17 speaks of Christ's sufferings and the agony
in Gethsemane. (c) Peter 2:21, of Christ's sinlessness,
and II Peter 1:16 of the Transfiguration. But these may
be references to our Gospels, as most of the similar passages in Acts. (d) *Interpolations* in the New Testament.
John 7:53, to 8:11, the story of the Woman taken in
adultery; John 5:4, the angel at the Pool of Bethesda;
Matt. 6:11, the doxology to the Lord's Prayer; Mark 16:
9-16 on the Resurrection. The first two may rest on a
trustworthy tradition.

44. **The Four Gospels,** by Matthew, Mark, Luke and
John, are our principal sources of information. (1) *Matthew,* also known as Levi, the son of Alphaeus, a tax collector at Capernaum, called by Jesus from his work. He
obeyed and made a feast in honor of Jesus to which he invited his fellow publicans. Nothing else is recorded of
him in the gospels. Tradition says that he worked for fifteen years in Judea and afterwards in Parthia and Ethiopia.
(2) His *book*. Matthew seems to have written two books:
(a) The Logia, a collection of sayings of our Lord, but
containing no historical narratives, written in Aramaic. This
is lost to us. (b) Our Gospel, which is not a mere translation of the Logia, but a work originally composed in Greek
by Matthew or an assistant, into which all, or the larger
part of the Logia was interwoven. (3) Among the *original
readers* were Greek-speaking Jews, for he finds it necessary
to interpret Hebrew words like "Immanuel" (1:23),
"Golgotha" (27:33), and Christ's Prayer (27:46). (4)
Date and Place. It was written a little before A. D. 70,
for there is no indication in it that Jerusalem had been destroyed, but rather an allusion to the approach of the crisis.

("Let him that readeth understand" Matt. 24). It was
written in Palestine, city unknown. (5) *Characteristics*.
(a) More Hebraistic than the others in following Hebrew
idioms ("Kingdom of Heaven" from the Jewish reluctance
to use the name of God) ; Old T. quotations not found in the
parallel gospels are made from the Hebrew and not from
the LXX; (b) his standpoint and atmosphere is Jewish, he
commences the genealogy with Abraham, frequently quotes
O. T. prophesies which he sees fulfilled in Christ. (c) But
he is no opponent of the Gentiles, for he alone records the
visit of the Magi, and the Great Commission.

45. **Mark's Gospel.** (1) *Author:* John Mark, probably the son of the man with the pitcher (Mark 14: 13) and
Mary, in whose house the Jerusalem church met, (Acts 12.
12). He probably is the young man in Gethsemane (Mark
14: 51, 52) ; he was a nephew of Barnabas, (Col. 4: 10),
with whom he came from Jerusalem to Antioch, the helper
on Paul's first missionary journey, later again with Paul,
(Col. 4: 10, Philemon 24), and with Peter (I Pet. 5: 13
"My son"). (2) The *book:* Mark received his material
from Peter whom he accompanied to Rome as "interpreter,"
translating Peter's Aramaic sermons into Greek. Later he
"wrote down accurately everything that he remembered."
(From "The Elder" quoted by Papias). Justin Martyr
therefore calls Mark's gospel, "Memoirs of Peter." (3)
Date and place of writing: Before 65 in Rome, *i. e.* after
Peter's death and before the destruction of Jerusalem. The
reason for this date, the same as in Matthew. (4) The
original readers were Gentiles, probably Romans. (5)
Characteristics: Graphic, concrete, animated, emphasizing
powerful deeds of Jesus which would appeal to the Romans.

46. **Luke's Gospel.** (1) *Author:* The only Gentile
among the Biblical writers (Col. 4: 14 omits him from the
list of "those of the circumcision"), probably a Greek from
Antioch, a physician (Col. 4: 14), and, according to an old
tradition, a painter; a co-worker of Paul (Philemon 24),
and during Paul's second imprisonment the only faithful

attendant (II Tim. 4:11). The "we" sections in Acts
show that he was with Paul from Troas to Philippi (Acts
16:16-17). He remains at Philippi and after six years ac-
companies Paul to Jerusalem (20:5 to 21-18), and on the
voyage to Rome (Acts 27 and 28). (2) The *Book*. In a
preface, (1:1-5) he states its object and his method. He
desires to confirm the faith of a "Theophilus," and as none
of the existing gospels suited him, he writes one himself.
His method is very thorough: (a) He collects documents,
(b) examines eye-witnesses, (c) employs critical canons in
sifting the material, and (d) aims at writing a complete
biography, in distinction from the fragments before him.
(3) *Date and Place*. About 75, probably at Philippi, that is,
after the destruction of Jerusalem, for, in place of the general language in Matthew and Mark, Luke 21:20 and 24
gives a clear description of the siege and its issue, and while
in Matthew and Mark the final judgment is closely associated with the doom of Jerusalem, in Luke it is distinguished from the local event, and an interval is placed between the two (22:24). (4) *Characteristics*. (a) Better
Greek style except in the "Hymns" in Chapter 1 and 2,
which are thoroughly Hebraistic and point to a Hebrew
document; (b) the longest account of the infancy probably
derived from the Virgin and others; (c) A long account
(Ch. 9-19) of the Perean period not found in the other gospels; (d) without bias he illustrates Paul's teaching of the
universality of the Gospel.

47. **Synoptic Problem.** (1) The first three Gospels are
called *Synoptists* (syn-opsis, i. e. a common view) because
they view the life of Christ from a common standpoint, in
contrast to John's altogether different treatment. (2) The
problem is to find a theory which will account for the re-
semblances and differences in those gospels. (3) *Resem-
blances* are, (a) a common plan (infancy,— the forerunner,
baptism and temptation—ministry in Galilee—passion);
(b) a common selection of incidents. Of 88 incidents, they
have 71 in common, and only 17 exclusive (Matt. 5, Mark

3, Luke 9) ; (c) similar groups of scenes (death of John is introduced parenthetically by all three to explain Herod's terror). (d) Verbal agreements, not only in sayings of Jesus, which might be due to tradition, but also in narrative passages. (4) *Differences:* (a) Accounts of different events—about 17; (b) differences in several accounts of the same events (order of temptations in Matt. and Luke, blind men at Jericho). (c) *Verbal differences.* (5) *Proposed Solutions:* (a) Theory of oral tradition. The rabbinical method of teaching, by constant repetition of the same forms, had fixed these forms so thoroughly in the minds of the early disciples, that when later they began to write their gospels independently each one naturally used these stereotyped phrases. (b) Theory of *original documents.* All three synoptists had access to older documents, such as referred to in Luke 1:1-5. Two are usually mentioned: Matthew's Logia, containing sayings of Christ, and a "Primitive Mark," (Ur-Markus), still simpler than our Mark, for the narrative. Besides these each had a few independent sources, as e. g. for the infancy, the Perean period and the resurrection. (c) Theory of *mutual dependence.* Matthew's Gospel is based on the latter process: Mark abbreviated Matthew and Luke used both. The order may be also reversed. (d) The second theory of the two original documents is the one generally accepted at present as furnishing the most scientific answer to the question: How did our present first three gospels originate?

48. **John's Gospel.** (1) *Author:* John, the son of Zebedee and Salome, brother of James the elder, called by Jesus at the Jordan after the temptation. Later banished to Patmos, dies at Ephesus about 100. Author of five New Testament books. (2) *Date and place:* Between 85 to 90, at Ephesus. (3) *Characteristics:* Clement of Alexandria called it the Spiritual Gospel (and the Synoptists, the "Bodily Gospels"), because it is more doctrinal and theological. (4) *Authenticity.* (a) *External evidence:* As early as 125, verses from this gospel are quoted by Basilides,

although he does not mention the author. The first one to mention John as the author is Theophilus of Antioch in 170. (b) *Internal evidence:* The gospel shows, (1) that it was written by a Jew (not a Gentile Gnostic), for he quotes the O. T. from LXX and the Hebrew, and his style and spirit is Hebraistic; (2) A Palestinian, for he is familiar with the minute topography (Cana, Jacob's Well, places in Jerusalem). (3) A contemporary with the events described. He knows that the Samaritans expect the Messiah. He makes no reference to Gnosticism of the 2nd century. (4) He was an eye-witness. Three times he claims this: 1:14; 19:35; 21:24. The vivid details of the gospel suggest the same. (5) *Objections:* (a) Inconsistency with the character of John. In the synoptists he is a "Son of Thunder," passionate, but in John he is "the beloved disciple." Answer: Cannot both go together? (b) Inconsistency with the book of Revelation in style, tone and teaching. The Gospel is in good Greek, but Revelation is faulty; Gospel is liberal, Revelation, narrow. Answer: Revelation was written before John came to Ephesus and the Gospel in his riper old age, when his language, views and experience had undergone changes; (c) Inconsistency with the Synoptists. The Synoptists speak mostly of Christ's work in Galilee, John of that in Judea; the Synoptists give one year, as the duration of Christ's ministry, but John three. Answer: Luke 13:34 shows that even the Synoptists indicate more than one passover and one visit to Jerusalem. (6) *Solution.* (a) There is indeed a difference between John and the Synoptists. The books of the latter are more objective chronicles, while in the fourth gospel the teaching of Christ went through the crucible of John's personality, and is a reproduction of Christ's life and teaching in John's own language and thought. Hence the similarities of the sayings of Christ, and the Baptist's to John's. (b) John's Gospel is avowedly an argument (20:30, 31). Its selection of material is confessedly partial, its aim being to confirm the faith of the

Christians. Many of the best histories are written from this standpoint (Sallust). (7) The *differences* of the gospels speak for their genuineness, for all four exhibit that agreement in substance combined with difference in detail that usually marks the accounts of witnesses to the same event.

49. **Reference Literature.** Keim, Jesus of Nazareth on the Agrapha I, pp. 34 to 40; Bennet & Adeney, Biblical Introduction, pp. 277 to 340; Rhees, Life of Christ, pp. 21 to 44; Hast. D. of Jesus, Apocryphal Gospels, I, 671, also the articles on "Gospel" I, 659, and the different gospels; Burton, Short Introduction to the Gospel; The Earliest Sources for the Life of Jesus, by F. W. C. Burkitt; Farrar, Messages of the Book. Also the N. T. Introductions by Dodd, Bacon and Reake. See the masterful standard works by Theodore Zahn, 3 Vol. Prof. Godet, 2 Vols., and Weiss, 2 Vols.; Chamberlain, Aussprueche Jesu, 160; Beyschlag, Leben Jesu I, pp. 59-72; Gilbert, Life of Jesus, 74-78; Knowling, Witness of the Epistles; On Agrapha see Seeberg, Worte Jesu (in Christoterpe 1906); Pope's Die Sprueche Jesu; Uckley, Worte Jesu, die nicht in der Bibel stehen; Grenfelt and Hunt, Sayings of Jesus; Resch, Agrapha. On lost and uncanonical gospels, see Salmon's Introduction, 175 and 580. For the text of the Apocryphal Gospels, see "Apocryphal New Testament;" Ante-Nicene Fathers VIII, 361-476; Ferris, Formation of the N. T.; Ebrard, The Gospel History, p. 532; Farrar, Exc. II, O. T. Quotations, II, Talmud on Christ; Exc. 15 Traditional Sayings of Christ; Zoeckler, Handbuch der Theologischen Wissenschaften I, 382.

CHAPTER 7.

The Chronology of the Life of Christ.

50. **The whole life of our Lord** may be divided into three great, but in point of time very unequal, periods: (1) his pre-existence from all eternity to his incarnation; (2) his incarnate life upon earth, 33 years; (3) his life as the God-man in glory. (2) *The earthly life* of Christ, which alone can be treated historically, may be divided as follows:

I. **The Thirty Years of Preparation,** Dec. 25 B. C. 5-Jan., A. D. 27.

II. The Three and One-half Years of Public Ministry, Jan., A. D. 27-April A. D. 30.

(1) *The Year of Obscurity,* Jan.-Dec., A. D. 27. So called (a) because little of it is recorded in the gospels. The Synoptists are almost silent, and even John disposes of at least six months in two verses (Jno. 3:22; 4:3); (b) because during it Jesus emerged only slowly into public notice. This period may be subdivided into:

(a) The Opening Events of Christ's Ministry, Jan.-April, A. D. 27.

(b) The Early Judean Ministry, April-Dec., A. D. 27.

(2) *The Year of Popularity,* Dec., A. D. 27-April, A. D. 29. So called, because during it Christ became known all over the land and was received with great favor. The subdivisions are:

(a) The First Galilean Period, Dec., A. D. 27-Summer, A. D. 28.

(b) The Second Galilean Period, Summer, A. D. 28-April, A. D. 29.

(3) *The Year of Opposition,* April, A. D. 29-April, A. D. 30.   So called because during it public favor ebbed away, and the enmity of the rulers increased. The subdivisions are:

(a) The Third Galilean Period, April-Nov., A. D. 29.

(b) The Perean Period, Nov., A. D. 29-April, A. D. 30.

III.   The Week of Passion. Palm Sunday, April 2- Easter Sunday, April 9, A. D. 30.

IV.   The Forty Days of Resurrection Life. Easter Sunday, April 9, to Ascension Day, Thursday, May 18, A. D. 30.

In connection with the above dates it should be observed, (a) that there is a distinction between absolute and relative chronology. The first aims to show how the principal events in Christ's life fit in with the course of universal history, and the latter tries to arrange the single events according to their inter-relation. (b) That all the above calendar dates are only approximate, because they are not contained in the gospels but are conjectured by comparing the facts given in the gospels (Matt. 2:1; Luke 2:1, 2; 3:1) with information gathered from contemporaneous history. (c) The assignment of dates is not essential for the study of the more important problems with which a life of Christ has to deal. (d) The dates for the chief events in the life of Christ, such as his birth, the beginning of his ministry and his death have resulted from the following calculations.

51. **When was Jesus Born?** About Dec. 25, B. C. 5, or 749 A. U. C. We calculate this from the following data: (1) Matt. 2:1, says: "In the days of Herod" (the Great) Jesus was born. Now, Josephus, in Ant. 17, 8, 1, tells us that Herod died in March, B. C. 4, shortly after the eclipse of the moon of March 12. As time must be allowed for Christ's circumcision, presentation, the preparation and long journey of the Wise Men, it is safe to decide that Christ was born about Dec., B. C. 5. (2) Luke 2:2 says Jesus was born when an enrollment was made under Quirinius as governor of Syria. There was indeed a census taken when Quirinius was governor of Syria, but this was in 8 A. D., or ten years later. (Acts 5:36). Some therefore hold that Luke made a mistake by bringing that census in connection with Christ's birth. But the two greatest authorities, Zumpt and Momsen, think they can prove that Quirinius was twice governor of Syria, the first time in 750, and that then he finished a census begun by his predecessor but called by his own name. Others hold that Quirinius took the census in some official capacity other than governor (Andrews p. 4; Rhees p. 52). (3) From John 2:20 we infer that near the beginning of Christ's ministry the Herodian temple had been in course of erection for 46 years. As Herod began the building in 733 A. U. C., we add to this figure the 46 years which gives us the year 779 as the opening of Christ's ministry. Subtract 30 years—the age of Christ at that time—(Luke 3:23) and we have B. C. 5 or 749 as Christ's birth. (4) Matthew 2:2 states that at Christ's birth a wonderful star appeared. The great astronomer Kepler observed in 1603 an unusual conjunction of stars and by diligent search he found that in 747 A. U. C. a similar conjunction of Jupiter and Saturn had appeared to which in

748 Mars was added. Chinese records affirm that in 749 and 750 a comet was visible. (5) There are no data in the N. T. to fix the *day and the month* of Christ's birth. Dec. 25, first mentioned in the 4th century, was selected more for symbolical and practical reasons than on historical grounds. At this season of the year the pagans observed feasts in honor of the victory of the god of light over the god of darkness, because from Dec. 25th the days lengthen. How natural it was to substitute the birthday of the Light of the World! Neander thinks that the church favored this date and season to keep its members away from these heathen feasts by offering them something better. (6) These things show that *our present system of chronology* ("The Christian, or Dionysian Era") is incorrect. It originated with Dionysius Exiguus ("The Little"), a Scythian by birth, who died in 556 as Abbot of a monastery in Rome, In his book "Cyclus Paschalis" he decided on the year 754 A. U. C. ("ab urbe condita"—"from the building of the city"—Rome), as the year of Christ's birth. All the specialists agree that he erred, but as there is no unanimity as to how much he erred, his chronology still stands for all mere practical purposes, while in all scientific statements we have to use the awkward expression that Christ was born 5 years before Christ. But right or wrong we must give credit to the monk for his bright and true idea of reckoning time to and from Christ, because all the lines of past history converge and focus in him and all the lines of subsequent history find their starting point in him.

52. **When did Christ Begin His Public Ministry?** About Jan., A. D. 27. This may be calculated from three different dates: (1) Lu. 3:23 says, that Christ began his ministry when he was about 30 years old. By counting these years from the date of his birth, Dec. 25, B. C. 5, we get about Jan., A. D. 27, as the approximate date of his baptism, with which his ministry begins. (2) At the first passover of Christ's ministry, the temple has been 46 years in building (Jno. 2:20). Josephus says that Herod com-

menced the building in 733 A. U. C. By adding to this figure the 46 years we have 779 (or A. D. 27) as the date of
the opening of Christ's ministry. (3) Lu. 3: 1 says that
John began preaching in the fifteenth year of Tiberius.
As this emperor became co-regent with Augustus about 764
(Jan. A. D. 12), we add the two figures and thus get about
summer, A. D. 26 (or 779 A. U. C.) as the date for the
beginning of John's ministry. About 6 months later, or in
Jan., A. D. 27, Christ was baptized.

53. **How Long was Christ's Public Ministry?** (1)
A few writers insist on only *one year*. They place a literal
interpretation on Isa. 61: 2 ("the acceptable year of the
Lord"), and point to the fact that the Synoptists mention
only one passover during Christ's ministry. (2) Others accept *three passovers* in Christ's ministry, as recorded in
John 2-13; 6: 4; 13: 1, which will make its duration two
and one-half years (the tripaschal theory). (3) Many
holding that the "unnamed feast" in John 5: 1 was a passover, figure out *four passovers*. (Quadripaschal theory),
which will make Christ's ministry last three and one-half
years. (4) The latter is the most probable interpretation
and has been accepted as the basis for this text-book.

54. **When did Christ Die?** On Friday, April 7 (15
Nisan), A. D. 30, about 3 P. M. (1) The *year* 30 A. D.
results from adding the 30 years before his baptism and
the 3½ years of his ministry to the date of his birth,
Dec. 25, B. C. 5. (2) The Synoptists and John agree that
the *day of week* was Friday (Mk. 15: 42; Lu. 23: 56; Jno.
19: 31, 42). The same result is reached by counting back
three days from the "first day of the week," remembering
that the Jews counted the periods of time inclusively, that
is, fractions for entire periods. (3) All three Synoptists
declare plainly that the *date of the month* was 15 Nisan
(April 7), the first day of the passover season which lasted
8 days (Matt. 26: 17; Mk. 14: 12; Lu. 22: 15). (4) Many
authorities, however, insist that John's gospel means to say
that the paschal meal was yet before them when Christ was

crucified, and that the Friday of Christ's crucifixion was therefore the 14th of Nisan (April 6). They base their opinion on four passages in John. (a) John 13:1, "Before the feast of the passover Jesus washed the disciples' feet:" Answer, "before" does not mean a whole day before the passover, but a few minutes before the eating began. (b) Jno. 13:27, 29 says that some disciples thought that Judas left the table because Jesus had said: "Buy what things we have need of for the feast." Answer, If this meal had been held on 13 Nisan, this belief of the disciples can hardly be understood, since there would have been no reason for Judas' hurrying out at that time to make the purchases for which the whole of the next day would have been free. (c) John 18:28, "It was early; and they (the rulers) went not into the judgment hall lest they should be defiled, but that they might eat the passover." Answer, The "passover" referred to was the offerings of the first paschal day (the "Chagigah"), and not the paschal meal with which the feast began. But even on the supposition that this was 14 Nisan, the pollution contracted would have ceased at sunset, which was the time for the meal. (d) Jno. 19:14: "And it was the preparation of the passover," that is, the day preceding the passover. Answer, "Preparation" always means Friday, hence, "preparation of the passover" means "Friday, on which the passover fell that year," and not the Friday before the passover. The day following Christ's death is called a "great sabbath" (Jno. 19:31), either because it fell in the passover week, or to distinguish it from the feast- or minor sabbaths, of which there were seven. (5) The view that according to John Christ died on 14 Nisan has recently received strong support by an opinion of the Astronomical Society of Berlin, Germany, according to which the passover of the year A. D. 30 began on Friday evening, at sunset, so that, if Jesus died on a Friday, it must have been 14 Nisan. (6) The defenders of this view say that even the Synoptists favor them, for they record various activities

which show that it cannot have been the 15th of Nisan.
(a) Mark 15:21, Simon comes from the country. Answer,
but not necessarily from work. He had his lodging outside the city. (b) Mark 15:46, Joseph buys linen. (c)
Lu. 23:56, the women prepare ointment. Answer, All
these activities may have occurred on the first feast day
which was one of the seven so-called "feast-sabbaths" (The
first and the seventh day of the passover; the day of Pentecost; the first and tenth day of the seventh month; the first
and eighth day of the Feast of Tabernacles). These were
not regarded as equal in sacredness to the week sabbath.
(7) Presumptive evidence is also in favor of holding that
all four evangelists agree on the 15th of Nisan. (a) It is
improbable that Matthew and Peter (Mark's informant)
should have forgotten such an important fact. (b) If John
had intended to correct the mistake of the Synoptists he
would have done so in a more intelligible way. (c) Jesus
who habitually kept the law would not celebrate the passover a day before the legal time.

55. **Relative Chronology.** (1) Of the 150 principal
events recorded in the gospels about 100 are fixed as to their
chronological order by the common consent of the leading
harmonizers; about 25 are agreed upon by the majority, and
the remaining 25 are altogether uncertain. This explains
the diversity of arrangement in the various Lives of Christ.
(2) For a detailed chart of approximate dates in the Life
of Christ, combining the absolute and relative chronology
of his life, see the "Table of Contents" in front of this
book. It should be thoroughly memorized and constantly
referred to.

56. **Reference Literature.** Farrar, Excursus I, Date of Christ's
Birth; Exc. 8, The Unnamed Feast; Exc. 10, Was the Last Supper
a Real Passover? Hastings D. of Christ I, p. 413, "Dates;" Hast.
B. D. I, 410, on Length of Ministry; Cambridge, Greek N. T. on
John, Appendix I; Andrews, on Date of Birth, p. 1; Date of Death,
p. 452; On the Divisions of Christ's Life, p. 125; Zoeckler, Hand-

buch der theol. Wissenschaften I, 481; Wieseler, Chronology; Ramsay, "Was Christ Born at Bethlehem? Deissmann, Light from the Ancient East, Ch. IV, on "Social and Religious history in the N. T."

CHAPTER 8.

Selected Bibliography.

57. **On the World in Which Jesus Lived.** The next best thing to possessing a considerable fund of useful information is to know reliable sources where to get more. Of the voluminous literature on our subject we will mention only a few of such books as are easily accessible. Additional references will be found throughout the book. (1) On the *World in Which Christ Lived:* Geo. A. Smith, Hist. Geography of the Holy Land, and his 2 vol. on "Jerusalem." Schuerer, History of the Jewish People in the Time of Christ, 5 vol.; the standard work on the subject. Mackie, Bible Manners and Customs. Schneller, "Kennst du das Land." Breed, Preparation of the World for Christ. Riggs, History of the Jewish People. Matthews, History of N. T. Times. (2) For the *historical background:* Five novels, "Quo Vadis," by H. Sienkiewicz; "Ben Hur," by Wallace; "The Last Days of Pompeii," by Bulwer Lytton; "The Prince of the House of David," by J. H. Ingraham; "Titus," by Kingsley. These stories must be read with discrimination, always remembering that they interweave with historical facts much imaginative detail; but for a historical background they are very helpful. (3) *Good Harmonies,* by Stevens and Burton, Kerr and Robinson.

58. **Lives of Christ.** *Andrews,* The Life of our Lord: excellent on all questions of chronology, geography and harmony; *Farrar's* Life of Christ; descriptive and picturesque; *Sanday,* The Life of Christ (in Hastings D. of the Bible, and in book form), clear, very learned and comprehensive; also Sanday, Life of Christ in Recent Research; *Edersheim,* Life and Times of Jesus; good on Rabbinical literature

Jewish archæology and theology; *Stalker,* The Life of Jesus Christ; terse and clear; *Gladstone, W. E.,* "Ecce. Homo," *Seeley, J. R.,*" Ecce Homo: A Survey of the Life and Work of Jesus Christ;" *Robertson,* Epochs in the Life of Christ. Other works on the Life of Christ, by B. Weiss, Beyschlag, Neander, Lange, Oehninger, Keim, Hanna, Geikie, Gilbert, Rhees, Schmidt, Burton and Matthews, Holtzmann, Hase, Strauss, Renan, Dawson. For articles from the Jewish and Roman Catholic standpoint, see under "Jesus" in "Jewish Encycl." VII, and in "Roman Catholic Encycl."

59. **Dictionaries and Encyclopedias.** Every up-to-date Bible student, minister or lay member, should constantly consult one or more reliable dictionaries of the Bible. They contain valuable and most necessary information in condensed and well-arranged form, and thus save time and money. (1) Dictionaries of one volume and low priced: Davis, (Presb. Board of Publ. very good); also Smith, Schaff; (2) of one volume, but larger and higher priced: Hastings, Piercy, Standard, Guthe, Kurzes Bibelwœrterbuch; (3) of several volumes: Hasting, D. of the Bible, five vol., D. of Christ and the Gospels, 2 vol., D. of Rel. and Ethics, 3 vol.; Smith's 3 vol.; Riehm, Real Woerterbuch; Mensel, Handlexicon, 7 vol.; Encycl. Biblica, 4 vol. (able, but radical); (4) Herzog's Realencyclopaedie für Theologie und Kirche, 20 vol.; the Schaff-Herzog Encycl. in 12 vol. (a condensed and adapted translation of the German work); Sanford, Encycl. of Rel Knowledge, all general Enc., especially the Brittanica and Meyer's Conversationslexicon contain articles on Bible subjects. (5) A Concordance of the Bible will sometimes be necessary to look up passages. Young's Analytical C., Cruden's C. and Calwer Bibelconcordanz are very good.

60. **Catalogues and Pictures.** (1) Hill, a Guide to the Lives of Christ; Votaw, Books for N. T. Study; Thayer, Books and Their Uses; Vincent, Student's N. T. Handbook; Appendix to Rhees' Life of Christ; Ayres, Bibliography of Jesus Christ. (2) Views of places and buildings are very

helpful, also models, as Herod's Temple by Herr Schick of Jerusalem, the original of which is in the archæological museum of Harvard University.   (3) Photographs of paintings by masters like Raphael, Guido Reni, Hofman, Tissot, and others. On this whole subject see McConaughy, "Great Events in the Life of Christ," p. 200, and also "Complete Handbook of Religious Pictures," at the S. S. Commission, 29 Lafayette Place, New York, 15 cents. Scenes in the Life of Christ by Famous Painters, Union Press, 1816 Chestnut Street, Philadelphia, Pa. Very helpful are "The Illuminated Lessons on the Life of Jesus," by Forbush (Underwood and Underwood, New York).

CHAPTER 9.

General Review.

61. **On the World of Jesus.** (1) Give and explain names of the *Holy Land,* its location, boundaries, size, roads, climate, natural and political divisions. To what empire did it belong? Locate and describe the mountains and bodies of water associated with the Life of Christ. (2) With reference to the closing period of *O. T. history,* give designation, events and date of its beginning and end, its periods; a sketch of Herod the Great's life; rulers of Palestine after Herod's death, and names of their capitals; give an account of the Jewish war and the revolt under Hadrian. Name the two branches of Jews, the languages of Palestine, the three names of the Jews. With reference to the Sanhedrin state origin, number of members, qualifications, president, meeting place, powers. What was the method of collecting taxes? Sketch the history of the Roman emperors of the first century. (3) What was the *intellectual* status of the world in Christ's time; the contribution of the Jews to culture? Name and describe the three classes of Jewish literature; their influence on Christ and the N. T. books. Describe the principal schools of Greek philosophy; What effect did philosophy have on religion and morality of the Gentiles? How did it pave the way for Christianity? What was the status of Roman culture and literature? (4) *Were the Jews religious?* What unique idea pervaded the O. T. and Jewish religion. Define Messianic prophecy. What was the popular idea of the Messiah in Christ's time? Describe the three religious sects, also the scribes, Herodians,

Zealots, the great Synagogue, the proselytes, the mission of the Jews. How many sacred buildings? Name and locate the six parts of the *Herodian temple,* the two porches. Explain the name "court of women," and state the contents of the Holy of Holies, formerly and in Christ's time. Describe the origin of the *Temple at Heliopolis.* With reference to the *synagogue* explain its name, origin, organization, furniture and its arrangement, services and influence. Name the *seven feasts* in chronological order, and state when, why and how each was observed. Trace the origin of the *Samaritans* and describe their religion. What was the religious condition of the pagan world? (5) What was the *moral condition* of the world in Christ's time in general and in particular with reference to labor, slavery, luxury, marriage and divorce, treatment of children? Quote from "Germania" what is said on the morals of Rome. State the *five lines of preparation* for the coming of Christ. Explain how a universal language, good roads and Roman government facilitated the spread of the gospel.

62. **Sources, Chronology and Bibliography.** (1) Name and describe the pagan, Jewish and extra-Biblical sources of information concerning Christ. What contributions to our knowledge of Christ's earthly life may be derived from Paul's and Peter's letters and also from the interpolations? State with reference to each gospel: by whom, for whom, when, where, with what purpose it was written; what is the "synoptic problem" and what is the present state of its solution? (2) State the *date of Christ's birth,* beginning of his ministry and death. In each case show from N. T. passages that these dates are approximately correct. What is the length of Christ's ministry. Name in order the periods of Christ's life and state with what event each begins and ends. Why does it seem natural to count time to and from Christ? Who was the author of the Christian system of chronology? (3) Name by title and author some of the most important books on "The World in which Jesus Lived" and on the Life of Christ.

PART II.

The Events of the Life of Christ

DIVISION I.

The Thirty Years of Preparation

From the Birth of Jesus until His Baptism. From December
25, B. C. 5, to January, A. D. 27.

CHAPTER 10.

The Introduction.

John 1: 1-18; Lu. 1: 1-4; 3: 23-38; Matt. 1: 1-17; Harmony
1-3.*

63. **John's Prologue.** The roots of the divine-human
life of which the gospels present a brief sketch reach into
the depths of eternity. (1) *The true nature of the word.*
John declares: In the beginning was the Word, and the
Word was with God, and the Word was God. All things
were made through him. In him was life, and the life was
the light of men. (2) *The Word Revealed to Men.* John,
a man sent from God came to bear witness of the light, that
all might believe through him. When Christ came unto
his own, they that were his own received him not. But as
many as received him, to them gave he the right to become
children of God, even to them that believed on his name.
(3) *The Word Reveals the Father.* The Word became

* These figures at the head of each chapter refer to the sections in
the "Harmony of the Gospels" by Profs. Stevens and Burton.

.iesh and dwelt amongst us (and we beheld his glory, a glory
as of the only begotten from the Father), full of grace and
truth.   No man hath seen God at any time; the only begotten Son who is in the bosom of the Father, he hath declared him.

64. **Luke's Preface.**   The divine-human life of Jesus on
earth is described with great care by the four evangelists.
Luke alone speaks of the method he pursued.   He says:
As many have drawn up a narrative of those matters which
have transpired among us (as they delivered them unto us,
who from the beginning were eye witnesses and ministers
of the Word), it seemed good to me also, having traced the
course of all things accurately from the first, to write unto
thee in order, most excellent Theophilus; that thou mightest
know the certainty concerning the things wherein thou
wast instructed.

65. **The two Genealogies.**   (1) The object of intro-
ducing into the gospels the genealogy of Jesus was to show
that he as the Messiah was the Son of David.   (2) Matthew's table begins with Abraham and traces his line in 14
generations to David; then through Solomon in 14 generations to the time of the Babylonian captivity; then in 14
generations to Jesus.   (3) *Luke* begins with Jesus and
traces his descent to Nathan the son of David; then back
to Abraham; but not stopping there as Matthew did, he
carries the pedigree back to Adam the son of God.

66. **Explanatory Notes.**   1. Name and compare the historical
sources of the section; memorize Jno. 1:18.   2. The *first clause*
of John 1:1 declares the eternity of the Logos, and the emphatic
word is *"was;"* the second, his distinct personality, and the emphatic word is, *"with;"* the third, his co-equality with the Father,
and the word *"God"* is to be emphasized.   3. *Arianism* (condemned
at the Council of Nicæa, 325) taught, "There was a time when he
was not."   Modern Unitarianism holds similar views.   4. *A word* is
that through which one makes himself known to others.   Jesus is
called "the Word," because through him God made himself known
to man.   5. *The application* of the term "Word" to Christ was
doubtless suggested by his own words in John 8:42; 12:44-50;

16:28; 17:8-14. The thought is in full accord with the teaching of Paul regarding the nature and work of Christ (Phil. 2:5-9; 2 Cor. 8:9; Gal. 4:4; Col., chaps. 1 and 2); and with Heb. 1:1-4. It is a philosophical statement of a vital element in the early Christian faith and thought. 6. *John gives the philosophy* of the incarnation while the Synoptists tell the story. 7. The *preface of Luke* emphasizes the credibility of his gospel. He first states the reason why he wrote it, namely, (a) to supplement the oral teaching of Theophilus, and to confirm his faith. (b) Because none of the existing gospels suited this purpose. Second, he explains his method; (a) he examined the existing gospels; (b) he compared the verbal reports of eye-witnesses; (c) all material thus furnished he sifted critically; (d) he aimed to write a complete sketch of the Life of Christ; (e) he arranged his material chronologically. 8. All admit that Matthew's genealogy refers to Joseph. As to Luke's table, some hold that it also refers to Joseph, while others believe that he means to give Mary's descent. 9. *The fact* of two different genealogies is perplexing. For if both tables are referred to Joseph, the dissimilarity of the names is remarkable, and if Luke's is referred to Mary, the similarity of names creates difficulties. 10. *The scope* of the two gospels explains why Matthew traces Christ's descent to Abraham and Luke to Adam. Matthew, writing for the Jews, shows that Jesus was the heir of David, being the legal son of Joseph, and he therefore begins with Abraham and descends through King David to Christ, his heir. Luke, writing for the Gentiles, begins with Christ, the second Adam, ascends to the first Adam, the son of God by creation.

67. **Reference Literature.** Consult the dictionaries; On the Logos, and the genealogies, especially Hastings D. of C. II, 49; "Only Begotten," Hastings D. of C. II, 281; for a full discussion of the genealogies, see Andrews, 60-65, and Smith, New Testament History, 192.

68. **Questions for Discussion.** 1. To what religious views is John's prologue opposed? 2. What great truth of the Gospel does it emphasize? 3. Why did only four of the early gospels survive? 4. What are the most marked differences in the two genealogies?

CHAPTER 11.

The Annunciations of John and Christ.

Lu. 1 : 5-56; Matt. 1 : 18-25.   Harmony, 4-7.

69. **To Zacharias.** (1) There was in the closing days
of Herod the Great (37-4 B. C.) a priest named Zacharias
and his wife's name was Elisabeth. They were both righteous but had no child, which in the O. T. was considered
a punishment; and both were now old. (2) While he
executed the priest's office in the order of his course (probably on Oct. 3, B. C. 6), his lot was to enter into the sanctuary and burn incense while the people were praying without. There appeared unto him an angel at which Zacharias
was troubled. But the angel said, "Fear not, thy supplication is heard and thy wife Elisabeth shall bear thee a son,
and thou shalt call his name John" (Hebrew, Jochanan—
"God is gracious"). (3) Thou shalt have joy and gladness, and many shall rejoice at his birth. He shall be great
in the sight of the Lord; he shall drink no wine nor strong
drink; and shall be filled with the Holy Spirit; he shall
work in the spirit and power of Elijah, to make ready for
the Lord a people. (4) Zacharias said, Whereby shall I
know this? for I and my wife are old. The angel said, I
am Gabriel that stand in the presence of God. Behold
thou shalt not be able to speak until the day that these things
come to pass, because thou believedst not my words. (5)
The people were waiting for Zacharias, and marveled because he tarried in the Temple. When he came out, he
dismissed them, making signs. When the days of his ministration were fulfilled, he departed unto his house at Hebron,
and the promise was fulfilled.

70. **To Mary.** (1) In the sixth month after the appearance to Zacharias (in March 25 B. C. 5), the angel
Gabriel was sent to Nazareth, to Mary, a virgin, betrothed
to Joseph of the house of David. (2) He greeted her.

"Hail thou, that art highly favored, the Lord is with thee."
When she was greatly troubled at this salutation, the angel
said, Fear not, Mary; for thou hast found favor with God.
Thou shalt bring forth a son and call his name Jesus.   (3)
He shall be great and be called the Son of the Most High.
(4) Mary said, How shall this be, seeing I know not a man.
The angel answered, The Holy Spirit shall come upon thee,
wherefore the holy thing which is begotten shall be called
the Son of God.   (5) Mary said, Behold the handmaid of
the Lord.   Be it unto me according to thy word.   And the
angel departed from her.

71. **To Joseph.** (1) Mary was betrothed to Joseph;
but before they came together, she was found with child
of the Holy Spirit.   (2) Joseph being a righteous man, and
not willing to make her a public example, was minded to
put her away privily.   (3) But an angel appeared unto
him in a dream saying, Fear not to take unto thee Mary thy
wife, for that which is conceived in her is of the Holy
Spirit.   She shall bring forth a Son and thou shalt call his
name Jesus: for it is he that shall save his people from their
sins.   (4) Joseph did as the angel commanded him, but
knew her not till she had brought forth a son.

72. **Visit to Elisabeth.** (1) Following the angel's suggestion (Lu. 1:36), Mary went to Hebron, to the house
of Zacharias, and saluted Elisabeth.   (2) When Elisabeth
heard the salutation of Mary, she was filled with the Holy
Spirit, and said, Blessed art thou among women, and blessed
is the fruit of thy womb.   And whence is this to me that
the mother of my Lord should come unto me?   (3) Then
Mary broke out into the words of the Magnificat: "My soul
doth magnify the Lord, and my spirit hath rejoiced in God
my Saviour."   (4) After three months, Mary left for
Nazareth, just before John's birth.

73. **Explanatory Notes.** 1. Name the historical *sources* of this
chapter, and notice the difference of Chaps. 1 and 2 of Luke from
the rest of the gospel. They show so strong a tinge of the Aramaic
idiom as to force the conclusion that the material must have come

from an Aramaic document, probably from Mary, whom Luke may have met while in Jerusalem, and at Cæsarea (Acts 27). 2. Locate the *places* on the map of Palestine and on the plan of the Temple; memorize Luke 1:46-47. 3. On *Herod the Great,* see ¶12. 4. As the *priests were so numerous* (20,000 at this time), that not all could officiate at the same time, they were divided into twenty-four courses, of which the course of Abiah was the eighth. (1 Chron. 24:10). Each of them officiated for one week. These weekly groups were again divided into five to nine subdivisions, each of which officiated one day. To avoid contentions, the various functions of the day were distributed every morning by lot. Of these functions, the offering of incense was considered the highest. It was offered twice a day before the morning and evening sacrifices, at 9 A. M. and 3 P. M. 5. On *Nazareth* see ¶7 and a Bible Dictionary. 6. Give a *sketch of Mary's life* from the material in the New Testament. 7. Tradition says, that *Mary's parents* were Joachim of Nazareth and Anna of Bethlehem; that at this time she was about 18 years old, whilst Joseph, a carpenter was much older (girls in the East were usually married between 14-17 years and even earlier). 8. On Dec. 8, 1854, *Pope Pius IX* went so far as to declare that Mary was conceived without sin. In memory of this event, he caused the erection of a monument in the Piazza di Spagna in Rome. In the church calendar the festival of the Annunciation falls on March 25 and is often called "Lady Day." 9. The seed of *Mariolatry* is not found in the New Testament where the virgin is invariably called "Mary." (Heb. Miriam), without any of the titles of dignity later applied to her. We find it rather in the marked propensity of paganism to deify human beings, and especially in the inclination of the male portion of the Latin race to worship a female in preference to a male idol. 10. "Hail" (Latin *"Ave."*) was an ordinary mode of salutation (Matt. 28:9). But these words of the angel (Luke 1:28) have been perverted into a ground for worship, and the "Ave Maria" is the daily prayer of millions. It is composed of the greetings by Gabriel and Elisabeth (Lu. 1:28, 42). The service is known as "Angelus" (the "Angels' Greeting"), of which the Catholic people are reminded in the evening by the ringing of a bell. 11. *"Jesus"* is the Greek form of Jehoshua, or abbreviated, Joshua, "Jehovah our Saviour," from Jehovah and Hoshea (a Saviour). As Joshua saved Israel from its enemies, so Jesus was to save the world from its greatest enemy. The title of Saviour in the sense of Conqueror is often applied to Christ by John, Rev. 2:7, 11; 3:5, 12, 21; 5:6. 12. The "Ave Maria" and the "Magnificat" are the first two of the five hymns dealing with the Advent of Christ, recorded by Luke. They took their names from the opening word of the Latin version of the Bible. The others are the Benedictus of Zacharias, the Gloria in Excelsis by the Angels, and the Nunc Dimittis of Simeon.

74. 1. *Betrothal* meant "the making sacred" and was usually accompanied by a social and festive ceremony; it was as strong as marriage, and could not be broken except by legal divorce. 2. Both *annunciations were necessary.* The one to Mary saved her from dreadful perplexity and suffering, and that to Joseph because he, on the mere testimony of Mary, could not have accepted so extraordinary a story. 3. On Jewish marriage customs, see D. B. There were seven days of feasting, lambs were sacrificed and there was also a procession of girls with lighted lamps and sprays of myrtle. 4. The *obvious sense* of Matt. 1:25 and Luke 2:7 refute the notion of the perpetual virginity of Mary. "Firstborn" implies subsequent children.   According to Matt. 13:55 she had after Christ's birth, four sons and at least two daughters. 5. The *visit to Elisabeth* was suggested by Gabriel (Luke 1:36), its object being sympathetic conference. 6. The *distance* from Nazareth to Jerusalem is 80 miles; and from Jerusalem to Hebron 17 miles; the whole journey would occupy 4 or 5 days. There were three routes: through Samaria, or Perea, or along the sea coast. 7. *Elisabeth's little hymn* of praise is a beautiful instance of humility; for, being the wife of a priest, Mary was her inferior in station as well as in age. 8. The *Magnificat* of Mary, borrows many expressions from Leah, Gen. 30:10, 13, and Hannah, 1 Sam. 2:1-10, which every Israelite knew by heart; but she enlarged and transfigured these expressions. She praises God for his great goodness (1) in permitting her to become the mother of the Messiah (vss. 46-49) and (2) in fulfilling to his people his ancient prophecies (vss. 50-55).

75. **Practical Lessons.** 1. As in the case of Mary, submission, obedience and faith prove our fitness for higher service. 2. Moody said, God always uses the one nearest him. 3. Zwingli (preaching in the church at Einsiedel, which claims a miraculous picture of Mary), said, "Not to Mary, but to the Son of Mary you must pray." 4. When Christ is born in man spiritually, the method is still: "The Holy Spirit shall come upon thee." 5. Birth, money and talent, make a man great in the sight of man; but humility and obedience in the sight of God (Lu. 1:15). 6. Unbelief and dumbness are like cause and effect. "I believed, therefore have I spoken." 7. The spirit of wine is a bar to the spirit of God. 8. True prayer, like incense, is composed of the sweet spices of praise, gratitude, petition, confession, intercession; love to God and men, faith and hope. 9. That an answer is delayed is no sign that the prayer is unheard (Goethe "Hermann and Dorothea").

76. **Reference Literature.** Sanford, on Immaculate Conception, Image Worship, Mariolatry, Angelus.—Andrews, 53-70; Edersheim, Life of Christ, Bk. II, Ch. 3, p. 133-155; Geikie's Life of Christ, Ch. 8; Schuerer, Jewish People, I. A. 216; Hasting's Dict. of Christ and the Gospels I, p. 76; Orr's and Sweet's books on the Virgin Birth; Goudnod's and Schubert's famous music to "Ave Maria;" Keble, "The Annunciation," a poem in his Christian Year; Photographs of Shick's model of the Temple; Guido Reni's, Degers, and Hofman's paintings of "The Annunciation;" Liddon's Sermons on the Magnificat; Hast. D. of C. Asceticism I, 128; Hast. D. of C. Ave Maria I, 159; Hast. D. of C. Jesus I, 859; Edersheim, The Temple and its Ministry, for a full description of this service.

77. **Questions for Discussion.** 1. Describe Zacharias' duty in the temple. 2. Why was it appropriate that the angel should appear to Zacharias just at this time and place? (See Ps. 50:23). 3. Was the sign given to Zacharias an encouragement or a rebuke? 4. To what kind of persons does God reveal his will? (Luke 1:6-13). 5. Nature and functions of angels (Heb. 1:14). 6. Why, in spite of these annunciations, is Jesus called the "Son of Joseph" in the N. T.? 7. Where did Luke receive the information for his first two chapters?

CHAPTER 12.

The Births of John and Jesus.

Luke 1:57-2:20; Matt. 1:18-25.   Harmony 8-10.

78. **John's Birth.** (1) About June 25, B. C. 5, John was born. Elisabeth's neighbors and kinsfolk rejoiced with her. (2) On the eighth day they came to circumcise the child, and would have called him Zacharias. But his mother, whose privilege it was to name the child, said, He shall be called John. (3) They said, There is none of thy kindred that is called by this name, and made signs to his father, what he would have him called. He wrote, and said, his name is John, and they marvelled all, but he blessed God. (4) All these sayings were noised abroad throughout all the hill country of Judea, and all that heard them

said, What then shall this child be? (5) Zacharias was filled with the Holy Spirit, and prophesied in the words of the Benedictus, saying, Blessed be the Lord, the God of Israel, for he hath visited and wrought redemption for his people. (6) The child grew and waxed strong in spirit, and was in the desert of Judæa, west of the Dead Sea, until the day of his showing unto Israel.

79. **The Birth of Jesus.** (1) In those days (Autumn, B. C. 5), there went out a decree from Cæsar Augustus that all the world should be enrolled. This was the first enrollment made when Quirinius was governor of Syria. (2) All went to enroll themselves every one to his own city. And Joseph also went up from Galilee to Bethlehem to enroll himself and with him went Mary, who was betrothed to him. (3) While they were there she brought forth her first-born son; and wrapped him in swaddling clothes and laid him in a manger because there was no room for them in the inn. (4) And there were shepherds in the field, and an angel of the Lord stood by them, and the glory of the Lord shone round about them, and they were sore afraid. The angel said, be not afraid, for I bring you good tidings of great joy which shall be to all people, for there is born to you this day in the city of David a Saviour, who is Christ the Lord. And this is a sign unto you, ye shall find a babe wrapped in swaddling clothes and lying in a manger. (5) Suddenly there was with the angel a multitude of the heavenly host, praising God and saying, Glory to God in the highest and on earth peace among men in whom he is well pleased. (6) When the angels went away from them, the shepherds said, let us now go to Bethlehem and see this thing which has come to pass. They came with haste and found Mary and Joseph and the babe. On the way they made known the saying which was spoken unto them about this child, and all wondered at the things. (7) But Mary kept all these sayings, pondering them in her heart. (8) The shepherds returned, glorifying and praising God for all the things they had heard and seen.

80. Explanatory Notes. 1. Name and compare the *sources* of the chapter. 2. Locate *places* on the map; memorize Lu. 2:11. 3. The *origin of circumcision* among the Jews dates from God's covenant with Abraham (Gen. 7). By it a boy was officially enrolled as a member of the Hebrew nation (For the law see Lev. 12:3). 4. John became a *Nazarite* (derived from "Nazar" to separate), one who vowed not to taste intoxicants or cut his hair (Num. 6:1-21). Other Nazarites were Samson and Samuel. That Paul was one (Acts 18:18) is a mere conjecture. The Nazarites were ascetics, i. e. men who abstained from things lawful in themselves (food, wine, marriage, etc.) for the purpose of attaining a higher stage of personal holiness. 5. According to Josephus there were *many pious Jews,* who, disgusted with the corruption of the times, retired to the deserts where they became teachers of divine things, and gathered about them many disciples. The case of John was therefore not an unusual one. 6. On the *time of Christ's* birth see "Chronology," ¶51. 7. On *Caesar Augustus,* see ¶18. 8. *Bethlehem* ("House of Bread") is beautifully situated on the eastern slope of a limestone ridge overlooking the wheat fields of Boas. It is covered with terraces and filled with vines and fruit trees. The city is six miles south of Jerusalem. Its population is from 5,000 to 8,000. 9. The castle-like *Church of the Nativity* is said to have been built by the Empress Helena, mother of Constantine the Great, in A. D. 330, and is the oldest church in Christendom. Much of the original construction still remains. The nave has 44 fine stone pillars but is bare and cheerless. It is occupied by the Greeks and Armenians. The transcepts and choir which are of very large proportions, are in charge of the Latins, and are richly ornamented with gifts of kings and queens. 10. On each side of the choir are steps leading to the *Cave of the Nativity,* which is under the altar and is about 40 feet long, and 12 broad and 10 high. It is paved with marble and lighted by 32 lamps. It is held in great veneration. The tradition that this is the place of Christ's birth reaches back to at least 140 A. D.. We find it first reported by Justin Martyr in his "Dialogue with Tryphon." It was confirmed by Jerome who spent thirty years of his life (370 to 400) in a cavern near Bethlehem, where he made his translation of the Scriptures known as the "Vulgate." In this cave we find to this day the form of a star and the Latin inscription, "Hic de virgine Maria Jesus Christus natus est." ("Here Jesus Christ was born of the Virgin Mary") 11. *Swaddling clothes,* were long bands of cloth, in which then as now in the east a babe was tightly wrapped, arms and all, for the first forty days after its birth.

81. 1. Schneller, a native of Palestine, in his "Kennst du das

Land" holds that *Joseph's* home had always been Bethlehem, and that he was a "tekton" (Matt. 12 : 55), a house builder, a mason, rather than a carpenter. As such he went wherever he found work, exactly as the builders of Bethlehem still do to-day. Working for a season at Nazareth, he met Mary and was betrothed to her; his intention to take her to his home city was precipitated by the decree concerning the census; they went to B. with a view of staying there, for after the Presentation they returned to B. and would also have done so on their return from Egypt if they had not feared Archelaus. 2. An *"inn"* (*khan*) is a low structure built of rough stones and generally only a single story in height, forming a square enclosure for the cattle and arched recesses for travelers. 3. Schneller contends that the place where Joseph and Mary stopped was not the public "inn," but *some private house,* for the Greek word "Batalyma" means simply "stopping place," while the word for a public inn is "Pandocheion." The legend that Christ was born in "a stable," he says, arose from the fact that a manger is mentioned. But this is sufficiently explained by the Oriental custom that very often men and beasts live close together under one roof. 4. If, as is said, the *flocks at Bethlehem* were destined for Temple sacrifices, these men cannot be regarded as ordinary shepherds. The site is now occupied by a few dilapidated houses, called the "Village of the Shepherds."

82. **Practical Lessons.** 1. Lives of usefulness are commonly traceable to pious parents (Lu. 1 : 6 and 15 to 17). 2. Inability to speak publicly for God is no sure sign that the heart is not right with God. (Lu. 1 : 22). 3. What shall the child be? A blessing or a curse? Every birth is an occasion for joy and hope but also for fear and awe. 4. "No man prepares for an emergency in a moment. What he is in an emergency is determined by what he has been habitually for a long time. This in turn will determine his future" (Lu. 1 : 80). Bosworth. 5. Imitate the Shepherds: they heard, went, found, made known, returned to work praising God. 6. No room in the inn. No rudeness was meant but only indifference. So it is to-day. Every chamber of our soul is already crowded with wealth, pleasure and business. Christ is crowded out of our families, politics, business, pleasure, literature and even of some churches. 7. The incarnation was a manifestation, (1) of God's love ("Jesus" a Saviour. Immanuel—God with us). (2) Of his wisdom (He came not as God or an angel). (3) Of his faithfulness (all was "fulfilled" concerning place, tribe, etc.). 8. A German mystic said: Though Christ a thousand times in Bethlehem be born, If he is not born in thee, thy soul is all forlorn. The cross of Golgotha thou lookest to in vain, Unless within thyself it be set

up again. 9. Christmas (from the Christ—Mass read at midnight of Dec. 25); German "Weihnacht," from weihen (consecrate) and night. The festival can be traced back to about 300 A.D.

83. **Reference Literature.** Farrar, Ch. 1; Andrews, 70-88; Stalker, Ch. 1. Consult a good Dict. of the Bible, on "Inn." Edersheim, Life of Christ II, 6. Geikie, Life of Christ, 9. Ramsey, W. M.—"Was Christ Born at Bethlehem?" For some of the early legends concerning the birth and childhood of Jesus see "Protevangelium of James," and the "Gospel of Thomas." For the Jewish calumnies, see Laible ("Jesus Christ" in Talmud, 9 to 39) and Jewish Encycl. under "Jesus." Virgil, in the fourth Eclogs says that a child from Heaven was looked for who should restore the Golden Age and take away sin. Longfellow's Golden Legend gives specimens of Apocryphal stories. Sermons by F. W. Robertson on the early development of Jesus. A tradition says that a Sibyl appeared to Cæsar Augustus at the Temple of Jupiter Capitolinus and announced to him Christ's birth. On the site of that temple there stands to-day the church Ara Cæli, with the "Bambino," (Baedeker. Ital. p. 250), a gorgeously clad image of the Divine infant carved in Jerusalem from the wood of an olive tree taken from Gethsemane in the 15th century. Birth and Infancy of Christ by L. M. Sweet. Pictures: "Holy Night" (Correggio, Dresden); "Birth of Jesus" by Murillo (Vatican); "Madonna" Raphael (Dresden); "Ben Hur," first pages. Beautiful Hymns: "Oh, little town of Bethlehem," Phillips Brooks; "It came upon the midnight clear," by Sears; "Stille Nacht," Adeste fideles!

84. **Questions for Discussion.** 1. Quote the first gospel sermon (Lu. 2:11). 2. What does the word "gospel" mean, who used it first and why is the term applied to the Christian message (Luke 2:10). 3. What is meant by the Incarnation? 4. Why was the birth of Jesus a cause of great joy? 5. Show from Mary's song what kind of a person she expected her son to be.

CHAPTER 13.

The Infancy of Jesus.

Lu. 2: 21-39; Matt. 2: 1-23.　Harmony 11-14.

85.　**Circumcision.**　On Jan. 1, B. C. 4, when Christ was eight days old, he was circumcised and his name was called Jesus.

86.　**Presentation in the Temple.**　(1) When Jesus was forty days old, February 2, B. C. 4, his parents brought him to Jerusalem to present him to the Lord (because he was the first-born son), and to offer a sacrifice,—a pair of turtle doves or two young pigeons.　(2) There was a man in Jerusalem whose name was *Simeon:* he was righteous, devout, looking for the consolation of Israel: and the Holy Spirit was upon him.　It was revealed to him that he should not see death till he had seen the Lord's Christ.　(3) When he came into the Temple, and there met the parents with the child Jesus, he received him into his arms, blessed God and spoke the "Nunc Dimittis," Now lettest thou thy servant depart, O Lord, according to thy word, in peace, for mine eyes have seen thy salvation.　(4) His parents marvelled at these sayings.　Simeon blessed them and said to Mary, This child is set for the falling and rising of many in Israel and for a sign which is spoken against.　And a sword shall pierce through thy soul.　(5) Also Anna, a prophetess, coming up at that very hour, gave thanks unto God and spake of him to all them that were looking for the redemption of Jerusalem.

87.　**Visit of the Wise Men.**　(1) Soon after the presentation, about Feb., B. C. 4, wise men from the East came to Jerusalem saying, Where is he that is born King of the Jews, for we saw his star in the East and are come to worship him.　(2) When Herod the Great heard this, he was troubled and all Jerusalem with him.　Gathering together all the chief priests and scribes he enquired where the Christ should be born. They said, In Bethlehem of Judea, for thus it is written through the prophet Micah. (3) Then Herod privily called the wise men and learned of them exactly what time the star appeared. And he sent them to Bethlehem and said, search out exactly concerning the young child and when you have found him bring me word that I also may come and worship him. (4) They went their way and the star went before them, till it stood over where the child was. They went into the house, saw the child with Mary, fell down and worshipped him and offered unto him gold, frankincense and myrrh (the customary gifts of subject nations, Gen. 43:11; I Kings 9:2-10). (5) Being warned of God in a dream that they should not return to Herod they departed into their own country another way.

88. **Flight into Egypt and Slaughter of the Innocents.** (1) When they were departed, an angel appeared to Joseph in a dream, saying, Arise and take the child and his mother and flee into Egypt and be thou there until I tell thee. For Herod will seek the child to destroy him. He did so and remained there until the death of Herod. (2) When Herod saw that he was mocked of the wise men, he was exceeding angry and slew all the male children in and around Bethlehem, from two years old and under, according to the time which he had exactly learned of the wise men. (3) When Herod was dead, about March, B. C. 4, an angel appeared in a dream to Joseph, saying, Take the young child and his mother and go into the land of Israel, for they are dead that sought the child's life. He did so, but when he heard that Archelaus was reigning over Judea, he was afraid to go thither and being warned of God in a dream, he withdrew into Galilee and dwelt in Nazareth.

89. **Explanatory Notes.** 1. Name and compare the *sources,* especially Lu. 2:39 with Matt. 2:22. Locate the places on the map and the plan of the temple; memorize Lu. 2:29. 2. The *presentation* of the first born male child was made on the forty-first day after the birth (Lev. 12:1-8), for a two-fold purpose: (a) for the

mother's purification from legal or ceremonial uncleanness. **If** the woman was rich, she brought a lamb for a sacrifice, if poor either two doves or two pigeons, each pair costing about 16 cents. One of these was for a sin offering in view of the ceremonial defilement, the other for a burnt offering to restore fellowship with the Lord. Mary brought the offering of the poor, which fact indirectly confirms the view that the Magi with their rich gifts came after the Presentation. (b) The child was brought into the temple also for the purpose of *redeeming him from priestly* service. When Jehovah destroyed all the first born sons of Egypt and spared all the first born of Israel, he ordained that this fact should be kept in everlasting remembrance by the consecration of the first born son of every Israelite to his own special service (Ex. 13:2). When later the tribe of Levi had been especially set apart for the priesthood (Num. 8), he allowed the first-born of the other tribes to be redeemed from the priestly service. This was done, first, by the presentation of the son in the Temple, by which act God's ownership was recognized and second, by the payment of five shekels (a shekel was variously estimated at from 50-80 cents) in exchange for the son. 3. The *presentation* in the time of Jesus took place at the magnificent Nicanor Gate, beyond which women were not allowed to go. 4. Simeon's conception of the Messiah was more universal and spiritual than that of most religious leaders of that day. He believed (a) that the Gentiles are to share in the Messianic glory; (b) that the Messiah will be a sufferer, not an earthly king; (c) that he will not meet popular expectation. Many will stumble over him and this opposition will be like a sword in the mother's heart. 5. Luke 2:39 does *not contradict* Matthew 2:22. Luke had said all he intended to say on the infancy of Jesus and he closes with the general statement that Christ passed his early youth and manhood at Nazareth, and not in Bethlehem. Either he did not know the story of the wise men or decided not to incorporate it in his life of Christ.

90. 1. The *Magi were a tribe of the Medes,* similar to the Levites, to whom were entrusted all the priestly functions, chief features of which were the study of astrology and the interpretation of dreams. They were the repositories of whatever science, philosophy, medical skill, and religious mysteries the Eastern people had. They came from a country outside of the Roman Empire, either Media, Arabia, or Persia. 2. The Magi no doubt received from the Jews in the Eastern dispersion their *knowledge of the Jewish Messianic hopes,* especially of the prophecy of Baalam (Num. 24:17), and Daniel. They shared the general expectation in the East at this time that a great King should be born in Judea to rule the world,

This rumor is even mentioned by the Roman historian Suetonius in his Life of Vespasian (ch. 4), and by Tacitus, in his History, v. 13. 3. *On the star* see ¶51, (4). 4. The belief that the *Magi were* kings, 3 in number, named Casper, Melchior and Balthasar, and the notion of "Ben Hur" that they represented Asia, Europe and Africa has no basis in history. The names and number were perhaps taken from one of the medieval "Mystery and Miracle Plays." 5. To commemorate this event, the festival of *Epiphany* ("Appearance") has been inserted in the church calendar on January 6th, and the Sundays following have been named after this day. 6. The famous *Cathedral of Cologne* in Germany claims to possess the bones of the Magi. 7. The *slaughter of the children* has been called into question, but it is in perfect keeping with Herod's otherwise well known extremely savage character. On this point Josephus says, "He was brutish, and a stranger to all humanities." It was only one and by no means the greatest of his crimes. He caused the murder of his wife, Mariamne and his three sons. And knowing that the Jews would rejoice over his death, he had thousands of the most promient Jews imprisoned in the circus at Jericho and gave secret orders that immediately after his death they should be killed, so that at least they and their friends might have cause to weep for his death. The order was not executed. When Herod's death was announced, his sister set all the prisoners free. Playing on the Greek words, Emperor Augustus said "He would rather be the "hus" (swine) of Herod than his "huios" (son), for being a Jew, he would not kill a swine. 8. *Rachel was the patron* saint of Bethlehem, because she died and was buried near the city. (Gen. 35: 16-20). 9. The church regarded the "innocents" of Bethlehem as the first martyrs and placed their names in the church calendar, on Dec. 26. 10. The flight involved a *journey of at least 225 miles.* if the tradition is true that the holy family abode in the Jewish colony at Memphis. 11. Galilee and *Perea under Herod Antipas,* a son of Herod the Great, were better ruled than Judea where Archelaus continued the oppressive policy of his father. For instance, not long after his accession he killed 3,000 Jews, in the Temple, at the Passover (Jos. Bell. Jud. II, 1, 3), and later he killed many Samaritans (Jos. B. J. 117-3; Ant. 17, 9, 3).

91. **Practical Lessons.** 1. Christ is the tester of men's hearts. 2. Simeon, a type of God-fearing old age, (a) the Spirit his guide, (b) faith his comfort, (c) the Saviour his joy, (d) heaven his desire. 3. If Simeon and Anna had not been constant attendants at the temple they would have missed the greatest experience of their lives. 4. It is not for lack of God's help that men do not find Christ, but lack of sincere purpose on their part. 5. The

scribes were like guide posts showing the way but not following it, a warning to all religious teachers. 6. The Magi were led by a sign suited to their peculiar mode of life. God speaks to every man in the language which he best understands. 7. The significance of this story lies in the fact that it is a symbol of what was to take place on a larger scale in the centuries to come. Israel rejected the Messiah and the Gentiles received him. 8. Wicked men are troubled by that which brings hope to the world: by preaching, revivals, moral reforms. Here is a test of our character. 9. Those are the truly wise men who use their learning to find God. 10. How often the very persons who live nearest to the means of grace are those who neglect them most. 11. The slaughter of the innocents by modern Herods is still going on, physically, morally, religiously, by neglect, ignorance, cruelty, fashions, over-work in factories, bad company, saloons, cigarettes, bad examples, harmful reading, low amusements, unclean habits, gross immorality. 12. Children have their guardian angels in the persons of faithful parents, teachers, friends, pastors, Christian spirit in the family, good literature, pure amusements, religious atmosphere, good state laws, good personal habits and local customs. 13. Types of four classes of men: (1) Those who earnestly seek the truth; (2) those who rest in the mere knowledge of the truth; (3) those who are fearfully alarmed at the truth; (4) those who are happy possessors of the truth. 14. Despotism drives the best people from the land. (Archelaus; later, the Huguenots, Puritans, the German Palatines to Pennsylvania). 15. Herod a type of men who try to suppress religion by cunning or force.

92. **Reference Literature.** Stalker, Ch. 1, 9; Farrar, Ch. 2, 3, 4; Andrews 89-108. Paintings: Simeon, by Dobson; the Magi, by Hofman, and Pfannschmidt; E. Frommel, Epiphanien, Christoterpe, 1882. Wallace, "Ben Hur," Ch. 1-5; Edersheim, Ch. 8; On "Unconscious Prophecy of Heathendom;" Trench's "Christ, the Desire of all Nations;" Herod's career and end are well illustrated by Shakespeare's "Richard III." On Herod's last days, see Josephus Antiquities, XVII, 6, 8. On the ministration of the angels, Beecher's Life of Christ, p. 39. Legends tell us that on the way to Egypt, the dragons, lions and leopards, adored Jesus, the palm trees bowed down to give them dates and all the idols fell from their pedestals when he entered the country. On Luke 2: 32, see Byrant's Library of Poetry and Song, p. 389, "Edwin and Paulinius;" On the Presentation: E. M. Myers' The Jews, their Customs and Ceremonies, p. 38; Edersheim, The Temple and its Services. One of Dr. Chalmer's famous "Astronomical Discourses" answers the objection to the coming of the Son of God, derived from the greatness of the universe; Robertson's sermons on the "Star of the East."

93. **Questions for Discussion.** 1. Why was Christ subjected to circumcision? (Gal. 4:4). 2. What did Simeon see in the Messiah that others had not seen? (Luke 2:32, 34, 35). 3. Why did God guide the Magi by the star instead of by an angel? 4. Why did the star lead them first to Jerusalem? 5. Why did Herod become so nervous? 6. What names and titles are here applied to Jesus? 7. How does God guide men now? 8. How do Luke and Matt. differ in their account of the movements of Christ's parents after the presentation?

CHAPTER 14.

Early Life in Nazareth.

Luke 2:39-52; Matt. 2:23. Harmony 15-17.

94. **Childhood.** The child Jesus grew, waxed strong, was filled with wisdom and the grace of God was upon him.

The Boy Jesus in the Temple. According to the law, Jesus' parents went every year to Jerusalem to the passover. When he was twelve years old, they took him along (April 8, A. D. 8). When they were returning, Jesus tarried behind in Jerusalem, but his parents knew it not. They missed him, but supposing him to be in the company ahead of them, they went a day's journey and sought him among their kinsfolk and acquaintances. When they found him not, they returned to Jerusalem seeking him. After three days they found him in the Temple, sitting in the midst of the teachers, hearing them and asking them questions. And all that heard him were amazed at his understanding and his answers. When his parents saw him, they were astonished; and his mother said, Son, why hast thou thus dealt with us? Behold thy father and I sought thee sorrowing. He said unto them, How is it that ye sought me? Knew ye not that I must be in my Father's house? They understood not the saying which he spake unto them, but his mother kept all these sayings in her heart.

95. **Eighteen Years of Silence and Growth.** Jesus went with his parents to Nazareth, was subject unto them,

advanced in wisdom and stature, and in favor with God and men.

96. **Explanatory Notes.** 1. Name the *sources,* locate the places; memorize Lu. 2:49. 2. *Christ's development* (Luke 2:40, 52), shows how real and normal a life he lived. He grew physically, intellectually, and spiritually, not out of sin, but into goodness. Growth is no sign of imperfection. A tree has in each stage of its development its own characteristic perfectness. 3. *Education.* Jesus' teachers were God, the Bible, nature, his godly parents, his teachers, his visits to Jerusalem. 4. *Jewish method* of child training: (a) As soon as Jewish children could talk they were made to commit the "Shema," the Jewish creed, consisting of 19 verses from Deut. 6:4-9; 11:13-21; Num. 15:37-41, and named from the first Hebrew word (as our Creed from "credo") and as they grew older (boys at least) were taught to write them out. (b) When six years of age boys were sent to school. Schools in most cases were attached to the synagogues in town (Luke 4:20). Compulsory attendance upon schools, according to the Talmud, dates from the famous Rabbi Simon Ben Shatach, the brother of queen Alexandria (about 75 B. C.). From this we infer that Jesus as a child also attended the village school of Nazareth. (c) There were institutions of higher learning in Jerusalem, corresponding somewhat to our theological and law schools, but these he never attended, John 7:15. (d) Besides, the education at school, the Jewish child was educated in his father's house, in the synagogue and the workshop. (e) The character of education among the Jews was exclusively religious and patriotic, its aim being to stimulate the conscience and engrave upon it the law of God. (f) As was the custom, Jesus followed the trade of his father. The Talmud says, "On the father lies the task of circumcising his son, of instructing him in the law, of teaching him a craft; for not to teach him a trade, is to teach him to steal." So Jesus is called a "tekton," Mk. 6:3, not a carpenter, as the Oriental houses were built of stone (see Schneller "Kennst du das Land," Ch. 7). 4. *Language.* The mother tongue of Jesus was Aramaic. He no doubt understood classical Hebrew, for although at his time it was a dead language, it was familiar to the Palestinian Jews. It is almost certain that he knew Greek for he seems to have spoken to non-Jews (Greeks, Pilate, centurion) without an interpreter.

97. **Christ's Brothers and Sisters.** (a) In Mk. 6:3 and Matt. 13:55 four brothers are mentioned by name: James, Joseph, Simon and Judas or Jude. (b) Two of these, James and Jude, became influential in the early Christian church. Both were authors of

epistles, and James was bishop of Jerusalem. (c) Sisters are also mentioned, but neither the number nor the names are given. The plural in Matt. 13:56 however, implies more than one (Consult Matt. 12:46-50; 13:55-56; Mk. 3:31; Luke 8:19; John 2:12; 7:3; Acts 1:14; 1 Cor. 9:5; Gal. 1:19). (d) In what relation did these stand to Christ? There are three theories, known by the names of their original or chief advocates: (1) The cousin or Hieronymian theory; (2) the half-brother, or Epiphanian; (3) the full-brother or Helvidian theory. (1) The *Cousin* theory. Jerome (died 420) held that the so-called brothers of the Lord were really his cousins, i. e. children of Mary, the sister of the Virgin, and Alpheus, or Clopas; and that two of them, James and Jude, became his apostles. Objections: (1) the Greek term denoting their relation is always "brothers and sisters" and never cousins or kinsman. Sound exegesis must hold to the primary meaning of these terms until compelled to depart from it. (2) The James mentioned in Gal. 1:19 is not called an apostle, for the correct translation of that passage is: "I saw none other of the apostles; but I saw James the brother of the Lord." This places James in contrast to the apostles and excludes him from them. (2) The *half-brother* theory. Epiphanias, bishop of Salamis in Cyprus (died 403), held that Christ's brothers and sisters were children of Joseph by an earlier marriage. This is possible, but (1) there is no hint of it in the N. T. (2) If Joseph had a son older than Jesus, that one would have been the heir of David and the N. T. argument that Jesus was the son of David, would lose its basis and force; (3) They always appear in connection with Mary as her children and younger than Jesus. (4) If older than Jesus, their continued presence with Mary is very unusual as they would have been married by the time Jesus was about 30 years old. (3) The *full-brother* theory. Helvidius, a layman, (living about 380 at Rome) held that they were Jesus' brothers and sisters in the full sense of the word. We favor this theory, because, (1) it takes the words in their natural meaning; (2) it is in harmony with Matt. 1:25 and Luke 2:7, for "firstborn" implies later born children. Against this view the Roman Catholics and others raise three objections: *Obj.* 1. It is derogatory to the dignity of the Virgin to suppose that after the birth of Jesus, she bore children to Joseph in the natural way. Answer: This would degrade Mary in the eyes of those only who, contrary to the teaching of the Bible, (a) regard celibacy as a higher state than God-ordained wedlock, and who (b) hold to the dogma, of the "Immaculate Conception of Mary," (made an article of faith on Dec. 8, 1854 by Pius IX), which dogma asserts that Mary "from the first instant of her conception by a singular grace and privilege of Almighty God was preserved from all stain of original sin." The "perpetual virginity of Mary" is based on a mistaken veneration of the Virgin. *Obj.* 2. Why did his brothers not believe on him? John 7:3. If younger than he, he could have molded their character. Answer: Their attitude was one of doubt, and not hostility. *Obj.* 3. Why did Christ on the cross commit Mary to John, if she had children living? Answer: (1) Very likely the brothers were not present. (2) John was Mary's nephew. (3) He was Christ's intimate friend and more congenial to her at this time than even her own children (Andrews, 111-123).

98. 1. Object of the stated attendance at the Feasts: (a) Promotion of the unity of the people. (b) Awakening of religious life by means of large, enthusiastic meetings. (c) Sociability. 2. The *twelfth year* being in Israel the dividing line between childhood and youth, marked a solemn period in the life of the young Israelite. At that age he was "confirmed" by being presented by his father to the elders in the home synagogue, who examined him as to his religious knowledge, blessed him and declared him a "son of the law." This made him a full member of the Jewish Church, bound to observe the law, which included the annual visit to Jerusalem at the three great feasts. 3. This incident illustrates the manner in which the *consciousness of his divine nature,* of his peculiar relation to the father, and of his mission developed itself in the mind of the child. 4. The *answer to his mother* is not beyond his tender years; it contains a presentiment nourished by his study of the O. T. 5. Jesus' *obedience was genuine,* there was no theatrical posing for the purpose of making an impression of piety. 6. The *attendance of women* at the great feasts was not required by the law. 7. Here is the *last mention of Joseph.* He seems to have died before the opening of Christ's ministry. 8. The early Christians surprised at the sobriety of the canonical gospels, tried to make up for their silence by composing the apocryphal gospels of the Infancy and Youth of Jesus. Read some of them.

99. **Practical Lessons.** 1. Every child should be trained to take an interest in Bible study, and should be taught, not by lecture only, but mostly by questions and answers. Encourage the child to ask questions. 2. Parents should be able to answer the question: Where is my boy to-night? 3. The places one freely and naturally resorts to are an index to one's character. 4. Children should never go where they are not willing to have parents and teachers find them. 5. The best parental oversight cannot always be perfect. 6. There is value in great religious gatherings. 7. Religion makes children obedient to parents and attractive to all. 8. Conversion belongs al-

most exclusively to the years between 10 and 25, for then the ability to reason arises. After 25, habits of thought and activity are more firmly fixed. Hence, train up the child when young in the way he should go. 9. Cheerful obedience to lawful authority is the most beautiful feature of a child's character and a great safeguard for it. It has also an ennobling effect on people of all ages. 10. Joseph's and Mary's home training: (1) their method: example, early teaching, taking him to the temple, seeking him when lost, reproof, meditation on the boy's sayings. (2) The result: normal development in body, mind, feeling and will power; obedience, usefulness in later years, care for his mother. 11. The boy Jesus an example to modern boys: (a) in his love for God's house. (b) His eagerness to learn God's word. (c) His desire to do God's will ("must"). (d) His obedience towards his parents. 12. Parental religious training should be supplemented by S. School and special pastoral instructions.

100. **Reference Literature.** Ramsay, "Education of Jesus;" Consult Bible dictionaries on all subjects. Farrar, Ch. 5, 6, 7; Stalker, 11-24; Andrews, 108-123; On Child Conversion, see Starbuck "Psychology of Religion," p. 21-36; On the Brethren of Jesus, Hastings B. D. I, 320; Lightfoot, "Galatians," pp. 252-291; Smith, "New Testament History, p. 281; On the methods of Jewish teaching, see Trumbull's "Yale Lectures on the Sunday School;" "Bedeutung der 30 Jaehrigen Stille," Christoterpe, 1889; Longfellow's "Golden Legend" gives some specimens of the Apocryphal stories of Jesus' childhood. See also the Apocryphal New Testament; C. Campbell Morgan's "The Hidden Years at Nazareth;" Lew Wallace's Boyhood of Christ;" Sermon by Robertson, "Early Development of Jesus; Thomas Hughes, "Manliness of Christ;" first 3 chaps. "Jesus, the Model Child." Painting by Hofman.

101. **Questions for Discussion.** Why do some Christians so strenuously assert that Jesus had no real brothers? Why did Jesus attend the Passover when he was just 12 years old? Describe the influences among which Jesus grew up, and his own inner experiences: (a) home, (b) school, (c) synagogue, (d) Scripture, (e) companions, (f) manual labor, (g) scenery and nature, (h) the moral condition and Messianic hopes of the people, (i) communion with God, (j) thought about God and feeling toward him, (k) thought about his future work. In what sense were the great feasts in Jerusalem religious revivals?

102. General Review.

1. With reference to the entire period of preparation, state, (a) length, (b) events and dates of its beginning and end, (c) sources

of information, (d) the 14 events in their proper order, (e) the leading persons, (f) locate the places on the map, the plan of Jerusalem and of the Temple, (g) name and locate the five hymns recorded by Luke. 2. Call to mind the four announcements of Christ's coming before, and the four after, his birth. State what classes of men they represented, assign a reason for each. Give the names applied to Jesus and how much of his nature and work they reveal. 3. Describe Christ's two visits to the Temple; the probable amount and character of his secular and religious education, his trade. 4. Give the names of Christ's four brothers, and outline the three theories as to their relation to him.

DIVISION II.

The Year of Obscurity

From Christ's Baptism to the Opening of the Galilean Ministry
—January to December, A. D. 27—the full calendar
year A. D. 27.

Two Subdivisions.

I. **The Opening Events of Christ's Ministry.** From Christ's Baptism to the first Passover of his Ministry, Jan.-April 11, A. D. 27.

II. **The Early Judean Ministry.** From the Passover to the Opening of the Galilean Ministry, April 11-Dec., A. D. 27.

I. The Opening Events of Christ's Ministry.

CHAPTER 15.

John's Ministry—Christ's Baptism and Temptation.

Matt. 3: 1—4: 11; Mark 1: 1-13; Lu. 3: 1-23; 4: 1-13.
Harmony, 18-20.

103. **John's Ministry.** (1) When the time was fulfilled the forerunner of Christ began his *great work* of announcing the presence of the Messiah and preparing the people. (2) This was in the *summer of A. D. 26*, in the 15th year of the reign of Tiberius Cæsar, Pontius Pilate being governor of Judæa, and Herod Antipas being Tetrarch of Galilee, and his brother Philip Tetrarch of the region of Ituraea, and Trachonitis, and Lysanias, Tetrarch of Abilene, in the high priesthood of Annas and

Caiaphas. (3) He came into all the region round about the Jordan, (Bethany; A. V. Bethabara in Perea). (4) His *raiment* was of camel's hair, held by a leather girdle about his loins, and his food was locusts and wild honey. (5) His message was, Repent ye, for the kingdom of Heaven is at hand. (6) As a *symbol* of moral cleansing, God directed him to baptize those who were penitent. (7) There went out unto him *Jerusalem,* all Judæa, and all the region about the Jordan. (8) All *classes came.* (9) To the *multitude* (Luke) and especially when he saw among them many Pharisees and Sadducees (Matthew), he said, Ye offspring of vipers who warned you to flee from the wrath to come. Bring forth fruit worthy of repentance, and think not within yourselves, we have Abraham to our father; for I say unto you, that God is able of these stones to raise up children unto Abraham. Even now the axe lieth at the root of the trees: every tree that bringeth not forth good fruit is hewn down and cast into the fire. (10) Then the *multitude* (not the Pharisees and Sadducees) asked him, what must we do? He said he that hath two coats let him impart to him that hath none, and he that hath food, let him do likewise. (11) The *publicans* said: Teacher, what must we do? He said, extort no more than that which is appointed to you. (12) The *soldiers* asked him, What must we do? He said, Extort from no man by violence, neither accuse any man wrongfully; and be content with your wages. (13) And as the people reasoned, whether *John were the Christ,* he said, I baptize you with water, but there cometh he that is mightier than I, the latchet of whose shoes, I am not worthy to unloose. He shall baptize you with the Holy Spirit and with fire. The fan is in his hand, thoroughly to cleanse his threshing floor and to gather the wheat into his garner, but the chaff he will burn up with unquenchable fire.

104. **Baptism of Jesus.** (1) About January, A. D. 27, after John had been preaching for over six months, came Jesus from Nazareth to John to be baptized. He was then

about thirty years old. (2) John would have hindered him saying, I have need to be baptized of thee, and dost thou come to me? But Jesus said, suffer it now, for thus it becometh us to fulfill all righteousness. Then he suffered him. (3) When Jesus was baptized and went up from the water, the heavens were opened unto him, and he saw the Spirit of God descending as a dove, and coming upon him, and a voice out of the heavens said: This is my beloved Son in whom I am well pleased.

105. **Temptation of Jesus.** (1) Immediately after his baptism Jesus was led up of the spirit into the wilderness, to be tempted of the Devil. Here he was with the wild beasts. (2) When he had fasted forty days and forty nights he hungered. Then the tempter said, if Thou art the Son of God, command that these stones become bread. He said, it is written, Man shall not live by bread alone, but by every word that proceedeth out of the mouth of God. (3) Then the Devil taketh him into the Holy City, and set him on the pinnacle of the temple, and said, If Thou art the Son of God, cast thyself down, for it is written, he shall give his angels charge concerning thee: and on their hands they will bear thee up, lest haply thou dash thy foot against a stone. Jesus said, Again it is written, Thou shalt not make trial of the Lord thy God. (4) Again the Devil taketh him into an exceeding high mountain, and showeth him all the kingdoms of the world, and the glory of them and said, all these things will I give thee, if thou wilt fall down and worship me. Then said Jesus, Get thee hence, Satan, for it is written, thou shalt worship the Lord thy God, and him only shalt thou serve. (5) Then the Devil leaveth him for a season, and angels came and ministered unto him.

106. **Explanatory Notes.** 1. This period is called the *"Year of Obscurity"* because so little of it is recorded. The reason for this silence seems to be that the Synoptists considered this year to be a part of the preparatory period, with negative results as far as the rulers in Jerusalem were concerned. 2. Name and compare the

sources, locate the places on the map and the plan of the temple; memorize Matt. 4: 10. 3. *On Tiberius* and other rulers in Luke 3: 1 see ¶13 and ¶18. 4. According to the law of Moses there could be only *one high priest* and he was to serve for life. But in Christ's time this law was disregarded. Annas was high priest A. D. 7-14, when the Roman procurator Gratus deposed him; but he controlled his successors, several of whom were of his own family. Caiaphas was Annas' son-in-law and ruled 18-36 A. D. In the N. T. we find both acting together, with a sort of joint authority. 5. *Locusts* are still used for food in the Orient. 6. *John's work* was threefold: (a) to announce that the kingdom of God was at hand and the Messiah about to appear, (b) to bring the nation to repentance, "to make ready a people prepared for the Lord," (c) to point out the Messiah personally to the nation when he should appear (Andrews, Life of our Lord, p. 129). 7. The Greek *"metanoia"* means "a change of mind" regarding God, one's self, final destiny, etc., such as leads to a corresponding change of the outward life. 8. *Kingdom of God:* (a) O. T. idea: God's dominion over the whole world and especially over Israel through the Messiah, (b) Current Jewish idea: Israel's political supremacy over the world preceded by the overthrow of Rome. (c) The term as used by Christ has not a constant meaning. There are at least four great ideas which are at times associated with it. (1) The dominion of God *realized within* and without (with emphasis on the realization within) Matt. 3: 2; 4: 17; 6: 10; 13: 44-45. The rule of God in the hearts of men. (2) *The people* who are under the dominion of God, Mark 8: 14; Matt. 13: 24-41. (3) *Blessing and privileges* that accompany the divine dominion (Matt. 5: 10). (4) *The Place* that is to be occupied in the future by those who are under the divine dominion (Matt. 7: 21; 8: 11; 13: 43; 25: 34; 26: 29). 9. The *form of baptism* was either original with John or adopted from the baptism of the proselytes. It signified moral cleansing as a preparation for entrance into the kingdom. The fact that it was performed only once shows that it was not one of the Levitical washings, but was designed to mark one decisive act in life. Neither is it exactly the same as the Christian sacrament of baptism, which was instituted three years later and is a sign and seal of conversion, and an initiation to church membership. 10. Christ's *"baptism in the Holy Spirit"* John views rather as a baptism of judgment, a holy breath of God sweeping away the wicked (Mal. 4: 1) and not so much as the sanctifying, life-giving influence as in Acts 1: 5. It must be noticed that he addressed people whom he called "offspring of vipers." Luke 3: 17 means that the Messiah would judge the people for their sins. "Fan" means a shovel for throwing grain into the air, so that the wind may blow the chaff out of the wheat. "Wheat" means God's true people. "Chaff" means the wicked. John's idea then was that the Messiah would be a strict judge, who would reward the good and punish the wicked. This was a great advance on the popular idea that he would be a great king and warrior. 11. If at that time the Jews required of the *proselytes* that they be baptized (which some deny), John must have angered the Pharisees by baptizing all classes of Jews, thus implying that the whole nation was spiritually unclean and morally not above the Gentiles. 12. The *shoe-lachet* was the thong or strap by which the sandal was bound to the foot. To unloose this or to bear the shoes (Matt 3: 11) was the office of the lowest slave.

107. 1. **Why did Jesus seek to be baptized?** 1. *Not for confession* and pardon, for he was sinless. 2. Not simply to encourage John's work and set an example to others. 3. Not as *our substitute,* for his disciples were also baptized; but (1) to provide a public mode of announcement, when in the presence of many the fact might be fully established that the Messiah had come (John 1 : 33). (2) To consecrate himself to his Messianic work by this kind of ordination. All priests in the Jewish church were inducted into office by baptism. (Ex. 29: 4.) Inasmuch as Christ was to be a priest (Heb. 5: 6) it was proper that he should enter by this door, thus fulfilling ceremonial righteousness. 2. The commencement of a *new course of life,* was the element which his and other people's baptism had in common: in the case of the people it prepared them to *receive* pardon, in the case of Jesus, to *bestow* it. 3. The *voice from heaven* was to John a revelation (Jno. 1 : 33) and meant for Jesus (a) divine approval of the step, (b) official anointing for his mission and (c) endowment with power. 4. The *dove* was considered a sacred bird in the East. The brooding dove was symbolical of the quickening warmth of nature. In Jewish writings, the Spirit hovering over the primeval waters is expressly compared to a dove. 5. *Christ was tempted,* (a) for his own sake, as a test of character (like the first Adam), (b) for men's sake that he could sympathize with us in similar circumstances (Heb. 4: 15-16). 6. *The form of temptation.* (1) Satan appeared in visible form (the text to be taken literally); (2) Some person, perhaps a Pharisee, urged him to carry out the Jewish ideal of the Messiah. (3) Christ had a vision of the powers of darkness which would attempt to turn him aside from his true mission to do the Father's will. (4) Satan presented evil thoughts to Christ's mind—tempting him as he does us. In this case the temptations were inward and spiritual, not outward and physical and all occurred in the wilderness when meditating upon his future plans. Later he communicated

his experiences in the allegory of our text. (5) But whether the objective or subjective form is accepted, Christ's experience in the wilderness proved a real temptation to him, that is, a strong solicitation to sin. 7. *The essence of Christ's temptation* was to take the short and easy road to the Messiahship by conforming to the popular ideal rather than the hard and slow way of a spiritual deliverer. 8. The objective preparation for Christ's public ministry was the work of John and the subjective preparation, his baptism and temptation. 9. The *traditional place* of Christ's temptation is the desolate Mount Quarantania, a high and precipitous wall of rock about 1500 feet above the plain and about 7 miles northwest of Jericho. It resembles Gibraltar and upon its summit are still visible the ruins of an ancient convent. Midway below are caverns hewn into the rock where hermits formerly retired to fast and pray in imitation of the 40 days' fast. 10. The *pinnacle of the temple* was either the highest part of the temple proper, or more likely the top of the Royal Porch, more than 200 feet above the Kidron Valley (see plan of the temple).

108. **Practical Lessons.** 1. God's word comes to us through (a) the Bible, (b) our conscience, (c) Providence in history, (d) the Holy Spirit, (e) the counsels of God's people. 2. There is no possible way to escape the unquenchable fire but to cease to be chaff. 3. The essence of true religion is always righteousness—right living—before God, judged by his standard, and neither ritualism nor emotionalism. 4. The wrath of God is a result of his love. Because sin ruins men, God hates it, but loves the sinner. 5. According to the law John should have become a priest, but obeying a higher call he worked as a layman. Meditate upon the immense streams of blessings which have flowed into the church from the work of laymen. 6. At conversion everyone must forsake his characteristic sins: the Sadducees, their false doctrine, worldliness and indifference; the Pharisees, their formalism, hypocrisy and self-righteousness; the publicans, their graft and deceit; the soldiers, their rudeness and thieving. And you? 7. To denounce popular sins and influential sinners is never a pleasant duty, often dangerous, but greatly needed. 8. Character draws. In Homer's Iliad an ill-tempered man delivers a fine speech against King Agamemnon, but without any effect on the army, because of the speaker's bad character. It is a rule to make the cannon one hundred times heavier than the shot. 9. Public pledges (such as baptism) are powerful means of sustaining character. The Spaniard Cortez, after landing in Mexico, burned the ships so that return was impossible. 10. Temptation means, (a) a test of character by trials (Jas. 1:2) and (b) more frequently, enticement to sin (Jas. 1:

13-14). 11. A favorable impression made on the heart by evil does not constitute sin, but only our yielding to it by the consent of our will. These evil suggestions came not from the soul of Jesus but to his soul from the outside. 12. The Devil leaves Christians only for a season; hence "Watch." 13. To originate doubt of God's truths is always one of Satan's methods. (Gen. 3:1). 14. Christ's three temptations are addressed to the three chief avenues by which sin enters the soul: gratification of the senses, love of praise, and desire for gain. 15. Means for winning the contest: (a) to know the real enemy (Luther: Satan is first black, then white, finally divine!), (b) to use the true weapon, (c) to stand firm, (d) to keep in view the crown of victory.

109. **Reference Literature.** Consult Dictionaries on John, Baptism, Temptation. Farrar, Ch. 8, 9; Stalker, Ch. 2, 3, 4; Andrews, 137-158; Goethe's "Faust," pledges himself to Satan (Faust I, 2nd Act); On the scene of John's ministry, see Smith's Historical Geography, 261, 312-317; On John's preparing the way, see Trumbull's Studies in Oriental Social Life; Robinson, Palestine I, 567; Thompson, The Land and the Book, 617; Campbell Morgan, Crises of the Christ, p. 137; Fairbairn, Studies on the Life of Christ, p. 93; Hanna, Life of Christ, 80-81.

110. **Questions for Discussion.** 1. What is repentance? 2. What phase of Christ's work did John emphasize? 3. What made it natural for the people to suppose that John was the Messiah? 4. Was duty repulsive to Jesus? 5. What should be our attitude toward religious rites? 6. What absorbed Jesus so that for forty days he was indifferent to food? 7. Is there any special significance in the number forty? (Ex. 24:18; 1 Kings 19:8; Jonah 3:4; Acts 1:3). 8. What was wrong in Satan's use of Scripture? 9. Could Satan have fulfilled his promises—Does he now? 10. What does worshiping Satan really mean? 11. In what one particular was Jesus' temptation unlike ours (Heb. 4:15). 12. Would the temptation be quite as real if the suggestions had come to Jesus as they do to us, by appealing to his mind and imagination? Would a visible appearance of Satan make the temptation stronger or not? 13 What does Christ's victory mean for us? (Heb. 2:17-18; 4:15-16).

CHAPTER 16.

First Disciples and First Miracle.

John 1 : 19—2 : 12.   Harmony 21-26.

111.   **John's Testimony before the Deputation.**   About
Feb. A. D. 27, when John was working at Bethany on the
Jordan (A. V. Bethabara), the Pharisees, just the day before Christ's return from the wilderness, (Jno. 1 : 29), sent
unto him from Jerusalem, priests and Levites, to question
him.   The following conversation ensued between them.
They: Who art thou? John: I am not the Christ. They:
Art thou Elijah? He: I am not. They: Art thou the
Prophet? He: No. They: Who art thou, that we may
give an answer to them that sent us. He: I am the Voice
of one crying in the wilderness, make straight the way of
the Lord. They: Why then baptizest thou, if thou art not
the Christ, neither Elijah, neither the Prophet? John: I
baptize in water: in the midst of you standeth one whom ye
known not, the one that cometh after me, the latchet of
whose shoes I am not worthy to unloose.

112.   **Jesus the Lamb of God.**   (1) On the following
day Jesus returned from the wilderness. When John saw
him coming, he said, Behold the Lamb of God that taketh
away the sin of the world. This is he of whom I said,
After me cometh a man who is before me (in dignity), for
he was before me (pre-existence). (2) I knew him not;
but that he should be made manifest to Israel, for this cause
came I baptizing in water. I beheld the Spirit descending
as a dove out of heaven, and it abode upon him. (3) I
knew him not (as the Messiah), but he that sent me to
baptize in water, said, Upon whom thou shalt see the spirit
descending and abiding the same is he that baptizeth in the
Holy Spirit. I have seen and bear witness that this is the
Son of God.

113.   **The First Three or Four Disciples.**   (1) On the

day following, John and two of his disciples looked upon
Jesus as he walked, and said, Behold the Lamb of God.
(2) The two disciples heard and followed Jesus. Jesus
turned and saith, What seek ye? They said, Rabbi, where
abidest thou? He saith, come, and ye shall see. They
came and abode with him that day, and it was about the
tenth hour. (3) One of the two was Andrew, Simon
Peter's brother, and the other was John the Son of Zebedee.
Andrew findeth first his own brother Simon, and saith, we
have found the Messiah. John probably also brought his
brother James afterwards. When Andrew brought Simon
to Jesus, he looked upon him and said, Thou art Simon, the
Son of John, Thou shalt be called Cephas (Peter).

114. **Philip and Nathaniel.** (1) On the following day
Jesus was minded to go into Galilee. He findeth Philip,
and saith, Follow me. Philip was from Bethsaida, the city
of Andrew and Peter. (2) Philip findeth Nathaniel and
saith, we have found him of whom Moses and the Prophets
wrote, Jesus of Nazareth, the Son of Joseph. Nathaniel
said, Can any good thing come out of Nazareth? Philip
saith, Come and see. (3) Jesus saw Nathaniel coming to
him, and saith unto him, behold an Israelite indeed, in whom
there is no guile. Nathaniel said, whence knowest thou me?
Jesus said, Before Philip called thee, when thou wast under
the fig tree I saw thee. Nathaniel answered, Rabbi, thou art
the Son of God, thou art the King of Israel. Jesus answered, because I said I saw thee under the fig tree believest thou? Thou shalt see greater things. Ye shall see
the heaven opened, and the angels of God ascending and
descending upon the Son of Man.

115. **The First Miracle at Cana.** (1) The third day
after leaving the Jordan, there was a marriage in Cana of
Galilee. The mother of Jesus was there. Jesus and his
disciples were also bidden to the marriage. (2) When the
wine failed, the mother of Jesus saith, they have no wine.
Jesus saith, woman, what have I to do with thee; mine hour
hath not yet come. His mother saith unto the servants,

whatsoever he saith, do it. (3) Now there were six water
pots of stone set there after the Jew's manner of purification, containing two or three firkins apiece. Jesus saith,
fill the water pots with water. They filled them up to the
brim. He saith, draw out now, and bear unto the ruler
of the feast, and they bare it. (4) When the ruler of the
feast tasted the water now become wine, and knew not
whence it was, he said to the bridegroom, every man set-
teth on first the good wine, and when men have drunk freely, then that which is worse. Thou hast kept the good wine
until now. (5) This sign manifested Jesus' glory and his
disciples believed on him.

116. **Brief Trip to Capernaum.** After the wedding
Jesus went down to Capernaum, with his mother, his
brethren and his disciples. There they abode not many
days, because the Passover was near. (April 11, A. D. 27).

117. **Explanatory Notes.** 1. Name the *sources* and locate the
places. 2. The Sanhedrin exercising spiritual oversight sent the
delegation because John's followers and influence increased to such
an extent that many were inclined to regard him as the Messiah.
3. To the deputation John states the *supremacy of Christ,* and to
the people later, his mission. 4. Jno. 1:20 and other passages
show that *"Christ"* was not originally a name but a title—"the
Christ," the anointed. After the resurrection this title gradually
passed into a name: "Jesus Christ," and later, "Christ Jesus." As
the Greeks and Romans did not understand the meaning they substituted their familiar name "Chrestos"=excellent, and Suetonius
regarded him as the leader of a Jewish faction in Rome in the
reign of Claudius (41-54), Vita Claud. 25. 5. *John's testimony.*
based on Isaiah 53, and referring to the Paschal Lamb, shows the
Baptist's belief in the idea of a Messiah, struggling with the corrupt part of the people, and suffering for man's sins. The term
"Lamb of God" suggests: (a) The spotless purity of Jesus, (b) the
vicarious character of his sufferings. 6. As among the *parts from
which the people* came to be baptized, prior to Jesus, Galilee is not
mentioned. It has been supposed that Jesus was the first Galilean
who came to John, and that Andrew and the rest came, while Jesus
was in the wilderness. 7. According to *Jewish reckoning,* (6 A. M.
to 6 P. M.) the tenth hour was four P. M. If John follows the
Roman reckoning as some suppose (from midnight to midnight)

it was 10 A. M. 8. The one disciple whose *name is not given* (Jno. 1 : 40), is undoubtedly John, who wrote this gospel. He never refers to himself by name, but several times as "the disciple whom Jesus loved" (John 13 : 23; 19 : 26, etc.). 9. Verses 47 and 51 contain *allusions to Jacob* and his vision (Gen. 28 : 12-17) (a) the patriarch showed guile, Nathaniel was without guile, (b) a new communication was to be opened between Heaven and earth through Jesus. 10. Either John 1 :42 is a *prediction* of such a development which later on should lead to the bestowing of the name Peter, or the name was given here and in Matthew 16 Jesus confirms it. 11. *Nathaniel* was of a prejudiced nature and had to be won by Christ's manifesting his supernatural knowledge. 12. John 1 : 42 is often interpreted as implying that as *Andrew found* his own brother (Peter) first, so later John also found his own brother (James). In this case, Jesus had six disciples.

118. 1. *Cana in Galilee* must be distinguished from Kana near Tyre. It was about four miles northeast from Nazareth on the road to Capernaum. To-day it is a dilapidated village with a small church reared on the ruins of St. Helena's Church. 2. Jesus had either received a *previous invitation* to this wedding, and was therefore expected, or he was invited when he unexpectedly arrived in the town. His disciples were certainly not expected. 3. From the *silence about Joseph,* we may conclude that he had died before this. 4. *Four points in the narrative* deserve special notice: (a) the contrast between the Baptist's conduct and that of Jesus. The Baptist practiced severe asceticism: Jesus went into the home to a marriage feast, thus sanctifying all human relations. This is still the spirit of Christian ethics. (b) Mary's request implies her belief that the Lord possessed a higher nature by virtue of which an unlimited power to work miracles stood at his disposal. (c) The miracle is called a sign, i. e., an index finger which points to his Messianic character, power, mission and hidden glory. (d) The address, woman, not mother, was selected to remind Mary solemnly, yet tenderly of the new changed relations between the Messiah and Mary of Nazareth. According to ancient usage, there is nothing derogatory in the address. 5. For the *Jew's manner of purification* see Mark 7 : 3, 4. 6. Sound exegesis must hold that *Jesus made real wine;* but it is blasphemous to infer that by so doing he justifies the ordinary drinking usages of American society of to-day, with its bars, treating customs, strong drinks, and all its attending evils. 7. *Capernaum* was our Lord's home during much of his early ministry and is therefore called "his own city." The town was situated on the northwest shore of the sea of Galilee, about 18 miles northeast of Cana, probably on the great road from Jeru-

salem to Damascus. It was a station for a Roman garrison and a custom house, and had at least one synagogue. The site of Capernaum is hotly contested, thus confirming Matt. 9:23. See D. B. and ¶7. 8. Jesus remained probably not more than a week or two at Capernaum. 9. His *reasons for going* to Capernaum may have been: (1) to join the caravans for Jerusalem for the Passover. (2) Because it was the residence of Andrew, Peter, John and James the elder (Matt. 13:1; Mark 1:19, 20), and lay very near Bethsaida, the home of Philip and the native place of Andrew and Peter (John 1:44).

119. **Practical Lessons.** 1. Reasoning is well, but an appeal to personal experience removes prejudice much quicker. 2. When working for Christ, do not overlook your blood relations. 3. Andrew's very first act of Christian service was probably the most far-reaching in all his life. 4. Public testimony and private interview are the two methods of enlisting followers for Jesus. 5. "Hand-picked fruit is the best." After general preaching, personal work is important (John 1:35). 6. Jesus encourages the slightest approach to him. 7. Christ's question, what seek ye, a test of sincerity and earnestness. 8. Christianity invites and rewards the most thorough investigations by all sincere seekers after truth. 9. Jesus is anxious to carry away the sins of the world, of its homes, business, government and institutions. Christ taketh away sin, its punishment, guilt and power, by expiation. 10. Four methods for winning men: (a) by entertaining in our home ("Come and see"), (b) by words of encouragement "thou shalt be called Peter (although vacillating), (c) by words of commanding authority (Philip), (d) by commendation (Nathaniel). 11. From this narrative the "Brotherhood of Andrew" (Episcopalian) and the "Brotherhood of Andrew and Philip" (founded by Dr. Rufus W. Miller) have derived their names and rules. 12. How may we to-day invite Jesus to the wedding? (a) by consulting him before the betrothal, (b) by observing the fifth commandment in consulting our parents (no clandestine marriages), (c) by asking the blessing of the church, (d) by observing decency at the marriage feast (no coarse jesting, immodest dress, or intemperance), (e) by having God's blessing invoked over the very first meal. 13. Christ's presence in the home, (a) sanctifies our joys, (b) shares our cares, (c) ends our troubles, (d) strengthens our faith. 14. Mary's words to the servants should be a guide for all who would serve Jesus. 15. "The conscious water saw its God and blushed" (an old mystic). 16. Christ's mission is to change the unspiritual into the spiritual. 17. Jesus came not to subtract from, but to add to, the wholesome joys of life. 18. That place of enjoyment is safe where Jesus may

go with us.   19. Jesus should be invited to the wedding and remain
a permanent inmate of our homes by means of the erection of the
family altar.

120.   **Reference Literature.** Farrar, Ch. 10, 11, 12; Stalker, Ch. 3;
Andrews, 157-165. Consult dictionaries; paintings by Dore; On Capernaum, see Robinson; Palestine I, 540; Thompson, The Land and
the Book; Walker's Jesus and his Surroundings, 72-79 (1st div.);
Trench, Notes on the Miracles; Robertson, First Miracle (two sermons), Vol. II, 11; Torrey, How to bring Men to Christ.

121.   **Questions for Discussion.** 1. In what sense was the Baptist
Elijah and in what sense was he not? 2. Where did John get his
clear conception of Christ's mission and how did it differ from
that of the Pharisees (Isa. 53: 6, 7). 3. Why does John by implication, and the apostles in words, call themselves "slaves of Christ?"
4. Was Christ's estimate of Peter's character correct? 5. Why
did Christ begin his ministry by enlisting disciples, rather than by
preaching or miracles? (Jno. 15: 27; Acts 1). 6. Can we know the
exact time of our conversion? Must we? 7. In what statement
does Philip's testimony follow popular impressions rather than
state facts? (Jno. 6: 42). 8. Why is Mary so concerned about the
failure of wine in the home where she was only a guest? 9. What
features of Christ's character are revealed at Cana?

SECOND SUB-DIVISION.

The Early Judean Ministry. From Christ's first Passover to the
Opening of the Galilean Ministry, April-December, A. D. 27.

CHAPTER 17.

First Ministry in Jerusalem and Judea.

John 2: 13—3: 26.   Harmony 27-30.

122.   **First Cleansing of the Temple.** (1) After **a**
brief sojourn at Capernaum Jesus went to Jerusalem to attend the first Passover of his ministry (April 11-17, A. D.
27); He found in the Temple those that sold oxen, sheep
and doves.   (2) When he saw the changers of money, he
made a scourge of cords, and cast all out of the temple, the
sheep and the oxen, poured out the changers' money, and

overthrew their tables. To them that sold the doves, he said, take these things hence, make not my father's house a house of merchandise. (3) His disciples remembered that it was written, Zeal for thy house shall eat me up. (4) The Jews said, What sign showest thou us of thy authority to do these things? Jesus said, Destroy this temple, and in three days I will raise it up. The Jews said, forty and six years was this temple in building, and wilt thou raise it up in three days? But he spake of the temple of his body. When he was raised from the dead, his disciples remembered that he spake this.

123. **Work in Jerusalem during the Feast.** In Jerusalem many believed on his name, beholding the signs which he did. But Jesus did not trust himself unto them for he knew all men and needed not that any should bear witness concerning man, for himself knew what was in man.

124. **Discourse with Nicodemus in Jerusalem.** (1) Nicodemus, a Pharisee and a ruler of the Jews, came to Jesus by night. The following conversation passed between them: Nicodemus: Rabbi, we know that thou art a teacher come from God, for no one can do these signs that thou doest, except God be with him. Jesus: Except one be born anew he cannot see the Kingdom of God. Nic.: How can a man be born when he is old? Jesus: Except one be born of water and the Spirit he cannot enter into the Kingdom of God. That which is born of the flesh is flesh, and that which is born of the Spirit is spirit. Art thou the teacher of Israel, and understandest not these things? If I told you earthly things and ye believed not, how shall you believe if I tell you heavenly things? As Moses lifted up a serpent in the wilderness, even so must the Son of Man be lifted up, that whosoever believeth may in him have eternal life.

125. **The Plan of Salvation.** For God so loved the world that he gave his only begotten Son that whosoever believeth on him, should not perish, but have eternal life. God sent not the Son to judge the world; but that the world

should be saved through him. He that believeth on him is not judged. He that believeth not, has been judged already, because he hath not believed on the name of the only begotten Son of God. This is the judgment, that the light is come into the world, and men loved the darkness rather than the light for their works were evil.

126. **Eight Months in Judea.** After the eight days of the passover were over, Jesus and his disciples left Jerusalem and abode in Judea, perhaps not far from where John was baptizing in Aenon, near Salim, because there was much water there. Jesus was also baptizing through his disciples.

127. **The Baptist's Last Testimony to Christ.** (1) John's disciples had a dispute with a Jew about purifying and said to their master: Rabbi, he that was with thee beyond the Jordan (Bethany in Perea) to whom thou hast born witness baptizes also and all men come to him. (2) John said: A man can receive nothing except it have been given him from heaven. Ye know that I said I am not the Christ, but I am sent before him. He that hath the bride is the bridegroom, but his friend rejoices at the bridegroom's voice. This my joy is now made full. He must increase, but I must decrease.

128. **Explanatory Notes.** 1. This is the second half of the Year of Obscurity, April-December A. D. 27. 2. Name the sources, locate the places on the map and the plan of the Temple. Note that the sources for this period are all contained in John (Chap. 2: 13 to 4: 3). The Synoptists make no allusions to it. They move from the temptation directly to the Galilean ministry. Memorize Jno. 3: 16. 3. The *offense* was not in the traffic itself, which was a necessity to those that came from a distance, and were required to exchange their foreign money for Jewish coins, and procure animals for sacrificial purposes, but that it was carried on so near the place of worship and, second, because there is reason to believe that the priests derived an exorbitant profit from it (See Edersheim, Vol. I, pp. 370 and 371). 4. *Josephus estimates* the number of lambs sacrificed at each passover feast, in the time of Nero (54-68) at 256, 500 (Bell. Jud. VI, 9, 3). 5. He cast out the men, *not by physical force,* but by the power of his righteous indignation, which was supported by the bad conscience of the traffickers themselves.

The uplifting of the hand was a symbol of the judgment which was soon to fall upon those who had corrupted the theocracy. 6. The temple could *only be cleansed* by the Sanhedrin, a Prophet, or the Messiah. Hence the demand. 7. *A paraphrase of John* 2:19. You will destroy this temple and the theocracy for which it stands by excluding from it the true spirit of worship and by killing the Messiah because he endeavors to purify it, and then I will soon establish the true temple, the church of God, by my redemptive work of which my resurrection will be the crowning event. This is Christ's first allusion to his death. The Jews interpreted his words as referring to the material temple, and were therefore enraged. Even at his trial (Matt. 26:60; 27:40; Mark 14:57) and at the cross (Mark 15:29) his enemies refer to this scene, but as they perverted his words, ("I will destroy") Matthew calls their testimony false. 8. The *faith of the converts* mentioned in John 2:23, rests entirely on the signs or miracles which Christ had done. They did not have whole-hearted belief in him as the Messiah, nor did they yield themselves up entirely to his service. He could not, therefore "trust himself" to them as the Messiah. 9. Some *clues as to the friends* he probably made at this time, are found in Matt. 26:17-19; Mark 11:1-6; Luke 23:50-53; John 11:1-5. 10. *Nicodemus* was one of the few in whom the recent deeds and words of Jesus had awakened a desire to know more about him. He was a speciment of the better class of the Pharisees. We meet him again in the tumultuous session of the Sanhedrin, John 7:51, and also at Christ's burial, Jno. 19:32. 11. The *plural "we know"* may indicate that he came with overtures from members of the Pharisaic party who, impressed by the Messianic act of cleansing the temple were disposed to join hands with him, to bring in the kingdom of God. 12. "By night," refers either to the particular point of time, or is probably an allusion to the fear of Nicodemus, who on account of the hatred of the Jews toward Jesus caused by the cleansing of the temple, dared not visit him openly. 13. The phrase, *"Born of water and spirit"* describes regeneration as to its two elements; negatively, as the purification of the soul, and positively as the implanting of the active principle of the new life. 14. John 3:14, contains Christ's *second allusion* to his suffering and death, his intention being to prepare the Jewish mind, to whom this feature was and remained the great stumbling block. 15. The *statement John* 3:16 seems to be from John, but the truth is from Jesus. The account of the interview closes with verse 15, for the words, "Only begotten" (verses 16 and 18) are never put in the mouth of Jesus, but always ascribed to John (1:18; 1 John 4:9). The point of view in verse 9 is that of the time when the gospel was written and not when Jesus spoke to Nicodemus (Similar comments of John, see 3:31 to 36; 12:36-43). 16. *"Eternal Life"* (A. V. "everlasting life") in John's writings means not only the life in Heaven, but the life on earth given by Christ to those who believe in him, a life whose blessings begin in this world, but which are fully realized only in the world to come.

129. 1. As John was *baptizing, at Aenon,* near Salim, it is probable that Jesus was also in the vicinity. Finding it inexpedient to remain longer in Jerusalem, and not wishing to begin an independent movement while John was still at work, the Lord attaches himself to John's work. The baptism by Christ's disciples was therefore not different from John's baptism, namely, a work of preparation. His recent experience in Jerusalem had shown him the need of making straight his own path. 2. *Jesus refrained from baptizing,* (1) because water baptism is a ministerial act, compared with baptism with the spirit, (2) because it might have resulted in spiritual pride in those baptized by Jesus. 3. Aenon means, *"place of springs"* and is derived from the Hebrew word "eye." Its location is uncertain. Robinson locates it four miles east of Shechem in Samaria. It was probably in, or near the territory of Herod Antipas (Galilee and Perea) for he seems to have arrested John while he was preaching at this place. 4. In answer to *petty jealousies* on the part of some of John's disciples, who did not fully understand their master's testimony concerning Christ, John with sincere humility meant to say, "I am the friend of the bridegroom;" one who, according to Jewish custom asked for the hand of the bride and arranged the marriage. My work is done, I have introduced the bride (the Jewish nation), to the bridegroom (the Messiah). And if as you say the people do indeed flock to him, this is exactly what it was my life work to bring about. John probably had a presentiment that the end of his career was at hand.

130. **Practical Lessons.** 1. Men engaged in any kind of iniquitous traffic always object to having their "personal liberty" interfered with. 2. Nicodemus, a character study; He came to Jesus, (a) by night (John 3), (b) in the twilight (John 7:26, 50), (c) in broad daylight (Lu. 24:20; John 19:39). 3. The teachers in Israel must learn from the teacher come from God. 4. The soul of all improvement is the improvement of the soul (Bushnell). 5. Points of comparison between Christ and the serpent. (1) Bite was painful and deadly; so is sin. (2) Wound was incurable by human means. (3) A serpent was the means of healing the bite of a serpent, so the Saviour must be a real man. (4) Both were lifted up. (5) Design was to save. (6) Condition, to look up with faith. 6. Luther calls John 3:16 a "gospel within the gospel" for

it contains all the essential elements of the plan of salvation, its author, motive, degree of love, ("so"), scope, means, condition, purpose. 7. It is the course of wisdom to recognize one's own mission in life, and it is useless to wish for another's career. 8. The inscription in the temple at Delphi: "Know thyself," became the motto of Socrates. 9. Goethe: In der Beschraenkung zeigt sich der Meister (Concentration is the secret of mastery). 10. Elements of greatness in John's character: (a) self-knowledge, (b) truthfulness, (c) confession, (d) humility.

131. **Reference Literature.** Farrar, Ch. 13, 14; Stalker, Ch. 3; Andrews, 167; consult D. of B. on each topic. Paintings by Hofman and Kirchbuck; On the "Biogenesis" see Drummond's Natural Law in the Spiritual World; Sermons on Regeneration, by Liddon.

132. **Questions for Discussion.** 1. What claim did Jesus make by cleansing the temple? 2. What new trait of Jesus' character does this claim reveal? 3. Has the cleansing of the temple any bearing on the question as to what uses our church buildings should be put to? 4. In what sense is a church building a "house of God?" 5. How did Jesus esteem faith which sprang from signs? 6. What are the points of similarity between the uplifting of Jesus and the serpent? 7. Had Jesus at this time the full consciousness of his mission and its results. 8. What spirit does John manifest toward Jesus? 9. What term would characterize the feeling of the Pharisees and John's disciples toward Jesus?

CHAPTER 18.

Christ's Ministry in Samaria.

John 4: 1-42; Matt. 4: 12; Mark 1 :14.   Harmony, 31-33.

133. **Reasons for Departing from Judea.** When the Lord knew that the Pharisees had heard that he was making and baptizing more disciples than John, (although Jesus himself baptized not, but his disciples), he left Judea and departed again into Galilee. A second reason was the imprisonment of John, which opened the way for Christ's independent ministry in Galilee.

134. **Jesus and the Samaritan Woman.** (1) On his road through Samaria Jesus came to Sychar, where Jacob's

well was. Being weary, he sat by the well, at about the sixth hour (noon). His disciples had gone into the city to buy food. (2) There cometh a woman of Samaria to draw water. Jesus: Give me to drink. The woman: How is it that thou being a Jew askest drink of me, a Samaritan woman? (3) Jesus: If thou knewest the gift of God, and who it is that saith unto thee, Give me to drink, thou wouldst have asked of him, and he would have given thee living water. Woman: Thou hast nothing to draw with and the well is deep. Whence then hast thou that living water? Jesus: Every one that drinketh of this water shall thirst again, but whosoever drinketh of the water that I shall give him, shall never thirst. Woman: Give me this water, that I thirst not, neither come all the way hither to draw. (4) Jesus' Omniscience. Jesus: Go call thy husband. Woman: I have no husband. Jesus: Thou saidst well; for thou hast had five husbands, and he whom thou now hast is not thy husband. (5) True worship. Woman: I perceive thou art a Prophet. Our fathers worshipped in this mountain, and ye say that in Jerusalem is the place that men ought to worship. Jesus: The hour cometh when neither in this mountain nor in Jerusalem shall ye worship the father. God is a spirit and they that worship him must worship him in spirit and in truth. (6) Jesus the Messiah. Woman: I know that the Messiah cometh; he will declare unto us all things. Jesus: I that speak unto thee, am he.

135. **Jesus and his Disciples.** (1) Their surprise. Upon this, came his disciples, and marveled that he was speaking with a woman, yet no man said, why speakest thou with her. (2) The woman's zeal. The woman left her water pot, went into the city, and saith to the people, come see a man, who told me all things that ever I did. Can this be the Christ? They went out of the city, and were coming to him. (3) Urging him to eat. Meanwhile the disciples prayed him, Rabbi, eat. But he said, I have meat to eat that ye know not. The disciples said, hath any man brought him aught to eat? Jesus saith, my meat is to do the will of

him that sent me, and to accomplish his work.   (4) **The**
spiritual harvest.   Say not ye there are yet four months and
then cometh the harvest?   Look on the fields, they are
white already to harvest.   Here is the saying true, one man
soweth, and another reapeth.   Others have labored (John,
the Baptist and this woman) and ye are entered into their
labor.

136. **Jesus and the Samaritans.** (1) Many of the
Samaritans first believed on him, because of the word of
the woman.   (2) When they besought him to abide with
them, he abode there two days.   (3) And many more believed because of his words and said to the woman, now we
believe, not because of thy speaking, for we have heard for
ourselves, and know that this is indeed the Saviour of the
world.

137. **Explanatory Notes.** 1. Name the sources, locate the places,
and trace the movements on the map; memorize Jno. 4:24. 2.
John: 4:1-3 implies that the *reason why Jesus left Judea,* was that
his work was giving occasion for comparison between his success
and that of John, to the disparagement of John. About the same
time Jesus heard that John had been imprisoned. The Synoptists
say that this was the reason for his departure, hence they date
the beginning of the Galilean ministry from the imprisonment of
John (Matt. 4:12). Some hold that Jesus withdrew from Judea
for the reason given by John, but that he delayed the actual beginning of work in Galilee as long as John was free and active.
At his arrival in Galilee, he dismissed his disciples for a brief space
of time. 3. The Lord took the *direct road from Judea* to Galilee
which passes through Samaria. Very scrupulous Jews went around
through Perea. 4. On the *Samaritans* see ¶11 (2), also ¶36 and
D. of B. 5. *Jacob's well* has been covered by a succession of
churches, the last of which was destroyed at the time of the
Crusades. Many of the ruins now remain. The mouth of the
well is several feet below the present surface of the ground and
is approached by steps leading to a small doorway into a vaulted
chamber about fifteen feet square. 6. By *"water,"* Jesus means
the spiritual life that he gives. Elsewhere he calls it seed, bread,
light, etc. 7. God *is a spirit,* i. e. he does not inhabit a material
body, hence his worship cannot be restricted to a material temple.
"Worship in the spirit" is such as is inspired by the Holy Spirit

and prompted by reverent thought and deep feeling. The Jews with their formalities did not worship in spirit, and the Samaritans with their imperfect idea of God did not worship in truth. Both have had followers in all ages. 8. The conversation with the woman is *important for four reasons*, (a) Jesus unlike the rulers of the time, was free from national prejudice and nativism, (b) he had a high regard for woman. It was considered improper for a rabbi to talk to a woman; even his disciples marveled. (c) His first plain announcement of his Messiahship was made to a non-Jew and a woman at that. (d) Jesus' consciousness of his Messiahship was not a gradual development, but was clear and positive at the very beginning of his ministry. 9. John 4:35 enables us to *determine the time* when Jesus went into Galilee. The commencement of the harvest was about April 1st. Upon 16 Nisan a sheaf of the first fruits of the barley harvest was waved before the Lord in the temple. Till this was done, no one might lawfully gather his grain. Counting back four months we have December as the month in which these words were spoken. 10. To *Christ's personal* work is undoubtedly due the religious awakening recorded in Acts 8:14.

138. **Practical Lessons.** 1. Notice the Lord's deep interest in persons casually met. 2. We can overcome the worldly spirit by deep interest in spiritual affairs. The woman in her zeal forgets her waterpot, and Jesus, his hunger. 3. Experience is an unanswerable argument. 4. The Greeks believed that before going into the Elysian fields all souls would drink from the river Lethe, and forget all sins and sorrows. Christ's water of life gives relief now.

139. **Reference Literature and Questions for Discussion.** Consult Dictionaries; Farrar, Ch. 15; Stalker, Ch. 3; Andrews, 183-188; Jos. Ant. 18, 5, 1; On Jacob's Well, Hast. D. B. II; H. Hofman's painting, Jesus and the Woman of Samaria. Point out features showing Christ's real humanity. What relation did Christ's baptism have to his work and self-consciousness? Did John and Jesus meet during the thirty years of preparation? What does Jesus mean by "Salvation is of the Jews?" Is the act in Jno. 2:15, 16 and the teaching in 4:21-24 in harmony? To what extent was Christ's work in this period a failure and to what extent was it a success?

140. General Review.

1. With reference to the whole "Year of Obscurity," state, (1) reason for the designation, (2) duration, (3) events and dates of beginning and end of period, (4) the two sub-divisions, (5) source of information by gospels and chapters, (6) trace Jesus' move-

ments, mentioning in their proper order, the places and what occurred in each, (7) names of disciples, (8) miracles. 2. State aim and general traits of the ministry during this period. 3. Which events prepared Christ for his ministry, and which prepared the people and how? 4. State time, place and subject of John's preaching; his personal appearance and mode of living; the classes of hearers, the popular opinion of him, his own explanation of his mission, some conspicuous features of his character and his different testimonies to Jesus' person and work. 5. How did Jesus show that he approved of John's work, and how did John show that he realized his true relationship to Jesus?

DIVISION III.

The Year of Popularity

From the Opening of the Galilean Ministry to the Crisis at Capernaum,—Dec., A. D. 27-April, A. D. 29—or about 16 months

TWO SUB-DIVISIONS.

I. **First Period of the Galilean Ministry.** From the Opening of the Galilean Ministry to the Choosing of the Twelve, December, A. D. 27-Early Summer, A. D. 28, or about six months.

II. **Second Period of the Galilean Ministry.** From the Choosing of the Twelve to the Crisis at Capernaum. From Early Summer, A. D. 28 to April A. D. 29, or about ten months.

First Sub-division.

FIRST PERIOD OF THE GALILEAN MINISTRY.

CHAPTER 19.

Opening of the Galilean Ministry.

Mt. 14: 3-5; Mk. 6: 17-18; Luke 4: 14-30; John 4: 43-54. Harmony 34-36.

141. **Imprisonment of John.** About Jan. A. D. 28, Herod Antipas cast John into the prison Machaerus, for the sake of Herodias, his brother Philip's wife whom he had married. For John had said to Herod, It is not lawful for thee to have thy brother's wife.

142. **Beginning of Christ's Galilean Ministry.** (1) After the two days' work in Samaria, Christ arrived in Galilee, with the intention of retiring; not to preach, for

Jesus himself testified that a prophet hath no honor in his
own country. (2) But contrary to expectation the Galileans
received him, having seen all the things that he did in Jerusalem at the passover, April 11, A. D. 27. (3) Moreover,
as John was now imprisoned Jesus decided to begin his
independent ministry. He preached the gospel of God, saying, The time is fulfilled and the kingdom of God is at
hand: repent ye, and believe in the gospel.

143. **Healing of the Nobleman's Son.** (1) On his
way to Nazareth Jesus again came to Cana. (2) A nobleman whose son was at the point of death at Capernaum,
heard of it and besought him to come and heal his child.
Jesus said: Except ye see signs and wonders, ye will in no
wise believe. The nobleman saith: Sir, come down ere my
child die. Jesus saith: Go thy way; thy son liveth. (3)
The man believed the word, and went his way. As he was
going down his servants met him, saying that his son lived.
(4) He inquired the hour when he began to mend. They
said: Yesterday at the seventh hour the fever left him.
The father knew that it was at that hour in which Jesus
said unto him: Thy son liveth: and he believed, and his
whole house. (5) This is the second sign that Jesus did.

144. **First Rejection at Nazareth.** (1) From Cana
Jesus went to Nazareth, and as his custom was he entered
into the synagogue on the sabbath day and stood up and
read from Isaiah 61, "The spirit of the Lord is upon me,
because he anointed me to preach good tidings to the poor:
and to proclaim the acceptable year of the Lord. Then he
sat down and said: To-day hath this scripture been fulfilled in your ears. (2) They all wondered at the words of
grace which proceeded out of his mouth: and said, Is not
this Joseph's son? (3) He said, Doubtless ye will say unto
me, Physician heal thyself: what we have heard done at
Capernaum (to the nobleman's son) do also here in thine
own country. (4) But he added, No prophet is acceptable
in his own country. There were many widows in Israel in
the days of Elijah, when there came a great famine and

unto none of them was Elijah sent, but only to Zarephath
in the land of Sidon, unto a widow. And there were many
lepers in Israel in the time of Elisha and none of them was
cleansed, but only Naaman the Syrian. (5) This reference
to Gentile preference filled them with wrath and they cast
him out of the city and led him unto the brow of the hill
whereon their city was built, that they might throw him
down. But he passing through the midst of them went his
way.

145. **Explanatory Notes.** 1. Name and compare *sources.* Locate the places on the map; memorize Luke 4:18. 2. *Herod Antipas* had put away his wife, the daughter of Aretas, king of
Arabia, after having been married 15 years, in order to marry a
princess of his own blood, Herodias, whom he had met at Rome, she
being the wife of his half-brother Philip. She consented on condition that Herod divorce his wife. When the latter learned of
this, she fled to her father, who thereupon made war upon Herod.
This adulterous union shocked the Jewish nation and John became
their mouth-piece. To punish the Baptist for his burning words,
Herod Antipas had him imprisoned in the fortress of Machaerus,
in the mountains of Moab, east of the Dead Sea, on the pretence that
the crowds which his preaching drew were a disturbance to the
public peace (cf. Josephus). 3. Supposing that he appeared in public
in the summer of A. D. 26, and that he was imprisoned in Jan.,
A. D. 28, *John's whole public ministry* lasted about 18 months. 4.
From this point the Synoptists begin their *continuous narrative* of
the Life of Christ. What precedes this in each of them is introductory. 5. The reason why the imprisonment of the Baptist is
made so prominent in the narrative of the Synoptists, and why the
beginning of Christ's ministry in Galilee is brought in so close connection with it is because this event marks the great turning point
in Christ's ministry. No doubt before, but certainly after Christ's
baptism, John repeatedly bore witness to the rulers that the Messiah was near at hand, and to the deputation he even said, "he is
standing in the midst of you." As the rulers took no steps to
seek him, Christ went to the Temple, cleansed it, met them, and
thus addressed himself to the Jewish people in their corporate
capacity as a nation represented by its ecclesiastical rulers. Had
the nation as a nation received the Messiah, the method for the pro-
pagation of the gospel might have become a different one. The
whole nation would have become the great missionary of the world.

But they disregarded the Baptist's and the Lord's work. When the imprisonment of John closed his peculiar work of preparation and the failure of his mission was plainly seen the Lord inaugurated another method. He went to Galilee, selected individuals from the nation who should still aim at national salvation, but, in case of failure, they should take the place of the hierarchy and become the builders of the kingdom. 6. Jno. 4:44 states either the *reason for leaving Judea,* which he could call "his own country" because he was born there, or a prophecy of his reception at Nazareth. It is also possible that "for" in Jno. 4:44 is used in the sense of "although." See also the narrative parts. 7. In Galilee Christ could *labor without hindrance:* (a) since Herod Antipas did not trouble himself concerning any religious movements that did not disturb the public peace, (b) the Galilean people were less under the influence of the hierarchy and were more open to his words. 8. After the Lord's arrival in Galilee, he *dismissed his disciples* for a time. They went to their respective homes until they were recalled later at Capernaum. 9. It is interesting to trace during this and the following periods (a) the Lord's progressive self-manifestation, (b) the gradual training of the Twelve, (c) the deepening and spreading hostility of the Jewish influential classes. 10. The Galilean ministry *began in great popularity* which was followed by criticism, hostility and opposition from the leaders, and loss of favor with the people because of his break with them at Capernaum. It resulted in the practical withdrawal from public work in Galilee, and in his devoting his attention to the training of the Twelve.

146. 1. The exact title of the nobleman is *"basilicos,"* "a king's officer," i. e. an official of the government of Herod Antipas. 2. Jesus did not wish to be known simply as a *worker of miracles.* The faith that rested exclusively on miracles was not regarded by Jesus as thoroughly trustworthy (Jno. 2:11, 23). 3. As the nobleman probably returned to Capernaum after sunset (about 9 P. M.) the healing is spoken of according to Jewish reckoning as having happened *"yesterday,"* i. e. at about 1 P. M. 4. On the *service* in the synagogue, see ¶34. 5 Very likely Isa. 61:1 which was read by the Lord was the *pericope* (the "haphtharim") appointed for the day. 6. While reading, the teacher in the synagogue *stood up;* when speaking *he sat down.* 7. Here we have Christ's *first recorded sermon:* 1 text, 2 exposition, 3 application, 4 result. 8. *This rejection* in Nazareth is to be *distinguished* from the one during the second Galilean period recorded in Matt. 18:53-58; Mark 6:1-6. (a) On this visit he is alone, on the other he is accompanied by his disciples; (b) here he escapes from the at-

tack and leaves the city at once, there he continued in the city for a time; (c) after this rejection he went to Capernaum, after the other, "he went round about the villages teaching." 9. Physician *heal thyself,* that is: work a miracle by which you, the carpenter, may rise to the dignity commensurate with your Messianic claims. 10. The *point in each* of the references to the Old Testament is that though there was plenty of opportunity for a prophet to do good in his own country, both prophets helped foreigners because of Israel's unbelief. Divine gifts are distributed on a different principle than local favoritism. 11. *The traditional site* of the brow of the hill is a long distance from the city. It may possibly be, however, that the modern town is not exactly in the same location as the ancient one was.

147. **Practical Lessons.** 1. The faith of the head of the household usually influences all its members (Jno. 4:53. Also Acts 4:14; 16:34). 2. The divine origin of Christianity is indicated by its great effects (Isa. 61:1). 3. It is foolish and wicked to hate the preacher for speaking the truth; destroying him will not change the truth. 4. Most of the best and greatest men have risen from social obscurity (Luther, Lincoln).

148. **Literary References.** Farrar, Ch. 17; Andrews, 209-244; the painting by Raphael, Miraculous Draught of Fishes; Edersheim's Life of Christ I, 422; On Nazareth, see D. of B. by Davis, p. 505; also D. B. by Piercy, p. 547; and by Hastings.

149. **Questions for Discussion.** 1. What was the connection between John's imprisonment and the beginning of the Galilean ministry? 2. Why is it not plausible that Christ left Judea for Galilee because of fear of Herod? 3. Did the Pharisees have anything to do with John's arrest? 4. What was the point in the two illustrations which Christ used at Nazareth? 5. Is there still danger of underestimating Jesus because we hear so much about him? 6. Are there reasons why most of our great men came from obscure families?

CHAPTER 20.

Removal to Capernaum, and First Preaching Tour.

Matt. 4: 13-23; 8: 2-4; Mk. 1: 16-45; Lu. 4: 1-44; 5: 12-15. Harmony 37-40.

150.   **Removal to Capernaum.**   After his rejection, and partly because of it, Jesus himself and either all or a part of his family removed to Capernaum on the Sea of Galilee, which from now on is frequently called "his city," that is, his home.

151.   **Recall of the Four Disciples.**   (1) Soon after his removal he recalled four of his six disciples who had gone home when, in Dec., A. D. 27, he went from Samaria to Galilee, namely, Peter, Andrew, John and James. (2) Walking by the sea, the multitude pressed upon him to hear the word of God.   He saw two boats standing, but the fishermen had gone out of them and were washing their nets. He entered into Simon's boat and asked him to put out a little from the land.   He sat down and taught the multitudes.   (3) Then he said unto Simon, Put out into the deep, and let down your nets for a draught.   Simon said, Master, we toiled all night, and took nothing; but at thy word I will let down the nets.   And they enclosed a great multitude of fishes; and their nets were breaking.   They beckoned unto their partners in the other boat, that they should come and help them.   They came and filled both the boats so that they began to sink.   (4) Simon, when he saw it, fell down at Jesus' knees, saying, Depart from me for I am a sinful man.   For he and James and John were amazed at the draught of fishes.   (5) Jesus said unto Simon, Fear not, from henceforth thou shalt catch men. And all four brought their boats to land, left all and followed him.

152.   **Teaching and Casting Out a Demon at Capernaum.**   (1) When he was teaching on the sabbath in the

synagogue of Capernaum the people were astonished, for his word was with authority. (2) There was a man, possessed with an unclean spirit who cried, Jesus, thou Nazarene, art thou come to destroy us? I know thee who thou art: the Holy One of God. Jesus rebuked him, Hold thy peace and come out of him. The demon threw him down and came out of him having done him no hurt. (3) Amazement came upon all and they spake together, What is this? A new teaching? For with authority and power he commandeth the unclean spirits and they come out. (4) There went forth a rumor concerning him into every place of the regions around about.

153. **Healing of Peter's Mother-in-law.** (1) He rose up from the synagogue and entered into the house of Simon whose wife's mother was holden with a great fever. When they besought him for her, he rebuked the fever, and it left her. (3) Immediately she rose up and ministered unto them.

154. **Healing on the Sabbath Evening.** (1) When the sun was setting all that had any sick brought them and he laid hands on them and healed them. (2) Demons also came out from many, crying out, Thou art the Son of God. (3) But rebuking them, he suffered them not to speak, because they knew that he was the Christ.

155. **First Preaching Tour in Galilee.** (1) On the following day, very early, he went into a desert place to pray; (2) The multitude sought after him, and would have stayed him, that he should not go from them. (3) Simon when he found him, said, all are seeking thee. But Jesus said, I must preach the good tidings of the kingdom of God to the other cities also: for therefore was I sent. (4) So he preached in the synagogues throughout all Galilee and cast out demons. (5) In one of the cities a man full of leprosy fell on his face, saying, Lord, if thou wilt thou canst make me clean. Jesus touched him and said, I will; be thou made clean. Straightway the leprosy departed from him. (6) Jesus charged him, tell no man; but show thyself to the

priest and offer for thy cleansing, according as Moses commanded, for a testimony unto them. (7) But he published
it, so that Jesus could enter no more into the city. (8)
Great multitudes came together to hear Jesus and to be
healed of their infirmities. But he withdrew himself in the
desert, and prayed.

156. **Explanatory Notes.** 1. Name and compare sources, especially Luke's report of the call with the others; locate places on the
map; memorize Luke 5 : 5. Draw a map of the Sea of Galilee, lo-
cating the chief cities. 2. On *Capernaum,* see ¶7 (2). 3. The *Sea
of Galilee* (Lake of Genesareth or Sea of Tiberias) is an expan-
sion of the Jordan and is 13 miles long, and at no point over 8 miles
wide. Its surface is 682 feet below the level of the Med. It is
enclosed on all sides by steep mountains except on the North East.
Of the nine populous cities mentioned in the New Testament which
stood upon its shores, all are now ruins with the exception of
Tiberias (See ¶5). 4. In the *selection of Capernaum* as the center of his activity Christ was probably determined chiefly by its
location on the sea and on one of the principal highways. This
gave him better facilities for intercourse with men than the more
secluded Nazareth. 5. It is generally supposed that the Lord
resided in the house of Peter. Some think that Peter furnished
him a house for his own exclusive use. It is certain that Jesus
did not own his own home (Matt. 8 : 20; 8 : 14; Mark 1 : 29). 6.
The change of abode seems to have included the *whole family* except the sisters (Mark 6 : 3; Matt. 13 : 56). 7. There were *three
stages* in the fellowship of the apostles with Christ: (a) A call
to *faith* in him as the Messiah, involving only an occasional absence
from their families and business. "Private Men Following Christ,"
(Lightfoot). During this stage they stood in a similar relation to
that which some of them had occupied toward the Baptist. (b)
A call to *work* involving the abandonment of secular occupations
and a constant attendance on his person. (c) A call to *lead,*
as special apostles. 8. To convince these men of his *ability to
supply* their temporal needs, the Lord worked the miracle of the
draught of fishes. 9. *Peter's exclamation,* Luke 5 : 8, did not express a real desire that Christ should go away, but showed his
awe at the divine power that Christ had manifested, and his feeling of unworthiness to be in Christ's presence. 10. The *mention of
two vessels* and hired servants together with John's acquaintance
with the Highpriest (Jno. 18 : 15) indicate that Zebedee was well-
to-do and explains how his wife Salome could supply the temporal

needs of Jesus. 11. At what time *Peter left his native city* Bethsaida (Jno. 1:44), and took up his residence at Capernaum is not known. From the fact, however, that his mother-in-law was in his house we may conclude that his wife was a native of Capernaum, and that at his marriage he moved to that city. 12. It is important to know that *Peter was married* when the Lord called him to the apostleship, because it shows that Jesus did not regard marriage as an impediment in his special service. They enjoyed a long period of married life, for at the time when the first epistle to the Corinthians was written (in 57), Peter's wife was not only living but strong enough to accompany her husband on his missionary journey (1 Cor. 9:5).

157. 1. He taught them as *having authority.* The scribes were professional teachers of the Law and their method of teaching was to quote copiously the opinions of their predecessors. Their teaching therefore impressed the people as discussion rather than truth. With Jesus precisely the opposite was true. He did not argue but presented his doctrine unsupported as eternal truth. 2. Luke's precise name *"great fever"* points to his professional knowledge of disease (Col. 4:10). Greek writers of medicine make a distinction between great and small fevers. 3. On the Miracles, see the chapter on "The Work of Christ." 4. One *reason for Christ's* going into the country may have been to allay the excitement among the people, lest the crowds should cause trouble with the Roman rulers, who dealt very severely with anything that might lead to an insurrection. But the chief reason was stated by Christ himself. 5. We have no data to decide the duration of the first preaching tour in Galilee nor of the particular parts of Galilee visited. It is probable that he was at Bethsaida and Chorazin, two places adjacent to Capernaum, because they are included in a later warning, and yet we have no record of our Lord's visit there. 6. *Leprosy* was one of the most terrible of diseases. It was contagious and incurable. Lepers were banished from society, and suffered terribly till death came to their relief. The healing of the leper was therefore an especially notable miracle. 7. Jesus showed *his fearlessness* and his sympathy by touching this leper when he healed him. 8. The *healing of the leper* must have been done privately. Christ enjoined silence upon him because he was unwilling that the people should look upon him as a mere miracle worker. It was the *Word* which he wished to make prominent.

158. **Practical Lessons.** 1. To-day men are just as thoroughly under Satan's control as the demoniacs, but it is usually evident in other ways. 2. We are saved in order to serve (Mt. 8:15). 3. The healing touch of Jesus cools the fevers caused by lust, love

of money, pleasure, undue ambition, worldliness, fanaticism. 4. No large growth in holiness was ever gained without taking time to be often and long alone with God (Mk. 1:35). 5. Even to-day some good people object to carrying the gospel to others. 6. Like the leper, saved people find it hard not to speak of Jesus. 7. Leprosy is a symbol of sin: (a) it defiles, (b) excludes from society (especially in its grosser forms), (c) is beyond human remedies, (d) leads to an early and awful death, (e) God only can heal it (culture can not).

159. **Reference Literature.** Farrar, Ch. 19; Andrews, 245; on the Sea of Galilee, see Davis' D. B., p. 233, and Stanley, Sinai and Pal., p. 375; on leprosy, Davis' D. B., p. 430; Hast. D. of C. II, 28; and Piercy's D. B., p. 472; on demoniacal possessions, Davis' D. B., p. 166; Piercy, p. 208; Nevin's "Dem. Possessions;" on miracles, Davis, p. 481; on the synagog, Davis, p. 714.

160. **Questions for Discussion.** 1. How did the synagogue service resemble our church services and how did it differ from them? 2. How can a man's business be made to advance the kingdom of God? 3. What was the purpose of the miraculous draught of fishes? 4. What is the difference in net fishing and hand fishing as applied to soul winning? 5. Why did Jesus silence this man's testimony? 6. Why did Christ command the leper to obey the laws (Lev. 14:1-9). 7. Did the report of this leper help or hinder his work? (v. 39). 8. What are the advantages and dangers of popularity? 9. How does the leper illustrate the danger lying in thoughtless earnestness?

CHAPTER 21.

Growing Hostility of the Pharisees at Capernaum.

Matt. 9:1-17; Mk. 2:1-22; Lu. 5:17-39. Harmony 41-43.

161. **The Paralytic borne of Four.** (1) After his return from the first preaching tour to Capernaum, one day when Jesus was teaching, and the Pharisees and doctors of the law who were come out of every village of Galilee from Judea and Jerusalem, were sitting by: four men bring a man lying on a bed sick of palsy. (2) Not finding by what way they might bring him in because of the multitude, they went up to the house-top and let him down through the

tiles with his couch before Jesus. (3) Seeing their faith he said, Man, thy sins are forgiven thee. (4) The scribes and Pharisees began to reason, Who is this that speaketh blasphemies? Who can forgive sins but God alone? (5) Jesus perceiving their reasonings said, Which is easier to say, Thy sins are forgiven thee; or to say, Arise and walk? But that ye may know that the Son of Man has authority on earth to forgive sins he said to the sick: Arise, and take up thy couch, and go into thy house. Immediately he did so, glorifying God. (6) They were filled with fear, saying, We have seen strange things to-day.

162. **Call of Matthew—Levi.** Soon after this, on his way to the seaside, Jesus beheld a publican named Matthew or Levi, sitting at the place of toll, and said: Follow me. And he did so.

163. **Levi's Feast of Honor.** (1) To express his gratitude to Jesus, Levi made a great feast in his house in honor of the Lord, and many publicans and others were present. (2) The Pharisees and scribes murmured against his disciples, saying: Why do ye and your master eat with the publicans and sinners? (3) Jesus said, They that are in health have no need of a physician; but they that are sick. I am not come to call the righteous but sinners to repentance.

164. **Jesus on Fasting.** (1) Levi's feast was probably held on one of the Pharisaic fast-days (Monday or Thursday). (2) So John's disciples (and the Pharisees) said to Jesus: Why do we and the Pharisees fast oft but thy disciples fast not? (3) Jesus said, Can ye make the sons of the bride chamber fast while the bridegroom is with them? The days will come when the bridegroom shall be taken away, then will they fast. (4) No man seweth a piece from a new garment upon an old garment, else he will rend the new, and also the piece from the new will not agree with the old. (5) No man putteth new wine into old wine-skins, else the new wine will burst the skins and itself will be spilled and the skins will perish. But the new wine must

be put into fresh wine skins. (6) Yet no man having drunk old wine desireth new, for he saith, The old is good.

165. **Explanatory Notes.** 1. Name and compare *sources;* notice Mark's graphic description, locate places on map; memorize Mk. 2: 17. 2. These Pharisees and doctors of the law, were, according to Josephus a sort of *village schoolmaster,* or a class of inferior municipal magistrates. 3. It is not necessary to suppose them to have been present *with evil intent.* Perhaps they came to judge by personal observation how far the popular reports concerning Christ were true. Some of them may even have expected to find him the Messiah, but were turned into enemies. 4. On *paralysis,* see D. B. 5. *Roofs in Palestine* were flat. The rafters and boards were often covered with a thatch or mat of grass, on which there were several inches of clay or mud trodden hard. Such a roof could easily be removed. The houses often had stairs on the outside leading up to the roof. 6. On their supposition that Jesus was a mere man, their *charge of blasphemy* was just. 7. By doing an act, the *truth or falsehood* of which can be instantly detected, Christ attests his power to be able to do that which in its very nature is outside the *regions of visible proof.* 8. On the *identity of Matthew* with Levi see ¶182. 9. It is probable that the *place of toll* where Levi sat was upon the road near its entrance into the city of Capernaum. 10. The manner of this call presupposes a former acquaintance of Jesus with Levi. It is not improbable that he was already a disciple in the wider sense of the word. 11. Matthew was no doubt one of the *good publicans,* for Jesus would hardly have called a dishonest man to be a leader in his church. 12. The call of Levi must have been a *stumbling block* to the Pharisaic party and to all Jewish patriots. for his occupation was odious to them, it being the sign of their national degradation. The Talmud says, "A Pharisee who turns publican must be turned out of the order." 13. From the *offense taken* we may infer that the supper was on Monday or Thursday, which two days were observed by the more scrupulous Jews as fast days. In the law only one day of fasting was commanded—the day of Atonement. 14. The *feast at Levi's house,* the wedding at Cana, the meal at the house of Simon the Pharisee (Luke 7: 30-50), the dinner given by Simon the leper (Mark 14: 3-9) and the banquet by one of the chief Pharisees (Luke 14: 1-5) show that Christ was no ascetic like John. He did not attend these feasts, however, merely for pleasure. They were opportunities for self-revelation and helpfulness to others. 15. *"Wine-skins"* (A. V. "bottles") were receptacles made of the skins of animals. These became stiff and

brittle with age. New wine in fermenting would break them. They were strong when new, but weak when old. 16. By the *old garments* and the old bottles Christ means the Mosaic law: by the new cloth and the new wine he means his own doctrine. Men, enlarged by Christ's spirit, need a wider garment, the liberty of the children of God. The new gospel will burst the old forms. Christ refused to sew his new faith like a patchwork upon a dispensation worn out and soon to pass away. 17. *"The old is good"* is the language of false conservatism. Progress under the guidance of the Spirit is the law of God's kingdom (Jno. 14:26).

166. **Practical Lessons.** 1. Sin is like paralysis—a weakness of the conscience and will to do good, hard to cure, ending in death. 2. It is our privilege to bring those to Christ who cannot or will not come of themselves. 3. Faith will find or make a way to come to Christ. 4. We can have faith for others as well as for ourselves. 5. Hasty and superficial judgment of the conduct of others is wicked. 6. The Church while contending for every particle of ascertained truth, must adapt itself in the presentation of the truth to new conditions and not indiscriminately decry "modernism."

167. **Reference Literature.** Farrar, Ch. 24:25; Andrews, 252; Edersheim I, 499; Trench on the Miracles. As to Eastern houses, see Land and Book II, p. 6-8. Consult D. of B. by Davis on Levi; How helpless man is to save himself may be illustrated by Aeschylus "Prometheus Bound," and Virgil's "Laocoon" with his sons in the coils of the great serpent.

168. **Questions for Discussion.** 1. What was the content of the faith of these men? 2. Has fasting in itself any value as a religious exercise? 3. What was Christ's attitude toward fasting? 4. How about seasons of self-denial? 5. Should religious people live mournfully or joyfully? Why? 6. What is the right relation of conservatism to progress?

CHAPTER 22.

The Sabbath Question at Jerusalem and Capernaum.

Jno. 5; Matt. 12:1-14; Mk. 2:23; 3:6; Luke 6:1-11.
Harmony 44-46.

169.   **The Healing of the Infirm Man.**   (1) Jesus attended the second passover of his ministry at Jerusalem on March 30-April 5, A. D. 28.   (2) By the sheep gate there is a pool which is called Bethesda, having five porches.   In it lay a multitude of sick, blind, halt, withered.   One of them had been thirty-eight years in his infirmity.   (3) When Jesus saw him, he saith, Wouldst thou be made whole? The man answered, I have no man, when the water is troubled to put me into the pool.   While I am coming, another steppeth down before me.   Jesus saith, Arise, take up thy bed and walk.   And he did so.

170.   **The Charge of Sabbath Breaking.**   (1) It being the Sabbath, the Jews said to him that was cured, It is not lawful for thee to take up thy bed.   He answered, He that made me whole, said, Take up thy bed and walk.   (2) They asked him, who said this?   But he knew it not, for Jesus had conveyed himself away; a multitude being in the place.   (3) Afterward, Jesus findeth him in the temple, and said, Thou art made whole.   Sin no more lest a worse thing should befall thee.   (4) The man now told the Jews that it was Jesus who had made him whole.   (5) For this cause the Jews persecuted Jesus.   (6) But Jesus, justifying himself said, my Father worketh until now and I work. Now the Jews sought the more to kill him because he not only brake the sabbath, but also made himself equal with God.

171.   **The Claims of Jesus.**   In his defense, Jesus claims (1) *a unique sonship*.   He said, The son can do nothing of himself, but what he seeth the Father doing.   (2) *Judgeship*.   The Father doth not judge any man but hath given

all judgment unto the Son: that all may honor the Son even as they honor the Father. (3) *Power to Dispense Eternal Life.* He that heareth my word and believeth him that sent me, hath eternal life. For as the Father hath life in himself, even so gave he to the Son also to have life in himself.

172. **Four Witnesses for Christ's Claims.** To establish these claims Jesus names four witnesses: (1) *John:* If I bear witness of myself, my witness is not true, but ye have sent unto John and he hath borne witness unto the truth (Jno. 1 : 19). (2) His *works.* Yet the witness which I have is greater than that of John, for the *works* which the Father hath given me to accomplish, the very works that I do, bear witness of me that the Father hath sent me. (3) The *Father:* The Father that sent me, he also hath borne witness of me. Ye have neither heard his voice at any time nor seen his form. (4) The *Scriptures.* Ye search the scriptures, because ye think that in them ye have eternal life; and these are they which bear witness of me. If ye believed Moses ye would believe me.

173. **Plucking Grain on the Sabbath.** (1) After the passover Jesus returned to Capernaum. (2) On a Sabbath as he was going through the grain-fields his disciples plucked the ears and ate. (3) The Pharisees said, Why do ye that which is not lawful to do on the sabbath day? (4) Jesus said, Have ye not read what David did when he was hungry, how he entered into the house of God, and ate the showbread, which is not lawful to eat save for the priests alone? (5) The Son of man is Lord of the sabbath. (6) The Sabbath was made for man and not man for the Sabbath.

174. **The Man with the Withered Hand.** (1) On another sabbath he entered into the synagogue at Capernaum and there was a man who had a withered hand. (2) The scribes and Pharisees watched him, whether he would heal him on the Sabbath day, that they might accuse him. So they asked him, Is it lawful to heal on the sabbath day? (3) He said, What man of you having one sheep, if this fall

into a pit on the sabbath day, will not lift it out? How much more valuable is a man than a sheep? (4) Then he saith to the man, stand forth, and addressing his audience he saith, Is it lawful on the sabbath day to do good, or to do harm? To save a life or to kill? But they held their peace. (5) When he had looked on them with anger, being grieved at the hardness of their hearts, he said unto the man, Stretch forth thy hand. When he stretched it forth his hand was restored. (6) But the Pharisees with the Herodians took counsel how they might destroy him.

175. **Explanatory Notes.** 1. Name and compare the *sources*. Locate places on map; on the "unnamed feast" see "Chronology;" memorize Jno. 5 : 39. 2. The *latter part* of Jno. 5 : 3 and the whole of v. 4 are omitted from the R. V. because they are not a part of the original Gospel. See footnotes in the R. N. Test. 3. This *pool* was fed by an intermittent spring, from which the water bubbled up from time to time; but the people thought that this bubbling was caused by an angel from heaven (A. V. vs. 4) and that whoever stepped into the water first thereafter would be healed. 4. The *traditional site* of this pool is the so-called "Birket Israel," just north of the temple area. It is over 50 feet deep, 131 feet wide and 365 feet long. Its depth seems to exclude it from consideration as the place spoken of by John. For this reason Robinson suggested the Fountain of the Virgin, outside the city wall on the east side. 5. The *sheep-gate* was in the north of Jerusalem and derived its name from the fact that through it the sacrificial animals were brought into the city. 6. The *"Jews"* in John's Gospel usually means the scribes and Pharisees—the enemies of Jesus. 7. The language in verse 14 perhaps suggests that the man's infirmity had been *caused by his sin.* What Jesus wishes in any case to save him from, is a worse than physical ill. 8. From verses 16-18 it seems probable that official action was taken by the Sanhedrin, and a resolution passed to kill Jesus if found in Judea. For this reason Jesus now left Judea and only returned to it after an interval of 18 months, and then only for brief periods at the feasts. At the very first opportunity, at the Feast of Tabernacles, Oct., A. D. 29 (Jno. 7 : 32), the Jews attempted to carry out their plan. 9. The *warrant for rejecting Jesus* they believed to have found in the instructions given in Deut. 13 : 1-5, by which the claims of one pretending to a divine mission were to be tested. His works and his words must be in conformity with the law. Of the Messiah it

was demanded: (a) that personally he should keep the law, (b) that he would set up the Messianic kingdom.

176.   1. The *prominent thought* in the Lord's defense, Jno. 5: 19-47 is his Messianic claim. He claims: (a) divine sonship (17-20), (b) power of judgment (21 and 22), (c) authority to dispense divine life (24 and 40). In support of this Messianic claim he appealed (a) to the witness of John (2:33), (b) to his own works (37), (c) to the Father at his baptism and transfiguration, (d) the Scriptures. 2. This *plucking of grain took place* near Capernaum in May or June, after Christ's return from "the unnamed feast." 3. Law and custom allowed the plucking of grapes and corn enough to satisfy hunger. 4. According to the *scrupulous Pharisees,* the disciples had broken the Sabbath in that they had reaped, threshed and winnowed, by pulling, rubbing and chewing the grain before eating it. The Mishna says: "He that reapeth corn on the sabbath to the quantity of a fig is guilty; and plucking corn is reaping." 5. *Showbread* was the sacred bread set before Jehovah in two rows of six loaves, on a table in the Holy Place of the Tabernacle. At the end of a week these loaves were eaten by the priests after the new ones had been put in their place. 6. By this *illustration Jesus showed* that as it was right for David to eat the showbread because he could get no other food, so it was right for the disciples, who were also hungry, to pick a little grain to eat on the Sabbath, the principle being that works of necessity are lawful on the sabbath. 7. That Jesus and his company resorted *to such means* of sustenance shows that they must have been living a very frugal life. 8. Verse 27 illustrates the *principle governing the observance of the Sabbath.* It must aid, not burden man, physically and spiritually. 9. On the *"Herodians"* see ¶31 (3). 10. The Herodians and the Pharisees were natural opponents. But hearing of Christ's Messianic claims, they united in opposing him. For should Jesus continue to gain popularity there was danger that what had seemed to them the religious and political foundation of society would be shaken.

177.   **Practical Lessons.** 1. Without a willingness to co-operate with God man cannot attain to the highest blessings (Jno. 5:66). 2. Notice (a) Christ's compassionate eye, (b) his words arousing interest and hope, (c) his deed of power. 3. By choosing the friendless one, Jesus rebukes the spirit of selfishness. 4. With Christ not only the first comers will be healed. 5. The best of one's deeds may be misunderstood. 6. Christ's teaching on the Sabbath: (a) it was made to help men live good, happy lives, and therefore should be used for that purpose, and not in such a way as to make men miserable. (c) Works of necessity and of mercy

are lawful on the Sabbath (Mt. 12:11, 12). (c) God does not command us to keep the Sabbath because it pleases him, but because it is best for ourselves. 7. In none of his defenses does Jesus call in question the obligation of the Sabbath law, but he emphasizes its original design, contrasting it with the Pharisaic perversion. 8. Far from abolishing the principle of the sabbath, Christ declared it was made for man, a universal, not Jewish ordinance, for his physical repose and spiritual culture. 9. Every command on God's part implies a promise of strength on man's part to obey (Mk. 3:5). 10. Religious fanaticism and political partisanship still conspire against Christ and religious liberty, even in free America.

178. **Reference Literature.** Farrar, Ch. 26 and 27. On the time, see Andrews, 50, 189, 255; on the miracle, see Trench and Dod. On Bethsaida see Davis, Hastings and Piercy's D. B., and Tristan's Land of Israel. On the Sabbath, see Piercy, D. B., p. 757; Davis, p. 627.

179. **Questions for Discussion.** 1. In what sense is sickness a result of sin? 2. Is special suffering always a sign of special sinfulness? 3. Is it the case sometimes? (Jno. 5:14). 4. What principles and motives should guide us in the observance of the Sabbath?

SECOND SUB-DIVISION.

Second Period of the Galilean Ministry.

From the Choosing of the Twelve to the Crisis at Capernaum. From Early Summer, A. D. 28 to the Passover, April 18, A. D. 29—or about ten months.

CHAPTER 23.

The Organization of the Kingdom.

Matt. 4:23-25; 12:15-21; 10:2-4; Chapt. 5, 6, 7; Mk. 3: 7-19; Luke 6:12-49. Harmony 47-49.

180. **The Widespread Fame of Christ.** (1) About summer A. D. 28 the popularity of Christ stood at its height. Large crowds flocked to him. All provinces and three cities are mentioned by name: Galilee, Judea, Decapolis, Perea,

Idumea, Jerusalem, Tyre and Sidon. (2) He preached the gospel, healed all kinds of diseases and cast out demons, who cried out, Thou art the Son of God. (3) The sick sought to touch him for power came from him and healed them. (4) But he charged all of them that they should not make him known.

181. **The Choosing of the Twelve.** (1) One of these days he and his disciples withdrew from Capernaum to the seaside and the multitude followed them. He asked his disciples to have a little boat wait on him, to cross the sea because the people thronged him. (3) North of Capernaum he left the boat and went into a mountain where he continued all night in prayer to God. (4) When it was day, he called his disciples and chose from them twelve whom he named apostles, that they might be with him and that he might send them forth to preach and cast out demons.

182. **The Names of the Twelve Apostles.**

First Group:

1. Simeon (Greek contraction Simon), the son of Jonas (Jno. 1:42; 21:16), called also Cephas (Heb.) or Peter (Greek), both meaning *a stone or rock,* native of Bethsaida.

2. Andrew, his brother (Matt. 4:18), a native of Bethsaida, and a former disciple of the Baptist.

3. James, the son of Zebedee (Matt. 4:21), and Salome (Mk. 15:40), also of Bethsaida, and

4. John, his brother, afterwards known as "the friend of Jesus," the "disciple whom Jesus loved" (Jno. 13:23), called "boanerges" from his ardent temperament.

Second Group:

5. Philip, a native of Bethsaida, and one of the earliest disciples (Jno. 1:43).

6. Bartholomew (Bar-Tolmai), "the son of Tolmai," a patronymic, his proper name was Nathanael.

7. Matthew or Levi, a collector of customs at Capernaum.

Third Group:

8. Thomas or Didymus (*a twin*), (Jno. 11:16; 20:24).
9. James, the son of Alphæus, or "James the Less."
10. Judas, a brother or, possibly, a son of James (Acts 1:13), and surnamed Thaddæus and Lebbæus (Matt. 10:3; Mk. 3:18), (from Hebrew "leb," heart=the courageous).
11. Simon the *Cananite* (Mk. 3:18) or *Cananaean* (perhaps derived from Cana) (Matt. 10:24), in Greek *Zelotes* (Lk. 6:15; Acts 1:13), one, probably, who before his call had belonged to the sect of the zealots.
12. Judas (called the son of Simon Iscariot=the man of Kerioth (Jno. 6:71; 13:26), or Judas Iscariot, Simon's son (Jno. 13:2), probably a native of Kerioth (Josh. 15:25), a little village in the tribe of Judah.

183. **The Sermon on the Mount.** After having appointed the earthly founders of the kingdom of God, at a private meeting on one of the peaks (Mk. 3:13), he descended to a level place on the mountain (Lu. 6:17), where the people stood who had followed him from Capernaum. In their presence he laid down the principles and laws of the kingdom in the famous "Sermon on the Mount."

Theme. THE KINGDOM OF GOD: ITS MEMBERS, LAWS AND PRINCIPLES OF CONDUCT.

1. *The Subjects of the Kingdom of Heaven* (Matt. 5:3-16).

   a. Their character and privileges (vss. 3-12).
   b. Their mission in the world (vss. 13-16).

2. *The Relation of Christ's Law to the Old Testament Law*
   (Matt. 5:17-48).
   a. Christ's law, a completion of the old law (vss. 17-20).
   b. Christ's law inward and spiritual; illustrated by the laws regarding murder, adultery, marriage, oaths, non-resistance, and neighborliness (vss. 21-48).

3. *The Righteousness of the Kingdom* (Matt. 6:1; 7:12).

    a. The general principle— to be seen of God, not of men —stated (6:1), and illustrated by almsgiving, prayer, and fasting (6:2-18).

    b. Right conduct toward God (6:19-34).

        (1) Serving both God and mammon impossible (vss. 19-24).

        (2) Trusting God for all needed things a duty (vss. 25-34).

    c. Right conduct toward men (7:1-12).

        (1) Harsh judgments rebuked (vss. 1-5).

        (2) Discrimination however to be used (vs. 6).

        (3) Wisdom to judge aright, as well as all other good, obtained by prayer (vss. 7-11).

        (4) The Golden Rule, or summary of right conduct toward men (vs. 12).

4. *Admonitions to the Members of the Kingdom* (Matt. 7: 13-27).

    a. To walk in the narrow way and not in the broad (vss. 13. 14).

    b. Not to be deceived by false teachers (vss. 15-20).

    c. To build on the rock of obedience to Christ (vss. 21-27).

5. *Impressions* (7:28, 29), (From Bible S. U. Sessions).

184. **Explanatory Notes.** 1. Name and compare the *sources,* especially those of the Sermon on the Mount, locate the places; memorize Matthew 5:2-10. 2. For a *proper understanding* of this greatest of sermons it is necessary to read and study it with the above analysis constantly in mind. 3. Christ *organized his forces,* (a) because his enemies began organizing theirs, (b) because thorough work in establishing his kingdom demanded it, (c) because his followers needed training for their future work. 4. Tradition makes the *Horns of Hattin,* a double peaked hill, four miles back from the Sea of Galilee and about eight miles S. W. of Capernaum the site where the twelve men were chosen, and the sermon preached, but the gospels give us no means of deciding on

the exact place. 5. The night before the appointment was *spent by Jesus in prayer* which fact emphasizes the significance that Jesus attached to this event. 6. The number of apostles corresponded to the twelve tribes of Israel, and pointed to Jesus' Messianic kingship over all Israel.

185. 1. The N. T. has *four lists of the apostles* (Matt. 10; Mk. 3; Luke 6, and Acts 1:13). Each list falls into three groups of four each. The name in each group are the same; the groups follow in the same order, and in all the lists the same names begin each group—Peter, Philip, James the Less. Only the order within the groups varies. The four fishermen constitute the first group in each list, Peter always leading. 2. Probably *all were Galileans.* Even Judas Iscariot (meaning "Man of Kerioth" in Judea), may have been a Galilean, as in Jno. 6:71; 13:26, the word "Iscariot" is attached to the father of Judas. 3. *Home towns:* Three apostles (Peter, Andrew and Philip) were natives of Bethsaida (Jno. 1:44). Six (James the Elder, John, Matthew, James the Less, Jude, and probably Thomas) were of Capernaum. Nathanael was of Cana (Jno. 21:2). 4. *Former connections.* The surnames of Simon ("the Zealot," and "The Canannean") mark him out as having once belonged to the furious followers of Judas of Giscala, the leader of an insurrection against the Roman government (Acts 5:37). And as the "Zealots" were most numerous in Galilee, Simon was no doubt a Galilean. The Greek names of Philip and Andrew, and the fact that the Greeks in Jno. 12 applied to Philip. and were referred by him to Andrew, may point to some connection on their part with the Greek colonists in Decapolis and the Hellenists (Greek-speaking Jews). Five or six of the twelve were formerly disciples of the Baptist (Jno. 1). 5. *Relationship to Jesus.* (a) If in John 19:25 the following punctuation is adopted, There stood by the cross of Jesus his mother; his mother's sister; Mary, the wife of Clopas, and Mary Magdalene, then the second woman was Salome mentioned in the parallel passage Matt. 27:58. In this case James and John the elder were cousins of Jesus. (b) The old punctuation distinguishes only three women, "The three Marys," making "his mother's sister" to be Mary the wife of Clopas (or Alpheus), and the mother of James the Less and Jude. In this case these two disciples were cousins of Jesus. But two sisters bearing the same name is improbable. (c) Again if Alpheus, the father of Matthew (Mk. 2:14) is identified with the father of James the Less and Jude, the three men were brothers and if the second punctuation be adopted, these three apostles were cousins of Jesus. 6. *The identity* of Matthew and Levi seems to follow (a) from the perfect agreement in the narrative of the

calling of Matthew (Matt. 9:10) and of Levi (Mk. 2:15; Luke 5: 29), (b) the absence from the lists of the Apostles of any trace of Levi while Matthew occurs in all. (c) It is not improbable that he changed his name Levi after his call, into Matthew=Theodore (gift of God), in grateful remembrance of God's mercy. 7. *The identity of Nathaniel* and Bartholomew appears highly probable: (a) John twice mentions Nathaniel (1:45; 21:2), but never Bartholomew; (b) the Synoptists speak of Bartholomew (Matt. 10:3; Mk. 3:18; Luke 6:14), but never of Nathaniel; (c) Philip first brought Nathaniel to Jesus and Bartholomew is mentioned by each of the Synoptists immediately after Philip; (d) Luke couples Philip with Bartholomew, precisely in the same way as Simon with his brother Andrew, and James with his brother John.

186. 1. The *education and social position* of the twelve is sometimes underestimated. Four only were fishermen and of these James and John belonged to a family of means and social standing. Their father had hired servants (Mark 1:20); their mother was one of the women who had means to support Jesus (Mark 15:41); John seems to have had a home in Jerusalem, (Jno. 19:27); he was also acquainted with the high priests (Jno. 18:15); Matthew must have been a man of some education and business ability. It may safely be assumed that all of the Twelve had a thorough Biblical education. 2. They were *selected with a view to complement* each other with reference to natural gifts, education and temperament, thus making the circle a perfect working body. Hence Christ received not many of the same cast of mind. The formative types were Peter, John and James, and even these three differed one from the other, forming a spiritual harmony however. 3. *Individual characteristics.* Peter is bold, impetuous, and sensitive; John is zealous, affectionate, and sympathetic; Thomas is cold, cautious, and skeptical; James is practical, energetic, and vehement; Philip is thoughtful, inquiring and decisive; and Simon, called Zelotes, most likely was fervent, radical and just a little fanatical. They were good men and true, but no one of them could have been mistaken for the other. A few of them were men of decided ability, and rose pre-eminently above their brethren in intellectual power and executive skill. But we really know very little of the majority of those who were apostles. They lived and toiled unnoticed, and died unsung, not even their great office being able to redeem them from obscurity.—(Lorimer, *Jesus the World's Savior,* p. 128). 4. The *immediate purpose* of the appointment was that they should assist Jesus in the rapidly accumulating work of spreading the gospel. The *ultimate* purpose was that these men after having received a special training might be able to plant the church after Christ's ascension (Mark 3:14; Acts 1:18).

187. 1. The *Sermon on the Mount* is not a collection of sayings of Christ uttered on various occasions, but a connected discourse, as affirmed by Matt. and Luke. These important and elementary teachings were of course repeated at other places, and this explains why we find many of them in other connections. 2. Luke, who speaks of a *"level place"* does not contradict Matt. who calls the place "a mountain." The spot was probably a level place on the mountain side or a plateau. 3. "Blessed" in these verses means "happy," full of the greatest possible happiness, or bliss. 4. *"Poor in spirit"* means being conscious of spiritual deficiency. 5. *"Meekness"* means self-control, ability to bear an affront with patience; not lack of courage and energy. 6. As *salt keeps food* sweet and good, so should Christians make the world better. Sometimes salt is adulterated with clay or sand, and when the genuine salt dissolves the refuse loses its savor, or saltiness, and becomes useless. In the same way when Christians lose the true spirit of Christ their influence for good is gone. 7. "To fulfil the law" means to reveal its deep and holy meaning and to obey its spirit. By "law" Jesus has in view the great principles of right living on which the law is based These are the same always and must be obeyed. 8. A "jot" (Matt. 5:18) is the smallest Hebrew letter, a "tittle" is a slight projection on certain Herbrew letters. To say "one jot or one tittle" would be like saying to-day "the crossing of a *t* or the dotting of an *i*." 9. *Raca,* a Chaldee word meaning "empty head," was at that time a very common word of slander. The teaching is that contemptuous language is at the root of murder and is worthy of punishment. 10. The *Lord's Prayer* contains (a) the Invocation, (b) six or seven petitions, of which the first three have a Godward and the last four a manword reference: six of them asking for spiritual and only one for material goods. (c) The Doxology which is a later insertion, due to liturgical usage. 11. The "eye" (Matt. 6:22) stands for the heart or the soul. "Single" means with one high, true purpose. The verse means that, as a healthy eye enables one to see to do one's daily tasks, so a true heart, full of desire to serve God, enables one to live aright. 12. "Mammon" (Matt. 6:24) here means worldly riches, which many worship instead of God. Christ does not say that a man cannot be rich and serve God too, but that he cannot serve God and riches with all his heart at the same time. 13. A mote (Matt. 7:31) is a very small particle of matter, a speck of dust. Here it means a trifling fault. A "beam" or stick of timber means a great fault. People who do not try to correct their own faults should not criticise others for small mistakes. 14. Hillel is said to have uttered a maxim similar to the Golden Rule (Matt. 7:12). Christ,

however, supplies the power to keep it. 15. "Rock" (Matt. 7:24) means obedience to Christ's teaching; sand, empty professions; rain, flood, winds refer to all that which tests moral character.

188. **Practical Lessons.** 1. In studying the Sermon on the Mount and the rest of Christ's ethical teaching it must be constantly remembered that they contain the law for the kingdom of God, and not for the Jewish Sanhedrin, or the Roman Senate, or a non-Christian modern state. They are workable in a nation only in proportion as the population has already become Christian. Under present conditions many of Christ's grandest precepts cannot be generally practised, even by his most devoted children. If, for example, the precept, "Lay not up treasures" (Matt. 6:19) should be literally obeyed, Christians would be excluded from the business affairs of the world. But under a more Christ-like condition of affairs, at a distant future, the reasonableness even of this and other precepts will be gloriously demonstrated. Under present conditions this grand precept must fade into the meaning that Christians should not lose themselves in amassing wealth. If these guiding principles are overlooked this grandest of sermons is in danger of being considered as a collection of most beautiful, but quite unattainable "counsels of perfection" (See Adeney, N. T. Theology, Ch. VII, on the New Ethics). 2. Guard well the Christian qualities of your character, and let not what is distinctively Christ-like evaporate from your life through contact with the worldly atmosphere about you. Let not society drag you down to its own savorless level of easy and conventional virtue. 3. A good man is not simply a witness for virtue but an instrument for repressing vice. 4. "The true servant unceasingly rebukes the wicked but he does it most of all by his conduct, by the truth which shines forth in his words, by the light of his example, by all the radiance of his life." (St. Francis of Assisi, died Oct. 3, 1226). 5. The characteristics of Christians are not to be creeds, professions and shibboleths, but graces. 6. Christ's religion has antiseptic properties keeping society from moral decay. 7. The Lord's Prayer is a beautiful expression of the Fatherhood of God and the Brotherhood of Man. We are to pray in the plural. 8. Matt. 7:1 does not forbid judicial action, but censoriousness and private judgments which are based on insufficient evidence, uncharitable thoughts, the imputing of bad motives, harsh language. 9. Apply the Golden Rule (a) in thought, and evil suspicions will vanish, (b) in word (abuse, detraction), (c) in deed (business dealings, labor questions). 10. What men are constantly doing in their relation to spiritual affairs, no man in his senses would do in relation to his material affairs. 11. It is too late to choose another foundation when the flood comes.

189. **Reference Literature.** Farrar, Ch. 18; Andrews, p. 265; Stalker, ¶105-108; Bruce, Training of the Twelve; Godet, Character of Peter, John, James and Paul (in his N. T. Studies); Lorimer, Jesus the World's Savior (p. 128 on the Characteristics of the Twelve); on the Sermon of the Mount; Tholuck, Die Bergrede (also in English); Achelis, Bergpredigt; Votaw, Sermon on the Mount in Hast. D. B. V, 1-45; Piercy, D. B., p. 808; on the Lord's Prayer, see books by Maurice, Boardman, H. J. Vandyke, Westin, Shorter and Heidelberg Catechisms; J. R. Miller, Practical Religion; on the Kingdom of God, see Piercy, p. 447, and Hast. D. of C. II, 607; on Mammon, Hast. D. C. II, 106; on "Raca," Hast. D. C. II, 467; Milton's Paradise Lost, I, 678 on Mammon; Whittier's poem, "Eternal Goodness."

190. **Questions for Discussion.** 1. In what sense is Christ and in what sense are Christians the light of the world? 2. Is Christianity the final religion or only the highest stage of present religious development looking to a still higher expression of the life of God? 3. Are there greater truths contained in the Sermon on the Mount than those which the church has as yet emphasized? 4. Do the principles of the Bible and especially the Sermon on the Mount cover all phases of our present complex political and social life? 5. Is the Sermon on the Mount livable under present conditions? 6. Are conditions conceivable under which it could be the basis of life? 7. Does Matt. 5:39 contain a principle of personal conduct or a law of government? (See Jno. 18:22, 23).

CHAPTER 24.

Christ's Second Preaching Tour.

Matt. 8:5-13; 11:2-19; Lu. 7:1-8, 3.   Harmony 50-54.

191. **The Centurion's Servant.** (1) After the sermon on the Mount, Christ returned to Capernaum. (2) When he entered, the elders, sent by a centurion, asked him to heal the latter's servant of the palsy, adding, He is worthy of it, for he loveth our people and built our synagogue. (3) Later the centurion himself came and asked him. Jesus said: I will come and heal him. (4) The centurion answered. Lord, I am not worthy that thou shouldest come under my roof; only say the word, and my servant shall be

healed. (5) For thou hast at least as much power as I, who though I am a man under authority, have under myself soldiers, and when I say to one, Go, he goeth, and to another, Come, he cometh; and to my servant, Do this, he doeth it. (6) Jesus marvelled and said to them that followed, I have not found so great faith in Israel. (7) Many shall come from the east and the west, and shall sit down with Abraham, and Isaac, and Jacob in the kingdom of heaven: but the sons of the kingdom shall be cast forth into the outer darkness: there shall be the weeping and the gnashing of teeth. (8) Jesus said unto the centurion, as thou hast believed *so* be it done unto thee. And the servant was healed in that hour.

192. **The Raising of the Widow's Son at Nain.** (1) On the next day (Summer, A. D. 28), Jesus left Capernaum for his second preaching tour, followed by his disciples and a great multitude. (2) When he drew near the gates of Nain there was carried out for burial the only son of a widow. (3) The Lord had compassion and said, Weep not. He touched the bier and said, Young man, I say unto thee, Arise. And he sat up, and began to speak. (4) They all feared and glorified God, saying, A great prophet is arisen among us. (5) This report went forth in the whole of Judea, and all the region round about.

193. **The Baptist's Last Message.** (1) John's disciples kept their imprisoned master informed of Christ's doings. (2) One day (Summer, A. D. 28), John sent two of them to the Lord. They met him somewhere on his second preaching tour and said, the Baptist hath sent us saying, Art thou he that cometh, or look we for another? (3) In that hour he cured many of diseases and he answered, Go and tell John the things which ye have seen and heard; the blind receive their sight, the lame walk, the lepers are cleansed and the deaf hear, the dead are raised up, the poor have good tidings preached to them. And blessed is he, whosoever shall find no occasion of stumbling in me.

194. **The Baptist Extolled.** (1) In order that the

people might not lose their great respect for John, Jesus said to them, when the messengers were departed, What went ye out into the wilderness to behold? a reed shaken with the wind? or a man clothed in soft raiment? (They that are gorgeously apparelled, and live delicately, are in kings' courts) ; or a prophet? (2) He is much more than a prophet. This is he of whom it is written, Behold, I send my messenger before thy face, who shall prepare thy way before thee. (3) Among them that are born of women there is none greater than John: yet he that is but little in the kingdom of God is greater than he. (4) From the days of the Baptist until now the kingdom of heaven suffereth violence, and men of violence take it by force. All the prophets and the law prophesied until John. He is Elijah, that is to come. (5) All the people and the publicans justified God, being baptized. But the Pharisees and the lawyers rejected the counsel of God, being not baptized of him. (6) Whereunto shall I liken this generation. They are like children that sit in the marketplace, and call one to another; We piped unto you, and ye did not dance; we wailed, and ye did not weep. John came eating no bread nor drinking wine; and ye say, He hath a demon. The Son of man is come eating and drinking; and ye say, Behold, a gluttonous man, and a winebibber, a friend of publicans and sinners! (7) But wisdom is justified of all her children.

195. **Anointed in the House of Simon the Pharisee.** (1) At an unnamed place on his second preaching tour, a Pharisee desired Jesus to eat with him. (2) When he entered the house a woman of that city, a sinner, heard of it and brought an alabaster cruse of ointment, and weeping, she began to wet his feet with her tears, and wiped them with the hair of her head, and kissed his feet, and anointed them. (3) When the Pharisee saw it, he spake within himself, If this man were a prophet, he would have perceived what manner of woman this is.(4) Jesus said, Simon, I have somewhat to say unto thee. A lender had two debtors: the one owed five hundred shillings, and the other fifty.

When they had not *wherewith* to pay he forgave them both. Which of them will love him most? Simon answered: He to whom he forgave the most. Jesus said, Thou hast rightly judged. (5) Turning to the woman, he said unto Simon, I entered into thy house, thou gavest me no water for my feet: but she hath wetted my feet with her tears, and wiped them with her hair. Thou gavest me no kiss: but she hath not ceased to kiss my feet. My head with oil thou didst not anoint: but she hath anointed my feet with ointment. (6) Wherefore her sins, which are many, are forgiven; for she loved much: but to whom little is forgiven, *the same* loveth little. (7) And he said unto her, Thy sins are forgiven. (8) They that sat at meat began to say within themselves, Who is this that even forgiveth sins. (9) Jesus said to the woman: Thy faith hath saved thee; go in peace.

196. **Women Disciples on the Second Preaching Tour.** Besides the Twelve, there accompanied him certain women who had been healed of evil spirits and infirmities: Mary that was called Magdalene, from whom seven demons had gone out, Joanna the wife of Chuzas, Herod's steward, Susanna, and many others, who ministered unto them of their substance.

197. **Explanatory Notes.** 1. Name and compare the *sources.* Note the variations between Matt. and Luke in the narrative of the Centurion; locate the places and trace the Lord's movements on the map; memorize Matt. 8:11. 2. It is probable that this healing occurred *on the same day* on which the sermon on the mount was preached. 3. This *centurion* was an officer in charge of a company of from 50 to 100 men and belonged either to a Roman garrison at Capernaum, or was in the service of Herod Antipas. The latter is more probable. He was evidently a man of wealth and a friend of the Jews. 4. That the *elders were willing* to make the request shows that at this time, no general hostility had yet developed itself against the Lord in Capernaum. 5. Twice the gospel states that *Jesus "marvelled."* Here because a Gentile's faith surpassed that of the Jews; and in Mark 6:6 on account of the unbelief of the people at Nazareth. 6. In Matt. 8:11-12 the Lord expresses the *universality* of the gospel and its benefits—one of the germs of Paulinism. 7. The *journey to Nain* and with it the

beginning of Christ's second circuit was commenced, "soon after-wards" (Luke 7 : 11), or according to the marginal reading: "On the next day," after the healing of the centurion's servant. 8. From Capernaum to Nain is a *distance of about 25 miles.* 9. Nain is now an *insignificant village.* Its name means "fair," pointing to its pleasant location in the plain of Esdraelon. 10. The Jews did not bury their dead in closed wooden coffins but carried them on a bier to a tomb where they were laid in little niches. 11. This is the first of the *three recorded cases* of Christ's raising the dead. The others are: the daughter of Jairus in Capernaum, and Lazarus of Bethany, the suburb of Jerusalem. These three persons were actually dead, both in the estimate of their friends and of Jesus. 12. Observe that no one recognized *Jesus as the Messiah.* In their opinion he was simply another great prophet. 13. This was the region in which Elijah and Elisha had worked their wonderful miracles nearly nine hundred years before, and the people thought that God had now given them another similar prophet.

198. 1. John's disciples met Jesus at some unnamed place on his second preaching journey. Some authorities place the meeting at Capernaum. 2. As this occurred about *summer A. D.* 28, the time elapsed since John's imprisonment (in Dec., A. D. 27) was possibly seven months. 3. The fact that *John could communicate* with his disciples shows that he was given some liberty in prison (Matt. 25 : 36; Acts 24 : 23; Socrates). 4. The Baptist had for the moment found a *stumbling block* to his faith in what he heard about the method of Christ and his lack of success. We find similar moments of despondency in the lives of Moses, Elijah, Huss, Luther. 5. The *Lord's testimony* to John was a plain though indirect assertion of his Messianic character. 6. Matt. 11 : 6 is a gentle *way of rebuking John* for his doubts concerning Jesus. "Occasion of stumbling" means anything which causes one to do wrong. Here it means John's temptation to disbelieve in Jesus as the Messiah. 7. This message would doubtless *recall to John the prophecies* in Isa. 29 : 18, 19; 61 : 1-3, and so would assure him that Jesus was really doing what the prophets had foretold concerning the Messiah. 8. Wishing to prevent his hearers from cherishing any depreciatory thoughts of his great forerunner, the Lord pronounced a *beautiful eulogy* on the Baptist. *He describes John,* (a) as a man of unflinching integrity who would break rather than bend, he is not a flattering courtier, (b) as a prophet, but (c) as one whose insight into the nature of the kingdom of God is inferior to the least of Christ's disciples, because these have higher privileges. 9. The figure in verses 11 and 12 is that of *soldiers carrying a city by storm.* It was intended to illustrate the dif-

ficulty which lay in the way of the Jews accepting Jesus as the
Messiah. 10. The comparison, Matt. 11:16-19, is drawn from the
games of children. One group is trying to induce the other to
play either "funeral" or "wedding." The point of the comparison
is the peevishness of one group who are satisfied with neither. So
the Jews would not be satisfied with an ascetic like John, nor with
the genial and social Son of man. 11. Luke 7:19 means to say that
God will ultimately be vindicated by men possessing the true wisdom from above.

199. 1. The invitation from Simon is evidence that the *break between Jesus* and the Pharisees was not yet complete. 2. The
houses in Palestine were less closed than ours and privacy is far
less observed in warm climates. 3. The Lord was *twice anointed*
—here at Capernaum and at Bethany, six days before his death
(Matt. 26.6). (a) Similarities: In both cases, the host's name
was Simon; it was a woman who anointed Jesus: both women
brought an alabaster box; offense was taken by persons present.
(b) The differences are: This Simon was a Pharisee, the one in
Bethany is called "the leper;" here Jesus was among people who had
no real sympathy with him, in Bethany he is among intimate friends;
here the woman is a notorious sinner, in Bethany she is a spiritually
minded friend; here the anointing is an expression of thankful
love for received pardon, in Bethany it is an anticipation of Christ's
burial. 4. *Tradition identifies* this woman with Mary Magdalene,
i. e. Mary from Magdala, a town in the southern end of the plain
of Genessaret, Luke 8:2; the "seven demons" are interpreted to
mean the passionate nature of the great sinner. Her name has become a synonym for accepted penitence and pardoned sin. Most
of the institutions to raise fallen women bear her name (Magdalene Asylums). But there is no real ground for such identifica-
tion. The fact that M. Magdalene's name appears in the narrative
closely following this should not be considered a sufficient reason.
5. The *"ointment"* was a very expensive perfume in a costly alabaster vase. In Jno. 12:5 a similar vase of perfume is said to
have been worth 300 shillings (A. V. "pence"), about $50, or a
year's wages at that time. 6. An *"alabaster cruse,"* or alabastron,
was a long-necked flask originally made of white or veined alabaster, but later of other materials also. 7. Among the Jews a
kiss of greeting, water for washing, and oil for anointing were
marks of respect for a guest. The Pharisee would have given
them to Jesus if he had wished to treat him politely, much more if
he had loved him. 8. The woman had *received pardon* and the
perfume was the expression of her gratitude. Hence the woman's
love is declared to be the proof and consequence of her forgiveness,

not the reason. The interpretation that her good work secured her pardon is against the context and the general teaching of the New Testament. 9. This *circuit is distinguished* from the former one by the attendance of women disciples. Nothing more is historically known of these persons than is here related. Their names appear again later. Herod's steward was the official in charge of Herod's estate or possibly the person attending to the domestic affairs of the royal palace in Tiberias. His wife therefore must have been a woman of some means. 10. Luke 8:3 offers an explanation of how Jesus and his companions could live without manual labor. In return for spiritual riches the woman provided for his temporal wants, as it was not his will to use his miraculous power to supply them.

200. **Practical Lessons.** 1. Let the young men arise from the death of sin. 2. Despondency has visited many great men. 3. Luther's wife in mourning, because "God has died," cheers the reformer. 4. Cause and cure of John's spiritual despondency. Cause: Close confinement, impatience, false reports, wrong preconceptions; Cure: Going directly to Jesus (prayer), Bible study, meditation, counsel from good men. 5. The proof of Christianity is its beneficial effect on the world. 6. On one pretext or another men find fault with God's ministers and their message. 7. One of the commonest sins is misjudging the acts and words of others. 8. Love is the fruit and proof of faith. 9. So far as Simon condemned vice he was right, but what had he done for the woman's reclamation? 10. The surest way to drive a penitent sinner back into sin is to treat him as an impertinent reprobate (Luke 7:39).

201. **Reference Literature.** Farrar, Ch. 20; Andrews, 275. Jewish forms in entertaining, in Geikie, Life and Words of Christ II, 123; on the six Marys, see Davis, B. D., p. 458, and on spikenard, p. 705; On Christ the Saviour of the Poor, see Walker's "Philosophy of the Plan of Salvation;" Eggleston, Christ in Literature, p. 128-130. Lange, Life of Christ III, p. 116; McCook, Women Friends of Jesus; J. R. Miller, Personal Friendship of Jesus.

202. **Questions for Discussion.** 1. Was it doubt or faith or both that led John to send the messengers? 2. In what particulars are modern Christians superior to John? 3. Had the woman been pardoned before she met Jesus at Simon's house? 4. Why is she persistently identified with Mary Magdalene? 5. Is it necessary to be a great sinner in order to love Jesus very much? 6. Is it not best to grow naturally into the love of God, as Jesus did?

CHAPTER 25.

Christ Teaching at Capernaum and by the Sea.

Matt. 12:22; 13:53; Mk. 3:19; 4:33; Lu. 11:14-33; 8: 19-21; 4:18. Harmony, 55-57.

203. **Anxiety of Christ's Friends.** Arriving at Capernaum from his second preaching tour (Autumn, A. D. 28), the people were so anxious to hear him and Jesus so enthusiastic to preach that he could not so much as eat bread. When his friends (not his family), heard it, they went out to lay hold on him: for they said, He is beside himself.

204. **Warning Against Blasphemy.** (1) The great popularity of Jesus attracted the attention of the leaders in Jerusalem and they sent scribes to Capernaum to watch him. (2) One day a man, possessed with a demon, blind and dumb, was brought to him and he healed him. (3) The multitudes were amazed, and said, Can this be the son of David? But the Pharisees said, This man casts out demons, by Beelzebub the prince of demons. (4) Jesus said, Every kingdom, city or house divided against itself shall not stand: If Satan casteth out Satan, he is divided against himself; how then shall his kingdom stand? (5) If I by Beelzebub cast out demons, by whom do your sons cast them out? therefore shall they be your judges. But if I by the Spirit of God cast out demons it is a sign that the kingdom of God is come upon you. (6) Or how can one enter into the house of the strong man, except he first bind the strong man? (7) He that is not with me is against me; and he that gathereth not with me scattereth. (8) Every sin and blasphemy shall be forgiven; but the blasphemy against the Spirit shall not be forgiven, for it is an eternal sin. Whosoever shall speak against the Son of man, it shall be forgiven him; but who shall speak against the Holy Spirit, it shall not be forgiven him, neither in this world, nor in that which is to come.

205. Demanding a Sign. (1) Then certain of the scribes and Pharisees answered, Teacher we would see a sign from thee. (2) He answered, An evil and adulterous generation seeketh after a sign; and there shall no sign be given to it but the sign of Jonah, for as he was three days and three nights in the belly of the whale; so shall the Son of man be three days and three nights in the heart of the earth. (3) The men of Nineveh shall stand up in the judgment with this generation, and shall condemn it: for they repented at the preaching of Jonah; and behold, a greater than Jonah is here. (4) The queen of the south shall rise up in the judgment with this generation, and shall condemn it: for she came from the ends of the earth to hear the wisdom of Solomon; and behold, a greater than Solomon is here.

206. Warning Against Relapse. The unclean spirit, when he is gone out of the man, passeth through waterless places, seeking rest, and findeth it not. Then he saith, I will return into my house; and when he is come, he findeth it empty, swept, and garnished. Then he taketh with himself seven other spirits more evil than himself, and they dwell there: and the last state of that man becometh worse than the first. Even so shall it be also unto this evil generation.

207. A Woman's Praise. As he said these things, a woman, moved by motherly ambition, said, Blessed is the womb that bare thee, and the breasts which thou didst suck. But he said, Yea rather, blessed are they that hear the word of God, and keep it.

208. The True Kindred of Christ. (1) While he was yet speaking his mother and his brethren stood without seeking to speak to him. (2) When one told him, he answered, Who is my mother? and who are my brethren? And he stretched forth his hand toward his disciples, and said, Behold, my mother and my brethren! For whosoever shall do the will of my Father who is in heaven, he is my brother, and sister, and mother.

209. **The Eight Parables by the Sea.** (1) On the same day, after the exciting discussion, Jesus left the house and went to the seaside, probably to avoid his enemies and the throng, and began to teach. (2) When the multitude increased, he entered into a boat that they might hear him better and for the first time he taught by means of parables. (3) The first five he spake in the presence of the people at the seaside, in the following order: 1. *The Sower.* After this the disciples seem to have interrupted him by the following question, showing their surprise at his new method of teaching: "Why speakest thou to them in parables?" (4) Jesus gave his reasons as follows: Unto you it is given to know the mysteries of the kingdom of heaven, but to them it is not given. For whosoever hath, to him shall be given, and he shall have abundance: but whosoever hath not, from him shall be taken away even that which he hath. (5) Therefore speak I to them in parables; because seeing they see not, and hearing they hear not, neither do they understand. (6) Many prophets and righteous men desired to see the things which ye see, and saw them not; and to hear the things which ye hear, and heard them not. (7) Then follows the interpretation of the parable of the sower, and the warning: A lamp is not put under a bushel. Take heed, therefore, how ye hear. Then follow in succession II. *The Tares;* III. *The Seed Growing Secretly;* IV. *The Mustard Seed;* V. *The Leaven.* At this point Jesus left the people and returned to the house. Here at the request of his disciples he interpreted the parables of the Tares, and spoke VI, the parable of The Treasure, VII, of the Merchantman and VIII. of the Draw-net. In conclusion Jesus added: Have ye understood all these things? They say to him, Yea. He said: Every scribe who hath been made a disciple to the kingdom of heaven is like unto a man that is a householder, who bringeth forth out of his treasure things new and old.

210. **Explanatory Notes.** 1. Name and compare the *sources.* Analyze accurately the contents of each parable; locate places on the

map; memorize Matt. 13:12. 2. *The "friends"* in Mk. 3:21 must not be identified with the members of his family (Mk. 3:31). They were simply what the term indicates. 3. What is here recorded occurred in the city of Capernaum after *his return* from his last circuit. 4. The *tremendous enthusiasm* of Jesus may have led to the opinion of his friends that he was insane. 5. This was the first time that the Messianic title *"Son of David"* was tentatively applied to Jesus. 6. The *powerful impression* recently made by Jesus induced a number of scribes from Jerusalem to come to Galilee for the purpose of counteracting his influence. 7. *Beelzebub,* composed of Baal—the supreme god of the Phoenicians—and the word "Ebub"—insect; means literally "the fly god," i. e. the defender against insects. In the New Testament the word is invariably applied to Satan, the ruler or prince of the demons (Matt. 10:25; Mark 3:22). 8. In his reply to their charge the *Lord emphasizes,* first, its folly and, secondly, its wickedness (Matt. 12:29, 31). Since Satan had made the possessed one his captive, Jesus, by dispossessing him showed himself the stronger. 9. *Exorcism* was a common profession among the Jews (Matt. 12:27; Mk. 9:38; Acts 19:13) Jos. Ant. 8, 2, 5 describes the juggleries practiced by them. 10. *They charge Jesus* with being possessed not with an ordinary demon but with the devil himself. 11. *Blasphemia* is derived from the Greek blapto—to slander, to revile the name or reputation of any one. 12. In the New Testament and in Christian usage blasphemy denotes *a condition of* spiritual deadness which often manifests itself by expressions of hatred against God and divine things. 13. This sin is known by *three names:* (a) Blasphemy against the Holy Spirit (never the *sin* against the Holy Ghost, Matt. 12:31). (b) The unpardonable sin (Heb. 6:4-10). (c) An eternal sin (Mk. 3:29). 14. From Matt. 26:24 it appears that in *Judas* we have a man who has committed the blasphemy against the Holy Spirit. 15. Blasphemy is called *"an eternal sin"* and unpardonable (Mk. 3:29) because it is incurable. By reason of spiritual insensibility the heart is rendered incapable of repentance, which is the condition of pardon, and this again is due to the fact that character has become fixed in its choice of evil. 16. Blasphemy must be *clearly distinguished* (a) from *sins* against the Holy Spirit, which consist in resisting the strivings of the Holy Spirit, and of which all believers are more or less guilty: (Eph. 4:30. "Grieve not the Holy Spirit." 1 Thess. 4:8); (b) from the sin against the Son of Man which consists in ascribing the works of Christ to the influence of demons. *This* sin the Lord himself declared was pardonable, because excusable, since the fulness of Christ's Godhead was veiled on earth and the experience of the Lord's power very limited. 17. Matt. 12:40 points to the resurrection as the great sign that Jesus is the Messiah. The point of comparison is: As Jonah was given up by the sea monster, so death will give back Jesus.

211. 1. The grave charge of the Pharisees that Jesus was in league with evil spirits may have aroused the *motherly instincts* of Mary and led her to dissuade him from overexerting himself. 2. Mary here showed the same spirit that Christ had twice before *gently rebuked* (Lu. 2:41; Jno. 2:8). In his father's work merely human bonds must give place to higher obligations. It is evident that Mary and his brothers were presuming too much on their near blood relationship. 3. Jesus insists that family ties are inferior to those of the kingdom of God. Mark 3:34 and 35 give us Jesus' beautiful definition of what constitutes true relationship to him. Those are the members of his family who do God's will. 4. On the *Lord's method* of teaching see the chapter on "The Work of Christ." 5. The growing emnity against him and the utter spiritual incapacity to see the true nature of his teaching induced the Lord to change the form of teaching and to adopt the parabolic method. This would hide his meaning from blasphemers and skeptics whose anger he was unwilling to excite too much at this time and would at the same time explain and open the secrets to the seekers after truth. The parable preserves like a husk that which it temporarily conceals in order that later it may come to light. 6. Mark 4:25 states a principle of modern pedagogy, namely: what one learns depends upon what one has learned. Progress in knowledge depends upon whether a solid foundation has been laid. 7. Notice the three pairs of parables: (a) Tares and Drag Net (the first emphasizes the present intermixture, the second, the future separation); (b) Merchantman and Treasure (One seeking, the other finding without seeking); (c) Mustard Seed and Leaven (external and internal growth).

212. **Practical Lessons.** 1. Nowhere is Satan cast out but by the stronger, as the history of civilization and present day experience prove. 2. Modern, so-called Christian nations have driven the devil into savage nations by giving them rum, gunpowder, slavery, smallpox and thereby causing extinction or deterioration of races. 3. There is no golden age for the world except the reign of Christ. 4. Apprehension felt that *blasphemy* has been committed is a sure sign that there has been no commission of it, for he who really sins in this way feels no contrition. 5. Jesus' friends try unconsciously to carry out the plans of his enemies by seeking to restrain him from work. 6. The claims of God and his kingdom take precedence over family ties; when they conflict the latter must yield to the former. 7. "Long is the road by precepts; short and

effective by illustrations" (Seneca). 8. The whole universe is a parable which hides God from the unworthy, while it reveals him to the devout. 9. The four classes of hearers are, (a) the heartless, (b) shallow-hearted, (c) half-hearted, (d) whole-hearted. 10. Spiritual stupidity is the characteristic of the first-class of hearers; shallowness and impulsive emotionalism that of the second; inconsistency and mixed motives of the third, the fourth avoids the danger of the other three classes. 11. Tares are not bad men in the world but counterfeit Christians in the church. As the field is the world outside of the church, evil men being of the world, have therefore no business in the church. 12. The origin of evil in the world is (a) not of God whose very essence is light, (b) not inherent in matter, as the Gnostics taught (Gen. 1:31), (c) not developed in man, (d) but imported from outside by the devil. Man is the victim of temptation, and, therefore, the object of God's mercy and redeemable, because his essence is not devilish. 13. As tares resemble wheat, so Satan often appears as an angel of light. Evil never professes to be evil, but endeavors to pass as virtue by applying well sounding names to sinful practices, e. g. business dishonesty calls itself smartness and foresight. 14. The kingdom of God is growing steadily. There is an irresistible trend in modern civilization toward higher and better conditions; forces for good are at work that are evidently beyond the control of any man or combination of men to stop or impede them. 15. The seed growing secretly teaches that true faith is active and progress gradual. 16. The church has ever been the place of refuge, defense, rest and security from all kind of oppression (cf. woman's condition among the heathen nations, treatment of children and aged, improvement of social conditions). All kinds of birds find shelter, alas, even birds of prey, heretics and oppressors. 17. Leaven is generally used as a symbol of corruption (1 Cor. 5:7), but here it is a symbol of the transforming influence of the truth. 18. Leaven is useless while it lies alone; Christians can improve the world, not by withdrawing from it, but by mixing with it. 19. The *parable of the Leaven* teaches the generative power of the Gospel, (1) in the life of the individual, (a) as to his mind, giving him a new view of life; (b) as to his soul, creating in him a new love to God and man; (c) as to his will, giving him a new aim; (d) as to his body, teaching him that it is to be a temple of the Holy Spirit. (2) In the family, teaching the husband, wife and children their respective duties. (3) In the State, (a) by securing to the ruler the necessary authority, Rom. 13; (b) by impressing on the authorities their solemn responsibility to the supreme Ruler; (c) by teaching all citizens that righteousness exalteth a people. 20. Personal religion is a treasure that can be had only at the cost of personal sacrifice. 21. The parable of the treasure hid in a field illustrates the doctrine of prevenient grace, by which is meant a divine influence which precedes any good effort on the part of the sinner. (Matt. 11:25; Rom. 9:16; John 15:16; "Das Glück," by Schiller). 22. The parable of the pearl teaches (1) that Christ must be personally appropriated. It is not sufficient to partake of many blessings under the shelter of the great mustard tree (church) or enjoy the benefits of the society leavened by the gospel; each man must make Christ his own by a distinct act of his own will. (2) The seeking of good pearls (virtues) is the way to find the one priceless pearl (Christ). So e. g. St. Augustine, Justin Martyr; Luther, Neander. 23. "Lord thou hast made us for thee and our heart is restless within us till it has found rest in thee." (Augustine's Confessions). 24. The final judgment will be a day of, (a) Revelation, (b) Separation, (c) Decision. 25. Kant's argument in favor of a final judgment: (1) (Major premise): Human conscience ("practical reason") demands that everyone should receive his due. (2) (Minor premise): But it is a fact that in this world virtue is crucified and vice crowned; (3) (Conclusion): Therefore there must come a final incorruptible judgment where every man shall receive his due.

213. **Reference Literature.** Farrar, Ch. 22 and 23; Andrews, p. 274; Davis on "devil," p. 169; on "Satan," p. 648; on parables, p. 541; Hast. D. of C. on blasphemy I, 208; on unpardonable sin II, 787; Herzog, Sünde wider den heiligen Geist; Bruce, Parabolic Teaching of Christ; on the scenery around the Sea of Galilee, see Stanley, Sinai and Palestine, p. 425; Trench, the Parables of Christ; Spurgeon's Sermons on the Parables; Thompson's Land and Book II, p. 111-114; Heid. Cat. Qu. 6 and 7 Westm. Shorter Cat. Qu. 1 Thiersch, Die Christliche Familie; Schmidt, Reconstruction of Ancient Society through Christianity; Farrar, Seekers after God; St. Augustine's Confessions; The Imitation of Christ by Thomas a Kempis.

214. **Questions for Discussion.** 1. Why did the friends of Jesus believe him to be insane? 2. Has such a charge been brought against other great persons? 3. What did the Pharisees mean by a "sign"? 4. What is the sign of Jonah? 5. What is the danger of merely giving up bad or questionable habits, instead of aiming at radical conversion? 6. Who are members of Christ's family? 7. Was Jesus indifferent to family relations? 8. Trace in these eight parables the history of God's kingdom on earth.

CHAPTER 26.

Miracles On and Near the Sea of Galilee.

Matt. 8:23-9:34; Mk. 4:35-5:43; Lu. 8:22-56. Harmony 58-61.

215. **The Stilling of the Tempest.** (1) In the evening of this eventful and exciting day Jesus said to his disciples, Let us go over to the other side. They take him, even as he was, in the boat. And other boats were with him. (2) There arose a great storm and the waves beat into the boat, so that the boat was now filling. But he was asleep. (3) They awake him, and say, Teacher, carest thou not that we perish? Then he rebuked the wind, and said unto the sea, Peace, be still. And the wind ceased, and there was a great calm. Jesus said, Why are ye fearful? have ye not yet faith? (4) And they feared exceedingly, and said, Who then is this that even the wind and the sea obey him?

216. **The Gadarene Demoniacs.** (1) When they landed on the Eastern shore, in the country of the Gadarenes (Gerasenes) there met him one or two possessed with demons coming forth out of the tombs, exceeding fierce, so that no men could pass by that way. (2) They cried, What have we to do with thee, thou Son of God; art thou come hither to torment us? Jesus said, What is thy name? The demon answered, My name is Legion for we are many. (3) Now, there was afar off a herd of swine feeding, and the demons besought him, If thou cast us out, send us into the herd of swine. He said, Go. And behold the whole herd rushed down the steep into the sea, and perished. (4) They that fed them fled into the city, and told everything. (5) And all the city came out to meet Jesus: and besought *him* that he would depart from their borders.

217. **Jairus and the Sick Woman.** (1) Probably on the following morning Jesus crossed over to Capernaum and the multitude welcomed him; for they were all waiting for

him. (2) Jairus, ruler of the synagogue, fell down at Jesus feet, and besought him to come for his only daughter, about twelve years of age, was dying. (3) As he went the multitudes thronged him. (4) A woman having an issue of blood twelve years, who had spent all her living upon physicians and could not be healed, came behind him and touched the border of his garment: and immediately the issue of her blood stanched. (5) Jesus said, Who touched me? When all denied, Peter said, Master, the multitudes press thee. But Jesus said, Some one did touch me; for I perceived that power had gone forth from me. (6) When the woman saw that she was not hid, she came trembling, and falling down before him declared for what cause she touched him, and how she was healed immediately. (7) Jesus said, Daughter, thy faith hath made thee whole; go in peace. (8) While he yet spake came one from the ruler of the synagogue saying, Thy daughter is dead; trouble not the Teacher. (9) But Jesus answered, Fear not: only believe, and she shall be made whole. (10) When he came to the house, he suffered none to enter in with him, save Peter, and John, and James, and the parents of the maiden. (11) As all were weeping, and bewailing her, he said, Weep not; for she is not dead, but sleepeth. And they laughed him to scorn. (12) But he took her by the hand and said, Talitha Kumi, (Maiden arise). And she rose up immediately: and he commanded that something be given her to eat. (13) And her parents were amazed: but he charged them to tell no man.

218. **Two Blind Men and a Dumb Demoniac Healed.** (1) As Jesus went home two blind men followed him, crying out, Have mercy on us, thou son of David. (2) When he was come into the house, they came to him, and Jesus saith, Believe ye that I am able to do this? They say, Yea, Lord. Then touched he their eyes, saying, According to your faith be it done unto you. And their eyes were opened. (3) Jesus strictly charged them, See that no man know it. But they went forth, and spread abroad his fame in all

that land. (4) There was also brought to him a dumb man possessed with a demon. And when the demon was cast out he spake: and the multitudes marvelled, saying, It was never so seen in Israel. (5) But the Pharisees said, By the prince of the demons casteth he out demons.

219. **Explanatory Notes.** 1. Name and compare *sources;* especially the variations; trace Christ's movements; locate places; memorize Lu. 8: 48; On Decapolis, see ¶6 (5). 2. On the demoniac see the chapter on "The Work of Christ." 3. *Gergesa,* on the east shore of the Sea of Galilee (R. V. Geresa) may have been the name of the district while Gadara was the name of the town in this dis‍trict. 4. Matthew, who was present, mentions two demoniacs, Mark and Luke, but one. The most probable explanation is that there were indeed two, but one of the two being more promi‍nent either by reason of his fierceness or because he was of a higher rank in society, or because later he became a disciple, is alone men‍tioned by Luke and Mark, who received their information at second hand. 5. The *request of the Gergasenes* that Jesus should with‍draw shows how material interests ruled their minds, and that their friends were of less value in their estimation than their swine. 6. Notice the language of *double consciousness* in Mark 5: 9. 7. *A "legion"* was a body of Roman soldiers numbering six thousand. With this instrument of oppression, a word of terror to conquered nations, is compared the cruel power which had gained the mas‍tery over these men. 8. The tombs were natural ravines in the mountains on the lake. 9. The keeping of swine is an indication of non-Jewish nationality. 10. Each synagogue had *one or more "rulers"* (Luke 13: 14) who had general charge of the synagogue worship. They were neither preachers nor pastors in our sense of the word; but presided at the service and selected from the congregation the person to read the Scriptures and to address the congregation, Acts 13: 15 (See ¶34). 11. "An issue of blood," i. e. *chronic hemorrhage.* It is more likely that Jesus exerted his power consciously and intentionally, although the woman in her crude con‍ception of the nature of Jesus believed that the Lord's power was exercised independently of his will. 12. The *selection of Peter,* James and John is the first instance recorded of special preference of these three above the other nine apostles (other instances are: Transfiguration, and in Gethsemane). 13. *Boisterous weeping* and wailing by hired mourners were the symbols of Oriental grief. 14. In Matt. 9: 27 is found the first record that Jesus was directly ad‍dressed by his *Messianic title.* In Matt. 12: 23 the people ask

æntatively, "Is this not the Son of David?" or as the American Revision says "Can this be the Son of David?" 15. Son of David was the most popular of the many designations for the Messiah current in the time of Jesus. Its use rested on the promise given to David (2 Sam. 7:13, 16; Ps. 89:35-37) that his throne should abide forever. This prediction was amplified by the prophets who identified this coming King of David's race with the Messiah (Isa. 9:6, 7).

220. **Practical Lessons.** 1. The Christian is not in peril from being in the world, but from getting the world into himself. (Mk. 4:37; Jno. 17:15). 2. You business men, make Jesus your senior partner, for the biggest mistake the disciples ever made was in thinking that Jesus couldn't manage a boat. 3. Seasons of calmness in life: (1) the evenings at home, (2) the "quiet hour" during the day, (3) Sabbath, (4) sickbed, (5) when ambitions subside, (6) at death's door, (7) in heaven. 4. When Satan has free rein he makes man an untamable beast, lost to decency, a terror to society, a destroyer of his own body and soul. 5. The demons are neither skeptics nor atheists (Mk. 5:6-13). 6. As Christ was excluded from Gadara he wanted the men to stay and bear witness. 7. A sordid commercial spirit still bids Christ depart where his presence interferes with material gain. 8. We are not lost in the crowd; Christ singled out the woman, as he observed the widow at the treasury and loved Martha and Mary and Lazarus. 9. Christ taught a new idea of death. The ancient Christians therefore called the resting place of the dead, "Koimeterion"—place of sleep, from which our word "cemetery" is derived.

221. **Reference Literature.** Farrar, Ch. 23; Andrews 294. Mrs. Hemans, O Thou: that in its wildest hour, etc.; On the violent and sudden tempests on the Sea of G. see Thompson, The Land and the Book, p. 374.—Trench, Miracles, p. 171, note; Davis, on "legion," p. 428.

222. **Questions for Discussion.** 1. How is the military term, legion, specially appropriate here? 2. Why did Jesus not take the man with him? 3. What were Christ's reasons for making the sick woman's act public? 4. What light does Lu. 8:55 throw upon Christ's method of healing. 5. What characteristics of Jesus appear in the incident of the raising of the maiden?

CHAPTER 27.

Christ's Third Preaching Tour.

Matt. 9:35-11:1; 14:1-12; Mk. 6:29; Lu. 9:1-9. Harmony 63-65.

223. **Second Rejection at Nazareth.** (1) It was about Jan., A. D. 29 when Jesus and his disciples left Capernaum for his third preaching tour. (2) They went to Nazareth, and on the sabbath he taught in the synagogue; (3) Many were astonished saying, Whence hath this man these things, and what mean such mighty works wrought by his hands? (4) Is not this the carpenter, the son of the carpenter and of Mary, and brother of James and Joses (Joseph) and Judas, and Simon? and are not his sisters here with us? And they were offended in him. (5) Jesus said, A prophet is not without honor, save in his own country, and among his own kin, and in his own house. (6) He could there do no mighty work, save that he laid his hands upon a few sick folk, and healed them. (7) And he marvelled because of their unbelief.

224. **The Preaching Tour Continued.** Leaving Nazareth Jesus went about all the cities and the villages of Galilee teaching in their synagogues and preaching the gospel of the kingdom, and healing all manner of disease.

225. **The Mission of the Twelve.** As Jesus considered the apostles sufficiently prepared he sent them out for the first time independently. (1) The *reason* for sending them was the great need. When Jesus saw the multitudes, he was moved with compassion because they were distressed and scattered as sheep not having a shepherd. Then saith he unto his disciples. The harvest indeed is plenteous, but the laborers are few. Pray ye therefore the Lord of the harvest that he send forth laborers into his harvest. (2) Their *spiritual equipment.* He gave them authority over unclean spirits, to cast them out and to heal all manner of

disease. (3) The *field*. Jesus charged them: Go not to the Gentiles and enter not into any city of the Samaritans; but go to the lost sheep of the house of Israel. (4) Their *Message and Mission*. Now as ye go preach, the kingdom of heaven is at hand. Heal the sick, raise the dead, cleanse the lepers, cast out demons. (5) *Simplicity of Life.* Freely ye received, freely give. Get you no money; no wallet, neither two coats, nor shoes, nor staff: for the laborer is worthy of his food. (6) *Their Support.* Into whatsoever city ye shall enter, search out who in it is worthy; and there abide till ye go forth. (7) *Wisdom* enjoined. I send you forth as sheep in the midst of wolves: be ye therefore wise as serpents, and harmless as doves. (8) *Help in persecution* promised: But beware of men: for they will deliver you up to councils, and in their synagogues they will scourge you; before governors and kings shall ye be brought. But be not anxious how or what ye shall speak: for it shall be given you in that hour what ye shall speak. For it is not ye that speak, but the Spirit of your Father that speaketh in you. (9) *Christ's example* should encourage them. A disciple is not above his teacher. If they have called the master Beelzebub, how much more them of his household. Be not afraid of them that kill the body, but are not able to kill the soul: but rather fear him who is able to destroy both soul and body in hell. (10) *Loyalty* enjoined: Every one who shall confess me before men, him will I also confess before my Father who is in heaven. But whosoever shall deny me before men, him will I also deny before my Father who is in heaven. (11) *Effect of their preaching.* Think not that I came to send peace on the earth: but a sword. For I came to set a man at variance against his father, and the daughter against her mother, and the daughter-in-law against her mother-in-law; and a man's foes *shall be* they of his own household. (12) *Christ before family.* He that loveth father or mother, son or daughter more than me is not worthy of me. He that doth not take his cross and follow after me, is not worthy of me. He that findeth his life shall lose it; and he that loseth his life for my sake shall find it. (13) *Reward for receiving them.* He that receiveth you receiveth me, and he that receiveth me receiveth him that sent me. (14) When Jesus had finished commanding his twelve disciples, he and they went out to teach and preach in the cities. The disciples cast out demons and anointed the sick with oil and healed them.

226. **Death of the Baptist.** (1) At that season (about March A. D. 29), Herod Antipas, the tetrarch of Galilee and Perea, heard the report concerning Jesus, and said unto his servants, This is John the Baptist; he is risen from the dead; and therefore do these powers work in him. (2) Others said, it is Elijah or one of the old prophets risen again. And Herod desired to see Jesus. (3) On Herod's birthday, it was that the daughter of Herodias danced, and pleased Herod. Whereupon he promised with an oath to give her whatsoever she should ask. (4) And she, being put forward by her mother, saith, Give me here on a platter the head of John the Baptist. (5) The king was grieved; but for the sake of his oaths, and of them that sat at meat with him, he commanded it to be given. (6) So his head was brought on a platter, and given to the damsel and she brought it to her mother. (7) John's disciples buried the body and told Jesus.

227. **Explanatory Notes.** 1. Name and compare the *sources;* trace the Lord's movements on the map; memorize Matt. 9:37. 2. For the features distinguishing the second rejection from the first one recorded in Luke 4:16, see ¶146 (6). 3. The Lord *adds to the proverb,* "and in his own house," because by this time even his own brothers had become doubtful as to his mission (Jno. 7:15). 4. The *plural "sisters"* shows that Jesus had more than one sister and that he was therefore one of a family of not less than seven children. 5. How long the third preaching tour continued can not be determined. Matthew's language that "Jesus went about *all* the cities and villages" suggests a considerable period. 6. *"Distressed and scattered"* i. e. spiritually uncared for. The figure of the harvest means that unless saved they will perish like ripe wheat that i

not reaped. 7. Notice the gradual *training of the Twelve.* In the Sermon on the Mount he instructs them in the principles of the kingdom; in the eight parables by the sea he taught them the development of the kingdom. For some time they accompanied him on his journeys; now he sends them out without him, yet in pairs. Later narratives show this training carried still farther. Let no one say the apostles had no Seminary training. 8. Their labors were *confined to Galilee.* They were forbidden to enter Samaria and it is unlikely that they went into Judea from which portion the Lord was excluded. 9. The *duration* of their labors was at least several weeks. Journeying two by two they could visit many towns in a few weeks. 10. *The mission* of the twelve was to announce that the Messiah had appeared and to confirm these words by miracles. 11. The *purpose of the injunction* in Mark 6:8 and 9 is to secure simplicity and freedom in their work. The customs of the land made it unnecessary to provide for travelling expenses since they went afoot and could obtain free entertainment everywhere. 12. The *dress of an ancient Oriental* was quite simple consisting of a pair of sandals, a turban, a tunic (a garment in form not unlike a long shirt round which the girdle was bound), and a cloak (scarcely more than a large square piece of cloth). Two tunics, one for Sabbath or festivals, were a sign of comparative wealth (Luke 3:11), and it was this that Jesus forbade. He himself apparently wore but one (Jno. 19:23). "Purses," literally "girdles,"were used not only for holding together the loose outer robe, but as a place to carry money. "Wallet" (A. V. "scrip") was a leather bag for carrying provisions. "Nor shoes:" Possibly meaning an extra pair, since Christ did not mean that His disciples should go barefooted (see Mk. 9). 13. The instructions are comprehensive and probably a summary of what Christ had told them on different occasions. They had prospective reference to their larger work after the Lord's ascension and even, in some measure at least, to all missionary work of the church. Some directions are plainly temporary, as for instance those not to visit the heathen or the Samaritans, and to make no provision of money or clothing. 14. "Shaking off the dust" was a symbolic act which meant that they would have nothing more to do with the people. It was a custom of the rabbis; as they considered the dust of a Gentile country defiling, they shook it off when entering Judæa (Mt. 18: 17; Acts 13:51; 18:6). 15: *"Salute it"* (Matt. 10:12) with the common Eastern greeting "Peace be unto you." "Peace" means the peace of the kingdom of heaven of which they were the messengers. 16. *During the mission* tour of the Twelve the Baptist's death occurred, about March, A. D. 29. After Christ's return to

Capernaum, John's disciples met him there and announced the sad event. 17. Notice the *manner* in which all synoptists introduce the report of John's death indicating the use of one and the same documents. 18. That Herod should not have *heard earlier* of one who crossed and re-crossed his dominions followed by great multitudes is best explained by the supposition that during Christ's ministry Herod was absent from Galilee, either living in Perea or on a visit to Rome or at war with Aretas, the father of his first wife whom he had put away. 19. The *occasion* of John's death was either Herod's birthday or his name day, or the anniversary of his accession to the throne. The latter would make the date of the Baptist's death April, A. U. C. 782, since Herod the Great died a few days before the passover in April, A. U. C. 750. 20. *Josephus* in Ant. 18: 52 says that John's death excited great consternation among the Jews because they regarded him as a prophet.

228. **Practical Lessons.** 1. Men are to witness to the truth as far as they know it. 2. The preaching of the gospel has ever been accompanied by the relief of bodily ills and acts of philanthropy. 3. Christians should not refuse all intercourse with or refrain from a second attempt to win those who reject Christ at the first presentation. 4. These rules were for a rapid mission whose main object was to arouse attention, and prepare for a future more extensive ministry. The principle contained in the Lord's instructions as to dress, namely great simplicity, is still binding on the minister. 5. Missionary motives: (a) Loyalty and obedience to Christ (Matt. 28: 19); (b) The need of men (Matt. 9: 36; Lu. 15); (c) Love to our neighbor (Matt. 22: 39); (d) Sense of stewardship (Matt. 10: 81); (e) The reflective influence on us (Acts 4: 20). 6. A promise may be broken if its fulfillment involves the commission of a crime. 7. A true instinct told John's disciples where to go for refuge in their great bereavement and loneliness.

229. **Reference Literature.** Farrar, Ch. 26 and 28; Stalker, ¶105; Andrews 307; Edersheim, Life of Jesus, I, 591; Davis, D. B. on Apostle, p. 42; on Herod, p. 289.

230. **Questions for Discussion.** 1. Why are a person's gifts very often not appreciated at his native place? 2. Why is faith a condition for obtaining blessings? 3. Give the evidence that the restriction of the missionary field was temporary. 4. What principle underlies Matt. 10: 9, 10? 5. Was it literally and always obeyed? (See Lu. 22: 35-36). 6. Why did the disciples use remedies (oil, Mk. 6: 13) when Jesus did not? 7. What was the harvest in Matt. 10: 5? 8. Why did not Herod hear of Jesus before this? 9. Must one keep a criminal promise?

CHAPTER 28.

The Great Crisis at Capernaum.

Matt. 14:13-15:20; Mk. 6:30-7:26; Lu. 9:10-17; Jno.
6:1-71. Harmony 66-69.

231. Seeking Rest near Bethsaida. (1) When Jesus
and all the apostles had returned to Capernaum from the
third missionary tour, he said, come apart to a desert place
and rest awhile. (2) For, as the passover was near (April,
A. D. 29) large multitudes were gathering in Capernaum,
so that they had not even leisure to eat. (3) Therefore
they rode in a boat to the western Bethsaida and sat down
on a mountain. (4) When the people saw this they followed on foot and outwent them. (5) He welcomed them,
healed their sick and taught them.

232. The Feeding of the Five Thousand. (1) When even
was come, the disciples said, send them away to buy food.
Jesus said, Give ye them to eat. (2) Turning to Philip he
asked, Whence are we to buy bread, that these may eat?
This he said to prove him: for he knew what he would do.
Philip answered, Two hundred shillings worth of bread is
not sufficient for them, that every one may take a little. (3)
Andrew saith, There is a lad here, who hath five barley
loaves, and two fishes; but what are these among so many?
(4) Jesus said, Make the people sit down. And they sat
down, about five thousand. (5) Jesus took the loaves; and
having given thanks, distributed to them; likewise also of
the fishes. (6) When they were filled, he saith, Gather up
the broken pieces which remain over, that nothing be lost.
So they gathered twelve baskets.

233. Offer to Make Jesus King. (1) When the people
saw the sign which he did, they said, This is of a truth the
prophet that cometh into the world. (2) Jesus therefore
perceiving that they were about to take him by force, to
make him king, constrained his disciples to go by boat to the

western Bethsaida (Mk. 6:45), then he sent the people away, and himself withdrew again into the mountain to pray.

234. **Jesus Walking on the Water.** (1) When the disciples had rowed about five and twenty or thirty furlongs, they beheld Jesus walking on the sea, drawing nigh unto the boat. (2) Supposing it was an apparition, they were afraid. But he said, It is I, be not afraid. (3) Peter said, Lord, if it be thou, bid me come. Jesus said, Come. Peter walked upon the waters. But when he saw the wind he was afraid, and beginning to sink, he cried out, Lord, save me. Jesus took hold of him and saith, O thou of little faith, wherefore didst thou doubt? (4) When both were in the boat, the wind ceased; and they that were in the boat worshipped him, saying, Of a truth thou art the Son of God.

235. **Landing at Genesaret.** (1) Probably on account of the storm they landed at Genesaret, the plain south of Capernaum, instead of at Bethsaida as they had intended (Mk. 6:45). (2) The men of that place knew Jesus had sent into all that region and brought all that were sick. These besought him that they might only touch the border of his garment, and as many as touched were made whole.

236. **Seeking Jesus.** (1) Many people remained over night at the place of the feeding expecting Jesus to return from the mountains as they knew that he had not left in the boat with his disciples. (2) In the morning, when they saw neither Jesus nor his disciples they went to Capernaum in boats which had meanwhile arrived, seeking Jesus. (3) They met him in the synagogue and said, Rabbi, when camest thou thither?

237. **Discourse on the Bread of Life.** (1) Exposing the selfish motive underlying their interest, Jesus said, Ye seek me, not because ye saw signs but because ye ate of the loaves. Work not for the food which perisheth but for the food which abideth unto eternal life. (2) They: What work must we do? Jesus: Believe on him whom God hath

sent. They: What doest thou for a sign, that we may see, and believe thee? Our fathers ate manna in the wilderness. Jesus: I am the bread of life; he that cometh to me shall not hunger, and he that believeth on me shall never thirst. The Jews murmured: Is not this the son of Joseph? How doth he say, I am come down out of heaven? Jesus: By this bread I mean my flesh, which I will give for the life of the world. The Jews: How can this man give us his flesh to eat? Jesus: Except ye eat the flesh of the Son of man and drink his blood, ye have not life in yourselves. He that eateth my flesh and drinketh my blood hath eternal life; and I will raise him up at the last day.

238. **Results of the Discourse.** (1) Many of his disciples said, This is a hard saying. Jesus explaining his mystical words said, It is the spirit that giveth life; the flesh profiteth nothing; the words that I have spoken unto you are spirit, and are life. But there are some of you that believe not. For Jesus knew from the beginning who they were that believed not, and who it was that should betray him. Upon this many of his disciples walked no more with him. (2) Then said Jesus unto the twelve, Would ye also go away? Peter answered, Lord to whom shall we go? thou hast the words of eternal life. And we have believed and know that thou art the Holy One of God. Jesus answered, Did not I choose you the twelve, and one of you is a devil?

239. **Eating with Unwashed Hands.** (1) Galilean visitors at the recent passover (April 18, A. D. 29), no doubt had spread the news of the feeding of the five thousand and of Christ's great popularity. This induced Pharisees and scribes from Jerusalem to come and watch him. (2) They noticed that some of his disciples ate bread with unwashen hands, and they ask him, Why walk not thy disciples according to the tradition of the elders? (3) Jesus said, Well did Isaiah prophesy of you hypocrites, This people honoreth me with their lips, But their heart is far from me Ye leave the commandment of God and hold fast the

tradition of men. (4) Moses said, Honor thy father and
thy mother; but ye say, If a man shall say to his father or
his mother, That wherewith thou mightest have been profited by me is Corban, that is to say, Given *to God;* ye
no longer suffer him to do aught for his father or his
mother; making void the word of God by your tradition.
(5) And he called to him the multitude, and said, There
is nothing from without the man, that going into him can
defile him; but the things which proceed out of the man are
those that defile and make him unclean. (6) Then came the
disciples and said, Knowest thou that the Pharisees were
offended, when they heard this saying? He answered,
Every plant which my heavenly Father planted not, shall be
rooted up. Let them alone: they are blind guides. And if
the blind guide the blind, both shall fall into the pit. (7)
When he was entered into the house from the multitude,
Peter and his disciples asked of him the meaning of the
parable. He saith, whatsoever from without goeth into the
man, cannot defile him; because it goeth not into his heart.
But that which proceedeth out of the man defileth the man.
(8) For from within evil thoughts proceed, fornications,
thefts, murders, adulteries, covetings, wickednesses, deceit,
lasciviousness, an evil eye, railing, pride, foolishness: all
these evil things proceed from within, and defile the man.

240. **Explanatory Notes.** 1. Name and compare the *sources;*
locate places; trace our Lord's movements; on Bethsaida, see ¶7;
memorize Jno. 6: 35. 2. The *purpose of* this retirement probably
was: (a) desire to obtain rest for himself and the Twelve; (b)
to hear their reports; (c) to calm his soul which was no doubt
agitated by the report of the death of his faithful forerunner. All
this could not be obtained at Capernaum. 3. Note that here is *one
passover mentioned* at which the Lord was not in Jerusalem, probably because the sentence of death was hanging over him and his
time had not yet come. (4) The *effect of this miracle* was to confirm the people in their false Messianic hopes that the Messiah
would bring chiefly temporal prosperity. The people evidently
recalled the promise of Moses, Deut. 18: 15—"The Lord thy God
will raise up unto thee a prophet from the midst of thee, of thy

brethren, like unto me; unto him ye shall hearken." And seeing
in this miracle a likeness to Moses who fed their fathers with
manna (Jno. 6:30 and 31), they concluded that Jesus was the
promised prophet. 5. The *"loaves"* here spoken of were thin, flat
barley cakes, something like large crackers. It took three such
loaves to make a meal for one man. The loaves and fishes used
in this miracle were purchased by the disciples from a boy who had
apparently brought his own luncheon (Jno. 6:9). 6. The Lord
had to *constrain his disciples* to depart, for two reasons: (a) they
were unwilling to leave him alone with this multitude that showed
signs of forcing him to become the leader of an insurrection; (b)
The desire to make him king created an atmosphere which was
unsafe for the disciples who themselves were not free from false
Messianic ideas. 7. This is the second instance mentioned of a
night spent alone in prayer (cf. Luke 6:12 and 13, the night prior
to the choice of the Twelve). A crisis and bitter conflict were
ahead of him in the coming weeks. 8. It is most instructive that
Jesus *did not dally with this temptation* for a moment. Though
on a small scale it was similar to that after his baptism (Matt.
8:10). 9. Some interpreters have labored to show that the
phrase *"upon the Sea"* may mean that Jesus walked along the
shore parallel to the vessel. But the records appear to describe
an amazing miracle. 10. "About the *fourth watch* of the night,"
i. e. between 3 and 6 A. M. The night beginning at 6 P. M. was,
according to the Roman method of reckoning, divided into four
watches of about three hours each. In Roman times the number
of watches was four, sometimes described by their numerical
order (Matt. 14:25), sometimes by the terms "evening" (closing
at 9 P. M.), "Midnight"—"cock crowing" (3 A. M.); "morning"
(6 P. M.). The old Jews recognized only three watches. See
D. B. 11. John 6:47-56 mentions the distance which they had
rowed when they saw Jesus, 25 or 30 stadia, about three miles, the
stadium being about one-ninth of a mile. As the lake was about
45 furlongs broad at the northern end, Christ's appearance occurred
about half way.

241. 1. *Genesaret* is a plain on the west side of the Sea of
Galilee, running from Magdala on the south to Capernaum on the
north and extending backward to the irregular line that bounds it
on the west. 2. This discourse was a *crucial test* of his worldly
minded followers and many of the larger circle of his adherents
left him. It marks also a crisis in the relation of the twelve to
him, but all the twelve remained steadfast. 3. This *confession of
Peter* is to be distinguished from that made later, (Matt. 16:16),
which displays a higher knowledge of the Lord's person. Here he

calls Jesus "The Holy One of God" expressing his Messiahship; there he calls him "The Son of the Living God" expressing the Deity of Jesus. 4. The terms *"eating his flesh* and drinking his blood" are synonymous with the term "Believing in him," appropriating him by vital faith, Jno. 6:53. They teach the so-called "Unio Mystica" (mystical union) and not the bodily presence of Christ in the Lord's supper. The Lord's own interpretation is decisive—"It is the Spirit that quickeneth," Jno. 6:63. 5. The *delegation* mentioned (Matt. 15:1), sent by the leaders from Jerusalem to watch and oppose Jesus in Galilee was the second for such a purpose. 6. The eating with unwashed hands shows that the disciples were becoming indifferent to the Pharisaic traditions. 7. On the tradition of the elders, see ¶30 (5). 8. "Corban" means "devoted to God" and thus excluded from use for other purposes. (See Edersheim, Vol. I, p. 19). If e. g. parents asked of a son any article, he could simply say, "corban," that is, it is consecrated to God, adding in his mind, "as far as my parents are concerned." Then he was not only permitted but bound to withhold it. But afterwards he was not bound to give the article to the temple. By such shameless hypocrisy the Jews were able to cover inhuman selfishness with the garb of religion, and to nullify the explicit command of God that children should honor their parents. 9. Note the severity of Christ's reply. For the first time he addresses them openly as hypocrites (lit.: "maskwearers," from the custom at the theatres). 10. John 6:22—40 records Christ's break with the Jewish political hopes, and Mk. 7:1-23 his decisive break with Jewish traditions. In the first instance he repulsed the people, and in the latter, the leaders. The words spoken in private to his disciples regarding the Pharisees suggested that he had given up the hope of impressing them.

242. **Practical Lessons.** 1. This miracle forms the brilliant inauguration of that continuous miracle of Christian charity which constantly multiplies bread for the hungry. 2. We must assimilate Christ, that is, his thoughts, feelings, habits, and thus become like him whom we love. 3. History furnishes examples of how hard it is to refuse a crown (Cæsar, King of Poland). 4. That Christ felt this as a recurrence of temptation is proved by his retirement for prayer, and the fact that he constrained his disciples, who may have urged him to accept the offer, to go away. 5. Perils of Tradition. It is *common* to attach the greatest weight to the oldest opinion. Yet it is not correct to look for the highest wisdom in antiquity; because, as Bacon reminds us, we are the ancients, and they who lived before us belonged to the childhood of the race. On the other hand, ideas that have stood the test of time

win a certain guarantee of their solidity in comparison with raw notions, suddenly springing from the imagination of a new thinker. But that is only the case when those ideas are being constantly tested by experience and criticism; and it does not apply after tradition has become petrified and has attained the rank of a venerated idol. Tradition sometimes claims to be of divine origin, handed down in the Church from the time of the Apostles in a line of authorized teachers. The extravagant pretensions of Romanism, founded on the authority of tradition, which the Council of Trent declared to be of equal value with that of Scripture, warn us against the danger of trusting such claims. Tradition may become an excuse for unfaithfulness to Divine revelation. Thus it was with the Jews, the Romanists and others. 6. In every religious community there is a tendency to place the keeping of certain observances that are added to the law above the law itself; to consider these extra things as the marks of a religious man, to call a man religious or irreligious according as he does or does not things that have as little to do with fundamental morality as the washing of hands before eating. We are apt, all of us, to pay attention to the means rather than to what is the great end of all religion; to wash our hands instead of our hearts.

243. **Reference Literature.** Farrar, Ch. 29, 30; Andrews, 320; Edersheim, Life of Jesus I, 676; II, 3-36; Davis, D. B. on Lord's Supper; Deems, Gospel of Spiritual Insight; How Jesus is the bread of life is made plain by Henry Drummond, in "The Changed Life," and "The Greatest Thing in the World." On the bearing of John 6 on the Lord's Supper, see Cambridge, Com. I, p. 152.

244. **Points for Discussion.** 1. Did Jesus believe in vacation periods? 2. Why did not Jesus attend this passover? 3. Do men to-day follow Jesus from similar motives as these people? 4. Why did not Jesus meet the murmurs about his supposed parentage and place of birth by revealing the mystery of his earthly origin? 5. Or is the stronger emphasis of his heavenly origin an indirect answer. 6. Has the old Pharisaic "corban" spirit died out among Christian children? 7. Why has ritualistic formalism the tendency to kill the real life of religion?

245. Review Questions.

1. Name the first two chief divisions of the Life of Christ? Also the subdivisions of each, and give the dates of chief and subdivisions? 2. Enumerate the events of each subdivision in the order of time. 3. Of the *Year of Popularity,* (a) explain the name; (b) state the provinces of the ministry; (c) the duration; (d)

the events and dates of the beginning and the end of the period; (e) the two subdivisions; (f) the sources of information by gospels and chapters. 4. Trace the Lord's movement on the map as contained in the first and second subdivisions and name the events connected therewith. (To assist the memory, group the events around Christ's principal movements: 1. Removal to Capernaum; first preaching tour; trip to his 2d passover at Jerusalem. 2. Journey to Mt. of Beatitudes; second preaching tour, to Gadara; to Bethsaida—See table of contents). 5. Enumerate in chronological order the more notable miracles of the period. 6. Give in the order of time the more prominent discourses. 7. Name the "Lake group" of the parables in the order spoken. 8. Mention some persons with whom Christ came in contact. 9. What was the general attitude of the rulers and the people toward Christ during this period? 10. Name some prominent characteristics of this period as to amount and kind of work, organization of forces, etc.

DIVISION IV.

The Year of Opposition

From the Crisis at Capernaum *to* the Triumphal Entry into Jerusalem; from the Passover, April 18, A. D. 29 to Palm Sunday, April 2, A. D. 30, or about one year.

TWO SUB-DIVISIONS.

I. **The Third Period of the Galilean Ministry.** From the Crisis at Capernaum, until the Final Departure for Jerusalem, From the Passover, April 18, to November, A. D. 29, or about seven months.

II. **The Perean Ministry.** From the Final Departure for Jerusalem until the Triumphal Entry into Jerusalem. From November, A. D. 29 to April 2, A. D. 30, or about five months.

First Sub-division.

THE THIRD PERIOD OF THE GALILEAN MINISTRY.

CHAPTER 29.

First Northern Journey to Tyre and Sidon.

Matt. 15:21-16:12; Mk. 7:24-8:26. Harmony 70-74.

246. **The Syrophoenician Woman.** (1) As after the crisis at Capernaum not only the leaders but also the people and even many of his disciples in the wider sense of the word became indifferent or hostile, Jesus left Capernaum and withdrew into the region of Tyre and Sidon with the intention of hiding himself (Mk. 7:24). (2) But a Canaanitish woman cried out, Have mercy on me, O Lord, thou

Son of David, my daughter is grievously vexed with a demon. But he answered her not a word. (3) His disciples besought him, Send her away, for she crieth after us. He answered, I was not sent but unto the lost sheep of the house of Israel. (4) She worshipped Him, saying, Lord, help me. He said, It is not meet to take the children's bread and cast it to the dogs. She replied, Yea, Lord; but even the dogs eat of the crumbs which fall from their master's table. (5) Then Jesus said, O woman, great is thy faith; be it done unto thee even as thou wilt. And her daughter was healed from that hour .

247. **Return through Decapolis.** (1) After a brief stay, Jesus departed from that region (in summer A. D. 29). Going through Decapolis he came nigh unto the Sea of Galilee, where he went up into the mountain. (2) Here came unto him great multitudes, having with them the lame, blind, dumb, maimed and many others and they cast them down at his feet; and he healed them; insomuch that the multitude wondered and glorified the God of Israel.

248. **Healing of a Deaf Mute.** (1) One of the sick was deaf, and had an impediment in his speech. (2) He took him aside from the multitude, put his fingers into his ears, spat, touched his tongue; and looking up to heaven, he sighed and said, Ephphatha, that "Be opened." (3) His ears were opened, the bond of his tongue was loosed and he spake plain. (4) Jesus charged them that they should tell no man; but the more he charged them, so much the more they published it. (5) They were beyond measure astonished, saying, He hath done all things well; he maketh even the deaf to hear and the dumb to speak.

249. **The Feeding of the Four Thousand.** (1) When there was again gathered together a great multitude, Jesus said to his disciples, I have compassion on the multitude, because they continue with me now three days and have nothing to eat, and I would not send them away fasting, lest they faint on the way. (2) The disciples say: Whence should we have so many loaves in a desert place as to fill so

great a multitude? Jesus said, How many loaves have ye? They said, Seven and a few small fishes. (3) Then he commanded the multitude to sit down on the ground and took the loaves and fishes, gave thanks, brake them, gave to the disciples, and the disciples to the multitude. (4) They all ate and were filled and took up of broken pieces seven baskets full. (5) They that did eat were four thousand men, beside women and children.

250. **Pharisees and Sadducees demand a Sign.** (1) After the feeding he sent away the multitudes and entered into the boat and came into the borders of Magadan (or Dalmanutha) on the southeast shore of the lake. (2) Here Pharisees and Sadducees trying him demanded a sign from heaven. (3) Sighing deeply, he answered: When it is evening, ye say, It will be fair weather; for the heaven is red. And in the morning, It will be foul weather to-day; for the heaven is red and lowering. Ye know how to discern the face of the heaven; but ye cannot discern the sign of the times. (4) An evil and adulterous generation seeketh after a sign; and there shall no sign be given unto it, but the sign of Jonah. (5) He left them, and again entering into the boat departed to the other side (to Bethsaida).

251. **The Leaven of the Pharisees.** (1) The disciples forgot to take bread along, having with them not more than one loaf. (2) So when he charged them, Beware of the leaven of the Pharisees, the Sadducees and of Herod, they reasoned: We have no bread. (3) Jesus perceiving it saith, Why reason ye because ye have no bread? Do ye not remember the five loaves among the five thousand and how many baskets ye took up? Neither the seven loaves among the four thousand and how many baskets ye took up? (4) Then they understood that He meant the teaching of His opponents.

252. **The Blind Man near Bethsaida Julias.** (1) When their boat landed at Bethsaida, they bring to him a blind man, and beseech Him to touch him. (2) He took him by the hand, brought him out of the village, spit on his

eyes, laid his hands upon him, and asked him, Seest thou aught? He looked up and said, I see men, as trees, walking. (3) Then again he laid his hands upon his eyes and he saw all things clearly. (4) He sent him away to his home, saying, Do not even enter into the village.

253. **Explanatory Notes.** 1. Name and compare the *sources;* locate places; trace the Lord's movements on the map; memorize Matt. 15:32. 2. Tyre is *about* 35 *miles,* in an air line northwest from the Sea of Galilee, and Sidon about 25 miles further north, both on the Mediterranean coast, chief cities of old Phœnicia which was at that time a part of the Roman province of Syria. 3. *Reasons* for the withdrawal: (a) Disappointment expressed by the 5,000 people whom he had fed, (b) abandonment of him by many of his followers, (c) intensified opposition on the part of the Pharisees, conditions all of which were unfavorable for further evangelistic work in Galilee; (d) Moreover, Christ desired to find the rest which he had sought in vain on the east side of the lake (Mk. 6:31). 4. As this journey was not for preaching but *for retirement* and intercourse with his disciples, he did not wish to have his presence known (Mark 7:24). 5. Christ did *not lower* himself to the level of Jewish prejudice and call this woman a "Gentile dog." The figure means to declare that to enter on Messianic activity among the heathen would be as much out of order as for a man to take his children's bread and cast it to the dogs. The time for the heathen would soon come. Christ's personal efforts were to be confined to the Jews. Yet this limitation is not absolute. For sufficient reasons he is willing to go outside as in this case. 6. *"Canaanitish"* describes her religion as a non-Jew; "Greek," or "Syro-Phoenician" denotes her nationality. 7. Mark 7:31 indicates an extended and somewhat *circuitous journey,* for the most part entirely outside of Jewish territory leading him perhaps into the city but at least into the vicinity of Damascus. 8. *Where the healing* of the deaf man occurred is not exactly stated. It probably took place on Jesus' return into the vicinity of the Sea of Galilee, as there is no suggestion that the man was a Gentile. 9. On *Decapolis* see ¶6 (5). 10. Some hold that the stories of the feeding of the 5,000 and of the 4,000 are two reports of one miracle. But the points favoring the view that there were two such events are as follows: (1) Matthew and Mark relate both, Mark especially distinguishing the two by the word "again," (Mark 8:1). (2) They differ: (a) as to the locality, the feeding of the five thousand took place near Bethsaida

in Galilee, the feeding of the four thousand in a desert place somewhere in the Decapolis territory or near the Sea of Galilee; (b) as to the quantity of food; (c) as to the quantity of fragments gathered up; (d) as to the time the multitude had been with Jesus; (e) as to the events both preceding and following the miracle. 11. *Magadan* and Dalmanutha are either two names for the same place or one denotes the district and the other the village, or both places were very near together. The place is located by Robinson on the S. E. shore of the Sea of Galilee (Mark 8: 13); others indentify it with Magdala, south of Capernaum. 12. This is the first time that the Sadducees are named as acting unitedly with the Pharisees in opposition to Christ. His teaching had begun to expose their errors also. Mark substitutes "Herod" for Sadducees, because he was one. 13. By *"a sign from heaven"* they meant some visible manifestation of God's glory, or some change in the heavenly bodies, or thunder and lightening. The miracles that He had already worked were sufficient to prove His claims to be the Messiah. It would have been wrong for Him to work a miracle merely to please His enemies. Even if He had done so, they would have found some excuse for rejecting it. 14. Here again Christ regards *his resurrection* as the chief sign of his Messiahship. 15. In Matt. 16, 2, 3 Jesus implies that it is *man's duty* to interpret current events, to read in passing history God's message without asking for portents from heaven. In the condition of the Jewish people and in Jesus' own life was all the evidence they needed that he was the Messiah. 16. By "leaven" Jesus *means principles* taught or exemplified which, like leaven, tend to transform man's character into likeness to themselves. 17. *From Dalmanutha* the Lord crossed the sea and probably went directly to Bethsaida Julias, east of the Jordan, without stopping at Capernaum. 18. Here, as in several other cases, *Christ does not wish* attention drawn to him as a healer because he did not regard relief of suffering as His highest duty, or happiness in the sense of physical comfort, the highest good.

254. **Practical Lessons.** 1. Many sons and daughters are vexed with the demons of lust, selfishness, dishonesty, envy, jealousy, intemperance. Jesus only can cast them out. 2. Difficulties are not intended to discourage but to strengthen our faith and character. 3. True faith is humble, earnest, persevering, importunate. 4. The blind man's gradual healing is a type of man's conversion and progress in holiness.

255. **Reference Literature.** Farrar, Ch. 34; Andrews, 332. On the miracle see the books of Trench, Macdonald; Edersheim, Life of Jesus II, 37 and 63; Land and Book II, 635. Poems: "Taulers

Faith" by Whittier, and the "Syro-Phœnician Woman," by Macdonald. Examine the paintings; Davis D. B. on Decapolis, p. 164.

256. **Questions for Discussion.** 1. How is this blind man's condition typical of the Gentile world? 2. What principle respecting his personal mission did Jesus enunciate in Matt. 15, 24? 3. On what ground did he make an exception to this rule? 4. What general principles are suggested in this conduct of Jesus? 5. How may Jesus' warning in Mk. 8: 15 be expressed in terms of our experience to-day?

CHAPTER 30.

Second Northern Journey to Cæsarea Philippi.

Matt. 16: 13; Mk. 8: 27-9: 13; Luke 9: 18-36.   Harmony 75-77.

257. **Peter's Confession.** (1) Leaving Bethsaida Julias Jesus came into the parts of Caesarea Philippi. (2) After praying alone, he asked his disciples, Who do men say that the Son of man is? They answered, some say, John the Baptist; some, Elijah; others, Jeremiah, or one of the prophets. (3) He saith, But who say ye that I am? Peter answered, Thou art the Christ, the Son of the living God. Jesus answered, blessed art thou, Simon Bar-Jonah, for flesh and blood hath not revealed it unto thee, but my Father who is in heaven. (4) Thou art Peter, and upon this rock I will build my church; and the gates of Hades shall not prevail against it. (5) I will give unto thee the keys of the kingdom of heaven; whatsoever thou shalt bind on earth shall be bound in heaven; and whatsoever thou shalt loose on earth shall be loosed in heaven. (6) Then charged he the disciples that they should tell no man that he was the Christ.

258. **First Announcement of His Death and Resurrection.** (1) After Peter's great confession, Jesus considered His disciples prepared to be told in plain words that he must go unto Jerusalem, and suffer many things of the

elders and chief priests and scribes, and be killed and the third day be raised up. (2) Peter began to rebuke him, saying, Be it far from thee, Lord; this shall never be unto thee. (3) But he said unto Peter, get thee behind me, Satan, thou art a stumbling block unto me; for thou mindest not the things of God, but the things of men.

259. **The Duty of Cross-bearing.** (1) Then said Jesus unto his disciples, If any man would come after me, let him deny himself and take up his cross and follow me. For whosoever would save his life shall lose it, and whosoever shall lose his life for my sake, shall find it. (2) For what shall a man be profited if he shall gain the whole world and forfeit his life? Or what shall a man give in exchange for his life? (3) The Son of man shall come in the glory of his Father with his angels, and then shall he render unto every man according to his deeds. There are some of them that stand here, who shall in no wise taste of death, till they see the Son of man coming in the kingdom.

260. **The Transfiguration.** (1) Six days after Christ's announcement of His death Jesus taketh with Him Peter, James and John into a high mountain to pray. (2) As he was praying, he was transfigured before them; his face did shine as the sun, and his garments became white as the light and dazzling. There appeared Moses and Elijah talking with him of his death at Jerusalem. (3) The disciples were heavy with sleep; but when they were fully awake they saw his glory and the two men. (4) Peter said unto Jesus, Lord, it is good for us to be here; if thou wilt, I will make here three tabernacles; one for thee, and one for Moses, and one for Elijah. (5) While he was yet speaking, a bright cloud overshadowed them; and a voice said, This is my beloved Son, in whom I am well pleased; hear ye him. (6) When the disciples heard it, they fell on their faces and were sore afraid. Jesus touched them and said, Arise and be not afraid. Lifting up their eyes they saw no one, save Jesus only. (7) As they were coming down from the mountain, Jesus commanded them: Tell the

vision to no man until the Son of man be risen from the dead.

261.　**The True Elijah.**　(1) On their way down from the mountain his disciples asked him: Why say the scribes that Elijah must come before the advent of the Messiah? (2) Jesus answered, Elijah is come already, and they knew him not, but did unto him whatsoever they would. Even so shall the son of man also suffer of them. (3) Then understood the disciples that he spake unto them of John the Baptist.

262.　**Explanatory Notes.**　1. Name and compare the *sources;* locate places; trace the Lord's movements; memorize Matt. 16: 18. 2. *From Bethsaida* Jesus went into the villages of (i. e. adjacent to) Cæsarea Philippi, 25 miles north of Bethsaida, at the foot of Mt. Hermon. 3. On the city, see ¶9 (3). 4. Here (Lu. 9: 18 and 29), as before *other important events,* Jesus engaged in solitary prayer. See also his baptism (Lu. 3: 21); the choosing of the twelve; the crisis at Capernaum and at Gethsemane. 5. The *answer of the disciples* shows that Jesus fell below the popular expectation of the Messiah. Christ's conduct being in striking contrast to their Messianic ideal, the people seemed to regard Jesus rather as the forerunner of the Messiah than as the Messiah himself. 6. Peter's answer is not the confession of a new faith, but of loyalty to the old one. This does not imply that his conception of the Messiah had remained unchanged. It had become more spiritual. Note the development of the disciples' conception concerning the person of Christ: (a) Andrew to Peter at Bethany, Jno. 1:41: "We have found the Messiah;" (b) after the feeding of the five thousand, "The Holy One of God;" (c) here the belief in Christ's Deity. 7. "Thou art Peter" may mean, (1) from now on you are to be known by your second name which you bore from childhood (like John Mark, Saul-Paul); or, (2) Jesus pointing back to John 1:42 means to say, "you have to-day made good the name which I prophetically gave you when I first saw you;" or (3) the name was given on this occasion and Jno. 1:42 was only a promise for the future: "thou shalt be called Peter." 8. *"Upon this rock."* Various interpretations (1) on the person of Peter; (2) on the faith in Christ's Deity (Chrysostom, Ambrose, Augustine), (3) on men of Peter's type and spirit. The best Protestant exegetes defend the first, as grammatically the most natural interpretation. No one would have thought of any other if it had not been the desire to escape Rome's astounding inferences from such an interpretation. But in order to demolish those pretenses we must not follow Rome's example by doing violence to the text. The demonstrative pronoun "this" points to the person of Peter, he being the first believer and confessor of Christ's Deity, and thus the first real Christian. Hence the meaning is: "on thee, as the first stone, I will lay others like you, in the building up of my church." This interpretation concedes Peter's primacy, but denies him any supremacy. The truth about Peter's position in the church is, (1) he was the leader among the apostles, (a) in Christ's time, (b) in the founding of the Church, (c) in the inauguration and defense of Gentile missions. (2) This primacy was personal, not official; he was a born leader; (3) the power of the keys (which Rome says implies *official* headship) was later given to all the apostles, and to any congregation (Jno. 20:23; Matt. 18:17); (4) According to Gal. 2:9 he was only one of the "three pillars." (5) He was not the founder of the Church at Rome, except perhaps very indirectly through Roman converts at Pentecost (Acts 2:10). (6) He was never bishop of Rome; (7) Consequently the pope is not his successor; (8) but even if he were, Jesus dealt here with Peter's person. Everything that is awarded to him rests on a personal act of faith, and therefore cannot be mechanically and legally transferred to other persons, especially not to popes, many of whom were worldly-minded men. (9) The legitimate successors of Peter are the believers in Christ's Deity. 9. Hades, from the Greek "a" privative—not—and "idein," to see, hence the unseen and therefore unknown land. It is a translation of the Hebrew "Sheol," the underground abode of the dead. In Old Testament times this was held to be a place of gloom and wretchedness. In the time of Jesus it was regarded as divided into two portions, "Paradise" (Lu. 23:43), or "Abraham's bosom" (Lu. 16:22), where the blessed enjoy great felicity, and "Gehenna," where the wicked suffer inconceivable torments (Lu. 16:23). Between the two there was an impassable gulf (Lu. 16:26). 10. The Gates of Hades. Two interpretations: (1) Hades is the world of the dead whose gates imprison all mankind. This power to destroy life shall not overpower the Church; she will remain forever. (2) "Gates" refers to the Oriental custom of holding counsel at the city gates ("The Porte"); hence the counsels of destruction shall not avail against my church." The translation "hell," meaning the place of the wicked, and the interpretation, "Satan shall not destroy the Church" are exegetically wrong, although containing a general truth taught in other places. 11. By *"the keys of the kingdom"* is meant the authority to teach the conditions on which men are admitted to the kingdom, as Peter did on the day of Pentecost; by binding and loosing is meant the power to declare what is right and what is wrong, as Peter did on many occasions; Peter enjoyed these powers in common with the other Apostles. 12. Key was an *oriental symbol of authority.* Peter was to open the treasure of divine truth and the kingdom of God, as a key opens a palace. Beyschlag says: "To bind is to declare anything to be either obligatory or forbidden; to loose is to declare anything to be not obligatory." The purport of this figurative utterance is that the church, as the representative of Christ,—but only in so far as she does represent Him,—is the norm of truth in the world (1 Tim. 3: 15). This binding and loosing is to be done by means of preaching and church discipline. Crafty priests have perverted also this saying into the authority to control the powers of the unseen world and to lord it over God's people.

263. 1. *After the confession* of the Twelve the Lord considered them prepared to be led into the deep mystery of the suffering of the Messiah. Having grasped the one truth (the Deity of Jesus), they must begin to learn the other—the necessity of the Atonement and the Resurrection. 2. Christ's teaching assumes a *new character.* This is the first of the three clear announcements of Christ's death. For previous allusions to his death in figurative language, see Jno. 2: 19 (Destruction of the temple of his body); Jno. 3: 14 (lifting up of the Son of Man); Mark 2: 20 (Removal of the bridegroom); Jno. 6: 5 (Giving his flesh for the life of the world). He foretells not only the fact but also the agents, form place and issue of his death. 3. Peter, although *intensely loyal,* was still ignorant. He could not yet associate death with his Messiah. Therefore from this time forward Jesus spoke with his disciples again and again concerning his death. See Mark 9: 30-32; 10: 32-34. 4. Every time that Jesus announced his death he also announced his resurrection. For previous references to his resurrection see Jno. 2: 19 (Destroy this temple, etc.); Luke 11: 30 (the sign of Jonah). 5. In Matt. 16: 23 Jesus meant to say that *Peter's words* were a temptation to Him to try to save His life by not doing His duty, just as Satan's words were at the time of the temptation in the wilderness (Matt. 4: 10). 6. The clause "till they see the kingdom of God" (Matt. 16: 28) may refer to (1) the transfiguration which was a temporary glory; (2) the resurrection; (3) the outpouring of the Holy Spirit; (4) the destruction of Jerusalem; (5) the guarantee that the Jewish race will continue till the Second Advent. 7. According to tradition the transfiguration took place on Mt. Tabor, a few miles from Nazareth.

1400 feet above the plain. Others determine on Mt. Hermon, in the vicinity of Cæsarea Philippi. This latter view is confirmed by Mark 9: 30-32. From the mountain of transfiguration Jesus went "through Galilee" to Capernaum, but a journey from Mt. Tabor would not have taken him through Galilee. Moreover, the top of Mt. Tabor was probably fortified at this time. 8. Luke speaks indefinitely of "about eight days," including the day on which Christ foretold his death and the day on which the transfiguration occurred. Matthew and Mark speak more definitely of six days, excluding from their reckoning these two days. 9. *Light is shed* on the interpretation of the transfiguration by the fact that it followed Christ's first explicit announcement of his death and his return in glory, a thought which greatly perplexed the disciples. The transfiguration taught the disciples: (1) That the death of the Messiah was a part of the Old Testament conception of the Messiah. (2) His temporary glory served as a pledge of the fulfillment of his recent words about entering into his glory through death. (3) The voice was a new confirmation of the Messiahship and Sonship of Jesus (2 Peter 1: 17 and 18). The meaning of the transfiguration for Jesus: (a) a foretaste of the glory as a reward after His sufferings (Phil. 2: 5-11); (b) assurance that the mystery of the cross was understood by the saints in heaven; (c) the approving voice of the Father. 10. The disciples thought that *Elijah's appearance* on the mountain was the fulfillment of Malachi 4: 5, and they expressed surprise that he had not come before the advent of Christ. Jesus corrected this misapprehension, telling them that the Elijah of whom they were thinking had already come in the Baptist. Because the people had hindered him from restoring all things, the other Scriptures regarding the suffering of the Son of man would now be fulfilled. 11. Why *"tell no man?"* The report of his Transfiguration would have aroused false hopes. After his resurrection these reports will help the truth. 12. John does not mention the Transfiguration. His counterpart is given Jno. 12: 23-41.

264. **Practical Lessons.** 1. Popular opinion about Christ may be interesting, but personal convictions are vital. 2. The Christian church is not built on creeds but on men filled with the Holy Ghost. 3. The most momentous question that confronts every man is what he thinks about Christ. 4. Take care of your character and your reputation will take care of itself (Mk. 7: 15). The relation is that of the substance to the shadow. 5. Obedience to God is better than popularity. 6. To deny ourselves means to say no to our inclinations. 7. It is good to be in the clear atmosphere of God's nearness and away from the misery, unbelief and

trouble of the world. 8. The presence of Moses and Elijah is a proof of the conscious, intelligent and useful life of believers after death.

265. **Reference Literature.** Farrar, Ch. 35, 36; Andrews, 351; on Cæsarea Philippi, Mt. Tabor and Hermon, see B. D.; Jos. Jewish war, 4, 1, 8; Stanley, Sinai and Palestine, p. 392. Raphael's famous painting in Rome, "The Transfiguration." On the "Rock" and "Keys" see Pinnock's Christ our King; Gunsaulus, "The Transfiguration;" Smith's Hist. Geog. of Pal.; Rhees, The Life of Jesus, 155-160. On Hades, see Piercy, D. B., p. 340; Hast. D. of C. I, 713; Schluesselgewalt, Herzog, Vol. 13; Davis on "hell," p. 286; on "church," p. 135.

266. **Questions for Discussion.** 1. Did Peter prove a rock in the High Priest's palace and at Antioch (Gal. 2)? 2. If not, was Christ's estimate of him erroneous? 3. How did Peter reach his conviction? 4. What question did the appearance of Elijah suggest to the disciples? 5. How does Peter's confession resemble Andrew's in Jno. 1:41, and how does it differ? 6. What was the central and permanent element in the disciples' faith in Jesus?

CHAPTER 31.

Journey from the Transfiguration to Capernaum.

Matt. 17:14-18:35; Mk. 9:14-50; Luke 9:37-49. Harmony 78-81.

267. **The Demoniac Boy.** (1) When, on the next day, Jesus and the three disciples came down from Mt. Hermon to the other nine disciples, they saw a great multitude about them, and scribes, questioning them. (2) The multitude when they saw him, were greatly amazed, and running to him saluted him. (3) He asked them, What question ye with them? There came a man, kneeling to him, and saying, Lord, have mercy on my son; for he is epileptic and suffereth grievously; for ofttimes he falleth into the fire and ofttimes into the water. And I brought him to thy disciples and they could not cure him. (4) Jesus said, All things are possible to him that believeth. The father said, I believe,

help thou mine unbelief. (5) Jesus said, O faithless and perverse generation, how long shall I bear with you? Bring him hither. Jesus rebuked him, and the demon went out of him, and the boy was cured. (6) Then the disciples said, Why could not we cast it out? He saith, Because of your little faith. If ye have faith as a grain of mustard seed, ye shall say unto this mountain, Remove hence to yonder place and it shall remove; and nothing shall be impossible unto you.

268. **Christ's Second Announcement of His Death.** (1) Leaving Mt. Hermon they passed through Galilee; and he would not that any man should know it. (2) For he taught his disciples, Let these words sink into your ears. The Son of man shall be delivered up into the hands of men, and they shall kill him; and after three days he shall rise again. (3) But they understood not the saying and were exceeding sorry and afraid to ask him.

269. **The Shekel in the Fish's Mouth.** (1) When they were first come to Capernaum, they that received the half shekel temple tax asked Peter, Doth not your teacher pay the half shekel? He saith, Yea. (2) When he came into the house, Jesus spake to him, What thinkest thou, Simon, from whom do the kings of the earth receive tribute? From their sons or from strangers? (3) When he said from strangers, Jesus said, Therefore the sons are free. But, lest we cause them to stumble, go thou to the sea and cast a hook, and take the fish that first cometh up; and when thou hast opened his mouth, thou shalt find a shekel; that take, and give unto them for me and thee.

270. **Discourse on Humility.** (1) On the way from Mt. Hermon the disciples had been reasoning as to who was the greatest in the kingdom of heaven. (2) When they had reached the house, Jesus asked, what were ye reasoning in the way? But they held their peace. (3) Then he set a little child in the midst of them and said, Except ye become as little children, ye shall in no wise enter into the kingdom of heaven. (4) Whosoever shall humble himself,

as this little child, the same is the greatest in the kingdom of heaven.

271. **Occasions of Stumbling.** (1) Whoso shall receive one such little child in my name receiveth me; but whoso shall cause one of these little ones that believe on me to stumble, it is profitable for him that a great millstone should be hanged about his neck and that he should be sunk in the depth of the sea. (2) Woe unto the world because of occasions of stumbling; for it must needs be that the occasions come; but woe to that man through whom the occasion cometh! (3) If thy hand or thy foot causeth thee to stumble, cut it off, and cast it from thee; it is good for thee to enter into life maimed or halt, rather than having two hands or two feet to be cast into eternal fire. If thine eye causeth thee to stumble, pluck it out and cast it from thee; it is good for thee to enter into life with one eye, rather than having two eyes to be cast into the hell of fire. (4) See that ye despise not one of these little ones; for I say unto you, that in Heaven their angels do always behold the face of my Father who is in heaven.

272. **Co-operation.** John said, Master, we saw one casting out demons in thy name; and we forbade him, because he followeth not with us. But Jesus said, Forbid him not, for he who is not against us, is for us.

273. **Brotherly Discipline.** (1) If thy brother sin against thee, show him his fault between thee and him alone. If he hear thee, thou hast gained thy brother. But if he hear thee not, take with thee one or two more, that at the mouth of two witnesses or three, every word may be established. If he refuses to hear them, tell it unto the church. If he refuses to hear the church, let him be unto thee as the Gentile and the publican. (2) What things ye shall bind on earth shall be bound in heaven; and what things ye shall loose on earth shall be loosed in heaven. (3) If two of you shall agree on earth as touching anything that they shall ask, it shall be done for them of my Father who is in

heaven. For where two or three are gathered together in my name, there am I in the midst of them.

274. The Duty of Forgiveness. (1) Then said Peter, Lord, how oft shall my brother sin against me, and I forgive him? Until seven times? Jesus saith, until seventy times seven. To enforce this precept, Christ spoke the *Parable of the Unmerciful Servant.* (Matt. 18:22-35).

275. Explanatory Notes. 1. Name and compare the *sources,* especially the variations in Matt. 18:1 and Mk. 9:33, and as to the time of the transfiguration; locate places; trace the Lord's movements; memorize Matt. 18:20. 2. From the *Mount of Transfiguration* Jesus passed through Galilee as secretly as possible (Mark 9: 30) because his object was no longer to teach the multitudes who had been seduced into rejecting him and among whom he could hardly appear in safety. 3. The *collectors of the half-shekel* must not be confounded with the publicans who collected money for the government. The tax demanded here was the temple tax (about 30 cents) which every Jew above the age of 20 was obliged to pay yearly (Ex. 30:13). This incident is illustrative of the attitude of Jesus towards the laws of the land. 4. The form of the *question implies* that this tax was then overdue and it is possible, as Edersheim holds, that it was the tax for the last passover which Jesus did not attend. Having also been absent from Capernaum for some time, the payment had been delayed. 5. The words that the *son of a king* is not taxed to support the king's house, echoes the consciousness of one who knew that he was "the Son" and greater than the temple. He paid the tax, but he put the payment on the ground that he would not give offense by causing them to regard him as opposed to the temple service. The point of the question evidently is that by reason of his unique relation to the kingdom of God, he is by right free from paying the tax. 6. Some regard the expression *"a shekel in the fish's mouth"* as an Oriental expression for the value in money of the fish caught. Is of course true!—*Vollmer.* 7. *The belief* that the long hoped for manifestation of the kingdom was approaching and the preference twice given to the three disciples may have occasioned the dispute about rank. 8. This address shows incidentally *Christ's estimate* of childhood, setting them up as teachers and showing the preciousness of the child-soul by telling them that the angels of children were especially near to God. 9. The *story of the unknown man* casting out demons in the name of Jesus belongs to the brighter side of the Galilean work, for it shows that there were here and there souls which had been profoundly influenced by the name of Jesus and which had become active in good works.

276. **Practical Lessons.** 1. Here the Lord illustrates a fixed principle of all reform, viz. the avoidance of actions which are not absolutely essential for the success of the reform and which, because easily misunderstood and thus arousing prejudice, would make it more difficult for others to join in the good movement. 2. The subjects of Christ's kingdom must be trustful, humble and unambitious, and these are the elements of true greatness. 3. Many church troubles would be nipped in the bud, if Matt. 18: 15-17 would be observed. 4. Sins once forgiven return unto the sinner through his after offenses, because all forgiveness is based on the condition that the pardoned man continues in that state of grace into which pardon has brought him. This condition is not arbitrarily imposed from without, but belongs to the very essence of salvation itself. A man rescued from the raging sea is safe on condition that he does not again cast himself into that water (Jno. 5:6; 1 Jno. 1:7). 5. The remembrance of the number and magnitude of our sins should keep us humble.

277. **Reference Literature.** Farrar, 37, 38; Andrews, 360. Consult D. of the Bible. Trench, Dod and Spurgeon on the parable; C. R. Robinson, The Childlike Spirit. There are many famous paintings of Christ and the Child; Davis, D. B. on the "disciples," p. 171.

278. **Questions for Discussion.** 1. Suggest modern applications of the lesson, in Matt. 17: 19-20. 2. What is the force of Jesus' argument respecting the temple tax? 3. As a reformer did Jesus always begin with the destruction of abuses? 4. Did he do so quite often? 5. State some of the beautiful elements of the child nature which makes it the type of a disciple of Christ? 6. What is meant by "having salt in one's self" (Mk. 9: 50)? 7. Where does the power of church discipline reside? 8. Show how Jesus' example illustrates his teaching as to forgiveness.

CHAPTER 32.

Jesus at the Feast of Tabernacles in Jerusalem.

Jno. 7: 1-8: 59. Harmony 82-85.

279. **Conversation with His Brethren.** (1) For about eighteen months (April, A. D. 28 to October, A. D. 29), Jesus had not been in Judea because the Jews sought to kill him (Jno. 5: 17). (2) When the Feast of the Tabernacles was at hand (Oct., 11-18, A. D. 29), his brethren said unto him: Go into Judea, that thy disciples there also may behold thy works. For no man doeth his works in secret, when he seeketh to be known openly. Manifest thyself to the world. (3) For even his brethren did not believe on him. (4) Jesus saith, My time is not yet come; but your time is always ready. Go ye up unto the feast; I go not up.

280. **The Secret Journey.** (1) When his brethren were gone, then went he also, but in secret, probably to avoid premature arrest. (2) The Jews sought Jesus at the feast. (3) Some said, He is a good man; others said: Not so, for he leadeth the multitude astray. Yet no man spake openly of him for fear of the Jews.

281. **Arrival and Discourse about the Sabbath.** (1) In the midst of the feast (about Oct. 14, A. D. 29), Jesus taught in the Temple. (2) The Jews marvelled, and said, How knoweth this man letters, having never learned? (3) Jesus said, My teaching is not mine but His that sent me. If any man willeth to do his will, he shall know of the teaching whether it is of God or whether I speak from myself. (4) Why seek ye to kill me? The multitude answered, Thou hast a demon: who seeketh to kill thee? (5) Jesus said, I did one work, (the healing of the infirm man), and ye all marvel. If a man receiveth circumcision on the Sabbath (that the law of Moses may not be broken), are ye wroth with me, because I made a man every whit whole on the sabbath?

282. **Opinions of the People.** (1) Some of the people of Jerusalem said, is not this he whom they seek to kill? And lo, he speaketh openly, and they say nothing unto him. Can it be that the rulers know that this is the Christ? (2) Yet we know this man, whence he is; but when the Christ cometh no one knoweth whence he is. Jesus cried, I am not come of myself, but he that sent me is true, whom ye know not. (3) Some sought to take him, but no man laid his hand on him, because his hour was not yet come. (4) Many believed on him, and said, When the Christ shall come, will he do more signs than those which this man hath done? (5) The chief priests and the Pharisees sent officers to take him and carry out their plan made eighteen months ago (Jno. 5: 16), to kill him. Jesus said, Yet a little while I am with you, and then I go unto him that sent me. (6) The Jews said will he go unto the Dispersion among the Greeks, and teach the Greeks?

283. **Discourse on the Last Day.** (1) On the last day (Oct. 18, A. D. 29), the great day of the feast, Jesus cried, If any man thirst, let him come unto me and drink. He that believeth on me from within him shall flow rivers of living waters. (2) This spake he of the Spirit, which they that believed on him were to receive.

284. **Effect of Christ's Teaching on the People.** (1) Some said, This is of a truth the prophet. Others: This is the Christ. But some said, Doth the Christ come out of Galilee? Hath not the scripture said that the Christ cometh of the seed of David? (2) On the officers of the Sanhedrin. The chief priests and Pharisees said to the officers, Why did ye not bring him? They answered, Never man so spake. The Pharisees answered, Are ye also led astray? Hath any of the rulers believed on him? But this multitude that knoweth not the law are accursed. (3) Nicodemus said, Doth our law judge a man except it first hear from himself? They answered, Art thou also of Galilee? Search and see that out of Galilee ariseth no prophet.

285. **The Woman Taken in Adultery.** (1) The night

following the "last day of the feast" Jesus spent on the Mount of Olives, probably with his friends at Bethany. Early in the morning, he came into the temple and taught the people. (2) The scribes and Pharisees bring a woman taken in adultery; and say, Teacher this woman hath been taken in adultery, in the very act. Moses commanded us to stone such: what sayest thou? (3) Jesus wrote on the ground. Then he said, He that is without sin among you, let him first cast a stone at her, and again he wrote on the ground. (4) They went out and Jesus was left alone with the woman. He asked her, where are they? Did no man condemn thee? She said, No. Jesus said, neither do I condemn thee; go thy way; from henceforth sin no more.

286. **Jesus the Light of the World.** (1) Probably on the evening of the great illumination, Jesus stood in the treasury and said, I am the light of the world; he that followeth me shall not walk in the darkness, but shall have the light of life. (2) The Pharisees said, Thou bearest witness of thyself; thy witness is not true. Jesus answered, Even if I bear witness of myself, my witness is true; for I know whence I came, and whither I go; but ye know not. (3) In your law it is written, that the witness of two men is true. I am he that beareth witness of myself and the Father that sent me beareth witness of me. (4) They said, Where is thy Father? Jesus answered, Ye know neither me, nor my Father; if ye knew me, ye would know my Father also. (5) Predicting his death, he added, I go away and ye shall seek me and shall die in your sin; whither I go ye cannot come. The Jews said "Will he kill himself?" (6) Jesus answered, when ye have lifted up the Son of man, then shall ye know that I am he, and that I do nothing of myself, but as the Father taught me. (7) As he spake these things many believed on him.

287. **Spiritual Liberty.** (1) Jesus said to those that believed him, If ye abide in my word, then are ye truly my disciples, and ye shall know the truth, and the truth shall make you free. (2) They answered, We are Abraham's

seed, and have never yet been in bondage to any man.   **(3)** Jesus said, Every one that committeth sin is the bondservant of sin.   If the Son shall make you free, ye shall be free indeed.   **(4)** If ye were Abraham's children, ye would do the works of Abraham.   But now ye seek to kill me. **(5)** They said, We have one Father, even God.   Jesus said, If God were your Father, ye would love me; ye are of your father the devil and the lusts of your father it is your will to do.   **(6)** Which of you convicteth me of sin?   If I say truth, why do ye not believe me?   The Jews answered, say we not well that thou art a Samaritan, and hast a demon? **(7)** Jesus said, If a man keep my word, he shall never see death.   The Jews said, Now we know that thou hast a demon.   Art thou greater than our father Abraham, who died? and the prophets died; whom makest thou thyself? **(8)** Jesus answered, Abraham rejoiced to see my day, and he saw it and was glad.   The Jews said, Thou art not yet fifty years old and hast thou seen Abraham?   Jesus said Before Abraham was born, I am.   **(9)** Then they took up stones to cast at him; but Jesus hid himself and went out of the temple.

288. **Explanatory Notes.** 1. Name the *sources;* locate places on map and plan of the temple; memorize Jno. 8: 12. 2. The *Feast of Tabernacles,* also called the Feast of Ingathering, was celebrated seven days as a harvest home feast and also in memory of the time when the Israelites dwelled in booths in the wilderness. For a description, see Ex. 23: 16; Lev. 23: 34; Deut. 16: 13. The booths were erected in the streets, outside the walls of Jerusalem and on the roofs. Four hundred and twenty-four priests were in attendance and there were brilliant illuminations at night. 3. The *Lord's brothers' advice* was in effect, "Do not stay in this remote province; go to the center of the theocracy." It confirms the fact that Jesus had recently avoided publicity. They had not yet true faith in him, and yet they seemed to have regarded him as equipped with some special authority. They could not understand his conduct sharing as they did the common opinion respecting the Messiah. Jerusalem being the ecclesiastical center, their advice to manifest himself openly was friendly rather than evil, though one of worldly wisdom. 4. The unbelief of Christ's brethren proves decisively that they were not his cousins, for on this theory, two of them

(James and Jude) were also apostles. 5. What John *records* is rather the controversy growing out of Christ's teaching than the teaching itself. The points are intensely personal. He claims a unique knowledge of the Father (Jno. 7:16), a unique mission from the Father (Jno. 7:28), and a unique union with the Father. His teaching on this occasion is urgent. Jesus called for immediate acceptance of His Messiahship on the ground that the time of his being with them was short (Jno. 7:33-36). 6. On the *last day of the feast* the priests, amid the loud hosannas of the people, brought water in a golden pitcher from the pool of Siloam into the temple and poured it on the altar in commemoration of the smitten rock at Horeb (Ex. 7:1-7). It was this ceremony, doubtless, which occasioned the words of Jesus in Jno. 7:37. 7. The *assertion* in Jno. 7:52 is not true, for at least two prophets had come from Galilee: Jonah of Gath and Elijah of Tishbeh; perhaps also Nahum and Hosea. Their contempt for Galilee made them lose sight of historical accuracy. 8. *The incident* in Jno. 7:53—8:1 is missing in all important manuscripts and can not have been in the original text of the gospel. But its early insertion into the gospel seems to prove that it is historical, and one of the many incidents unrecorded by any evangelists but preserved and handed down by a reliable tradition (cf. e. g. the word of Jesus quoted by Paul, Acts 20:35). Augustine (died 430), however, considers it a part of the original gospel and accounts for its later omission from the fear that it might be perverted into an excuse for sin. 9. Lev. 20:10 provides *death as the penalty* of adultery, but owing to the corrupt morals of the times, divorce was generally substituted. The snare laid for Jesus was this: If he declared for the law, his rigor would make him unpopular, but if for acquital, they would have denounced him as a law breaker. Christ saw her penitence and mercy triumphed over justice (Jam. 2:13). 10. The metaphor, "I *am the Light* of the World," might have been suggested by the 2 or 4 great candelabra (75 feet in height) which stood in the court of the women and which were lighted every night in memory of the pillars of light which guided the Israelites in their 40 years' journey through the wilderness. On at least one night during this feast the temple was brilliantly illuminated, probably also in commemoration of the pillar of fire in the wilderness. Ex. 13:21, 22. 11. As the *Pharisees* had charged him with idle self-glorification, Christ appealed to his Father's testimony and to the self-authenticating evidence of the Light. 22. On the *treasury*, see ¶33 (4). 13. According to Jno. 7:37 compared with Jno. 7:53 the discourses on the Light of the World and Spiritual Freedom were spoken on the day after the close of the feast. Hence, if in them Christ alluded to the illumination we must suppose that it was repeated after the feast. If, however, the interpolated incident of the adultress is eliminated, both discourses may be placed on the "last day" (Jno. 7:37). 14. The word *"freedom,"* inspiring to every man, touched especially a Jew's innermost heart. The Lord, however, is careful to explain that he did not intend to become a political Messiah, but desired to lead them to moral emancipation through the truth he taught. This of itself would eventually issue in political freedom. 15. *Abraham* rejoiced when he received the promise of the seed (Gen. 15); he saw Christ's day, when God informed him of Christ's birth. 16. Jno. 8:58 means that *before Abraham* was born Christ existed. Here Jesus clearly affirms His own divinity by identifying Himself with the "I am" or Jehovah, of the Old Testament (Ex. 3:14). 17. *"We have never yet* been in bondage" sounded strange from persons who were under the Roman yoke. Probably they meant, "lawfully" or, "with our consent."

289. **Practical Lessons.** 1. Men who do not believe in Christ are not the ones to give advice as to his, or his followers' conduct (Jno. 7:5; 1 Cor. 2:14). 2. The world lies in the darkness of ignorance, of sin, of death; Christ is the Light. 3. Christ compels even his enemies to bear testimony to his superlative greatness. (Jno. 7:46). 4. Official ecclesiastics are often the most indifferent to the real needs of the people. 5. Streams of holy influence go forth from many Christians. 6. To be unappreciated, misunderstood, misrepresented is a trial that falls to many (Heb. 4:15).

290. **Reference Literature.** Farrar, Ch. 39, 40; Andrews, p. 347-350. For a full account of the pouring of water, see Edersheim, Life of Christ, B. IV, Ch. 7; Schaff, The Person of Christ. Consult D. of the Bible. Also Hunt's painting, "Jesus the Light of the World."

291. **Questions for Discussion.** 1. How did the invitation (Jno. 7:37) show great courage? 2. Do the "rulers" in science, art, commerce, government believe on Christ? 3. Was the taunt addressed to Nicodemus true? (2 Kings 14:25). 4. Show from Israel's history that their boast in Jno. 8:33 was not true. 5. What are the marks of the Devil's sons? (Jno. 8:44). 6. How could the declaration of Jno. 8:56 be true? (Heb. 11:13). 7. What are the various arguments used by the Jews at this time in favor of and against the Messiahship of Jesus? 8. On what grounds does Jesus defend his trustworthiness. 9. What is the effect of truth? (Jno. 8:32). 10. What is the chief reason to-day why men do not appreciate Jesus? 11. What is the best way to gain more truth than we have at present? (Jno. 7:17). 12. In what respects is Jesus the Light of the World to-day?

The Perean Ministry

CHAPTER 33.

The Opening of the Perean Ministry.

Matt. 19:1-2; 8:18-22; 11:20-28; Mk. 10:1; Lu. 9:51-
10:37.   Harmony, 86-88.

292. **Final Departure from Galilee.**   (1) After the
Feast of Tabernacles, Jesus returned to Galilee, probably to
Capernaum, for a short time (end of Oct.-Nov., A. D. 29).
(2) When the days were well nigh come that he should be
received up, he steadfastly set his face to go to Jerusalem
by way of Perea.   (3) He sent messengers into a village of
the Samaritans to make ready for him.   And they did
not receive him, because his face was as though he were
going to Jerusalem.   (4) James and John said, Lord, wilt
thou that we bid fire to come down from heaven, and con-
sume them?   But he rebuked them.   And they went to another village.

293.   **Meeting with three Men.**   (1) On their way a
scribe said to Jesus, *I will follow thee* whithersoever thou
goest.   And Jesus said, The foxes have holes, and the birds
have nests; but the Son of man hath not where to lay his
head.   (2) To another man he said, Follow me.   But he
said, Lord, suffer me first to go and bury my father.   But
he said, Leave the dead to bury their own dead; but go thou
and publish the kingdom of God.   (3) Another said, I will

follow thee, Lord; but first suffer me to bid farewell to
them that are at my house. But Jesus said: No man, having put his hand to the plow and looking back, is fit for
the kingdom of God.

294. **The Mission of the Seventy.** (1) Perea was the
only section of Palestine which had not been evangelized.
As the time was short, Christ appointed seventy disciples
and sent them two and two into every place whither he was
to come, to announce him. (2) *Reason:* He said, The harvest is plenteous, but the laborers are few: pray ye therefore the Lord of the harvest, that he send forth laborers into
his harvest. (3) *Their support:* Carry no purse, no wallet, no shoes; and salute no man on the way. Into whatsoever house ye shall enter, first say, Peace be unto this
house. In that same house remain, eating and drinking
such things as they give: for the laborer is worthy of his
hire. Go not from house to house. (4) *Their mission:*
Heal the sick, and say, The kingdom of God is come nigh
unto you. (5) *Treatment of opponents:* Whatever city
receive you not, go out and say, Even the dust from your
city, we wipe off against you: nevertheless know this, that
the kingdom of God is come nigh. It shall be more tolerable in that day for Sodom, than for that city. (6) Woe
to the rejecters: Woe unto thee, Chorazin! woe unto thee,
Bethsaida! for if the mighty works had been done in Tyre
and Sidon, which were done in you, they would have repented long ago. But it shall be more tolerable for Tyre
and Sidon in the judgment, than for you. And thou, Capernaum, shalt thou be exalted unto heaven? thou shalt be
brought down unto Hades. (7) *Their authority:* He that
heareth you heareth me; and he that rejecteth you rejecteth
me; and he that rejecteth me rejecteth him that sent me.
(8) *Return and Report:* They returned with joy, saying,
Lord, even the demons are subject unto us in thy name.
Jesus said, I beheld Satan fallen as lightning from heaven.
In this rejoice not, that the spirits are subject unto you;
but rejoice that your names are written in heaven.

295. **A Remarkable Prayer.** (1) Moved by the success of these plain men, Jesus rejoiced in the Holy Spirit, and said, I thank thee, O Father, Lord of heaven and earth, that thou didst hide these things from the wise and understanding, and didst reveal them unto babes. (2) All things have been delivered unto me of my Father: and no one knoweth who the Son is, save the Father; and who the Father is, save the Son, and he to whomsoever the Son willeth to reveal him. (3) And turning to the disciples, he said privately, Blessed are the eyes which see the things that ye see: for I say unto you, that many prophets and kings desired to see the things which ye see, and saw them not; and to hear the things which ye hear, and heard them not. (4) And to the people he said: Come unto me, all ye that labor and are heavy laden, and I will give you rest. Take my yoke upon you, and learn of me; for I am meek and lowly in heart: and ye shall find rest unto your souls. For my yoke is easy, and my burden is light.

296. **The Good Samaritan.** (1) Somewhere in Perea, a lawyer made trial of him, saying, Teacher, what shall I do to inherit eternal life? He said: What is written in the law? The lawyer answered, Thou shalt love the Lord thy God with all thy heart, and with all thy soul, and with all thy strength, and with all thy mind; and thy neighbor as thyself. (2) Jesus said, Thou hast answered right: this do and thou shalt live. (3) But he, desiring to justify himself, said: Who is my neighbor? Jesus made answer in the words of the *Parable of the Good Samaritan.*

297. **Explanatory Notes.** Name and compare *sources;* locate places; trace the Lord's movements; memorize Matt. 11: 27-28. 2. *Christ's movements* during this period were as follows: After the Feast of Tabernacles the Lord left Jerusalem for Galilee. After a brief stay, probably at Capernaum, he went south again. He intended to travel by way of Samaria, but when repulsed he went directly to Perea. His final destination was Jerusalem in order to be present at the feast of Dedication (December 25), but the chief scene of action during the remaining months was Perea. 3. During this period he made *three journeys to Jerusalem,*

(a) to the feast of Dedication, (b) to the home of Lazarus, (c) from Ephraim. 4. The *principal source* for this period is Luke's gospel whose record covers ten chapters, from 9:51-19:23, while Mark has but one chapter (the tenth) and Matthew two (19 and 20). 5. *The order of the events* is in a large part conjectural, especially as Luke's report has somewhat the appearance of being a collection of events and teachings largely without reference to places and order. 6. He must have had the use of an *independent source* which document he may have introduced here in its entirety. 7. *The Perean Ministry* was a repetition of the Galilean ministry. First he was very popular, but the shadow of the cross was deepening. The rulers in Jerusalem definitely plot his death and seek a convenient season for the execution of their purpose. His disciples become increasingly aware that a crisis is aproaching and are torn with hopes of a glorious coronation and fear of a terrible catastrophy. 9. Note the Lord's *pedagogical wisdom* shown in his treatment of the three would-be disciples. To the first who was in danger of taking impulsively a step the significance of which he had not considered, Jesus points out the cost and seriousness of discipleship; to the second, its paramount claims; to the third, the danger of irresolution and the need of prompt decisive choice. 10. *Pollution contracted* by the presence of a dead body lasted seven days (Num. 19:11-12).

298. 1. These seventy were probably sent out *from Capernaum* a short time before Christ's final departure from that place. 2. The *pressure* arising from the nearness of his end and the great amount of work yet to be done may have led to the sending of a second group of helpers. It is evident that Jesus planned quite an extensive evangelistic tour, intending himself to visit no less than 35 towns, probably more. 3. That *Jesus was able* to send out seventy trusted followers besides the Twelve proves that the Judean and Galilean ministries could not have been so barren of results as they are sometimes represented. 4. The *number* may have been suggested by the seventy nations into which the Jews divided mankind (Gen. ch. 10) or the 70 members of the Sanhedrin, but more likely by the seventy elders appointed to help Moses (Num. 11:16, 17, 24, 25). 5. The Twelve had been sent out *to assist Jesus* in His work; the Seventy were sent to prepare the way for his own arrival, so that there should be no needless loss of time, which at the best was short for the great work that remained to be done. 6. As the work of the *two missions* was in some respects similar, the instructions were substantially the same in both cases. But note that, while the Twelve were forbidden to go to the Gentiles or to the Samaritans (Matt. 10:5), no such restriction was

put on the Seventy whose work lay in a district where Gentiles were numerous. 7. After the *feast of Dedication,* in December, they returned to him at that place on the Jordan where he abode (Jno. 10:40), viz.: Bethabara or Bethany, not all at once, but from time to time, as their itinerary was completed. 8. The yoke of Christ is his word and spirit. The figure comes from the Jews who spoke of the law with its discipline as a yoke (Acts 15:10). 9. Babes here means the unlearned, the common people, like his disciples, contrasted with the learned proud Pharisees. 10. The lawyer desires to put Jesus to the test to see whether he will not give some answer to the law. On the "lawyers" see ¶32.

299. **Practical Lessons.** 1. There are critical periods in the life of men, when that which is not done at the moment will never be done. 2. The parable of the Good Samaritan teaches that one's neighbor is any one whom it is within our power to help. 3. Truer conceptions of the gospel, Christian missions, modern science, the newspaper, commerce and foreign travel operate powerfully to give a world-wide meaning to the term "neighbor." 4. Race prejudice disappears before the feeling of the brotherhood of men and sincere piety. Nativism and jingoïsm are survivals of barbarity, when a foreigner was considered by the Greeks a barbaros, and by the Romans an enemy (hostis—strangers and enemy). 5. In America the "ignorant foreigner" is often used as a scapegoat for all national sins, while in truth, as shown by official statistics, he compares favorably with the better class of natives. 6. We are naturally prejudiced against large bodies of men, on account of their religion, race, color, nationality, business and social station. This is against the first elements of the idea of Christian brotherhood. 7. This parable abolishes the word "foreigner" and transfigures the word "neighbor," making the whole world kin. How significant are the modern expressions "international law," "comity of nations," "world congresses"—Christ teaches us to pray in the plural: "our, we, us." 8. The finest virtues are often found where least expected. 9. Philanthropy is the child of Christianity. 10. Neighbor, upon Christ's lips, is synonymous with "humanity."

300. **Reference Literature.** Farrar, Ch. 42, 43; Andrews, 365-388; Edersheim, II, 135, 177, 226. Trench and Spurgeon on the Parables; Davis D. B. on the Samaritans, p. 633.

301. **Questions for Discussion.** 1. Is the number 70 significant? (Num. 11:24, 25); Matt. 18:22). 2. What is the peculiar peril of success? (Lu. 10:20). 3. What is the precise thing for which Jesus gives thanks in Lu. 10:21? 4. What does Jesus say of his own character in Matt. 11:29? 5. Suggest modern appli-

cations of the principle contained in Matt. 11 : 20-24. 6. What principle is implied in Lu. 10 : 16? 7. In the parable of the Samaritan
did Jesus make use of a real occurrence?

CHAPTER 34.

Christ at the Feast of Dedication in Jerusalem.

Lu. 10 : 38-42; Jno. 9 : 1-10 : 42. Harmony, 89-92.

302. **Visit to Bethany.** (1) On his way to Jerusalem
(Dec., A. D. 29), Jesus visited two of his women disciples at
Bethany, Martha and her sister Mary. (2) The latter sat
at the Lord's feet and heard his word, but Martha was cum-
bered about much serving. (3) She said, Lord, dost thou
not care that my sister did leave me to serve alone? bid her
that she help me. (4) The Lord answered, Martha, Martha, thou art anxious and troubled about many things; but
one thing is needful: Mary hath chosen the good part, which
shalt not be taken away from her.

303. **Healing of the Man born Blind.** (1) Passing
through the streets of Jerusalem he saw a man blind from
his birth. (2) His disciples asked, Rabbi, who sinned, this
man, or his parents, that he should be born blind? (3)
Jesus answered, Neither did this man sin, nor his parents:
but he was born blind that the works of God should be
made manifest in him. (4) He spat on the ground, made
clay, anointed his eyes and said, Go, wash in the pool of
Siloam. He did so and came seeing. (5) *The neighbors*
said, is not this he that sat and begged? Some said: It is
he: others said, No, but he is like him. He said, I am *he.*
They said, How then were thine eyes opened? He told
them. They said, Where is he? He saith, I know not.
(6) Some of the Pharisees said, This man is not from
God, because he keepeth not the sabbath. But others said.
How can a man that is a sinner do such signs? So there
was a division among them. (7) They ask the man: What

sayest thou of him? He answered, He is a prophet. (8) Then the Pharisees asked his *parents,* Is this your son? They answered, This is our son, he was born blind; but how he now seeth we know not; or who opened his eyes, we know not; ask him; he is of age. (9) These things said his parents, because they feared the Jews: for they had agreed already, that if any man should confess him *to be* Christ, he should be put out of the synagogue. (10) The Pharisees said to the man: Give glory to God: we know that this man is a sinner. He answered, Whether he is a sinner, I know not: one thing I know, that, whereas I was blind, now I see. (11) They said unto him, How opened he thine eyes? He answered, I told you, wherefore would ye hear it again? would ye also become his disciples? They reviled him, Thou art his disciple; but we are disciples of Moses. We know that God hath spoken unto Moses: but as for this man, we know not whence he is. (12) The man answered, Why, herein is the marvel, that ye know not whence he is, and yet he opened mine eyes. We know that God heareth not sinners. Since the world began it was never heard that any one opened the eyes of a man born blind. If this man were not from God, he could do nothing. (13) They answered, Thou wast altogether born in sins, and dost thou teach us? And they cast him out. (14) Jesus heard that they had cast him out; and finding him, he said, Dost thou believe on the Son of God? He answered, Who is he, Lord, that I may believe on him? Jesus said, He it is that speaketh with thee. (15) He said, Lord I believe and worshipped him. (16) Jesus said, For judgment came I into this world, that they that see not may see; and that they that see may become blind. (17) Those of the Pharisees who heard these things said, Are we also blind? Jesus said, If ye were blind, ye would have no sin: but now ye say, We see: your sin remaineth.

304. **The Good Shepherd.** (1) In contrast to the treatment accorded to the blind man by the official shepherds of Israel, Jesus presents himself as the Good Shepherd. (2)

The marks of the good shepherd: He that entereth in by the door is the shepherd of the sheep. He calleth his own sheep by name and leadeth them out. He goeth before them and the sheep follow him: for they know his voice. (3) Jesus the Door: Jesus said, I am the door of the sheep. All that came before me were thieves and robbers; but the sheep did not hear them. By me if any enter in he shall be saved, and shall go in and go out and shall find pasture. (4) Jesus the good shepherd. I am the good shepherd. The good shepherd layeth down his life for his sheep. I know mine own and mine own know me. (5) And other sheep I have, which are not of this fold: them also I must bring and they shall hear my voice; and they shall become one flock and one shepherd. (6) There arose a division again among the Jews because of these words. Many said he hath a demon, and is mad; why hear ye him? Others said, These are not the sayings of one possessed with a demon. Can a demon open the eyes of the blind?

305. **Discourse at the Feast of Dedication.** (1) When Jesus was walking in Solomon's porch, the Jews said, How long dost thou hold us in suspense? If thou art the Christ, tell us plainly. (2) Jesus answered, I told you, and ye believe not: the works that I do in my Father's name, bear witness of me. I and the Father are one. (3) The Jews took up stones but Jesus answered, Many good works have I showed you, for which of those works do ye stone me? (4) The Jews answered, For a good work we stone thee not, but for blasphemy; because that thou, being a man, makest thyself God. (5) Jesus answered, Is it not written in your law, Ye are gods? If he called them gods, unto whom the word of God came, say ye of him, whom the Father sanctified and sent into the world, Thou blasphemest; because I said, I am the Son of God? (6) They sought again to take him: but he went forth out of their land beyond the Jordan into the place where John was at the first baptizing; and there he abode.

306. **Explanatory Notes.** 1. Name *sources;* locate places, and trace the Lord's movements; memorize Jno. 10: 15. 2. *Bethany* ("House of Dates"), the suburb of Jerusalem, was located on the eastern slope of the Mt. of Olives. 3. This is the *first mention* of the greatly beloved (Jno. 11: 5) family at Bethany. Probably Jesus had made their acquaintance during his early Judæan ministry. 4. *Jesus did not object* to their preparing food for him, but he administered a gentle rebuke for dishonoring him by assuming that he cared more for fine food than for the joy of imparting truth (Jno. 4: 34). 5. The *pool of Siloam,* still existing and known as "Ain Silwan," is situated outside the city walls at the southeast corner of the city. Its present dimensions are 18 feet from west to east by 55 feet from north to south, and 25 feet deep. It was formerly much larger. It is fed by the so-called Virgin Fountain through a tunnel 1760 feet long. 6. To assist the memory the story of the miracle may be analyzed as follows: The blind man and (a) the disciples, (b) Jesus, (c) the neighbors, (d) the Pharisees, (e) his parents, (f) the Pharisees again, (g) Jesus again. 7. *This miracle* is biographically important in several respects: (a) It again caused a division among the people and created a party favorable to Jesus, which made it possible for him to appear in public again. (b) Stringent ecclesiastical action (excommunication) was now taken against any one who should accept Jesus. (c) This extreme measure shows that the rulers considered Jesus a dangerous enemy even in Jerusalem, the center and stronghold of their power. (d) Jesus uses means. Saliva and clay were supposed to have medicinal effects. By using them Christ helped the blind man to believe that he would be cured. 8. The Talmud recognizes two kinds of excommunication, the minor and the major. The first lasted thirty days and could be repeated. It did not exclude from the temple. The latter excluded from the temple, the synagogue and all association with the faithful. 9. The *discourse* of the Good Shepherd grew out of the harsh conduct which the blind man had received from the acknowledged religious leaders. 10. "Hireling" means one who is a religious teacher for his own profit, not for the good he can do, and who deserts his post as soon as any danger or "wolf" appears. 11. The *feast of Dedication* was celebrated for eight days in the month. "Chislev" from December 20-27. Its name is misleading as it does not refer to the dedication, but the rededication of the temple. It was instituted by Judas Maccabeus in 164 B. C., to commemorate (a) the national deliverance by the Maccabees from Syrian oppression, (b) the cleansing of the temple, (c) the restoration of the appointed Jehovah worship after Antiochus Ephiphanes had polluted the tem-

ple by heathen sacrifices. 12. *Solomon's porch* is the colonnade on the east side of the temple. See map of temple. 13. *The question* "how long dost thou hold us in suspense" seems to be an honest seeking after the truth on the part of some and indicates that his mighty works had induced them to think better of his Messianic claims. But it may also be a trap to get from him a statement which would alienate the sympathy of the people or one which would enable them to proceed against him in a legal manner. 14. *Referring to Ps.* 82: 6, Jesus argues: If the title "God" is sometimes applied even to unjust judges, because they represent God, how much more to him whose works prove that the Father was in him. 15. *They desisted* from throwing the stones which they had taken up probably for the reason that there were present too many who sympathized with Jesus. 16. At the end of the discourse Jesus left the city a fugitive, and went to Bethany beyond the Jordan (Bethabara). As at Nazareth (Lu. 4: 30) and at the Feast of Tabernacles (Jos. 8: 59), Jesus escaped premature death.

307. **Practical Lessons.** 1. The two types of piety, receiving and serving, meditating and working, are still with us. 2. Many things are desirable, one thing is needful. 3. Thousands have laid down their lives for a great cause, but Jesus only had power "to take it up again." 4. Responsibility is proportionate to knowledge (Jno. 9: 41).

308. **Reference Literature.** Farrar, Ch. 41, 45; Andrews, p. 346; on the Maccabees, see Davis, D. B., p. 445; on Antiochus Epiphanes, p. 3; on excommunication, see Encycl. Brit. VIII.

CHAPTER 35.

Teaching Concerning Trust in God and the Judgment.

Lu. 11: 1-13: 30.   Harmony 93-98.

309. **Discourse on Prayer.** (1) At a certain place in Perea, one of his disciples said, Lord, teach us to pray, even as John also taught his disciples. (2) In answer, Jesus repeated the Lord's Prayer in an abbreviated form. (3) To encourage them to persistency in prayer, he added the parable of the *Importunate Friend,* closing with the application, Ask and it shall be given unto you: seek, and ye shall find; knock, and it shall be opened unto you.

310. **Woe against the Pharisees.** (1) Somewhere in Perea, a Pharisee asked him to dine with him, and marveled that he had not first bathed before dinner. (2) The Lord said, The Pharisees cleanse the outside of the cup, and of the platter, but your inward part is full of extortion and wickedness. (3) Woe unto you Pharisees! for ye tithe mint and rue and every herb, and pass over justice and the love of God: but these ought ye to have done, and not to leave the other undone. (4) Ye love the chief seats in the synagogues, and the salutations in the marketplaces. (5) Ye are as the tombs which appear not, and the men that walk over them know it not. (6) One of the lawyers saith, Teacher, in saying this thou reproachest us also. (7) And he said, Woe unto you lawyers also! for ye load men with burdens grievous to be borne, and ye yourselves touch not the burdens with one of your fingers. Ye build the tombs of the prophets, and your fathers killed them. (8) The blood of all the prophets, which was shed from the foundation of the world, may be required of this generation; from the blood of Abel unto the blood of Zachariah, who perished between the altar and the sanctuary. (9) Ye took away the key of knowledge; ye entered not in yourselves, and them that were entering in ye hindered. (10) When he was come out the scribes and the Pharisees began to press upon him vehemently, and to provoke him to speak, laying wait for him, to catch something out of his mouth.

311. **Trust in God.** (1) Christ's popularity was great in Perea. (2) At this time many thousands were gathered together, insomuch that they trod one upon another. (3) His teaching contained many truths which he had uttered on other occasions. Some of these gems are as follows: Beware ye of the leaven of the Pharisees, which is hypocrisy. But there is nothing covered up, that shall not be revealed; and hid, that shall not be known. (4) Be not afraid of them that kill the body, and after that have no more that they can do. Fear him, who after he hath killed

hath power to cast into hell.   Everyone who shall confess me before men, him shall the Son of man also confess before the angels of God.

312.   **Warning Against Covetousness.**   (1) One of the multitude said, Teacher bid my brother divide the inheritance with me.   Jesus answered, Man, who made me a judge or a divider over you.   (2) Keep yourselves from all covetousness, for a man's life consisteth not in the abundance of the things which he possesseth.   (3) To impress this lesson, Jesus spoke the parable of *The Rich Fool.* (4) Evidently to still more impress this parable, Christ repeated some sayings from the sermon on the mount: Be not anxious for your life; consider the ravens and the lilies; fear not, little flock.

313.   **The Steward's Duty in his Lord's Absence.**   (1) Let your loins be girded about and your lamps burning, and be ye yourselves like unto men looking for their lord when he shall return from the marriage feast.   (2) Peter said, Lord, speakest thou this parable unto us or unto all?   The Lord said, Blessed is that servant whom his lord when he cometh shall find faithful.   He will set him over all that he hath.   (3) But that servant, who knew his Lord's will, and did not according to his will, shall be beaten with many stripes.

314.   **Baptism of Fire and Christian Prudence.**   (1) I came to cast fire upon the earth; and what do I desire, if it is already kindled?   But I have a baptism, to be baptized with; and how am I straitened till it be accomplished?   (2) Think ye that I am come to give peace upon the earth? Nay; but rather division: They shall be divided, father against son, and son against father; mother against daughter, and daughter against her mother; mother-in-law against her daughter-in-law, and daughter-in-law against her mother-in-law.   (3) And he said to the multitudes, When ye see a cloud rising in the west, ye say, There cometh a shower; And when ye see a south wind blowing, ye say, There will be a scorching heat.   (4) Ye hypocrites, ye

know how to interpret the face of the earth and the heaven; but how is it that ye know not how to interpret this time?

315. **The Galileans slain by Pilate.** (1) There were some present who told him of the Galileans whom Pilate had killed while engaged in the sacred act of sacrificing. (2) Jesus answered, Think ye that these Galileans were sinners above all the Galileans, because they have suffered these things? I tell you, Nay, but except ye repent, ye shall all in like manner perish. (3) Or those eighteen upon whom the tower in Siloam fell, think ye that they were offenders above all the men that dwell in Jerusalem? I tell you, Nay, but except ye repent ye shall all likewise perish. (4) To illustrate the patience of God, Jesus added the *Parable of the Fig Tree.*

316. **The Woman healed on the Sabbath.** (1) When he was teaching in one of the synagogues on the sabbath, he met a woman that had a spirit of infirmity eighteen years. (2) Jesus said, Woman, thou art loosed from thine infirmity. and immediately she was made straight and glorified God. (3) The ruler of the synagogue, being moved with indignation because Jesus had healed on the sabbath, said to the multitude, There are six days in which men ought to work; in them come and be healed. (4) The Lord said, Ye hypocrites, doth not each one of you on the sabbath loose his ox or his ass from the stall, and lead him to watering? Ought not this woman, whom Satan had bound these eighteen years, to have been loosed on the Sabbath? (5) And all his adversaries were put to shame: and all the multitude rejoiced for all the glorious things that were done by him.

317. **Whether Few are Saved.** (1) As he was teaching, a man asked him: Lord are there few that are saved? (2) He said, Strive to enter in by the narrow door; for many I say unto you, shall seek to enter in and shall not be able.

318. **Explanatory Notes.** 1. Name *sources;* locate places and trace movements of the Lord; memorize Lu. 11:9. 2. *It is difficult* to locate particular events and discourses as the evangelists do

not mention a single place in Perea by name, excepting the allusion, Jno. 10:40. 3. Either Jesus *repeated the Lord's Prayer* on this occasion, or, for the purpose of unity of subject, Luke, in his independent document, found it inserted here as a fitting introduction to the parable of the Importunate Friend. The same may be said of other thoughts which we find in the sermon on the mount, in the commission to the Twelve and in the discourse on mount Olivet. 4. *The invitation* by the Pharisee was probably given with the evil intention of entrapping him. The severity of Christ's words against Pharisaism rather than against individuals present indicates this. 5. This slaughter and the violation of the sanctity of the temple may have happened at the feast of Dedication observed a few weeks before. It may have caused the enmity between Pilate and Herod (the ruler of these Galileans, Luke 23:12), or it may have been the effect of it. Such deeds of revolting atrocity were frequent in those times. 6. The *accident at Siloam* may possibly have happened at the building of the aqueduct erected by Pilate from funds taken from the temple treasury. (See Jos. Jewish War Bk. II, ch. 9, sec. 4). 7. *The teaching here* is that exceptional suffering is no proof of exceptional sinfulness and that the long-suffering of God should lead sinners to repentance.

319. **Practical Lessons.** 1. Note again the Lord's *pedagogical wisdom* in giving to a purely speculative and useless question a practical and personal turn. 2. *Luther* was asked, how God spent his time before the creation and answered, He sat in a forest and cut sticks to punish those who would ask such foolish questions. 3. *Mere consumers* without returning any benefits to society are worthless parasites whatever their wealth and social rank (Lu. 12:16). 4. A drowning man is in no position to speculate about the peril of others: his own salvation is paramount (Lu. 13:22). 5. Divine judgments on other men should be taken, not as opportunities to impute evil to them, but as calls to personal self-examination and repentance.

320. **Reference Literature.** Farrar, Ch. 44; Andrews, 393; Trench and Dod on the Parables; Land and Book, II, 262; Davis, D. B. on Pilate, p. 583.

321. **Questions for Discussion.** 1. Distinguish between conscious and unconscious hypocrisy. 2. Are educated people to-day liable to the same charge as that made against the lawyers in Lu. 11:52? 3. Did Jesus commit a breach of etiquette in the house where he was a guest? 4. What is it to confess Christ? 5. What does Jesus teach about the relation of suffering and sin? 6. What will God do with nations and individuals who do not live up to their privileges? 7. Does history prove him right? 8. What theory of disease is suggested by Lu. 13:16?

CHAPTER 36.

From the Warning Against Herod to the Raising of Lazarus.

Lu. 13:31-17:10.   Harmony, 99-104.

322. **Warning against Herod.** (1) In that very hour, somewhere in Perea, probably in Jan., A. D. 30, came some Pharisees, saying, go hence: for Herod would kill thee. (2) He said, Say to that fox, I cast out demons and perform cures to-day and to-morrow, and the third day I am perfected, for it cannot be that a prophet perish out of Jerusalem. (3) O Jerusalem, Jerusalem, that killeth the prophets, and stoneth them that are sent unto her! how often would I have gathered thy children together, even as a hen gathereth her own brood under her wings, and ye would not!

323. **Healing of the Man with the Dropsy.** (1) When he went into the house of one of the rulers of the Pharisees on a sabbath to eat bread, they were watching him. (2) Here was a man that had the dropsy. (3) Jesus spake unto the lawyers and Pharisees, Is it lawful to heal on the sabbath or not? But they held their peace. (4) He healed him and said, Which of you shall have an ass or an ox fallen into a well, and will not draw him out on a sabbath day? (5) And they could not answer him.

324. **Discourse at a Pharisee's Table.** (1) When he saw how the guests chose out the chief seats he said, When thou art bidden to a marriage feast sit not in the chief seat, lest happily a more honorable man be bidden of him, and the host shall say to thee, Give this man place; and then thou shalt with shame take the lowest place. (2) But when thou art bidden sit in the lowest place; that he that hath bidden thee may say, Friend, go up higher: then shalt thou have glory in the presence of all that sit at meat. (3) For every one that exalteth himself shall be humbled; and he

that humbleth himself shall be exalted.   (4) He also said to him that had bidden him, When thou makest a dinner or a supper, call not thy friends, nor thy brethren, nor thy kinsmen, nor rich neighbors; lest haply they also bid thee again, and a recompense be made thee.   (5) But when thou makest a feast, bid the poor, the maimed, the lame, the blind: and thou shalt be blessed; because they have not wherewith to recompense thee: for thou shalt be recompensed in the resurrection of the just.   (6) When one of them that sat at meat heard these things, he said, Blessed is he that shall eat bread in the kingdom of God.   (7) Christ answered him by telling the parable of the *Great Supper.*

325. **Counting the Cost.**   (1) When there went with him great multitudes, he said, If any man cometh unto me and hateth not his own father, and mother, and wife, and children, and brethren and sisters, yea, and his own life also, he cannot be my disciple.   (2) To impress this truth, Jesus added the parables of *Building a Tower* and of the *King Going to War.*

326. **Three Parables of Grace and Two of Warning.** (1) When all the publicans and sinners were drawing near to hear him, the Pharisees and the scribes murmured, saying, This man receiveth sinners and eateth with them.   (2) In answer to this taunt, Jesus spoke the parables of the *Lost Sheep,* the *Lost Coin,* and the *Prodigal Son.*   (3) To teach foresight in heavenly things, he utters the parable of the *Unjust Steward,* and to warn them of the fate of self-indulgence, he speaks the parable of the *Rich Man and Lazarus.*

327. **Forgiveness and Faith.**   (1) Probably with reference to the controversy with the Pharisees, Jesus said unto his disciples, It is impossible but that occasions of stumbling should come; but woe unto him, through whom they come! It were well for him if a millstone were hanged about his neck, and he were thrown into the sea, rather than that he should cause one of these little ones to stumble.   (2) The apostles said, Increase our faith. The Lord said, If ye had

faith as a grain of mustard seed, ye would say unto this sycamine tree, Be thou rooted up, and planted in the sea; and it would obey you. (3) But who of you, having a servant plowing or keeping sheep, will say, when he is come from the field, Sit down to meat and will not rather say, Make ready wherewith I may sup, and serve me, and afterward thou shalt eat and drink? (4) Doth he thank the servant because he did the things that were commanded? (5) Even so ye also, when ye shall have done all the things that are commanded you, say, We are unprofitable servants; we have done that which it was our duty to do.

328. **Explanatory Notes.** 1. Name *sources;* locate place; memorize Lu. 17:10. 2. The *Warning against Herod* shows that at this time Christ was under Herod Antipas' jurisdiction, in Perea. 3. *These Pharisees* were either (a) friends who possessed some information of the purpose of Herod, or (b) they were sent by Herod to frighten Jesus from his territory, or (c) they were Christ's enemies who intended to drive him into Judea where he could be more readily arrested by the Sanhedrin. 3. Jesus *refused to hasten his fate* and to leave important work unfinished. 4. The *term "fox"* (a) shows that Christ understood Herod's crafty character, and (b) it favors the second interpretation. 5. *"On the third day"* must not be taken literally; it stands for "in the immediate future" and means: "My course is determined and cannot be changed by the schemes of men." 6. Note the *cutting words* in the last clause of Lu. 13:33; the one fatal place for the messenger of Jehovah was in the center of Jehovah worship. Outside of orthodox Jerusalem a prophet was safe. 7. *Incidentally* we have in verse 34 of Lu. 13 ("How many times") a hint of several visits made to Jerusalem, a fact mentioned only in John's gospel. 8. On the *"chief of the Synagogue"* see ¶34 (4). 9. The motive of this Pharisee in inviting Jesus was evil (Lu. 24:1). 10. There was no *little scheming* among the rabbis for the best place, and much anxiety on the part of the host not to give offense. In the days of Jannaeus a rabbi seated himself between the king and his queen, giving as the reason that "wisdom made its scholars sit among princes." 11. *"Resurrection of the Just"* means when the just shall rise at the inauguration of the *Messianic kingdom.* 12. The parable of the Great Supper was *suggested* by the complacent remark of a guest and was intended to show that no people had a monopoly of the divine favor. 13. In the East *it*

is customary to send two invitations, one some time beforehand and another when the feast is ready. The guests are then expected to come at once. 14. The *"certain man"* here means God, the "great supper" is the kingdom of heaven, and the "servant" is Christ, who gives the invitation. 15. On "the publicans," see ¶16 (9). "Sinners" were either people who did not obey the Pharisees' strict religious rules or immoral persons. Both classes were regarded as outcasts not worth saving. 16. In all three *parables of grace* we find the three elements: (a) loss, (b) restoration (c) joy. 17. The parable of the *prodigal* marks out (a) separation, (b) the wages of sin, (c) repentance, (d) father's welcome, (e) note of discord. 18. The *object* of the parable of the prodigal is to emphasize the subjective condition of salvation; the objective condition, the atonement, is taken for granted. 19. The parable of the *Unjust Steward* teaches Christian foresight, and the duty of using earthly goods so as to make them helpful to one's eternal welfare; and that of Dives and Lazarus condemns worldliness and reveals the doom of those, who, unmindful of the sufferings at their very doors, use their riches only for their own gratification.

329. **Practical Lessons.** 1. A man may give a hundred excuses and never hint at the real reason. 2. An "excuse" is often a pretext which men invent so as to shun without self-reproach, a plain duty. 3. Compel men to come to the church, (a) by sound teaching, (b) good example and (c) noble deeds. 4. The parables of grace are designed to show that no people have a monopoly of the divine favor. (5) Just as the progress of science is marked by the utilizing of what was formerly thought to be worthless, so Jesus makes useful men out of forsaken sinners. 6. He who sows wild oats must not expect a crop of good grain. 7. Satan begins by being an obedient slave to men's pleasures, and ends by being a terrible tyrant. 8. No hunger is so pitiful as that of a soul that has exhausted the joys of life. 9. Though sin can drag down a man into the companionship of beasts, it cannot extinguish his sense of a higher destiny. 10. The elder brother is a type of negative goodness without any filial spirit.

330. **Reference Literature.** Farrar, Ch. 44; Andrews, 402; Taylor, The Lost Found. Hast. D. B. under "heir;" On the teaching of Jesus on wealth, see Matthew's Social Teaching of Jesus, Ch. 6; Spurgeon and Trench on the Parables.

331. **Questions for Discussion.** 1. What is Jesus' teaching about the real nature of hospitality? 2. What truth do the parables in Lu. 15, teach? 3. What are the different aspects of this truth that each parable illustrates? 4. What is the one truth which the parable of the Unjust Steward teaches?

CHAPTER 37.

Raising of Lazarus and Flight to Ephraim.

Jno. 11 : 1-54. Harmony, 105-106.

332. **The Message Sent.** (1) Probably in Feb., A. D. 30, Martha and Mary of Bethany sent to Jesus in Perea the message, Lord, he whom thou lovest, Lazarus, is sick. (2) Jesus said, This sickness is not unto death, but that the Son of God may be glorified thereby. (3) After a two days' delay he saith to the disciples, Let us go into Judea. (4) The disciples say, Rabbi, the Jews were but now seeking to stone thee; and goest thou thither again? Jesus said, If a man walk in the day he stumbleth not, because he seeth the light of this world. (5) Thomas said to his fellow-disciples, Let us also go that we may die with him.

333. **Arrival at Bethany.** (1) When Jesus came, Lazarus had been in the tomb four days' already. (2) Martha met Jesus on the way, but Mary sat in the house. (3) Martha said, Lord, if thou hadst been here my brother had not died. Jesus said, Thy brother shall rise again. (4) Martha saith, I know that he shall rise again in the resurrection at the last day. Jesus saith, I am the resurrection and the life; he that believeth on me, though he die, yet shall he live, and whosoever liveth and believeth on me shall never die. Believest thou this? (5) Martha saith, Yea, Lord, I have believed that thou art the Christ, the Son of God. (6) Then Martha went to call Mary, and said: The Teacher is here and calleth thee. (7) She arose quickly and went unto him, for Jesus was still in the place where Martha met him. (8) The Jews who were consoling her followed, supposing that she was going unto the tomb to weep there. (9) Mary fell down at Jesus' feet, saying, Lord, if thou hadst been here my brother had not died.

334. **The Raising of Lazarus.** (1) When Jesus saw

her and the Jews weeping, he groaned in the spirit and said,
Where have ye laid him? They say, Lord, come and see.
(2) Jesus wept and the Jews said: How he loved him!
Some said, Since he opened the eyes of the blind man,
could he not have caused that Lazarus should not die? (3)
Jesus again groaning, cometh to the tomb and saith, Take
away the stone. Martha saith, Lord by this time the body
decayeth; for he hath been dead four days. Jesus answered, Said I not that if thou believedst, thou shouldst see
the glory of God? (4) They took away the stone, and
Jesus lifting up his eyes, said: Father, I thank thee that
thou heardest me. And he cried with a loud voice, Lazarus,
come forth, and he came forth. Jesus saith, Loose him
and let him go.

335. **The Effects of the Miracle.** (1) On the *Jews.*
Many of the Jews believed on him. But some of them told
the Pharisees the things which Jesus had done. (2) On
the *Sanhedrin:* (a) The chief priests and the Pharisees
gathered a council and said, What do we, for this man
doeth many signs? If we let him thus alone, all men will
believe on him, and the Romans will come and take away
both our place and our nation. (b) But Caiaphas, being
high priest that year, said, It is expedient for you that one
man should die for the people, so that the whole nation perish not. (c) This he said not of himself, but being high
priest that year, he prophesied that Jesus should die for
the nation. (d) So from that day forth they took counsel
that they might put him to death. (3) *On Jesus' Movements.* Jesus walked no more openly among the Jews but
departed to a city called Ephraim, probably in February,
A. D. 30. There he tarried with his disciples.

336. **Explanatory Notes.** 1. Name *sources* and analyze them
carefully, locate places and trace the Lord's movements; memorize
Jno. 11:25. 2. The *raising of Lazarus took place* about the end
of February, A. D. 30, or about six weeks before the Passover,
which that year fell on April 7. 3. John 11:4 means that *this
sickness* was to become an occasion for showing the power and

glory of God and of his Son. 4. The *Jews believed* that for three days the soul hovered about the sepulchre anxious to re-enter the body. Had Jesus arrived within three days, it might have been pronounced no miracle. 5. Jno. 11:9, 10 *means:* my ministry has its appointed length sufficient to complete my work, if I only do not forsake God's will for the darkness of self-will. 6. Notice the *various emotions* recorded; Mary and the Jews wailed, Jesus wept and groaned. On Palm Sunday it is also recorded that Jesus wept. 7. For other indications of *Thomas' tendency* to despondency and pessimism, see Jno. 14:5; 20:25. 8. The sepulchres in Palestine were caves with recesses in the sides for the bodies; either natural (Gen. 23:9) or hewn in the rock (Mt. 27:60); often in a private garden (Jno. 19:41) or some field (Gen. 23:9). 9. The silence of the synoptists respecting this miracle has often been urged against its historicity. This objection would have force were this silence an isolated instance. It must be weighed in connection with their silence concerning the entire ministry in Judea and Jerusalem. On the other side the raising of Lazarus fits in with the scheme of John's gospel, which confines itself almost wholly to this omitted portion of Jesus' ministry, as it does not fit in with the scheme of synoptists. 10. The raising of Lazarus and the great popular effect brought on a crisis. The Sanhedrin felt that it was now high time that something decisive should be done and in a formal session Caiaphas advised the death of Jesus, insisting that the plan agreed upon two years ago,—to put Jesus to death—should now be resolutely carried out. He gave this as his official opinion (Jno. 11:51). 11. Joseph Caiaphas held the office eleven years from A. D. 25, when Valerius Gratus placed him there till A. D. 36, when Vitellius removed him. 12. The religious completion of the council was as follows: Annas and Caiaphas were Sadducees and most resolute and resourceful church politicians. The majority of the "chief priests" at this time were also Sadducees, but the Pharisees seem to have had the majority in the Sanhedrin. Thus we see here a union of the two parties which were usually antagonistic. With the Pharisees the motive for opposing Jesus was religion, but with the Sadducees it was politics. 13. John 11:48 shows that the Sadducees feared a Messianic movement, which the Romans might treat as treason and punish by taking from the Jews the large measure of "home rule" which they enjoyed. Thus having much to risk and nothing to gain by a change the aristocratic party of the Sadducees was anxious to keep things quiet, so as to offer no excuse to the Romans for interference. 14. Caiaphas' pernicious advice was couched in language the deep meaning of which he himself did not understand. To the evangelist these words so appropriately and exactly described the actual mission of Jesus that he can only account for them by considering them as spoken by inspiration, which is itself accounted for by the sacred office that Caiaphas held. The conception of the high priest as a medium of divine communication and the idea of "unconscious prophecy" both belong to Jewish thought. 15. The Hill of Evil Counsel is the name still given to the traditional site of the house of Caiaphas where this meeting is supposed to have been held. See the map of Jerusalem. 16. After this Jesus left Jerusalem secretly for Ephraim, in February or early March. The location of Ephraim is disputed. Most maps locate it in the northeast part of Judea, about 16 miles from Jerusalem. 17. Of the sojourn in Ephraim we know nothing. It was probably a time of quiet and of preparation for the end. It is plain that Jesus retired to the place to escape from the Jews, Jno. 11:54, and it is therefore not likely that his place of retirement was known.

337. **Practical Lessons.** 1. The presence of Jesus in individual and national life exerts a preventive influence upon evil. 2. Trouble also enters the homes of those whom Jesus loves. 3. After Jno. 11:11 the early Christians called their grave-yards "cemeteries," that is sleeping rooms, from the Greek koimeterion. 4. It is never right to do evil that good may come.

338. **Reference Literature.** Farrar, Ch. 47; Andrews, 408; Trench on the Miracles; Davis D. B. on Annas, p. 34, and Caiaphas, p. 102; a famous sermon by Robertson on the Atonement, based on Jno. 11:50; On Eastern funeral customs, see Trumbull's studies in Oriental Social Life; Tristran's Eastern Customs; Tennyson, "In Memoriam," 31, 32; Arnold's Light of the World.

339. **Questions for Discussion.** 1. How much did Martha know about the resurrection, and what did Jesus add to her knowledge. 2. Why did the Jews refer to the healing of the blind man and not to the two raisings in Galilee? 3. Why was Lazarus silent at the trial of Jesus? (Jno. 12:10-11). 4. Why did Jesus not go to Bethany at once when he was called. 5. Explain Caiaphas' words in the light of the political status of Palestine?

CHAPTER 38.

Journey from Ephraim to Jericho.

Lu. 17: 11-18: 34; Matt. 19: 3-20: 19; Mk. 10: 2-34.
Harmony, 107-113.

340. **The Ten Lepers.** (1) About two weeks before his death, at the end of March, A. D. 30, Jesus left Ephraim to go to the passover at Jerusalem. (2) Probably to meet some Galilean caravans, he first went northward. (3) As he was passing along the borders of Samaria and Galilee, there met him ten lepers who stood afar off saying, Jesus, Master, have mercy on us. (4) He said, show yourselves unto the priests. As they went they were cleansed. (5) One of them turned back, with a loud voice glorifying God, and fell upon his face at Jesus' feet giving him thanks, and he was a Samaritan. (6) Jesus said, were not the ten cleansed, where are the nine? Were there none found that returned to give glory to God, save this stranger? (7) Then he said to the man, Arise and go thy way: thy faith hath made thee whole.

341. **The Coming of the Kingdom.** (1) At an un-named place he was asked by the Pharisees when the kingdom of God cometh? He said, The kingdom of God cometh not with observation; neither shall they say, Lo, here; or there! for the kingdom of God is within you. (2) Then said he unto the disciples, The days will come, when ye shall desire to see one of the days of the Son of man, and ye shall not see it. (3) When they shall say, Lo, there! Lo, here! go not away, for as the lightning, when it lighten-eth out of the one part under the heaven, shineth unto the other part; so shall the Son of man be in his day. But first must he suffer many things and be rejected of this genera-tion. (4) Indifference will reign as in the time of Noah and Lot. They ate, drank, bought, sold, planted, married, until they were destroyed. (5) Remember Lot's wife. Who shall seek to gain his life, shall lose it.

342. **Two Kinds of Prayer.** In order to encourage prayer without ceasing, and to warn them of self-righteous worship, Jesus spoke the parables of *The Unjust Judge,* and of the *Pharisee and Publican.*

343. **Concerning Divorce.** (1) Either in Perea, the territory of Herod Antipas, or already in Judea, some Pharisees tempting him, said, Is it lawful *for a man* to put away his wife for every cause? (2) Jesus said, God made them male and female. For this cause shall a man leave his father and mother, and shall cleave to his wife; and the two shall become one flesh? What therefore God hath joined together, let not man put asunder. (3) They say, Why then did Moses command to give a bill of divorcement. He saith, Moses for your hardness of heart suffered you to put away your wives: but from the beginning it hath not been so. (4) Whosoever shall put away his wife, except for fornication, and shall marry another, committeth adultery: and he that marrieth her when she is put away committeth adultery. (5) The disciples say, If the case of the man is so with his wife, it is not expedient to marry. (6) But he said, There are eunuchs that were so born, and there are eunuchs that were made eunuchs by men; and there are eunuchs that made themselves eunuchs for the kingdom of heaven's sake.

344. **Blessing Little Children.** (1) Probably in Perea there were brought unto him little children, that he should lay his hands on them, and pray. (2) The disciples rebuked them. But Jesus said, Suffer the little children, and forbid them not, to come unto me: for to such belongeth the kingdom of heaven. And he took them in his arms and laid his hands on them.

345. **The Rich Young Ruler.** (1) At an unnamed place, probably in Perea, a ruler asked him, Good Teacher, what shall I do to inherit eternal life? (2) Jesus said, Why callest thou me good? none is good, save one, even God. Thou knowest the commandments, Do not commit adultery, Do not kill, Do not steal, Do not bear false wit-

ness, Honor thy father and mother. (3) The ruler said,
All these things have I observed from my youth up; what
lack I yet? Jesus looking upon him loved him, and said:
One thing thou lackest yet: sell all that thou hast, and dis-
tribute unto the poor, and thou shalt have treasure in
heaven: and follow me. (4) When he heard these
things he became exceeding sorrowful; and went away;
for he was very rich. (5) Jesus said, How hardly
shall the rich enter into the kingdom of God! It is
easier for a camel to enter in through a needle's eye,
than for a rich man to enter into the kingdom of God.
(6) They that heard it said, Then who can be saved?
He said, The things which are impossible with men
are possible with God. Peter said, Lo, we have left
our own and followed thee. What shall we have? (7)
Jesus said, There is no man that hath left house, or wife, or
brethren, or parents, or children, for the kingdom of God's
sake, who shall not receive manifold more in this life, and
in the world to come life eternal. (8) But many shall be
last that are first and first that are last. (9) To illustrate
this truth Christ added the parable of the *Laborers in the
Vineyard*.

346. **Third Plain Announcement of Christ's Death.**
(1) Again he said to the twelve, Behold, we go up to Jerusalem, and all the things that are written through the
prophets shall be accomplished unto the Son of man. (2)
For he shall be delivered up unto the Gentiles, and shall
be mocked, and shamefully treated, and spit upon: and they
shall scourge and kill him: and the third day he shall
rise again. (3) And they understood none of these things.

347. **Explanatory Notes.** 1. Name and compare *sources;* locate places; trace the Lord's movements; memorize Lu. 18: 17. 2.
The words *"through the midst* of Samaria and Galilee" suggest
a brief journey from Ephraim to the north to meet caravans of
Galilean friends bound for the passover. Jesus joined them and
on his way to Jerusalem he meets these lepers at a place in Perea
not named. 3. It is *doubtful* whether the question in Luke 17: 20,

so interesting to all Jews, was asked in mockery, or to tempt him to say something treasonable or whether in an honest spirit. 4. Note the *two translations* of Lu. 17:21: (a) the kingdom of God is "in the midst of you," in the person of Christ and his few followers. It is not a political regime to be set up on some future day; it is a new moral order which has already begun. (b) The kingdom of God "is within you"—It is God's rule in the hearts of men, through whom he would influence society, church and state, science, literature and art. 5. *Justified* means forgiven, made acceptable to God. The Pharisee could not be forgiven because he was not penitent. This parable shows that the so-called Pauline idea of justification by faith is germinally contained in the teaching of Christ. 6. The Pharisees *"tempted him"* (a) either to get an expression on divorce from Jesus which would arouse Herod Antipas against him, (if this was the intention Jesus must have still been in Herod's dominion) or (b) to entangle him in the controversy between the liberal school of Hillel and the stricter views of Schammai's followers. 7. *The law permitted* a man to divorce his wife, "if she find no favor in his eyes, because he hath found some unseemly thing in her" (Deut. 24:1). The ambiguity of this statement made it one of the standing puzzles of the Jewish schools. The strict school of Shammai interpreted it as referring only to unfaithfulness to the marriage vow. The liberal school of Hillel extended it to the most trivial displeasure, such as burning the dinner, or if he saw a woman whom he liked better, etc. 8. *Jesus admits* that Moses allowed divorces to protect women from worse treatment, but he considered it as an accommodation to the rude nature of primitive civilization. The original law is Gen. 1:27; 2:24. 9. Jesus' *teaching on divorce* was as follows: Mere legal divorce does not break the marriage tie; adultery does break it and hence is the only exception to the prohibition of divorce (Matt. 19:9). 10. Dr. Woolsey sums up *Christ's teaching* very clearly in the following sentence: "The general principle, serving as the groundwork of all these declarations, is, that legal divorce does not, in the view of God, and according to the correct rule of morals, authorize either husband or wife thus separated to marry again, with the single exception that when the divorce occurs on account of a sexual crime, the innocent party may, without guilt, contract a second marriage." 11. *Eunuchs* (from the Greek eune-echo, to have the bed, i. e. a keeper of the bedchamber) were persons who had been emasculated and set over the harem. They often obtained other high positions and great authority.

348. 1. The fact that *these mothers* valued Jesus' blessing shows that the Lord was held in high esteem by the people of the region

where he was at that time and that they regarded him as a holy man. 2. Christ *welcomed the children* both for their own sakes and as a type of the material of which the kingdom of heaven consists. 3. Jesus does not deny that the title "good" belongs to him, but it must be intelligently given. The ruler regarded Jesus as a mere man. 4. As the *popular conception* of the Messianic kingdom included temporal blessings in great abundance, therefore Christ's demand greatly surprised the young ruler. 5. This incident shows *the insight* which Jesus had into the hearts of men. This young ruler was of blameless morality of the legal sort. But the Lord saw beneath the surface the dangerous point in the young man's character, viz. his attachment to his wealth. Jesus tested him and the correctness of his estimate is shown by the result. 6. Matt. 19:24 contains a *hyperbole* for an impossibility. The largest familiar animal cannot pass through the smallest familiar opening. 7. A *new element* in the third announcement of his death is his declaration that they shall deliver him unto the Gentiles. Yet this was a necessary consequence of the political status of Judea, if he was not to be slain by a mob, since the Jewish courts did not possess the power of life and death. Matthew's word "crucify" is a reference to the Roman mode of punishment, that of the Jews being stoning.

349. **Practical Lessons.** 1. Efforts to discourage us in reaching Christ should make us the more resolute. 2. To appeal to the good in men rather than to denounce the evil is often a good way to win them. 3. Better than arguing and antagonizing men is to set before them a higher standard (Lu. 18:23). 4. There are many handicaps in riches (Matt. 19:24-30). 5. Christ applies various tests to men. 6. Only love to God displaces love of money. 7. We may have both, God and Mammon, but we cannot love and serve both. 8. Eternal life is received rather than inherited. 9. The function of the commandments is not to show the way to life, but the way to live after life is obtained through faith. (Paulinism). 10. The *principal teaching* of the parable of the Laborers is the true nature of the reward in the Kingdom of God. Peter's question, "What shall we have?" showed a tendency to bring the disciples' obedience to a calculation of so much work so much reward. The Lord's answer is "Not of works lest any man should boast" (Rom. 4:1-4). 11. The *successive hours* may be taken as an image (a) of the different periods of man's life, when God calls him: Childhood (instruction at home and in the Sabbath School); youth; manhood, and old age, or (b) of the call to the different races, viz.: the Jews, the Greeks, the Romans, the Teutonic race, mission field of modern times. 12. All activity

which disregards man's chief end is in God's sight *idleness.* A Roman was called idle, "otiosus" when not engaged in state affairs, however busy he might be in his private affairs. He was regarded as occupied busy "negotiosus," only when in office working for the good of the state. Worldly minded people may be busily engaged in their own personal affairs, incessantly hunting after wealth, honor, pleasure and pleading lack of time to attend to their souls, yet as Christ sees them they are idle, playing with pebbles on the ocean of time, neglecting the highest interest of their life. 13. Matt. 20:8 teaches in parabolic form the doctrine which many passages of Scripture teach in plain language, and which is common to all Protestants, "That the souls of believers are at their death made perfect in holiness and do immediately pass into glory." Westmin. Shorter Cat., Ques. 37; Heid. Cat., Ques. 58, "After this life I shall inherit perfect salvation," 14. *Opposed to this* common Protestant doctrine is (1) the notion that the soul exists during the interval between death and the resurrection in a state of unconscious repose commonly called, "sleep of the soul." (2) The Roman Catholic dogma which divides the world beyond into five compartments, viz.: (a) *Limbus Patrum,* place where the Old Testament saints are; (b) *Limbus Infantum,* for unbaptized children; (c) *Hell,* place of torment; (d) *Heaven;* (e) *Purgatory,* place of cleansing. 15. Does Matt. 20:16 imply that there will *be degrees of glory in heaven?* In one sense there will not; for objectively, the penny, which is the vision of God, is the same for all. In another sense, however, there will be degrees, for subjectively, the penny is to every one exactly what he will make of it. There is one vision of God but there are very different capacities for enjoying that vision. Augustine compares it to the "light which gladdens the healthy eye, but torments the diseased."

350. **Reference Literature.** Farrar, Ch. 46; Andrews, 410; on the eunuchs, see Davis' D. B., p. 211, and Hast. D. of C. I, 547; and Robinson's Greek Dict. under "eunuch;" on marriage and divorce, Hast. D. C. I, 137; Encl. by Herzog, Schaff-Herzog and Sanford; Davis, p. 458. A famous sermon by Chalmers on the Expulsive Power of a New Affection; J. R. Miller, Wedded Life.

351. **Questions for Discussion.** 1. Notice the variations in the discourse on divorce as given by the synoptists. 2. What is the relation of Jesus' teaching to the O. T. law on divorce? 3. Does Mark 10:4-6 teach that the morality of the O. T. was progressive? 4. Did Jesus in Mk. 10:18 intend to deny that he was God? 5. Why did Jesus love the young ruler? (Mk. 10:21). 6. Is Matt. 19:21 a universally applicable command?

CHAPTER 39.

Jesus at Jericho and Bethany.

Matt. 20:20-34; 26:6-13; Mk. 10:35-52; 14:3-9; Lu. 18:
35-19:28; Jno. 11:55-12:11. Harmony, 114-118.

352. **An Ambitious Request.** (1) Not far from Jericho came to him Salome with her two sons, John and James, worshipping him and requesting him, Command that these, my two sons, may sit, one on thy right hand and one on thy left hand, in thy kingdom. (2) Jesus answered, Ye know not what ye ask. Are ye able to drink the cup that I am about to drink? They say, We are able. (3) He saith, My cup indeed ye shall drink; but to sit on my right hand and on my left hand, is not mine to give; but it is for them for whom it has been prepared of my Father. (4) When the ten heard it, they were moved with indignation. (5) Jesus said, Ye know that the rulers of the Gentiles lord it over them. Not so shall it be among you; but whoever would become great among you shall be your minister; even as the Son of man came not to be ministered unto, but to minister, and to give his life a ransom for many.

353. **The Blind Men Near Jericho.** (1) As they went into Jericho a great multitude followed him. (2) Bartimæus, sitting by the wayside begging, inquired what this meant. When they told him that Jesus of Nazareth passeth by, he cried, Jesus, thou son of David, have mercy upon me. (3) They that went before rebuked him that he should hold his peace, but he cried out the more, Thou Son of David, have mercy on me. (4) Jesus commanded him to be brought and asked, What wilt thou that I should do unto thee? He said, Lord, that I may receive my sight. Jesus said, Receive thy sight, thy faith hath made thee whole. (5) Immediately he received his sight and followed him, glorifying God; and all the people gave praise unto God.

354. **Visit to Zacchæus.** (1) When Jesus passed

through Jericho, Zacchæus, a chief publican and rich, sought to see him. (2) As he could not for the crowd because he was little of stature, he ran on before and climbed up into a sycamore tree. (3) When Jesus came to the place, he looked up and said, Zacchæus make haste and come down, for to-day I must abide at thy house, and he received him joyfully. (4) But all murmured, saying, he is gone in to lodge with a man that is a sinner. (5) Zacchæus said unto the Lord, the half of my goods I give to the poor, and if I have wrongfully exacted aught, I restore it fourfold. (6) Jesus said, To-day is salvation come to this house. For the Son of man came to seek and to save that which was lost.

355. **Parable of the Minae.** (1) Because he was now nigh to Jerusalem his disciples and others supposed that the kingdom of God was immediately to appear. (2) To teach them that a long time would elapse before the consummation of the kingdom, Christ spoke the *Parable of the Pounds or Minae.*

356. **Excitement at Jerusalem.** (1) The passover being at hand many had already arrived at Jerusalem to purify themselves. (2) They sought Jesus and spake with one another, What think ye? Will he come to the feast? (3) Now the chief priests and the Pharisees had given commandment that if any man knew where he was, he should show it, that they might take him.

357. **Anointing at Bethany.** (1) On Friday, March 31 (Nisan 8), A. D. 30, six days before the passover, Jesus came to Bethany. (2) In his honor his friends made him a supper in the house of Simon the leper. (3) Martha served; Lazarus was one of them that sat at meat. (4) Mary took a pound of ointment of pure spikenard, very precious, and anointed the feet of Jesus and wiped his feet with her hair, and the house was filled with the odor of the ointment. (5) Judas, followed by the other disciples, saith, Why was not this ointment sold for above three hundred shillings and given to the poor? (6) Now this Judas said, not because he cared for the poor, but because he was

a thief, and having the bag took away what was put therein. (7) Jesus said, Suffer her to keep it against the day of my burying. For the poor ye have always with you, but me ye have not always.

358. **The Life of Lazarus in Danger.** (1) When the common people learned that Jesus was at Bethany they came, not for Jesus' sake only, but that they might see Lazarus also. (2) But the chief priests took counsel that they might put Lazarus also to death; because that by reason of him many of the Jews believed on Jesus.

359. **Explanatory Notes.** 1. Name and compare the *sources,* especially the variations in the narratives of the blind men and of the ambition of James and John; locate places; trace the Lord's movements; memorize Matt. 20:28. 2. The *variation* between Matt. 20:20 and Mk. 10:35 may be solved by supposing that Salome opened the subject and her two sons afterward joined her in her request. 3. Perhaps *Salome had* in mind the promise in Matt. 19:23, that the apostles shall occupy twelve thrones. 4. Notice that the teaching of the death of Christ being of the nature of a *ransom,* is not an idea invented by Paul. 5. *Jericho,* about 17 miles from Jerusalem, was an important city in the time of Christ; to-day it is inhabited by about 60 families living in miserable hovels. 6. The *three narratives* of the blind men have exercised the ingenuity of harmonizers. Luke and Mark have one, Matthew mentions two; Luke represents the miracle as taking place when Jesus was approaching Jericho; Matthew and Mark, when He was leaving it. The following solutions have been suggested: (1) There were three different healings. (2) As Christ entered Jericho, Bartimæus called for help, and was not healed; he then joined a second blind man, and with him made an appeal as Jesus left Jericho, and then both were healed. (3) One blind man was healed as He entered, Bartimæus, and another as He left. (4) One was healed as He entered and one as He left; and Matthew combines the first with the second. (5) There were two Jerichos, old and new, and Luke means that Jesus was approaching new Jericho, Matthew and Mark that He was leaving old Jericho, although there is no evidence that old Jericho was still inhabited. The narrative of Mark, who gives the name Bartimæus and other details, is probably the most exact of the three. 7. These *trivial variations* in detail are probably due to variations in the original sources from which these narratives were derived. 8. The *meaning of Zac-*

chaeus (the "Just") was an irony in view of his business. 9. This visit to Zacchæus was regarded by many as an act unworthy of Christ's Messianic claims (Luke 19:7). 10. A *chief publican* was one who had bought the right to collect the customs in a certain district or on certain articles. Strictly speaking Zacchæus was not an official, but a contractor. He doubtless sold to others the right to collect the customs at certain points or on certain articles of commerce. 11. Balsam from the numerous palm groves was the chief article of commerce at Jericho. 12. From Luke 19:5 (and vs. 7, "lodge") it seems to follow that *Jesus stayed* in Jericho over night. 13. *Restoration* of goods taken by fraud was demanded by the law (Ex. 22:1, 4 and 7; 2 Sam. 12:6). 14. The *introduction* to the parable of the Pounds states the reason for uttering it, viz.: (a) to repress impatience in his loyal disciples and (b) to enjoin active work for him until his return. Verses 14 and 27 are meant for his wavering followers who might be tempted to forsake his cause when his personal presence should be withdrawn from them and when his ignominious death should have seemed to belie his lofty pretensions. 15. *Two features* of this parable are taken from contemporaneous history. (a) Both Herod the Great and Archelaus were obliged to repair to Rome to obtain their kingdom; (b) Fifty Jews followed Archelaus to Rome and 8,000 of the Roman colony joined them beseeching Augustus in the temple of Apollo to free them from Archelaus and rather unite Judæa with Syria. In Jericho where this parable was spoken stood a royal palace which Archelaus had built.

360. 1. Jesus *arrived at Bethany* on the Friday before Palm Sunday, March 31 (8th of Nisan). This house was his home until he was arrested. 2. The *supper* took place on the day following his arrival, i. e. on the Sabbath, Saturday, April 1st (9th of Nisan), probably after sunset, although feasting was also allowed during the Sabbath (Lu. 14:1), provided the food and the tables were prepared beforehand. 3. John *places the feast* in the home of Simon but Matt. and Mark in that of Mary and Martha. Solution: (a) Simon was the father of Lazarus and his sisters, or (b) the husband of Martha. 4. The *character of the feast,* (a) a thank-offering by Simon for having been healed by Christ from leprosy; (b) a feast of welcome by his friends. 5. *"Pure nard"* (A. V. "spikenard") was a very costly perfumed ointment imported from India. A pound of it was worth about fifty dollars, a year's wages in Christ's time, and equal to about five hundred dollars now. 6. *John puts* this supper six days before the passover, but the Synoptist seemingly only two days before. John puts it in the right place. The Synoptists bring it in parenthetically

for the purpose of explaining the action of Judas and the San-hedrin's change of plan as to the time of arresting Jesus. The "two days" in Matt. 26:2 refers to the meeting of the Sanhedrin and not to this meal. 7. On the differences between the two anointings, see ¶199. 8. John's casual remarks about the bag shows (a) that the Twelve had a common treasury; (b) that they supported the poor; (c) that Judas was their steward; (d) that even before this he had proved unfaithful. 9. Jesus accepted Mary's act as an anticipation of the customary funeral honors.

361. **Practical Lessons.** 1. Murmurings against God's dealings with us are inspired more by feelings of envy at the good fortune or the supposed good fortune of others than by a sense of injustice to ourselves (Matt. 20:24). 2. To set wrong matters right is the best evidence of a real change of heart. 3. Christ's nearness exerts a sanctifying influence (Alcibiades and Socrates). 4. Do not wait till friends are dead to pour out upon them the perfume of kind words and loving deeds.

362. **Reference Literature.** Farrar, Ch. 48; Andrews, 410; Stalker, Ch. 6; Davis, D. B. on spikenard, p. 705; the six Marys, p. 458; Edersheim, Life of Jesus II, 344-360; Hofman's painting of the Anointing.

363. **Questions for Discussion.** 1. What two errors betray themselves in the request of James and John? (Mk. 10:36). 2. What principle of primacy is laid down in Mk. 10:42-44? 3. What is its modern application? 4. What false view of the kingdom of God did he correct in the parable of the Minae? 5. Did Mary intend to anoint Jesus for his burial? (Mk. 14:8).

364. Review Questions.

1. Name the first three chief divisions of the Life of Christ; also the subdivisions of each and give the date of the three chief and their subdivisions. 2. Enumerate the events of each subdivi-sion in the order of time. 3. Of the *Year of Opposition,* (a) ex-plain the name; (b) state the provinces of the ministry; (c) the duration; (d) the events and dates of the beginning and the end of the division; (e) the two subdivisions, with dates; (f) the sources of information by Gospels and chapters. 4. Trace the Lord's movements on the map as contained in the first and second subdivisions and name the events connected with each place. (To assist the memory, group the events as follows: I. Feeding of the 4,000; transfiguration; feast of Tabernacles. II. The three visits to Jerusalem; 1. to the feast of Dedication; 2. to the raising of Lazarus; 3. from Ephraim to Triumphal Entry). 5. Enumerate in

chronological order the more notable miracles. 6. Give in the order of time the more prominent discourses; also the parables in the order spoken. 7. Name some persons with whom Jesus came in contact. 8. What was the general attitude of the rulers and the people toward Jesus during this period? 9. Name some prominent characteristics of this period as to amount and kind of work, etc. 10. What feasts did he attend?

DIVISION V.

The Week of Passion.

Palm Sunday to Easter Sunday, April 2 to April 9, A. D. 30

CHAPTER 40.

The Days of Triumph and of Authority.

Matt. 21: 1-19; Mk. 11: 1-19; Lu. 19: 29-48; Jno. 12: 12-19. Harmony 119-121.

365. **The Triumphal Entry.** (1) On Sunday, April 2, Jesus and his disciples drew nigh to Jerusalem, and came unto Bethphage, unto the mount of Olives. (2) From here he sent two disciples, saying, Go into the village over against you, and ye shall find an ass tied, and a colt with her: bring them unto me. If any one say aught, ye shall say, The Lord hath need of them; and straightway he will send them. (3) The disciples did as Jesus appointed them. (4) Then they put their garments on the animal and he sat thereon. (5) The multitude, re-enforced by people coming from Jerusalem, spread their garments in the way; others cut branches from the trees, and spread them in the way. And the multitudes that went before him, and that followed, cried, Hosanna to the son of David: Blessed is he that cometh in the name of the Lord; Hosanna in the highest.

366. **Attitude of the Pharisees.** (1) Some of the Pharisees said, Teacher, rebuke thy disciples. He answered if these shall hold their peace, the stones will cry out. (2) They therefore said among themselves, Ye prevail nothing; the world is gone after him. (3) When the city came in sight, probably at a certain turn of the road, Jesus wept

211

over it, saying, If thou hadst known in this day the things which belong unto peace! but now they are hid from thine eyes. (4) For the days shall come when thine enemies shall cast up a bank about thee, and shall dash thee to the ground, and thy children; and shall not leave thee one stone upon another; because thou knewest not the time of thy visitation. (5) When he was come into Jerusalem, all the city was stirred, saying, Who is this? The multitudes said, This is the prophet, Jesus, from Nazareth of Galilee. (6) He went into the temple and when he had looked round about upon all things, it being now eventide, he went out unto Bethany with the twelve.

367. **The Cursing of the Fig Tree.** On Monday morning, April 3, as he returned to the city, he hungered. And seeing a fig tree, he came to it and found nothing but leaves only; then he saith, Let there be no fruit from thee henceforward forever. And immediately the fig tree withered away.

368. **Christ's Work in the Temple.** (1) *Second Cleansing.* Jesus entered into the temple and cast out all them that sold and bought in the temple, overthrew the tables of the money-changers, and the seats of them that sold the doves; saying, It is written, My house shall be called a house of prayer: but ye make it a den of robbers. (2) *Healing the Sick.* The blind and the lame came to him in the temple; and he healed them. (3) *Praise of the Children.* But when the chief priests and the scribes saw the wonderful things that he did, and the children that were crying in the temple, Hosanna to the son of David; they were moved with indignation, and said, Hearest thou what these are saying? Jesus saith, Yea: did ye never read, Out of the mouth of babes and sucklings thou hast perfected praise? (4) *Hatred of the Rulers.* The chief priests and the scribes and the principal men of the people sought to destroy him: and they could not find what they might do; for the people all hung upon him, listening. (5) Every day he was teaching in the temple; and every night he went out,

and lodged in mount Olivet. All the people came early in the morning in the temple, to hear him. (6) In the evening of Monday, he returned to Bethany, probably to his friends, Lazarus, Mary and Martha.

369. **Explanatory Notes.** 1. Name and compare the *sources,* especially Mt. 21 : 2 with Mk. 11 : 2 and Mt. 21 : 8 with Jno. 12 : 13; locate places on map and plan of Jerusalem; memorize Mt. 21 : 9. 2. About one-third of the combined narratives of the four gospels is concerned with the last week of Christ's life and with his resurrection. This is due to three reasons : (a) Jesus filled the closing days with intense activity. (b) The events of the last days naturally impressed themselves most deeply on the minds and hearts of his disciples. (c) The apostles regarded Christ's death as of fundamental importance and dwell at length on the events connected with it. 3. *The language* of Christ and the willingness of the owner of the ass to accede to the request seem to indicate that they were friends. 4. *"The village"* in Mark 11 : 2 is possibly Bethphage or Bethany, but quite as likely neither. 5. *Bethphage* has never been certainly identified but it was on the Mount of Olives near Bethany. Some scholars have regarded it as the name not of a village but of a district. The name means, "House of Unripe Figs." 6. *This entrance* into the city of the great king was the most formal assertion of his Messianic claims yet made. 7. *The palm branches* were regarded as a symbol of gladness and victory (Lev. 23 : 40 and Rev. 7 : 9). The spreading of garments was a recognized act of homage (2 Kings 9 : 13). 8. Matt. 21 : 5 is not an exact quotation, but is the substance of the prophecy in Zech. 9 : 9.

370. 1. There was *nothing especially humble* in those times in riding on an ass. As compared with walking it was an entrance in state; as compared with riding on a horse it was a peaceful act typical of the character of his kingdom. 2. Luke 19 : 43 and 44 contains a *striking prediction* of what actually happened at the capture of Jerusalem by the Romans under Titus in 70 A. D., after a most terrible siege. A "bank" (A. V. "trench"), was a palisade or fortification of a double fence of stakes and branches filled in with earth. 3. *Four times* in the last week Christ predicted the destruction of Jerusalem (a) near Jericho (Parable of Pounds), (b) here on Palm Sunday, (c) on Mt. Olivet on Tuesday, (d) on his way to Calvary. 4. *The place* where Jesus wept is supposed to have been that bend in the road where the city hitherto hidden from view, suddenly burst upon his sight in all its grandeur. 5. *Several nights* in the passion week the Lord spent at Bethany. But as the Lord was hungry on the morning of the cursing of the

fig tree (Monday) it has been supposed that he spent the preceding night in solitude and prayer and not at his friends' house; or that he left without breakfast. 6. This, the *only miracle of destruction,* was not an outbreak of unholy passion, but an acted parable addressed to the eye. As on fig-trees the fruit appears before the leaves, this tree challenged Jesus to refresh himself. When he accepted the challenge he found that it was, like other trees at this time (Mk. 11:13), without fruit. Its fault lay in pretending to be in advance of other trees. The tree was a hypocrite, and this fact made it a type of Israel, especially in that very point which has been ignorantly supposed to be illogical, namely, that "it was not yet the season of figs." True; but neither was it in that case the season for leaves. There should be no show without the reality. Hence, the tree was cursed, not for being barren, but for being false. 7. This *second cleansing* became necessary because the first (Jno. 2:13-17) had wrought no permanent results and the old abuses were restored in full vigor. Notice the Lord's greater severity in action and words: he overthrew the seats of dove-sellers and used the term "den of thieves." 8. *The common people* being so largely in sympathy with Jesus, the leaders feared to seize him and so he could continue his public teaching. 9. This is *the only record of sick* being brought to him even into the temple. 10. *The applause* of these children should not be confused with that of the people on Palm Sunday. These children probably repeated what they had heard the day before at the time of the triumphal entry. 11. *The primary meaning* of Ps. 8:2 is that the children wonder at the marvels of creation.

371. **Practical Lessons.** 1. Public applause is fickle; the idol of to-day may be crucified to-morrow. 2. The New Testament does not mention that Jesus ever laughed, but it reports twice that he wept; here and at the tomb of Lazarus. What inference may be drawn from this fact? 3. The time of visitation comes in one form or another to every one—a time when God seems very near. Such a time demands immediate action, for it may never return.

372. **Reference Literature.** Farrar, Ch. 49 and 50; Andrews, p. 429; Stalker, Ch. 6. Stanley, Sinai and Palestine, p. 193; Trench, Miracles, p. 440; W. J. Bryan's famous lecture, The Prince of Peace; on the spreading of garments, see, The Week of Passion, p. 152. Paintings by Plockhorst and Deger; on the Temple, see Davis, D. B., p. 725.

373. **Questions for Discussion.** 1. In what sense did the triumphal entry mark a new policy on Christ's part? 2. What would have been the result if the rulers had accepted Jesus as the Messiah? 3. Show proofs for two cleansings of the temple. 4. Enumerate times of visitation in the individual, in church and national life.

CHAPTER 41.

Last Controversy With the Rulers.

Matt. 21 : 20-Ch. 23 ; Mk. 11 : 20-12 : 40; Lu. 20: 1-47 ; Harmony 122-127.

374. **The Fig Tree Withered.** On Tuesday morning, April 4 ("the Day of Conflict"), on their way from Bethany to Jerusalem, they passed the fig tree, and Peter said, Rabbi, the fig tree which thou cursedst is withered away. Jesus saith, Have faith in God. Whosoever shall say unto this mountain, Be thou taken up and cast into the sea ; and shall not doubt in his heart, but shall believe that what he saith cometh to pass : he shall have it.

375. **Christ's Authority Challenged.** (1) When he was come into the temple, the chief priests and the elders came as he was teaching, and said, By what authority doest thou these things ? (2) Jesus answered, I also will ask you one question, which if ye tell me, I likewise will tell you by what authority I do these things. The baptism of John, whence was it ? from heaven or from men ? (3) They reasoned with themselves, If we shall say, From heaven ; he will say, Why then did ye not believe him ? But if we shall say, From men ; we fear the multitude ; for all hold John as a prophet. So they answered, We know not. (4) He said, Neither tell I you by what authority I do these things.

376. **Three Parables of Warning.** (1) In order to warn the rulers of their fate, if they continue opposing God, he spoke three parables : (a) *The Two Sons;* (b) *The Wicked Husbandmen;* (c) *The Marriage of the King's Son.* (2) The application of the second parable was very pointed. He said, The Kingdom of God shall be taken away from you, and shall be given to a nation bringing forth the fruits thereof. (3) He that falleth on this stone shall be broken to pieces : but on whomsoever it shall

fall it will scatter him as dust. (4) When the chief priests and the Pharisees heard his parables, they perceived that he spake of them. But when they sought to lay hold on him, they feared the multitudes, because they took him for a prophet.

377. **Three Catch Questions.** (a) About the *Tribute-Money*. (1) Worsted so far in the controversy, the Pharisees and Herodians took counsel how they might ensnare him in his talk. (2) They send to him their disciples saying, Teacher, we know that thou art true, and teachest the way of God in truth, and carest not for any one: for thou regardest not the person of men. Tell us therefore, Is it lawful to give tribute unto Cæsar, or not? (3) But Jesus perceived their wickedness, and said, Why make ye trial of me, ye hypocrites? Show me the tribute money. And they brought unto him a denarius. He saith, Whose is this image and superscription? They say, Cæsar's. Then he saith, Render unto Cæsar the things that are Cæsar's; and unto God the things that are God's. They marvelled, and left him. (b) On *the Resurrection.* (1) On the same day came the Sadducees saying, Teacher, Moses said, If a man die having no children, his brother shall marry his wife, and raise up seed unto his brother. (2) Now there were with us seven brethren: and the first married and deceased, and having no seed left his wife unto his brother; in like manner the others unto the seventh. After them all, the woman died. Now in the resurrection whose wife shall she be of the seven? (3) Jesus answered, Ye do err, not knowing the scriptures, nor the power of God. (4) For in the resurrection they neither marry, nor are given in marriage, but are as angels in heaven. (5) But as touching the resurrection of the dead, have ye not read that which was spoken unto you by God, saying, I am the God of Abraham, and the God of Isaac, and the God of Jacob? God is not the God of the dead, but of the living. (6) And when the multitudes heard it, they were astonished at his teaching. (c) On the *Great Commandment.* (1) When the Pharisees

heard that he had put the Sadducees to silence, a lawyer, trying him, asked, Teacher, which is the great commandment in the law? (2) He said, Thou shalt love the Lord thy God with all thy heart, and with all thy soul, and with all thy mind. This is the great and first commandment. And a second like unto it is this, Thou shalt love thy neighbor as thyself. On these two commandments the whole law hangeth, and the prophets. (3) This impressed even the scribe and he said, Of a truth, Teacher, thou hast well said that he is one; and there is none other but he: and to love him and one's neighbor is much more than sacrifices. (4) When Jesus saw that he answered discreetly he said, Thou art not far from the kingdom of God. And no man after that durst ask him any question.

378. **Christ's Unanswerable Question.** (1) When they had finished, Jesus asked the Pharisees a question: What think ye of the Christ? whose son is he? They say, *The son* of David. (2) He saith, How then doth David call him Lord, saying,

> The Lord said unto my Lord,
> Sit thou on my right hand,
> Till I put thine enemies underneath thy feet?
> If David calleth him Lord, how is he his son?

(3) And no one was able to answer him a word, neither durst any man from that day forth ask him any more questions.

379. **Woes against the Rulers.** (1) Then spake Jesus to the multitudes and to his disciples against the rulers, denouncing them in the severest terms as hypocrites. (2) He admits that they sit on Moses' seat: all things whatsoever they bid you, these do, but do not ye after their works; (3) They are *tyrants,* for they bind heavy burdens and lay them on men's shoulders; but they themselves will not move them with their finger. (4) They are *hypocrites,* for all their works they do to be seen of men: for they make broad their phylacteries, and enlarge the borders *of their garments,* and love the chief place at feasts, and the chief seats in the synagogues, and the salutations in the market-places, and to be called of men, Rabbi. (5) Ye shut the kingdom of

heaven against men: for ye enter not in yourselves, neither suffer ye them that are entering in to enter. (6) Ye compass sea and land to make one *proselyte;* and when he is become so, ye make him two fold more a son of hell than yourselves. (7) Your oaths lead to immorality, for ye teach that whosoever shall swear by the temple, it is nothing; but whosoever shall swear by the gold of the temple, he is a debtor. Ye fools and blind: which is greater, the gold, or the temple that hath sanctified the gold? And, whosoever shall swear by the altar, it is nothing; but whosoever shall swear by the gift that is upon it, he is a debtor. Ye blind: which is greater, the gift, or the altar that sanctifieth the gift? (8) Ye tithe mint and anise and cummin, and have left undone the weightier matters of the law, justice, and mercy, and faith: but these ye ought to have done, and not to have left the other undone. Ye blind guides, that strain out the gnat, and swallow the camel! (9) Ye cleanse the outside of the cup and the platter, but within they are full from extortion and excess. (10) Ye are like unto whited sepulchres, which outwardly appear beautiful, but inwardly are full of dead men's bones, and of all uncleanness. Ye also outwardly appear righteous but inwardly ye are full of hypocrisy and iniquity. (11) Ye build the sepulchres of the prophets, and garnish the tombs of the righteous, and say, If we had been in the days of our fathers, we should not have been partakers with them in the blood of the prophets. (12) O Jerusalem, Jerusalem, that killeth the prophets, and stoneth them that are sent unto her! how often would I have gathered thy children together, even as a hen gathereth her chickens under her wings, and ye would not!

380. **Explanatory Notes.** 1. Name and compare *sources,* locate places on map and plan of the temple, memorize, Lu. 20: 38. 2. *A comparison* between this acted and the spoken parable of the fig tree in Luke 13: 6-9, shows that, according to the latter, the Jewish people had still a little time for repentance. Judgment is threatened but yet in the future. This incident foreshadows the fast approaching doom of the nation. 3. To destroy the Lord's influence

with the people the leaders questioned his authority for his course on Monday, and his teaching in general. Jesus silenced them with a counter question to which they could not answer yes or no, without either stultifying themselves on account of their not believing John's testimony concerning Christ, or bringing upon them the hostility of the people, for the Baptist still had a firm hold upon them and it continued for years. (Acts 19: 1-7.) 4. *Paraphrase* of Mt. 21: 25: Was John's ministry, including his testimony to the deputation and the people (Jn. 1: 26) from God? If you say, yes, then you know that I am the Messiah, for he told you so, and if I am the Messiah, you know that I have the right to cleanse the temple. 5. Mt. 22: 15 seems to indicate that a *formal council* was held for making plans to ensnare Jesus. 6. *To teach while walking about,* and to stop a teacher and ask him questions was very common with Rabbis and philosophers ("Peripatetics"). 7. These *three parables* were spoken in the temple. For the first time the Lord uttered plainly the truth in the hearing of the Pharisees that they would kill him, and that in consequence the kingdom would be taken from them. Their only reply was to plot violence. 8. The *Herodians* and Pharisees were under ordinary circumstances mutual enemies, but here, as on several other occasions, they were united by the danger coming from a greater common adversary. 9. The *question* as to the tribute money was designed to force from him some unpopular or treasonable answer which would give them an excuse for arresting him. An affirmative answer would have been incompatible with popular Messianic ideals. A negative answer would have laid him open to the charge of treason against Rome in the eyes of the Herodians. His answer recognized the claims both of Jehovah and Cæsar. 10. The coin bore the head of Tiberius, the reigning emperor of Rome, encircled with a wreath of laurels; and the inscription running around was "Tiberius Cæsar, Divi Augusti filius Augustus, Imperator." (For an illustration see any D. of B.)

381. 1. *The question of the Sadducees* was intended to cast ridicule both upon him and upon the Pharisees by showing the inconsistency and absurdity of the doctrine of the resurrection. Jesus in his masterly answer simply denied the truth of their premises (that the earthly relations and the law of Moses would be binding in eternity), and by so doing their case fell to the ground. 2. *Their question* was based on the Levirate law (from the Latin, levir—brother-in-law) in Deut. 25: 5, 6, the object of which was to preserve the name of the man who died childless. 3. *The grotesque illustration* of the woman with seven husbands had no doubt been invented for the purpose of making the doctrine of the resurrec-

tion ridiculous. 4. *The Lord teaches* the Sadducees (a) that earthly relations cease at death and in the next world man will be exalted to a higher order of beings; (b) that in the life beyond men were not governed by the law of Moses, for their new natures will determine their relations; (c) that precisely as the presence of death in this world makes marriage necessary for the perpetuation of the human race, so the absence of death in the next world makes marriage unnecessary. 5. *Jesus found immortality* at the very heart of the Mosaic law, involved in the distinctive name of God, Yahveh, the living one, the creative. 6. *The lawyer's question* respecting the comparative value of the commandments was designed either to test his knowledge of the law, and to discredit him in the eyes of the people in case he could not answer, or to mix him up in the controversies of the scribes on this question. His answer is a comprehensive summing up of the Old Testament teaching. 7. *The Jews inferred* that because the Messiah was David's son his coming would signify the restoration of David's political kingdom. To correct this narrow view Christ shows that David himself considered him a higher being by calling him "Lord." 8. According to Matthew 23:3 Jesus did not desire to bring about an abrupt break with the rulers in Israel, but rather that the people should follow them till, under the influence of his own teaching and of providential circumstances, better leaders should arise. 9. *The malice veiled* under the show of righteousness explains the terrible severity of Christ's language. 10. I* *is not certain* who the Zacharias son of Barachias of Matt. 23:35 was. Many identify him with Zachariah, son of Jehoiada, "who was stoned at the commandment of the king in the court of the house of the Lord," (2 Chron. 24:20 and 21). 11. *Phylacteries* were small leather cases bound to the forehead or left arm and containing four texts (Ex. 13:1-10, 11-16; Deut. 6:4-9; 11:13-21) written on parchment. By their varying size they were supposed to measure the wearer's zeal. They were also called "frontlets" (Ex. 13:16; Deut. 6:8). 12. *The borders* of their garments were the fringes or tassels which all Jews were commanded to wear (Num. 15:38). By enlarging these things the Pharisees pretended to be very pious. 13. As touching a dead body or sepulchre made one ceremonially unclean, graves were covered with slabs of stone which were whitewashed on the outside so that people would see them and keep away from them. Hence the term, "whited sepulchres."

382. **Practical Lessons.** 1. In its modern application the parable of the two sons teaches, not that there is more hope for a flagrant sinner than for a virtuous man, but that the flagrant sinner who forsakes his sins enters the kingdom of heaven before the

orthodox man who clings to his sins. The first son is commended, not because of the daring wickedness of his reply, but because he regretted it and showed his regret by his action. 2. The parable of the Wicked Husbandmen teaches that unfaithfulness puts individuals and nations in danger of losing God's gifts altogether. 3. Luther, in his famous book "Admonition to my Beloved Germans" says: "What's gone, is gone; the Jews had Christ, but they rejected him and they are now scattered abroad; Greece had the pure Gospel, but now they have the Turks; Rome and the Latin nations had the truth, but now they have the pope; Germany has now its great opportunity, but unfaithfulness will drive it away." ("Hin ist hin!") 4. The *Parable* of the Marriage of the King's Son teaches that it is not sufficient to be a member of the visible Church, for many within the pale of the Church will not be owned by God, because they despise the mercies of the Covenant. (Matt. 6:21.) 5. The guest without the wedding garment represents those who profess Christ but do not make progress in holiness. 6. Nature says, Love thyself alone; domestic education says, Love your family; the nation says, Love your country; Christ insists, Love all mankind. 7. The tendency of a formal and lifeless religion is always to multiply needless burdens, such as (a) vexatious observances and rites; (b) difficult doctrines as essential to salvation; (c) fancied duties. 8. It is better to make no profession at all than to practice hypocrisy. 9. Professional religious guides are often blinder to religious truth than the people whom they profess to lead. (Matt. 21:26.) 10. Christianity should be judged by what it accomplishes in the best of its followers and not by its misrepresentations in hypocrites. (Mk. 23:13-31.) 11. No pious appearance can take the place of holy living.

383. **Reference Literature.** Farrar, Ch., 51 and 52; Stalker, Ch. 6; Andrews, p. 438; on the authority to teach, see Edersheim's L. of C., II, p. 381; on Immortality, see Fairbairn's Studies in the Life of Christ, p. 236; on hypocrisy, see Hast. D. of C., I, 765; Salmond, Christian Doctrine of Immortality; Charles, Critical Hist. of the Doctrine of the Future Life.

384. **Questions for Discussion.** 1. Why did the disciples not notice on their return on Monday that the tree was withered? 2. How did Christ's question convey an answer to that of the rulers concerning his authority? 3. What does Jesus teach as to politics? 4. Why did he ask the Pharisees to hand him a coin, instead of using one of his own? 5. When quoting O. T. books by the name of the author does Jesus attempt to give definite teaching as to the authorship of such writings? Did Jesus show ability as a debater?

CHAPTER 42.

Last Experiences in the Temple and Discourse on the Last Things.

Mk. 12:41-14:11; Lu. 21:1-22:6; Matt. 24-26:16; Jno. 12:20-50. Harmony 128-132.

385. **The Widow's Two Mites.** (1) At the close of these exciting controversies, which probably took place in the court of the Gentiles, Jesus retired to the court of the women and sat over against the treasury, and beheld how the multitude cast money into the treasury. (2) Many rich cast in much, and a poor widow cast in two mites. (3) He called his disciples, and said, This poor widow cast in more than all, for they all did cast in of their superfluity; but she of her want, all that she had.

386. **Greeks Seeking Jesus.** (1) While Jesus was still resting in the court of the women, proselytes of Greek nationality, probably from Decapolis, said to Philip, of Bethsaida, Sir, we would see Jesus. Philip telleth Andrew and both tell Jesus. (2) Jesus answereth, The hour is come that the Son of man should be glorified. Except a grain of wheat fall into the earth and die, it abideth by itself alone; but if it die, it beareth much fruit. (3) Now is my soul troubled; and what shall I say? Father, save me from this hour. But for this cause came I unto this hour. Father, glorify thy name. (4) There came a voice out of heaven, I have glorified it, and will glorify it again. (5) The multitude said that it had thundered: others said, An angel hath spoken to him. (6) Jesus said, This voice hath not come for my sake, but for your sakes. Now is the judgment of this world; now shall the prince of this world be cast out. And I, if I be lifted up from the earth, will draw all men unto myself. (7) But this he said, signifying by what manner of death he should die. (8) The multitude answered, We have heard that the Christ abideth for ever:

(9) Jesus said, Yet a little while is the light among you. (10) While ye have the light, believe on the light, that ye may become sons of light.

387. **Leaving the Temple.** (1) When Jesus had spoken these things he departed from the temple, never to return, and hid himself from them. (2) But though he had done so many signs before them, yet they believed not on him: that the word of Isaiah might be fulfilled,

Lord, who hath believed our report?

And to whom hath the arm of the Lord been revealed?

(3) Nevertheless even of the rulers many believed on him; but because of the Pharisees they did not confess it, lest they should be put out of the synagogue: for they loved the glory that is of men more than the glory that is of God. (4) And as he was walking out of the temple Jesus cried, He that believeth on me, believeth not on me, but on him that sent me. (5) If any man hear my sayings, and keep them not, I judge him not: for I came not to judge but to save the world. He hath one that judgeth him: the word that I spake, shall judge him in the last day. (6) For I spake not from myself; but the Father that sent me, hath given me a commandment, what I should say.

388. **Discourse on the Last Things.** (1) It was Tuesday, towards evening when Jesus left the temple. (2) As they were ascending Mt. Olivet the disciples, pointing to the sun-bathed temple, said, Master, behold, what manner of stones and what manner of buildings! Jesus answered, There shall not be left one stone upon another. (3) When Jesus had sat down on Mt. Olivet, Peter, James, John and Andrew asked him privately three questions: When shall these things be, and what shall be the sign of thy coming, and the sign of the end of the world? (4) The Lord's answer may be analysed as follows:

I. *Events which precede the End* (Mt. 24: 4-14):

(1) *False Messiahs:* Take heed that no man lead you astray. For many shall come saying, I am the Christ; (2) *Wars and famines:* Ye shall hear of wars and rumors of

wars; there shall be famines and earthquakes. But all these things are the beginning of travail. (3) *Persecutions and false prophets:* Then shall they deliver you up unto tribulation, and shall kill you: and ye shall be hated of all the nations for my name's sake. And then shall many deliver up one another. Many false prophets shall arise, and shall lead many astray. Iniquity shall be multiplied and the love of the many shall wax cold. (4) This gospel of the kingdom shall be preached in the whole world for a testimony unto all the nations; and then shall the end come.

II. *The Sign of the Approach of the End* (Matt. 24:15):

This sign is the abomination of desolation (most likely the Roman army) which was spoken of through Daniel the prophet, standing in the holy place (let him that readeth understand).

III. *Warning against Delay* when the sign appears (Matt. 24:16-18):

Let them that are in Judæa flee unto the mountains: let him that is on the housetop not go down to take out the things that are in his house: and let him that is in the field not return back to take his cloak.

IV. *Terrors of those Days* (Matt. 24:19-22):

Then shall be great tribulation, such as hath not been from the beginning of the world until now, no, nor ever shall be. And except those days had been shortened, no flesh would have been saved: but for the elect's sake those days shall be shortened.

V. *Warning against the Supposition that then the Son of Man shall come* (Mt. 24:23-28):

(1) Then if any man shall say, Lo, here is the Christ, or, Here; believe *it* not. For there shall rise false Christs, and false prophets, and shall show great signs and wonders; so as to lead astray, if possible, even the elect. (2) For as the lightning cometh forth from the east, and is seen even unto the west; so shall be the coming of the Son of man. Wheresoever the carcase is, there will the eagles be gathered together.

VI. *The Manner of Christ's Second Coming* (Mt. 24::29-31):

(1) But immediately after the tribulation of those days the sun shall be darkened, and the moon shall not give her light, and the stars shall fall from heaven, and the powers of the heavens shall be shaken: (2) Then shall appear the sign of the Son of man in heaven: and then shall all the tribes of the earth mourn, and they shall see the Son of man coming on the clouds of heaven with power and great glory. (3) And he shall send forth his angels with a great sound of a trumpet, and they shall gather together his elect from the four winds, from one end of heaven to the other.

VII. *The time of Christ's Coming* (Mt. 24: 32-36):

(1) From the fig tree learn her parable: when her branch putteth forth its leaves, ye know that the summer is nigh; so when ye see all these things, know ye that he is at the doors. (2) This generation shall not pass away, till all these things be accomplished. Heaven and earth shall pass away, but my words shall not pass away. (3) But of the exact day and hour knoweth no one, not even the angels of heaven, neither the Son, but the Father only.

VIII. *Condition of the World at Christ's Coming* (Mat. 24: 37-44):

(1) As were the days of Noah, so shall be the coming of the Son of man. They were eating and drinking, marrying and giving in marriage, until the day that Noah entered into the ark, and the flood took them all away. (2) Then shall two men be in the field; one is taken, and one is left: two women shall be grinding at the mill; one is taken, and one is left. Watch therefore: for ye know not on what day your Lord cometh. (3) But know this, that if the master of the house had known in what watch the thief was coming, he would have watched. Therefore be ye also ready; for in an hour that ye think not the Son of man cometh.

IX. *Description of the Judgment upon four classes* (Matt. 24:45-25:46):

(1) *Judgment upon Christ's Servants* (Matt. 24:45-51): (a) Blessed is that servant, whom his lord when he cometh shall find faithful; he will set him over all that he hath. (b) But if that evil servant shall say in his heart, My lord tarrieth; and shall begin to beat his fellow-servants, and shall eat and drink, the lord of that servant shall come in a day when he expecteth not, and shall appoint his portion with the hypocrites: there shall be the weeping and the gnashing of teeth. (2) Judgment upon the Church as a whole. See the Parable of the *Ten Virgins* (Mt. 25:1-11). (3) Judgment upon the individual. See the parable of *The Talents* (Mt. 25:14-30). (4) Judgment upon the world. See the thrilling word picture in Matt. 25:31-46.

389. **Conspiracy against Jesus.** (1) *Fourth announcement of Christ's death.* When he had finished the great discourse on the last things he said unto his disciples, Ye know that after two days the passover cometh, and the Son of man is delivered up to be crucified. (2) *Plan of the Sanhedrin.* Probably on the same Tuesday evening, there were gathered the chief priests, and the elders, unto the court of the high priest Caiaphas; and took counsel that they might take Jesus by subtlety, and kill him. But they said, Not during the feast, lest a tumult arise among the people. (3) *The offer of Judas.* Either when Jesus left the temple or after the discourses, Judas Iscariot, went unto the chief priests, and said, What are ye willing to give me, and I will deliver him unto you? And they weighed unto him thirty pieces of silver. From that time he sought opportunity to deliver him. (4) *The Quiet of Wednesday.* There is no record of this day. It is generally assumed that Jesus and the Twelve spent it in quietness with the friends at Bethany.

390. **Explanatory Notes.** 1. Name and compare the *sources* especially of the eschatological discourses; locate the places on the map of Jerusalem and the plan of the temple; memorize Mt.

24:35. 2. *Two mites* were about equal to three-fifths of a cent, or about one-fortieth of a laborer's day's wages. 3. *The women's court* was so called, not because reserved to women only, but because women might not go further. (Just as the "Court of Gentiles.") 4. *Before the passover* free will offerings, in addition to the half shekel temple tax, were generally received. 5. *The term* indicates that these Greeks were not Hellenists (Greek-speaking Jews) but Gentiles, probably proselytes of the gate who had come to the passover. As the two apostles with Greek names introduced them to Jesus, it has been supposed that they came from the region of Decapolis and that Philip and Andrew had some intimate connection with them, and the Greek speaking population of that region. 6. Sepp, a Catholic theologian, regards these Greeks as deputies of Abgarus, king of Edessa, of whom there is a spurious correspondence with Jesus in existence. A legend says, that Jesus gave them a letter and his picture for the king. 7. As they requested a *private interview* it has been conjectured that, having witnessed the bitter attacks of the rulers during the day, they decided to invite him to preach to the Gentiles. At any rate their visit proved a great comfort to Jesus, for they just came when Jesus felt most keenly the bitterness of being "despised and rejected of men," and it was an assurance of the Gentiles' readiness. 8. *Three times* the Father bore audible witness to his Son: at his baptism, at the transfiguration and here.

391. 1. The disciples were justly proud of their temple for it was one of the most beautiful buildings, and when bathed in the setting sun its gold and ornaments must have made an enchanting impression. 2. *Some of the stones* in the outer temple wall were of enormous size; one over thirty-seven feet long, and large in proportion, still remains; also several others nearly as large. 3. *The Jews divided* the history of the world into two parts: the time before the coming of the Messiah to set up His glorious earthly kingdom, and the time after His coming. By the "end of the world," or "age" (as it should be translated), the disciples meant the end of the former of these two periods. They were anxious to know when His kingdom would begin. His reply showed how widely different His idea of the future was from theirs. 4. Mt. 24:2 has been fulfilled with terrible accuracy. There is only one stone of which it is certain that it belonged to that temple. That is a block of marble from the screen that separated the inner courts from the court of the Gentiles. The inscription warns Gentiles to go no further on penalty of death. The stone is now in the museum at Constantinople. 5. *The eschatological* (Greek: "eschatos" last) discourses treat of two subjects: the destruction of Jerusalem and Christ's

second coming. But it has always proved one of the greatest exegetical difficulties to ascertain what portions relate to each event and what relation of time the two events sustain to each other. Certain points seem to indicate that Jesus thought of his advent as indefinitely remote, e. g.; the gospel must be extensively preached; the reference to the time of the Gentiles during which Jerusalem would be trodden down (Luke 21:24); the prophecy of many wars, and of many false prophets; the declaration that these things were only the beginning of the travail pains (Mark 13:4-8). Other passages seem to represent the advent as quite near: e. g. Matt. 24:42, "Watch therefore; for ye know not on what day your Lord cometh;" Matt. 10:23 which states that he will come before the disciples shall have finished the evangelization of Palestine. Dr. Sheldon thinks that the evangelists in compiling these sayings of Christ, either by omission or imperfect arrangement, have obscured the original connection of some of his words. 6. *Among the many interpretations* of these discourses we mention three: (a) the first part predicts the fall of Jerusalem, A. D. 70, and the second part foretells the end of this age and Christ's second coming at a remote future. The difficulty of this interpretation consists in the fact that according to Mt. 24:29 the two parts of the drama will follow each other "'immediately," and according to Mk. 13:24 both fall within the same period. (b) Christ expected both parts to be fulfilled in his generation. This would involve an error in Christ's teaching and should therefore be rejected. (c) The first part was fulfilled A. D. 70, and the coming of Christ is to be taken spiritually of his coming at his resurrection or on Pentecost. This interpretation harmonizes with John's Gospel, which always speaks of Christ's second coming as being of a spiritual nature. According to this interpretation the "signs" are not events but figurative descriptions of the greatness of the doom of God's judgment such as are found in O. T. imagery (Isa. 13:10; 34:4; Ezek. 32:7, 8; Joel 2:30, 31; 3:15). 7. Mt. 26:64 shows (a) that there is a sense in which the coming of Christ is *not a single event,* (b) that it was to begin with the very day of Christ's departure, (c) that he is to assume power in heaven and exercise it on earth by interferences in the world's history, beginning with the destruction of Jerusalem. 8. *Some have tried* to harmonize both classes of passages in the discourses on the last things by saying that Christ looked upon his advent as a process rather than as one definite historical event, and that he gave to his disciples two scenes out of that long process, viz: its beginning, the destruction of Jerusalem falling within the present generation and the culmination of the process, his coming, the time of which was known to the Father only. 9. After *indescribable suffering* and cruelty Jerusalem was taken on Aug. 10, A. D. 70. Josephus says, "If the miseries of mankind from the creation were compared with those which the Jews then suffered, they would appear inferior." He also tells us that 1,100,000 Jews perished during this war nd siege, and that all the 97,000 miserable survivors who were captured when the city fell were either slain or sold as slaves. The "elect" (vs. 22) were the Jewish Christians who would be in Jerusalem at that time. 10. *The Greek "parousia"* means literally "presence" as opposed to absence. But as his presence is made possible only by his coming, the latter translation is also correct. The expression "second coming" is not found in the Bible.

392. 1. *The plans of the Sanhedrin* agreed upon at this meeting (to arrest Jesus "not during the feast") were soon afterwards changed because of the offer of Judas who seems to have entered into the room towards the close of their session. With his aid they believed to be able to do that which they had a little while ago judged impossible, viz: to arrest Jesus during the feast without causing an uproar. Now they agreed to leave the details as to the opportune time, etc., to Judas. They may also have taken into account that after the feast he might escape as he had often done before. It is to be noted that in all accounts Judas and not the Sanhedrin takes the initiative. 2. *Thirty shekels* (120 denarius) was the value of a slave. As one denarius was at that time the wages for a day's labor (Matt. 20:2), 30 shekels amounted to 4 months wages. 3. *Among the motives* which led Judas to the betrayal we may give prominence to five: (a) avarice, which led to (b) embezzlement of trust funds (Jno. 12:6); (c) disappointment of his Messianic expectations; (d) gradual growth of hostility toward Jesus, as he became aware, through Christ's rebukes (Jno. 6:70; 12:6) that his real character was known; (e) anger, because he came to believe that Jesus, by misrepresentations, had induced him to follow him.

393. **Practical Lessons.** 1. God has regard not only to what a man gives, but to what he keeps. 2. Gentiles were present at the Lord's manger, on his last visit to the temple and at his cross. 3. The world gains little or nothing from those who live for themselves. It is the unplanted seed that remains unfruitful. 4. The law of the seed is the law of human life. 5. Use your life for selfish gratification and you lose it forever; spend it for the common good and it will find its highest development and exert the most enduring influence. 6. Longfellow's Psalm of Life: "Lives of great men all remind us we can make our lives sublime, etc." 7. Christ promises an immortality of influence, but also an immor-

tality of personal life. 8. Great are the blessings from Christ's life, but greater those from his death. 9. The aim of the discourse on the last things is not to gratify curiosity respecting the future, but to inculcate watchfulness and service. 10. Every great religious movement whereby Christ's kingdom is advanced may be regarded as a coming of Christ. 11. Every age begets religious imposters who enrich themselves by leading people astray (Dowie, Mrs. Eddy) Matt. 24:4. 12. The more preposterous and shameless the claims of deceivers, the more readily they seem to win followers. 13. Kant's famous proof of a final judgment is as follows: major premise—conscience demands that every one should receive his due; minor premise—but in this world virtue is often crucified and vice is crowned; conclusion—therefore reason demands that there be a final righteous judgment by an incorruptible judge. 14. Commotions in the political, religious, social and industrial world are often signs of the advancement of God's kingdom. 15. Schiller's famous saying, "Die Weltgeschichte ist das Weltgerichte" (The world's history is the world's judgment) is only partially true. 16. Talents are given according to natural ability. He who receives one talent is just as perfectly equipped for his work as the others. Unfaithfulness narrows the vessel, and fidelity has the tendency to enlarge it, so that one with inferior natural gifts will often bring in a more abundant return than another with superior gifts. 17. The doom of the slothful servant is a warning to those who choose "a goodness solitary and particular rather than generative and seminal" (Lord Bacon). St. Augustine on the anniversary of his installation as Bishop of Hippo in North Africa (died 430) preached on this feature of the parable and spoke of the temptation to withdraw from active labor in the Church, and cultivate a solitary piety. 18. The reward of the faithful worker is not merely that he receives more, and the punishment of the slothful servant is not only that he loses, but the very gift which the one forfeits the other obtains. Continually we see men taking hold of opportunities which others neglected. (Esau: Gen. 25:34; 27:36. Also Gen. 49:4, 8; 1 Sam. 16:1-13; 1 Kings 2:35; Acts 1:25; Rom. 11:11.)

394. **Reference Literature.** Farrar, Ch. 53, 54; Andrews, p. 443; Stalker, § 146; on the "Abomination" see Davis, D. B.; Hast. D. of C., I, 6; on false Christs: Davis D. B.; Hast. D. of C., I, 574; on eschatology, Hast: D. of C., I, 525; on the treasury, Hast. D. C., II, 748. Sanford on eschatology; Herzog II, Chiliasmus; on the interpretation of Matt. 24 and 25 see Internat. Crit. Com. on Mk. by Gould, p. 240; Steven's N. T. Theol., p. 150; Sheldon's N. T. Theol., p. 119; Moffat, Hist. N. Test., p. 641; Haupt, Die eschatol-

ogischen Aussagen Jesu, p. 22, 45; on the second coming viewed
as a process, see Clark, Christ. Theol., p. 390; on the probable
date of the flight of the Christians to Pella, see Hanna, Life of C.,
p. 561; on the view of Jerusalem from Mt. Olivet see Milman's
Hist. of Christianity, I, p. 294, quoted by Maclear N. T. Hist. p.
276; on the temple buildings, see Jos. Bell Jud. 5:5, 6; Ant. 11:5.
The Arch of Titus in the Forum Romanum. Funk, The Widow's
Mite. On the "Warning Tablet," see Barton's Week of Passion, p.
172.

395. **Questions for Discussion.** 1. How may Christ's commendation of the widow's mite be abused? 2. What constitutes a
giver's "mite"? 3. What did the coming of the Greeks suggest
to Christ's mind? 4. Does the principle set forth in Jno. 12:24
apply to all men? 5. What is the main purpose of the discourse
on the last things? 6. What is each of the parables intended to
teach? 7. What is to be the basis of God's judgment? 8. Why does
this not contradict "Salvation by grace on condition of faith"
(Jno. 3:16)? 9. What was the exact bargain between Judas and
the rulers, and in what particulars did it change their former plans?

CHAPTER 43.

Last Supper and Farewell Addresses.

Matt. 26:17-35; Mk. 14:12-31; Lu. 22:7-38; Jno. 13:1-
Chap. 17. Harmony 133-135.

396. **Preparation for the Passover.** (1) After his
last sleep on earth, on Thursday, April 6 (Nisan 14), which
was the first day of unleavened bread on which the passover must be sacrificed, the disciples came to Jesus, saying,
Where wilt thou that we make ready for thee to eat the
passover? (2) And he sent Peter and John, saying, When
ye are entered into the city, there shall meet you a man
bearing a pitcher of water; follow him into the house, and
say unto the master of the house, The Teacher saith, Where
is my guest-chamber, where I shall eat the passover with
my disciples? (3) He will show you a large upper room
furnished: there make ready. (4) They found as he had
said

397. **First Part of the Passover Meal.** (1) When Peter and John had made ready the passover they returned to the rest at Bethany. (2) In the evening all went to Jerusalem and sat down to the meal. (3) After the usual "benediction" Christ said: I have greatly desired to eat this passover with you before I suffer, for I shall not eat it anymore until it be fulfilled in the kingdom of God. (4) Then he took the "first cup," gave thanks and said, divide it among yourselves. I will not drink from henceforth of the fruit of the vine until the kingdom of God shall come.

398. **Strife for Seats of Honor.** (1) Probably when selecting their places there arose a contention among them, which of them was accounted to be greatest. (2) Jesus said, The kings of the Gentiles have lordship over them; but ye shall not be so; but he that is the greater among you, let him become as he that doth serve. I am in the midst of you as he that serveth. (3) But ye are they that have continued with me in my temptations; and I appoint unto you a kingdom, even as my Father appointed unto me, that ye may eat and drink at my table in my kingdom; and ye shall sit on thrones judging the twelve tribes of Israel.

399. **Feet Washing.** (1) To impress the lesson of service still more, Jesus, in place of the usual washing of the company's hands, arose from the supper and began to wash the disciples' feet. (2) When he cometh to Simon Peter he saith, Lord, dost thou wash my feet? Jesus answered, What I do thou knowest not now: but thou shalt understand hereafter. (3) Peter saith, Thou shalt never wash my feet. Jesus answered, If I wash thee not, thou hast no part with me. (4) Peter saith, Lord, not my feet only, but also my hands and my head. (5) Jesus saith He that is bathed needeth not save to wash his feet for he is clean every whit: and ye are clean, but not all. (6) For he knew him that should betray him. (7) When he had washed their feet, he said Know ye what I have done to you? Ye call me, Teacher, and, Lord: and ye say well; for so I am. If I then, the Lord and the Teacher, have washed

your feet, ye also ought to wash one another's feet. (8) I have given you an example, that ye also should do as I have done to you. A servant is not greater than his lord. (9) If ye know these things, blessed are ye if ye do them. (10) I speak not of you all; I know whom I have chosen: but that the scripture may be fulfilled, He that eateth my bread lifted up his heel against me.

400. **The Betrayer Pointed Out.** (1) As the meal proceeded, Jesus was troubled in the spirit and said, One of you shall betray me. (2) The disciples looked one on another, doubting of whom he spoke, and each one asked, Is it I, Lord? (3) As John was reclining in Jesus' bosom, Peter beckoned to him, Tell us who it is of whom he speaks. John said, Lord, who is it? Jesus answereth, He it is, for whom I shall dip the sop, and give it him. (4) The Son of man goeth, even as it is written of him: but woe unto that man through whom the Son of man is betrayed! good were it for that man if he had not been born. (5) Then he gave the sop to Judas, and he also asked, Is it I, Rabbi? Jesus said, Thou hast said. (6) After the sop entered Satan in him. (7) Jesus said, What thou doest, do quickly. Now no man at the table knew for what intent he spake this unto him. Some thought, because Judas had the bag, that Jesus said unto him, Buy what things we have need of for the feast; or, that he should give something to the poor. (8) Judas went out straightway: and it was night.

401. **Institution of the Lord's Supper.** (1) When Judas had left, and as they were eating, Jesus took bread, blessed, and brake it; and gave to the disciples, and said, Take, eat; this is my body. (2) And he took a cup (probably the "third cup"), gave thanks, and gave to them, saying, this is my blood of the new covenant, which is poured out for many unto remission of sins.

402. **Farewell Conversations.** As was customary, Jesus and his apostles remained a long time after the meal at the table engaged in serious conversation on the following subjects:

1. *Christ's triumph.* When Judas had left the spell was broken, and Jesus exclaimed, Now is the Son of man glorified, and God is glorified in him: Little children, yet a little while I am with you. Ye shall seek me: and as I said unto the Jews, Whither I go, ye cannot come.

2. *The New Commandment.* A new commandment I give unto you, that ye love one another even as I have loved you. By this shall all men know that ye are my disciples.

3. *Testing of the Disciples.* (1) Peter said, Lord, Why cannot I follow thee now? (2) Then saith Jesus unto them, All ye shall be offended in me this night: for it is written, I will smite the shepherd, and the sheep of the flock shall be scattered abroad. But after I am raised up, I will go before you into Galilee. (3) But Peter said, If all shall be offended in thee, I will never be offended. Jesus said, Simon, Simon, behold, Satan asked to sift you as wheat; but I made supplication for thee, that thy faith fail not; and when once thou has turned again, establish thy brethren. Peter said, Lord, with thee I am ready to go to prison and death. Jesus replied, This night before the cock crow twice, thou shalt deny me thrice. But he spake exceeding vehemently, If I must die with thee, I will not deny thee. And in like manner also said they all.

4. *Instructions for the Future.* Jesus said, When I sent you forth without purse and wallet, and shoes, lacked ye anything? They said, Nothing. He said, But now, he that hath a purse, let him take it, and likewise a wallet; and he that hath none, let him sell his cloak, and buy a sword. For I say unto you, that this which is written must be fulfilled in me, He was reckoned with transgressors. They said, Lord, behold, here are two swords. He said, It is enough.

5. *Comfort for Troubled Hearts.* Jno. 14: 1-11.
    (1) I go to prepare a place for you. (2-6).
    (2) I have revealed the Father. (7-11).

6. *Promises for Those left Behind.* Jno. 14: 12-24.
    (1) Greater works than Christ's. (12).

(2) Answered Prayer. (13-15).

(3) An Abiding Comforter. (16-17).

(4) The Indwelling Christ. (18-24).

(5) The Gift of Peace. (25-31).

7. *New Relationships.* Jno. 15: 1-17.

    (1) Union with Christ: vine and branches. (Jno. 15: 1-11).

    (2) Union with one another in Him. Love one another. (12-17).

8. *The Hatred of the World* against him and them. Jno. 15: 18-25.

9. *The World and the Paraclete.* Jno. 16: 1-11.

It is expedient that I go. The Spirit will convict the world.

10. *The Disciples and the Paraclete..* 16: 12-15.

The Spirit shall guide you into all the truth.

11. *The Sorrow of Christ's Departure* turned into joy by his return (Jno. 16: 16-24). "A little while."

12. *Summary and Conclusion* of the whole discourse, Jno. 16: 25-33. "I have overcome the world."

13. *The High-priestly Prayer.* Jno. 17.

    (1) 1-5 prayer for himself. Glorify thy Son;

    (2) 6-19, prayer for his disciples; manifest thy name to them; keep them from evil in this world; sanctify them in the truth;

    (3) 20-24, prayer for all future believers; that they all may be one in me, that they may be where I am to see my glory.

    (4) 25-26. Summary of his Mission; I made known to them thy name; I communicated thy love to them.

403. **Explanatory Notes.** 1. Name and compare *sources;* trace the Lord's movements on the map; memorize John 14: 1-2. This Thursday is called *Maundy Thursday* from the Latin words, dies mandati, day of command, because on that day was instituted the Lord's Supper, or because he gave "the new commandment" (Jno. 13: 34). The Germans call it "Gruendonnerstag" (Green Thurs-

day), because the introitus to the service of that day was Ps. 23:2, the "green pasture" referring to the Lord's Supper, as the bread of life. Others call the day, "Hoher Donnerstag" (High Thursday). 3. The Jews named this feast (a) "passover" because in the night before the exodus the angel passed over the houses of the Hebrews; (b) feast of unleavened bread, because their fathers could not wait for the bread to rise. It commemorated Israel's deliverance from Egypt (First Commandment). The celebration began on the 14th of Nisan at even with the paschal supper and lasted one week. 4. Christ probably did not mention his host's name because he did not wish Judas to know beforehand where the supper was to take place, as he might have him arrested before he had kept the feast. 5. *Pitchers* of water were usually carried by women, so that a man carrying a pitcher would be conspicuous. 6. The man carrying the pitcher, or better the "good man" of the house, was, according to tradition, the father of John Mark, the author of the second gospel. His wife's name was Mary (Acts 12). The form of the message ("my guest-chamber") seems to indicate that Jesus had some previous understanding with the man. Many non-resident Jews rented guest-chambers for the feast. 7. The *tradition* with reference to the "upper room" is as follows: It was the home of the disciples when in Jerusalem. Here the Risen One appeared to them on the evening of the resurrection day, and a week later; here the prayer meeting of the 120 and the election of Matthias were held; here the Holy Spirit was poured out on Pentecost and the first Christians held their meetings (Acts 12:12). The house is one of the few buildings that survived the destruction of Jerusalem and forms a part of a complex of buildings known as Neby Daud, on the southwest hill. It is known as the Coenaculum (from the Latin coena-supper). It is now in possession of the Mohammedans who are unwilling to part with it. 8. The *house adjoining* the Coenaculum is called "Dormitio Sanctae Virginis" (abode of the Holy Virgin). Here according to old legends Mary lived and ascended into Heaven. This house has been donated by the Sultan to Emperor William of Germany at the occasion of his visit to Jerusalem for the purpose of dedicating the German Protestant Church of the Redeemer (Die Erloeserkirche). The Emperor in turn gave the house to the Roman Catholic Historical Society of Germany, and the German Catholics are now erecting a magnificent church on the spot. 9. The *paschal supper* consisted of (a) a lamb, selected on the tenth of Nisan and killed in the temple on the afternoon of the 14th; (b) unleavened bread; (c) bitter herbs, in remembrance of the bitterness of their fathers' sufferings and (d) wine. 10. The *passover supper* was a full meal, not simply a ceremonial eating as in our Lord's Supper. Yet it was a strictly religious sacramental meal, interspersed with prayer and various ceremonies, and was eaten according to a strict ritual, in the following order: (1) benediction; (2) cup of wine; (3) hands of company washed by master of the feast, who recites a prayer; (4) bitter herbs dipped in sauce and eaten; (5) lamb brought in with other portions of the meal; (6) benediction and second eating of bitter herbs; (7) second cup of wine with question and answer as to origin of the feast (Ex. 12:26); (8) first part of the Hallel (Pss. 113, 114) sung with the benediction; (9) leader washes his hands, makes a "sop" by wrapping a bit of the lamb with the unleavened bread in bitter herbs, dipping it in the sauce, eating it and making similar sops for the others present; (10) each eats what he likes, finishing with a piece of the lamb; (11) hands are washed, and a third cup of wine taken; (12) second part of the Hallel (Pss. 115-118) is sung, which concludes the supper; (13) fourth cup of wine.

404. 1. The *"contention"* probably occurred soon after the Twelve entered the room. It was doubtless about the order of places at the table, the middle place on each couch being considered the best, and to be as near to the Lord's right as possible might be an index of rank in the future kingdom. 2. When Jesus had rebuked their pride, and they had arranged themselves on the couches, the first cup (rit. 2) was taken. After this the master of the feast would arise for the handwashing (rit. 3); For this part of the ritual Jesus seems to have substituted the washing of the feet, which had been omitted on entering the room, because no one of the Twelve was willing to take the part of a servant (Jno. 13:2-4). After the "sop" (rit. 9) Judas went out to betray Christ. 3. The Last Supper, by Leonardo da Vinci, represents the consternation of the disciples on being told by Jesus that one of them should betray him. Their names beginning on the left are: Bartholomew, James the son of Alphæus, Andrew, Judas, Peter leaning behind Judas, John, James the brother of John, leaning behind Thomas, Thomas, Philip, Matthew, Thaddæus, and Simon the Cananæan. 4. *John reclined* on the Lord's bosom and Judas seems to have been next to Jesus on the other side, and Peter more remote (Jno. 13:26-29; Mark 14:20; Matt. 26:23). 5. *Of the institution* of this memorial we have *four* accounts in two groups, Matthew and Mark, Luke and Paul (1 Cor. 11:23-26). From these we learn that after the eating of the paschal lamb (ritual 10), but before the concluding ceremonies, Jesus "took bread," one of the unbroken loaves, and "the cup," the "third cup" (ritual 11). 6. Luke 22:21 says that Judas was present at the institution of the Lord's Supper, but

John 13:26 favors the view that he went out before. The latter is probable, because the supper was instituted towards the end of the passover (See No. 10 and 11 of the ritual), while Judas left immediately after the exposure when the sop was handed him (No. 9 of the ritual). This is also intrinsically probable, for Jesus would naturally desire that Judas, whose heart was now hopelessly alienated from him, should not by his presence break the sympathetic circle to which he was about to give his last tender words of farewell. 7. *The movements* of Judas, after leaving the paschal supper, were probably as follows: he went to the rulers and hurried the soldiers to the upper room; before they arrived, Jesus had departed; Judas knowing the usual place of the Lord's retirement led the soldiers to Gethsemane; John Mark, the son of the house, being aroused from his sleep by the noise of the soldiers quickly followed them without stopping to dress fully (Mk. 14:51, 52). 8. Where were the *warning to Peter* and the Farewell Addresses delivered? Matthew and Mark say, On the way from the upper room to Gethsemane; Luke and John: in the upper room. Solution: (a) The warning was first given in the upper room and repeated on the way; (b) Luke and John report the right order; (c) the first part to Jno. 14:31 was spoken in the upper room. Then they left the room and the rest was spoken on the way; (d) the part to Jno. 14:31 was spoken while reclining; then the Lord said, "Arise, let us go hence." While preparing to leave, Jesus spoke the words in Jno. 15:16, 17, at the close of which they left for Gethsemane. 9. *The last part of the "hallel"* (hymn) was sung either before all the discourses, or at Jno. 14:31, or at the close (Jno. 18:1). 10. *The chief object* of the farewell discourses was to prepare the disciples for the coming shock of disappointment and despair. 11. *The subjects in* the farewell addresses are not kept distinct; they cross and interlace like the strands in a rope. 12. *The "greater works"* refer to the results of Pentecost, the victory over Judaism and Paganism which for the moment were victorious over Jesus. (Lu. 22:53).

405. **Practical Lessons.** 1. The term sacrament was taken from a military custom. The *'sacramentum'* was the oath taken by the Roman soldier that he would never desert the standard, never turn his back on the foe, and never be disloyal to his commander. By our presence at the sacrament we pledge each other before God, that with His help we will be true men, more courageous, more pure, more victorious, than before" (Lu. 22:19). 2. The four historical theories as to the mode of Christ's presence in the Lord's Supper are based on the four principal interpretations of the words of Christ, "This is my body:" (a) The Roman

Catholic: this bread is changed into my body (transubstantiation),
(b) Luther: This bread is accompanied by my body (my body is
"in, with and under" the bread); (c) Zwingli: this bread signifies
my body (Memorial view); (d) Calvin: this bread is not only a
sign (Zwingli) but also a seal of my (spiritual) body. 3. The
significance of the Lord's Supper: (a) it is the Lord's table; he
prepares and invites to it; (b) Christ is really present, but in
a spiritual manner (Calvin); (c) it is only for real disciples (Heid.
Cat. 81, 82; West. Cat. 53; 1 Cor. 10:16); Judas was therefore
not present. In the ancient church the unbaptized were dismissed
when the celebration began. The minister would say, "congregatio
est missa," from which are derived the terms, "Mass" and the
German "Messe;" (d) Christ and Paul emphasize the memorial
feature of the supper. "This do in remembrance of me" (Lu. 22:
19), and, "For as often as ye eat this bread, and drink the cup, ye
proclaim the Lord's death till he come" (1 Cor. 11:26); (e) it is
a communion, a "union with" God and the brethren—a love feast.
(f) it emphasizes the manner of Christ's death. The wheat must
be bruised and broken and the grape crushed and bleeding, before
we can eat the bread or drink the wine. It is by the death of
Christ that we have life. (g) It shows the necessity of appropriating Christ. The bread and wine enter into and become part of our
flesh and blood, and so the support of our life. It is Christ *in us*
who is the hope of glory. (h) Historically it is connected with
and grew out of the passover, which prefigures and interprets it.
Thus it memorializes our deliverance from the bondage of sin by
the death of Christ, who is our passover (Rom. 8:2; 1 Cor. 5:7).
(i) It prophetically points to the future marriage supper of the
Lamb (Mt. 26:29; Mk. 14:25). (j) It is the clearest expression
of the importance claimed by Jesus for his own person (bread equal
to the body; wine equal to the blood; broken unto remission). 4.
"I am the way:" to (1) pardon; (2) peace; (3) power; (4) hope;
(5) heaven. The Japanese call Christianity "the Jesus-way." 5.
Jesus reveals the Father to us. He shows us his (1) holiness; (2)
love; (3) fatherhood. 6. To abide in Christ means (a) to hold
fast to his truth; (b) to have the spirit dwell in us. 7. Many that
are indifferent to the truth are like men of whom Plato says, that
they resemble people who live in a cave; they see the light only
as it filters down through their obstinate pride and tenacious pre-
judices. 8. Christianity is to be propagated by patient witnessing
for the truth, not by force. 9. The necessary qualifications for
successful witness-bearing are (a) Bible knowledge; (b) Christian
experience; (c) courage and (d) patience. 10. Method of witness-bearing (a) by words; (b) deeds; (c) the pen and (d) by

death (Martyrs). 11. The two functions of the spirit are (a) to impart new truth which however must harmonize with the old, (b) to interpret old truth.

406. **Reference Literature.** Farrar, Ch. 54, 55, 56; Andrews, p. 450; Rhees, p. 181-187; Stalker, p. 160; Gilbert's Life of Christ, p. 344; on the coenaculum, see Smith's "Jerusalem" II, 567; on "unity," see Hast. D. of C. II, 781; "Brodbrechen," Herzog II; Leonardo's famous "Last Supper" in Milan; on the ritual of the passover, see Maclear's N. T. Hist., p. 280; Maundy Thursday, see Barton's Week of Passion, p. 176; on the "upper room," p. 176; Holy Grail, p. 179; on passover, p. 176; on the hallel, Hast. D. of C. I, 699; on the Lord's Supper, Davis, D. B., p. 443.

407. **Questions for Discussion.** 1. Explain the ready consent of the "good man." 2. Why does Jesus not mention the precise place of eating the passover? 3. What point is emphasized in each of the names "Lord's Supper," "eucharist," "communion." 4. Point out the variations in the four accounts of the Lord's Supper. 5. How was the promise in Jno. 14: 12 realized? 6. What is the difference between union, unity and uniformity? 7. As applied to church life what is the difference between Christian union and Church union; between co-operation, federation and organic union? 8. Did our Lord in Jno. 17: 21 pray that they may be one organization, or, one in him (mystical union), or one in faith, hope and love? 9. Which interpretation can best stand the test of sound exegesis?

CHAPTER 44.

Agony and Arrest in Gethsemane.

Matt. 26: 36-56; Mk. 14: 32-52; Lu. 22: 39-53; Jno. 18: 1-11.   Harmony 136-137.

408. **Agony in Gethsemane.** (1) When they had sung the closing hymn they went, as his custom was, over the brook Cedron, to the Mount of Olives, to a garden called Gethsemane. (2) Here he said to his disciples, Sit ye here, while I go yonder and pray. He took with him Peter and the two sons of Zebedee (James and John). (3) He began to be sorrowful, and saith unto them, My soul is exceeding sorrowful, even unto death: abide ye here, and

watch with me. (4) He went forward a little, and fell on
his face, and prayed. My Father, if it be possible, let this
cup pass away from me: nevertheless, not as I will, but as
thou wilt. (5) When he cometh unto the disciples, and
findeth them sleeping, he saith unto Peter, Simon sleepest
thou? Could ye not watch with me one hour? Watch
and pray, that ye enter not into temptation: the spirit indeed
is willing, but the flesh is weak. (6) A second time he
went away, and prayed, My Father, if this cannot pass
away, except I drink it, thy will be done. And he came
again and found them sleeping, for their eyes were heavy.
(7) He went away, and prayed a third time, saying the
same words. (8) Then there appeared unto him an angel,
strengthening him. (9) And being in an agony he prayed
more earnestly; and his sweat became as it were great drops
of blood falling down upon the ground. (10) Then cometh
he to the disciples, and saith, Sleep on now, behold, the
hour it at hand, and the Son of man is betrayed into the
hands of sinners. (11) Arise, let us be going: behold, he
is at hand that betrayeth me.

409. **The Betrayal and Arrest.** (1) While he yet spoke
came Judas (who knew the place, for Jesus often resorted thither), with a great multitude, with swords, staves,
lanterns and torches, from the chief priests and elders. (2)
Judas gave them a sign, saying, Whomsoever I shall kiss,
that is he: take him. And straightway he came to Jesus,
and said, Hail, Rabbi; and kissed him. Jesus said, Friend,
do that for which thou art come. Judas betrayest thou the
Son of man with a kiss? (3) Then Jesus saith unto them,
Whom seek ye? They answered, Jesus of Nazareth. Jesus
saith, I am he. When he said this they fell to the ground.
Again he asked, Whom seek ye? And they said, Jesus of
Nazareth. Jesus answered, I told you that I am he; if
ye seek me, let these go their way: that the word might be
fulfilled which he spake, Of those whom thou hast given
me I lost not one. (4) Then they laid hands on Jesus and
took him. (5) But when his disciples saw what would fol-

low, they said, Lord, shall we smite with the sword? And
Peter drew his sword and cut off the right ear of the high
priest's servant, whose name was Malchus. But Jesus said
unto Peter, Put up the sword into the sheath: the cup which
the Father hath given me, shall I not drink it? All they
that take the sword shall perish with the sword. Or thinkest thou that I cannot beseech my Father and he shall even
now send me more than twelve legions of angels? How
then should the scriptures be fulfilled, that thus it must be?
(6) In that hour said Jesus to the multitudes, Are ye come
out as against a robber with swords and staves to seize me?
I sat daily in the temple teaching, and ye took me not. But
this is your hour and the power of darkness. (7) Then all
the disciples left him and fled. (8) Only a young man followed with him, having a linen cloth cast about him. They
laid hold on him; but he left the linen cloth, and fled naked.

410. **Explanatory Notes.** 1. Name and compare *sources;* locate places; trace Christ's movements; memorize Matt. 26:41. 2.
About midnight of Thursday (according to Jewish reckoning, from
sunset to sunset, it was already Friday Nisan 15) the Lord reached
Gethsemane ("valley of oil" or "oil press"). 3. *Its precise location*
is not known. The traditional site is a grove on the western slope
of the Mt. of Olives, just above the valley of Kidron (Jno. 18: 1-
3), about 50 paces square, containing very ancient olive trees,
eight of which are said to be 2,000 years old. 4. *The brook Kidron* ran through the valley between Jerusalem and the Mt. of
Olives. At present its bed contains no water except during the
rainy season or immediately after a heavy rain. 5. *Reasons why
Jesus withdrew* to Gethsemane: (a) He did not wish to involve
the owner of "the upper room" in trouble. (b) He wished to
have a secluded spot for prayer. 6. *Jesus desired* his disciples to
watch, partly, perhaps, because He was afraid the enemy might
surprise them at any moment, but especially because He wanted
human sympathy in the great struggle through which He was passing. 7. *The "cup" signifies* that portion of good or evil which is
appointed to man by God. 8. *"This cup"* does not mean his crucifixion and death, but the agony, anguish and soul struggle in Gethsemane. This is in accordance with Mark 14:35, where the cup is
defined as "the hour," and with Heb. 5:7, which says that "he was
heard." These passages show plainly that Jesus did not shrink

from the death on the cross but from anguish which might have resulted in death in the garden. Such a death would have made him a martyr but not an atoning Saviour. There was reason for such a fear, for Luke, with a physician's knowledge, speaks of the agony and the bloody sweat (22:44), which in cases of extreme anguish have been the immediate precursor of death. 9. *In Gethsemane,* Christ's sufferings were pre-eminently mental and spiritual, and at Calvary chiefly physical. 10. The arresting force was large, consisting of the temple police (Luke 22:54), and a Roman cohort (margin of Jno. 18:3), a body of soldiers which generally numbered 600 men. The authorities evidently feared resistance if not a popular uprising, especially when considering the enthusiasm for Jesus on Palm Sunday. 11. Although it was *full moon* the soldiers carried torches and lanterns in case Jesus should retreat into caverns, grottos or houses. 12. *The crowd,* many of whom knew Jesus as a wonder-worker, recoiled at his approach, being over-awed by the power of his personality and fearing that he might use his miraculous power against them. 13. *The Malchus* incident shows that Jesus, although he expects to be defended by his friends, will not have it done by carnal weapons. 14. *"Twelve legions"* is a figurative expression, in round numbers—72,000. 15. *The young man* in Mark 14:51 is generally supposed to have been the author of the gospel, which alone reports the incident, John Mark himself. Being aroused from sleep by Judas and the soldiers when they came to his father's house, he threw a loose garment around himself and followed them. When the disciples fled, he seems to have endeavored to follow Jesus and protect the Lord, but was driven away.

411. **Practical Lessons.** 1. Some of the ingredients of Christ's cup were (a) an inconceivable sense of the horribleness of sin by the sinless one. (b) A shrinking of holy love from being rejected. (c) The natural aversion to death. 2. The prime object of true prayer is to bring the human will into submission to the Divine will. Petition is a subordinate feature. 3. Every life has its Gethsemane, where the question of supremacy between God's will and self-will must be fought out. 4. Unbelief is always tempted to resort to illegitimate means for promoting the kingdom of God (Peter with the sword). 5. The last deed of Christ's hands before they were bound was to heal. He is indeed the Saviour, "der Heiland" ("the healer").

412. **Reference Literature.** Farrar, Ch. 57; Andrews, p. 497; Stalker's L. of C., ¶161 and ¶162; on Gethsemane, see D. B., especially Encycl. Bibl. II, 1712; and Davis, D. B., 244; Stalker's Trial and Death of Jesus, Ch. 1; Hofman's paintings, Gethsemane; Kiss of Judas: Stalker, Imago Christi (last chapter).

413. Questions for Discussion. 1. What was the original source of information for the account of the agony in Gethsemane? 2. Does a comparison of the second with the first prayer show that the feeling of submission increases? 3. Wherein consisted the bitterness of Christ's agony in Gethsemane and at the cross (See Heb. 12:2; 13:13; Gal. 3:13; 1 Cor. 1:23). 4. Why did Christ shrink from suffering when martyrs and even bad men faced death calmly? 5. Does the presence of a Roman cohort indicate that Pilate had any knowledge of the arrest? 6. How does the Malchus incident throw light on Luke 22:35-38? 7. Does Christ want to be defended, and how?

CHAPTER 45.

The Three Trials Before the Jewish Courts.

Matt. 26:57; 27:10; Mk. 14:53-72; Lu. 22:54-71; Jno 18:12-27.   Harmony 138.

414. Led to the Highpriest Annas. (1) The band and the chief captain and the officers of the Jews, bound Jesus and led him to Annas first; for he was father-in-law to Caiaphas, who was high priest that year.

415. Peter's First Denial. (1) Peter and John followed Jesus afar off unto the court of the high priest. (2) John was known unto the high priest, and entered in with Jesus into the courtyard, but Peter was standing at the door without. (3) So John went out and spake unto her that kept the door and brought in Peter. (4) When they passed her the maid said to Peter, Art thou also one of this man's disciples? He said, I am not. And the cock crew the first time. (5) Now the servants and the officers having made a fire of coal were warming themselves: and Peter also warmed himself.

416. Informal Trial by Annas. (1) The high priest asked Jesus of his disciples, and of his teaching. (2) Jesus answered him, I have spoken openly to the world; I ever taught in synagogues and in the temple, where all the Jews come together; and in secret spake I nothing. Why askest thou me? ask them that have heard me, what I spake unto them. (3) When he had said this one of the officers struck Jesus with his hand, saying, Answerest thou the high priest so? (4) Jesus answered, If I have spoken evil, bear witness of the evil: but if well, why smitest thou me? (5) Then Annas sent him bound unto Caiaphas the high priest.

417. **Night Trial Before the Sanhedrin.** (1) Meanwhile, at the house of Caiaphas, the council gathered together. (2) They sought false witness against Jesus, that they might put him to death, and they found it not. Though many false witnesses came, their testimony agreed not together. (3) But finally came two, and said, This man said, I am able to destroy the temple of God, and to build it in three days. But not even so did their witness agree together. (4) Then in his desperation the high priest stood up and said, Answerest thou nothing? what is it which these witness against thee? But Jesus held his peace. (5) Then the high priest said, I adjure thee by the living God, that thou tell us whether thou art the Christ, the Son of God. Jesus saith, Thou hast said, for I am; nevertheless I say unto you, Henceforth ye shall see the Son of man sitting at the right hand of Power, and coming on the clouds of heaven. (6) Then the high priest rent his garments, saying, He hath spoken blasphemy: what further need have we of witnesses? behold, now ye have heard the blasphemy: what think ye? They answered and said, He is worthy of death. (7) Then did they spit in his face and buffet him: and some blindfolded and smote him with the palms of their hands, saying, Prophesy unto us, thou Christ: who is he that struck thee?

418. **Peter's Second and Third Denials.** (1) During this trial of Jesus Peter went into the porch, and another maid (Lu. 22:58; "man") saw him and saith unto them that were there, This man also was with Jesus of Nazareth. Again he denied with an oath, I know not the man. (2) After a little while (about one hour) they that stood by

came and said to Peter, Of a truth thou also art one of them, a Galilean; for thy speech maketh thee known. (3) One of the servants of the high priest, being a kinsman of him whose ear Peter cut off, saith, Did I not see thee in the garden with him? (4) Then began he to curse and swear, I know not the man. And straightway the cock crew the second time. (5) At the same moment the Lord turned and looked upon Peter. And Peter remembered the word which Jesus had said, Before the cock crow twice, thou shalt deny me thrice. And he went out, and wept bitterly.

419. **Morning Trial by the Sanhedrin.** (1) As soon as it was day the assembly of the elders was gathered together. (2) They led him into their council and said, If thou art the Christ, tell us. (3) But he said, If I tell you, ye will not believe: and if I ask you, ye will not answer. But from henceforth shall the Son of man be seated at the right hand of the power of God. (4) Then they all said, Art thou then the Son of God? And he said unto them, Ye say that I am. They said, What further need have we of witness? for we ourselves have heard from his own mouth.

420. **Remorse and Suicide of Judas.** (1) Judas, when he saw that he was condemned, repented and brought back the thirty pieces of silver to the chief priests and elders, saying, I have sinned in that I have betrayed innocent blood. But they said, What is that to us? see thou to it. (2) And he cast down the pieces of silver into the sanctuary, and departed; and hanged himself. And he fell down headlong and burst asunder and all his bowels gushed out. (3) The chief priests took the pieces of silver, and said, It is not lawful to put them into the treasury, since it is the price of blood. And they bought with them the potter's field, to bury strangers in. Wherefore that field was called, The field of blood.

421. **Explanatory Notes.** 1. Name and compare *sources*, especially the reports of the denial of Peter; locate places; trace the

Lord's movements; memorize Matt. 26:63. 2. *Note that John* has no report of the trials before the Sanhedrin, and the synoptists none on the examination by Annas. But the Syriac version "Peshito," which is older than our oldest manuscripts, places the statement of Jno. 18:24 immediately after that of 18:14. Should this order be accepted we have no record of what transpired before Annas. Jno. 18:19-23 then describes a private examination before Caiphas, and the term "high priest" is used in its exact rather than a loose sense. This would also meet the difficulty as to the place of Peter's denials. 3. *Annas* was appointed high priest 7 A. D., by Quirinius, the imperial governor of Syria. He was deposed by Gratus, procurator of Judea, 14 A. D. He is mentioned in Luke 3:2; Jno. 18:13, 24; Acts 4:6, where he is reported assisting in presiding over the Sanhedrin which sat in judgment upon Peter and John. Some suppose that Caiphas was the actual high-priest and Annas president of the Sanhedrin; others hold that Annas held the office of substitute of the high-priest. He lived to an old age, having had five sons in the high-priestly office. He was father-in-law to Caiphas. 4. *The two questions* of Annas indicated that he suspected Jesus as being the head of some secret organization (like the Essenes), with dangerous doctrines. In his reply to Annas Jesus demanded his legal rights as a prisoner. No charge had been preferred against him; the private examination before Annas was contrary to express provisions of the Rabbinical criminal code; hence his refusal to bear testimony against himself was thoroughly legal. He also demanded that his prosecutors introduce witnesses. 5. *Caiaphas,* son-in-law of Annas (Lu. 3:2; Jno. 18:13) and high priest from A. D. 18-36, was a Sadducee (Acts 5:17), a hard and crafty man. The fact that he remained so long in office shows that the Romans found in him a subservient tool. Jno. 18:14 refers to his prejudice against Jesus which made him unfit as a judge. 6. *The regular place of meeting* for the Sanhedrin was in the temple, but that was not available for the trial of Jesus, at least not for the night trial, since the gates of the temple were closed at night. 7. *The House of Caiaphas* (Matt. 26:57), the high priest's palace probably stood on the southern slope of the western hill, a short distance outside of the present city wall, but in what was then the finest part of the city. It was doubtless a splendid building surrounding a large central court. One side of the quadrangle would naturally be retained by Annas. The preliminary hearing took place in one of the apartments belonging to Annas. When Jesus was brought before Caiaphas and the informal assembly of the Sanhedrin, He merely crossed the courtyard where Peter stood warming himself by the fire. 8. On the membership and powers of the Sanhedrin, see the "Introduction." 8. The witnesses are called false because they perverted the Lord's warning in Jno. 2:19 "Destroy this temple," into a threat, "I will destroy." 9. Jesus, aware of his legal rights, several times refused to testify against himself, but when, in his desperation, the High Priest challenged him to give true information as to his real nature, Jesus affirmed under a solemn oath, that he was the Son of God. 10. The Lord's answer to Caiaphas reveals three cardinal traits of his character (a) courage in confessing himself the son of God, when death was the inevitable consequence; (b) confidence in the success of his cause upon earth; (c) the admission that only the future could unfold the real meaning of his person.

422. 1. *The following* are *some* of the *illegal features* of Christ's trial: Trying a criminal in the night; passing judgment of death before one night had elapsed after the trial; trying a criminal case on the day before the Sabbath or a feast; undue haste; compelling the prisoner to testify against himself; the judicial use of the prisoner's confession; the seeking (probably buying) witnesses; the neglect to warn the witnesses solemnly before giving evidence; the failure to release Jesus when the two witnesses did not agree, as concurrent testimony of two witnesses was necessary to framing an indictment. 2. *The trial* was illegal provided that we have a full report of proceedings and that the Talmudic law was enforced in Palestine during the lifetime of Jesus. But not a few hold that the Talmud represents a later phase of Jewish jurisprudence, and that the letter, though not the spirit, of the then existing law was observed. 3. *About ten years ago* there was a movement on foot among Jewish rabbis in Russia to re-open the case of Jesus and grant him a new trial conducted by a modern Sanhedrin selected from the rabbis; first, on the ground of the many illegalities at his first trial, and secondly, because new evidence had come to light; the course of history having shown that Jesus was indeed the Messiah. 4. *The morning trial* seems to have been held simply to confirm the decision of the night trial and to hold a consultation how best to present the matter to Pilate. Luke who has the fullest report indicates that they merely reviewed the proceedings of the night trial. 5. *Either Joseph* of Arimathea and Nicodemus, two members of the Sanhedrin, were not present at the two sessions, or in the great uproar and confusion their protests were not heeded; hence the decision was announced as being unanimous. 6. *The denial* of Peter recorded in Matt. 26:69, 70 is apparently the same as that recorded in Jno. 18:15-18, and occurred while Jesus was before Annas. The other two denials (Mt. 26:71-75) probably took place after Jesus had been taken across the courtyard to the

palace of Caiaphas. 7. *John places* Peter's denial in the palace of Annas, the Synoptists in the house of Caiaphas. This is natural since John does not report the trial before Caiaphas, and the Synoptists are silent on the examination before Annas. To harmonize the records it has been supposed that the two priests occupied the same palace. 8. *At the third denial,* the Lord "turned." Two explanations: (a) Jesus was tried in one of the halls which surrounded the inner court of an Oriental house. As these were open to view Jesus could hear Peter curse and swear and deny; when he became very vehement, Jesus "turned" towards him; (b) After his condemnation the Lord was led from the hall of judgment to the apartments of the servants, there to wait until the morning trial. Just when Jesus passed him Peter cursed and the Lord "turned" towards him. 9. *The double cock* crowing is true to nature and furnishes a valuable note of time, for the cock always crows soon after midnight and again at the break of day. 10. *Although in Matt.* 27:9 all the earliest manuscripts read "Jeremiah" it should read "Zechariah" (11:12-13). A similar incident is recorded in Jer. 32:8-10, and possibly the two may have become confused in the writer's mind. Matt. 27:7 says, the priests bought the field and Peter in Acts 1:18 says that Judas did, meaning probably that his money bought it. The "field of blood" is still shown in the valley of Hinnom. See D. B.

423. **Practical Lessons.** 1. Jesus betrays no man. Annas's questions were designed to ascertain how many adherents Jesus had in the council. 2. Christ's answer to Annas reminds one of Socrates, who said to his judges, "If any one says he ever learnt from me in private what all other people did not hear, be sure he is not speaking the truth." (Apologia xxi). 3. There is majesty in silence. 4. It is absurd to say that Jesus was a good man but not the Son of God. If he was not the Son of God he swore falsely and this certainly does not indicate a good character. 5. If we regard Jesus simply as a Jewish citizen, and not the Son of God, his conviction was strictly according to law, though the trial may not have been legal in all its forms. The bearing of this inference on radical theology is plain. 6. Half-way loyalty to Christ invites, while complete loyalty delivers from, many dangers. John took no pains to conceal his discipleship and no one troubled him. How different with Peter. 7. Genuine repentance does not lead to suicide, remorse often does. 8. Before the sin, it is the gain we see; after the sin, the guilt. 9. Many traitors are aghast at the consequences of their treason, never imagining any fatal issue.

424. **Reference Literature.** Farrar, Ch. 58 and 59; Andrews, p. 505; Stalker, [164-173; Innes, The Trial of Jesus. On the legal

procedure, see Hast. D. of C. II, 749; Gess, Jesus vor Gericht, in Christoterpe of 1881; on the House of Caiaphas, see The Week of Passion, p. 182; a description of Oriental houses, see Maclain, N. T. Hist., p. 290; examine some of the famous paintings on the subject, as Harrach's Peter's Denial, also poetry as "Jesus and shall it ever be;" Stalker, Trial and Death of Jesus, ch. 2 and 3; Chandler, Trial of Jesus from a Lawyer's Standpoint; Illegality of the Trial in The Week of Passion, p. 187; on Annas, Davis, D. B., p. 34; on Caiaphas, p. 102.

425. **Questions for Discussion.** 1. Why did Annas question Jesus as to his disciples? 2. What did Jesus mean in Matt. 26:64? 3. Why was Peter pardoned and Judas was not? 4. Did Judas show his estimate of Jesus by the price he demanded for his betrayal? 5. Is there a price for which you will part from him? 6. How may Christ to-day be denied and betrayed?

CHAPTER 46.

The Trials before Pilate and Herod.

Matt. 27:11-31; Mk. 15:1-20; Lu. 23:1-25; Jno. 18:28-19:16.   Harmony 139.

426. **The Rulers demanded Christ's death.** (1) They led Jesus from Caiaphas into the Prætorium: and it was early; (2) They themselves entered not into the Prætorium, that they might not be defiled, but might eat the passover. (3) Pilate therefore went out and saith, What accusation bring ye against this man? They answered in effect, you need not reopen the case; if this man were not an evil-doer we should not have delivered him up unto thee. (4) Pilate replies in scorn, Then take him yourselves, and judge him according to your law. The Jews said, It is not lawful for us to put any man to death.

427. **Three Charges Preferred.** (1) When the rulers saw that Pilate insisted on reviewing the case, they said not a word about the charge on which they had condemned Jesus, but preferred against him the charge of treason under three specifications, saying, We found this man per-

verting our nation, and forbidding to give tribute to Cæsar, and saying that he himself is Christ a king.

428. **Examination by Pilate and First Acquittal.** (1) The last charge very naturally arrested Pilate's attention. He took Jesus into the Prætorium and examined him as follows: Pilate: Art thou the King of the Jews? Jesus: Sayest thou this of thyself, or did others tell it thee concerning me? Pilate: Am I a Jew? Thine own nation and the chief priests delivered thee unto me: what hast thou done? (2) Jesus: My kingdom is not of this world: if my kingdom were of this world, then would my servants fight, that I should not be delivered to the Jews. Pilate: Art thou a king then? Jesus: I am a king. To this end have I been born, that I should bear witness unto the truth. Every one that is of the truth heareth my voice. Pilate: What is truth? (3) And when he had said this, he went out unto the Jews, and saith, I find no crime in him.

429. **Renewed Accusations and Jesus' Silence.** (1) But the chief priests accused Jesus of many things, to which he answered nothing. (2) Then saith Pilate, Hearest thou not how many things they witness against thee? And he gave him no answer, not even to one word: insomuch that the governor marvelled greatly.

430. **Christ before Herod Antipas.** (1) In their desperation the rulers now press the first of the three charges, saying, He stirreth up the people, teaching throughout all Judæa, beginning from Galilee. (2) Pilate asked whether the man were a Galilæan. When he knew that he was of Herod's jurisdiction, he sent him unto him who also was at Jerusalem to observe the passover. (3) When Herod saw Jesus, he was exceeding glad: for he was of a long time desirous to see him, because he had heard concerning him; and he hoped to see some miracle done by him. (4) He questioned him in many words; but he answered him nothing. (5) The chief priests and the scribes vehemently accused him. (6) But Herod with his soldiers mocked him, and arraying him in gorgeous apparel sent him back to

Pilate.   (7) Herod and Pilate became friends with each other that very day: for before they were at enmity.

431.   **Second Acquittal and Proposed Compromise.**
(1) Now Pilate called together the chief priests, the rulers and the people and said, Ye brought unto me this man, as one that perverteth the people: and I have examined him before you and found no fault in him, nor yet Herod.   (2) I will therefore chastise him (to please you) and then release him (to satisfy my sense of justice).

432.   **Jesus and Barabbas.**   (1) While Pilate was still wrangling with the rulers a new crowd of people arrived who knew nothing of what had been going on all morning.   They came for a different purpose.   (2) At the passover, the Roman governor was wont to release unto the multitude one prisoner, whom they would, and this crowd came to ask Pilate to do as he was wont to do.   (3) This request Pilate now tries to use for extricating himself out of an unpleasant situation.   At that time he had a notable prisoner called Barabbas, who was one of those who had made an insurrection, and in it had committed murder. Pilate said, Whom will ye that I release unto you? Barabbas or Jesus who is called Christ?   For he knew that for envy they had delivered him up.   (4) While he was sitting on the judgment seat, waiting for Barabbas to appear, his wife sent unto him, saying, Have thou nothing to do with that righteous man; for I have suffered many things this day in a dream because of him.   (5) Meanwhile the rulers persuaded the multitudes that they should ask for Barabbas, and destroy Jesus.   But the governor, desiring to release Jesus, said, which of the two will ye that I release unto you? Shall I release the King of the Jews?   But they cried out altogether, saying, Away with this man, and release Barabbas.   Pilate saith unto them, What then shall I do unto Jesus who is called Christ?   They all say, Let him be crucified.   And he said, What evil hath he done?   But they cried out exceedingly, Let him be crucified.   (7) So when Pilate saw that he prevailed nothing, but rather that a tu-

mult was arising, he took water, and washed his hands before the multitude, saying, I am innocent of the blood of
this righteous man; see ye to it.   And all the people said,
His blood be on us, and on our children.   (8) Then released he unto them Barabbas; but Jesus he delivered up to
their will.

433. **Scourging and Mocking.** (1) Then the soldiers
of the governor took Jesus into the court yard of the Prætorium where they stripped and scourged him, a punishment which usually preceded crucifixion.   (2) Then they
put on him a scarlet robe, plaited a crown of thorns and
put upon his head, and a reed in his right hand, kneeled
down before him, and mocked him, saying, Hail, King of
the Jews!   And they spat upon him, and took the reed and
smote him on the head.

434. **Pilate's Final Attempt to Release Jesus.** (1)
After the scourging and abuse Pilate went out again and
saith, I bring him out to you that ye may know that I find
no crime in him.   (2) Jesus came out wearing the crown
of thorns and the purple garment.   And Pilate saith unto
them, Behold, the man!   (3) When the chief priests and
the officers saw him, they cried out, Crucify him, crucify
him!   Pilate saith, Take him yourselves, and crucify him:
for I find no crime in him.   (4) The Jews answered, We
have a law, and by that law he ought to die, because he
made himself the Son of God.   When Pilate heard this he
was the more afraid: and entered into the Prætorium, and
saith unto Jesus, Whence art thou?   But Jesus gave him no
answer.   (5) Pilate saith, Speakest thou not unto me?
knowest thou not that I have power to release thee, and to
crucify thee?   Jesus answered, Thou wouldest have no
power against me, except it were given thee from above:
therefore he that delivered me unto thee hath greater sin.
Upon this Pilate sought to release him: (6) The Jews cried
out, If thou release this man, thou art not Cæsar's friend.
every one that maketh himself a king speaketh against
Cæsar.   (7) When Pilate heard these words, he brought

Jesus out, and sat down on the judgment-seat at a place
called the Pavement (Hebrew, Gabbatha). It was the
Preparation of the passover about the sixth hour. And he
saith unto the Jews, Behold, your King! They cried out,
Away with him, away with him, crucify him! Pilate saith
unto them, Shall I crucify your King? The chief priests
answered, We have no king but Cæsar. Then he delivered
him unto them to be crucified. (8) They took off from
him the robe, and put on him his garments, and led him
away to crucify him.

435. **Explanatory Notes.** 1. Name and compare *sources;* give
an accurate outline of the trial; locate places and trace the Lord's
movements on the map; memorize Jno. 18:37. 2. *The Sanhedrin*
could condemn but it could not execute the criminal. Singularly
enough the power to execute was taken from the Sanhedrin just a
few years before the death of Christ. Thus it happened that both
Jews and Gentiles became guilty of the Lord's death. The governor might simply confirm the decision of the Jewish judges,
or he might give the prisoner a new trial. 3. *Pilate was the sixth*
Roman procurator of Judea after the banishment of Archelaus and
reigned from 26-36 A. D., usually residing at Caesarea. He became
odious both to Jews and Samaritans for his cruelty and, being
accused by the latter, was banished by the emperor Caligula to
Vienne in Gaul and while there he committed suicide. According
to a legend he sought refuge in the recesses of a mountain near
Lucerne which mountain still bears his name, "Pilatus." He was
born in Seville, Spain, one of the four cities which enjoyed the
right of Roman citizenship. He was twice married. Having abandoned his first wife, he subsequently married Claudia, the youngest
daughter of Julia, the prostitute daughter of emperor Augustus.
The reputed father of Claudia was one Tiberius a Roman knight.
She was married to Pilate at the age of sixteen years. Notwith-
standing the unfavorable record of her ancestors she seems to
have been a woman of tender and noble impulse. 4. *Praetorium*
was the name for the headquarters of a Roman general or governor,
wherever he happened to be. The capital of the Roman procurator
of Judea was Cæsarea. During the feasts he usually came up to
Jerusalem to keep order and quickly suppress any insurrection.
Here he resided either in the tower of Antonia, adjoining the northern part of the temple or in the splendid palace of Herod the
Great. 5. *Pilate scornfully refused* the audacious demand of the

rulers to execute Jesus without even knowing the charges against him. 6. *They accused him* of treason, knowing that the charge of blasphemy would not stand in a Roman court. At the very last, when even this charge seemed to fail to secure a conviction they brought out the original accusation before the Sanhedrin. 7. *Pilate being only* a procurator had neither quaestor ("asker"), nor lictor ("scourger"). Hence he himself had to conduct the examination and the soldiers scourged Jesus. These little details testify to the accuracy of the Gospels. 8. *In John* 18: 34 Jesus means to say, "Do you ask this question of your own initiative, or is this the charge that the Jews preferred against me?" Jesus knew that the charge before the Sanhedrin was blasphemy. 9. *What is truth:* An expression (a) of contempt by a practical politician for speculations on questions of morality; (b) of scepticism which denied the objective reality of truth (Academics); (c) or, of despondency. 10. *When Pilate* heard the word "Galilee" he determined on a double stroke of diplomacy: (a) to rid himself of a troublesome responsibility; (b) to conciliate Herod, with whom he was on unfriendly terms, due perhaps to the slaughter of the Galileans (Lu. 13:1). 11. *On Herod Antipas,* see chapter on "The Political World." He lived either in his father's palace or in the palace of the Maccabees (Jos. Ant. 20, 8, 4). 12. *Herod probably* thought that Jesus was a juggler or magician, and that He would perform some tricks to amuse him. But his foolish questions received no answers. 13. *Herod for some reason* shrank from settling the case which Pilate had committed to him. Perhaps the memory of John the Baptist troubled his conscience. His return of the prisoner to Pilate seems to have been regarded by Pilate as a flattering recognition of his superior wisdom, and so served to bring the two rulers into a friendly relation to each other. 14. *The custom of* releasing a prisoner on the passover was probably of Jewish origin, to remind the people of their father's release from Egypt, and was continued by the Romans from motives of policy. 15. Barabbas is a patronymic, "bar"—son; "abba"—father. A remarkable coincidence. Some MSS. give the name as "Jesus Barabbas"—Jesus, Son of the Father. 16. *Pilate's wife* had her dream either in the night before, and in that case we must assume that she knew something of the conspiracy going on; or during a brief rest while Jesus was led to Herod. 17. *The instrument* for scourging was a whip with leather lashes loaded with lead and iron; nails and pieces of bones being stuck into the scourges. It cut the flesh to the bone and sometimes itself caused death. 18. *The name "Son of God"* (Jno. 19: 7-8) made Pilate afraid of the wrath of some unknown deity. Hence the question and his renewed endeavor to free Jesus. 19.

Note in John 19:12 how skillfully the priests compel Pilate to balance the life of Jesus against his own interests. He could never have justified himself before the emperor Tiberius for having released a man "speaking against Cæsar" and whom the head of the Jewish nation denounced as a traitor and rebel. Moreover, Pilate had already given offence to the Jews. His administration was marked by severity and he was regarded by the Jews as a bad governor and a bad man. He therefore chose to protect his own interests.

436. 1. *The judgment seat* ("bema") was a portable tribunal which symbolized the majesty of the law. So necessary was this considered to the form of justice that Julius Cæsar carried about with him on his expeditions pieces of marble which could readily be fitted into a "bema." In Jerusalem it stood on a "pavement," which was a mosaic floor (Suet. Cæsar, 461). 2. Recently a portion of this pavement has been uncovered under the convent of the Sisters of Zion, just north of the temple area near the "Ecce Homo" arch. At any rate this pavement was evidently used at some time by Roman soldiers, since it has scratched upon it gambling devices, such as were numerous on the Roman pavements in Italy. 3. *The Scala Santa* in Rome is believed by many to be the stairway which led up to the "pavement." These 28 steps were consequently touched by our Lord, and therefore sacred. An indulgence for 9 years is granted to all who ascend the 28 steps on their knees. 4. *Outside of the N. T.* we have a brief notice of Christ's death from the Roman historian, Tacitus, who in speaking of the Christians says, "The author of this name was Christ, who was capitally punished in the reign of Tiberius by Pontius Pilate." 5. *The tradition* that Pilate sent a report of Christ's trial to the emperor Tiberius (14-37), is intrinsically probable. The early Fathers mention such an account as circulating in their day. 6. In 1280 a *plate of brass* was discovered in Aquilla, Italy, which contains the "judgment against Jesus," engraved in Hebrew letters. It is one of twelve plates which were sent by the Sanhedrin to the twelve tribes. The writing is as follows: In the seventeenth year of the reign of the Emperor Tiberius, and on the 24th day of the month, in the most holy city of Jerusalem, during the pontificate of Annas and Caiaphas, Pontius Pilate, intendent of the province of Lower Galilee, sitting to judgment in the presidential seat of the praetors, sentences Jesus of Nazareth to death on a cross between robbers, because the numerous and notorious testimonies prove: 1. Jesus is a misleader. 2. He has excited the people to sedition. 3. He is an enemy to the laws. 4. He calls himself the Son of God. 5. He calls himself, falsely, the King of Israel. 6. He went to

the temple followed by a multitude carrying palms in their hands. Pilate orders the centurion, Quirrillis Cornelius, to bring him to the place of execution. Forbids all persons, rich or poor, to prevent the execution of Jesus. The witnesses who have signed the execution of Jesus are: 1. Daniel Robani, Pharisee. 2. John Zorobable. 3. Raphael Roban, 4. Capet. Jesus to be taken out of Jerusalem through the gate of Tournes. 7. *A careful study* of the reports of the four gospels leave it extremely doubtful whether Jesus really had a trial in the strict sense of the term or whether he was not rather "lynched;" Pilate, indeed, made an attempt to try Him, but later he failed to recognize any rights on the part of Jesus, and for personal considerations he finally ratified the sentence pronounced by the Jewish Sanhedrin.

437. **Practical Lessons.** 1. The representatives of church and state, of the Jews and the Romans united in compassing the death of Jesus. 2. Foolish or inquisitive questions receive no answer. 3. Wives should be the guardian angels of their husbands. 4. It is a remarkable fact that we read of no woman contributing anything to the sufferings of the Lord. The "maid" in Peter's denial simply repeated what she had heard the men say. 5. What will you do with Jesus? 6. Pilate shows that moral weakness makes a man capable of any wickedness.

438. **Reference Literature.** Farrar, Ch. 60; Andrews, p. 528; Stalker, ¶174-189. See D. B. on Pilate and Herod; on Pilate's considerate treatment of Jesus, see Hanna, p. 700; Hobs, The Court of Pilate (a story); on the Praetorium, see The Week of Passion, Edersheim II, 533-618; Chandler, Trial of Jesus from a Lawyer's Standpoint, 2 vol.; Stalker, Trial and Death of Jesus, Ch. 4-8. Rodemeyer, Frauen der Bibel. On the crown of thorns and Barabbas, see Barton's Week of Passion, pp. 185, 186. On the charges of the Samaritans against Pilate, see Maclair's N. T. Hist., 308; Davis, D. B. 38, on Tower of Antonia; On Cæsar, Davis, p. 100; Pilate, p. 583; scourge, p. 653.

439. **Questions for Discussion.** 1. Does not Jno. 18:28 contain an illustration of the parable of the mote and beam? 2. Why were the rulers unwilling to prefer charges against Jesus before Pilate? 3. How do the charges before the Sanhedrin and before Pilate differ? 4. Why did the last charge of Christ's kingship attract Pilate's attention first? 5. Show how and where the cry, "his blood come over us and our children," was fulfilled? 6. What does Paul call Christ's declarations before Pilate? (1 Tim. 6:13).

CHAPTER 47.

Crucifixion and Burial.

Matt. 27:32-66; Mk. 15:21-47; Lu. 23:26-56; Jno. 19: 16-42. Harmony 140-141.

440. **The March to Calvary.** (1) When they led Jesus away, he first bore his cross *himself*. But probably he soon broke from exhaustion. (2) For they compelled *Simon of Cyrene,* coming from the country, the father of Alexander and Rufus, to bear his cross. (3) There followed him a great multitude of the *people,* and of *women* who bewailed him. But Jesus said, Daughters of Jerusalem, weep not for me, but weep for yourselves, and your children. For if they do these things in the green tree, what shall be done in the dry? (4) *Two malefactors* were also led with him to be put to death. (5) They brought him to a place which is called *The Skull* (in Hebrew Golgotha).

441. **The Crucifixion.** (1) Here they *offered him wine* mingled with gall or myrrh. But when he tasted it, he would not drink. (2) Then they *crucified* him, and the *malefactors,* one on the right hand and the other on the left. (3) It was the *third hour* (9 a. m.). (4) Pilate wrote a superscription of his accusation which they set over his head, namely, JESUS OF NAZARETH, THE KING OF THE JEWS. This title read many of the Jews, for the place was nigh to the city; and it was written in Hebrew, in Latin, and in Greek. The chief priests said to Pilate, Write not, The King of the Jews; but, that he said, I am King of the Jews. Pilate answered, What I have written I have written. (5) The soldiers took his garments and made four parts, to every soldier a part; but as the coat was without seam, woven from the top throughout, they said, Let us not rend it, but cast lots for it, whose it shall be. (6) Then they sat down and watched him.

442. **Attitude of the people.** Four classes are men-

tioned. (1) The people stood beholding. (2) They that passed by railed on him, wagging their heads, saying, Thou that destroyest the temple, and buildest it in three days, save thyself: if thou art the Son of God, come down from the cross. (3) The rulers and the chief priests mocking him, with the scribes and elders said, He saved others; himself he cannot save. He is the King of Israel; let him now come down from the cross, and we will believe on him. He trusteth on God; let him deliver him now, if he desireth him: for he said, I am the Son of God. (4) The soldiers also mocked him.

443. **The Seven Last Words.** (1) While, or soon after, Jesus was nailed to the cross, he prayed: *Father, forgive them; for they know not what they do.* (2) At first both robbers cast upon him the same reproach as the others. One of them said, Art thou not the Christ? Save thyself and us. But later the other rebuking him said, Dost thou not fear God, seeing thou art in the same condemnation? And we indeed justly; for we receive the due reward of our deeds: but this man hath done nothing amiss. And he said, Jesus, remember me when thou comest in thy kingdom. And he said unto him, *Verily I say unto thee, To-day shalt thou be with me in Paradise.* (3) There were standing by the cross of Jesus 4 women: his mother; his mother's sister (Salome, Matt. 27:56); Mary the wife of Clopas, and Mary Magdalene. When Jesus saw his mother and the disciple standing by whom he loved (John), he saith unto his mother, *Woman, behold thy son!* Then saith he to the disciple, *Behold, thy mother!* And from that hour the disciple took her unto his own home. (4) Now from the sixth hour there was darkness over all the land until the ninth hour. And about the ninth hour Jesus cried with a loud voice, saying, *Eli, Eli, lama sabachthani?* that is, *My God, my God, why hast thou forsaken me?* And some of them that stood there, when they heard it, said, This man calleth Elijah. (5) While they were yet speaking Jesus said, *I thirst.* There was set there a vessel full of vinegar; so

one put a sponge full of the vinegar upon hyssop, and brought it to his mouth, but the rest said, Let be; let us see whether Elijah cometh to save him. (6) When Jesus had received the vinegar, he said, *It is finished.* (7) Then he cried with a loud voice, *Father, into thy hands I commend my spirit.* After these words he bowed his head and gave up his spirit.

444. Happenings after Christ's death. (1) When Jesus died the veil of the temple was rent in two from the top to the bottom. (2) The earth did quake; and the rocks were rent. (3) The tombs were opened; and many bodies of the saints were raised; and coming forth out of the tombs after his resurrection they entered into the holy city and appeared unto many. (4) The centurion, and they that were with him watching Jesus, when they saw the earthquake, and the things that were done, feared exceedingly, saying, Truly this was a righteous man and the Son of God. (5) When the multitudes beheld these things they returned home smiting their breasts. (6) The Jews because it was the Preparation, that the bodies should not remain on the cross upon the sabbath (for the day of that sabbath was a high day), asked of Pilate that their legs might be broken, and that they might be taken away. The soldiers brake the legs of the first, and of the other that was crucified with him: but when they came to Jesus, and saw that he was dead already, they brake not his legs: Yet one of the soldiers with a spear pierced his side, and straightway there came out blood and water.

445. The Burial of Jesus. (1) Joseph from Arimathea, a rich man, a counsellor of honorable estate, who had not consented to their counsel and deed, a disciple of Jesus, but secretly for fear of the Jews, went boldly to Pilate on Good Friday afternoon and asked for the body of Jesus. (2) Pilate marvelled if he were already dead: and calling unto him the centurion, he asked him whether he had been any while dead. And when he learned it of the centurion, he granted the corpse to Joseph. And he bought a linen cloth, and took away the body. (3) There came also Nicodemus, bringing a mixture of myrrh and aloes about a hundred pounds. Both men bound the body of Jesus in linen cloths with the spices, as the custom of the Jews is to bury. (4) Now in the place where he was crucified there was a garden; and in the garden Joseph had a new tomb hewn out in the rock wherein was never man yet laid. There then because of the Jews' Preparation (for the tomb was nigh at hand) they laid Jesus. (5) They rolled a great stone to the door of the tomb. (6) Mary Magdalene and Mary the mother of Joses were sitting over against the sepulchre and beheld where he was laid.

446. **The Watch at the Sepulchre.** (1) On Saturday which is the day after the Preparation, the chief priests and the Pharisees said to Pilate, Sir, we remember that that deceiver said while he was yet alive, After three days I rise again. Command therefore that the sepulchre be made sure until the third day, lest haply his disciples come and steal him away, and say unto the people, He is risen from the dead; and the last error will be worse than the first. Pilate said, Ye have a guard: go, make it as sure as ye can. So they made the sepulchre sure, sealing the stone, the guard being with them.

447. **Explanatory Notes.** 1. Name and compare *sources;* locate places; give an accurate and detailed outline of the events of the chapter; memorize the seven words on the cross. 2. The *day of Christ's death* is called Good Friday, because on it men were redeemed; the German "Charfreitag" may be derived from "carus," dear, which would mean the same; others derive char from a root which means "care"; hence a "care-Friday," a Friday of trouble. 3. *The cross* was the most disgraceful and one of the most awful instruments of torture among the Romans. A Roman citizen was therefore not allowed to be crucified; only slaves and foreigners. The Jews never crucified any one, their mode of execution was stoning. 4. *As to the shape* of the cross a distinction should be made between the cross as an instrument of torture, the cross of history, and the cross as an emblem, the cross of Christian art. Of the latter there are many forms. Of the cross as an instrument of punishment there were five shapes: (1) the simple "crux," a mere

stake; (2) the "Tau cross," with the cross-piece straight across
the top of the upright, resembling the Greek letter "tau"; (3) the
"crux immissa," or the Latin cross, with the cross-piece below the
top; (4) the "crux commissa," or Greek cross, with the four arms
of equal length; (5) the "crux decussata," or St. Andrew's cross,
with the arms crossed obliquely.

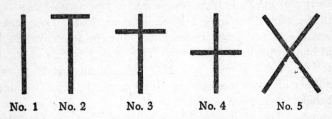

No. 1   No. 2   No. 3   No. 4   No. 5

5. *From Mark* 15 : 26, saying that a superscription was placed *above,*
it has been inferred that it was the traditional cross, the crux immissa, on which Christ died. 6. *The crosses* were not nearly so
high as generally represented, the body being often only about
one or two feet above the ground. On the crossbar the hands
of the condemned man were nailed or in some other way fastened.
The body rested on a peg driven into the upright post. The person
ordinarily died from starvation and pain, not from any fatal in-
jury. 7. On the way to the place of execution the condemned man
carried the crossbar (not the entire cross). He was preceded by a
herald bearing a piece of wood upon which was written the name
of the crime he had committed. This would be nailed to the cross.
(Mark 15 : 26.) 8. The *Roman soldiers* being too proud and the
Jews too superstitious or hateful to carry the crossbar of Jesus,
when his strength failed, they pressed a passer-by into service. 9.
Simon was either already a friend of Jesus or the cross-bearing
led to his conversion. At any rate his two sons, Alexander and
Rufus, became prominent members of the early church and should
almost certainly be identified with those mentioned in Rom. 16 : 13
and Acts 19 : 33. 10. *Luke* 23 : 31 draws the comparison between his
sufferings and those threatening his people by the use of a current proverb. The green tree representing innocence and the dry
tree guilt. 11. The *traditional site* of Golgotha (Hebrew) or Calvary (Latin), meaning place of skull, or Schaedelstaette, is about
a quarter of a mile west from the n. w. corner of the temple,
within the walls of the present city, under the church of the Holy
Sepulchre which was erected by the Empress Helena A. D. 335,
who decided on this spot by miracles of healing by means of the
cross. But of late years many scholars favor the skull-like emi-

nence just outside the present wall, north of the city, near Jeremiah's Grotto. The narrative calls for a place without the city (Heb. 13:12), near some public highway (Mk. 15:29), visible from afar (Lu. 23:4, 9), containing a garden (Jno. 19:41). Nowhere in the gospels is Calvary called a "mount." 12. *The place was* named Golgotha (The Skull), either because of the shape of the hill, or, because it was the public place of execution, strewn with the remains of condemned criminals. 13. *If Jesus was tried* in the tower of Antonia or its immediate vicinity, the distance which he walked may have been a third of a mile. 14. *That Jesus* was placed between two robbers may have been done at the instigation of the priests who thus unconsciously would have helped to fulfill the prophecy.

448. 1. *The superscription* was evidently drawn up by Pilate himself and, in order that everyone might understand it, it was composed in three languages—Hebrew or Aramaic, the local speech of the people, Greek, the language of commerce and culture, and Latin, the official language of the Roman empire. It is variously reported by each of the four evangelists. This may have been because the inscription itself differed in each of the three languages, or perhaps because each evangelist records only a part of what Pilate wrote, as shown in the following scheme.

Pilate:	This is Jesus of Nazareth, the King of the Jews.
Matthew:	This is Jesus ...., the King of the Jews.
Mark:	.... The King of the Jews.
Luke:	This is ....the King of the Jews.
John:	...... Jesus of Nazareth, the King of the Jews.

2. *This inscription* was unquestionably intended by Pilate as a revenge on the haughty and implacable priests for their momentary triumph over him, and in derision of their present impotence. That a crucified malefactor should be so described they took as a deadly insult. It is difficult to think of Pilate as not providentially guided in proclaiming a truth so profoundly significant. 3. *On crucifixes* these four letters are often seen: I. N. R. I., which mean in Latin: Jesus Nazarenus Rex Judaeorum—Jesus of Nazareth, King of the Jews. 4. *The differences* in the inscription in the four gospels is a decisive proof that true inspiration does not preclude varieties of expressions, even in quoting important documents. 5. *The clothes* of the condemned were a perquisite of the executioners. Of the outer garments they made four parts, probably by loosing the seams. The tunic, a close fitting undergarment, perhaps the skillful work of some loving hand, had no seams, and was so precious that they decided to cast lots. 6. Mk. 15:25 says that Jesus was *crucified at the third hour* (9 a. m.); but according to Jno. 19:14

the trial was not quite over at "about the sixth hour" (12 noon),
and therefore the crucifixion was still later. It is probable that
both writers reckoned the time roughly by the position of the sun
in the heavens, and did not know the exact hour. People did not
carry watches. John's estimate accords better with the probabil-
ities of the case; moreover, he was present at the cross. 7. *The
soldiers' business* was to watch, so that the bodies might not be
taken down by friends, or unduly molested by enemies. 8. *An old
tradition* says that Dionysius, who later became a member of the
council at Athens, was studying at Heliopolis in Egypt on the day
of Christ's death. When suddenly the sun darkened, a priest of
that temple exclaimed, "Either Divinity suffers or the earth is near
its destruction." Later, when Paul preached at Athens, Dionysius
became a Christian (Acts 17). 9. *This darkness* was not due to an
eclipse of the sun, because the passover fell at the time when the
moon was full. 10. *Either they did* not understand the Aramaic
"Eli," or Mt. 27:49 was spoken in mockery. The appearance of
Elijah was by the Jews, universally accepted as the sign of the coming of the Messiah. They seemed to understand the words as a
reproach to Elijah for failing to come to his aid. 11. *The word
"woman"* in this tender address (Jno. 19:26) shows clearly that
the same term in Jno. 2:4 does not indicate lack of respect. 12.
Jesus committed his mother to John and not to his four brothers,
because he was present and they were not. They may not have
been in Jerusalem even, and immediate help was necessary. Probably Mary was in danger of collapsing on the spot. 13. *The punctuation* of Jno. 19:25, and in the text of this chapter shows that
there were not three but four women standing at the cross. (a) This
avoids the improbable supposition of two sisters having the same
name; (b) The natural inference from a comparison of Jno. 19:
25 with Mk. 15:40 is that Salome is the same as "his mother's sister." (c) If this is correct, John's silence about the name of "his
mother's sister" is explained. She was his own mother and he is
reserved about his relatives. He never mentions his own name,
nor his brother's, nor the Virgin's (his aunt); (d) The very ancient
Syriac version Peshito, adopts this view by inserting "and" before
"Mary, the wife of Clopas." On the bearing of this interpretation
on the relationships to Jesus, see § 185 (5).

449. 1. *For the full symbolism* of the rending of the veil read
Heb. 9:3; 10:19. This miracle may explain why subsequently a
great number of the priests became Christians. (Acts 6:7.) 2. *The
rising of the saints* was the result, not the immediate accompani-
ment, of the opening of the tombs. It was "after his resurrection" that they appeared. 3. *According to opinions* which carry

weight the centurion was a German. Investigation of the old
Roman military annals has shown that the legion stationed at
Jerusalem at this time was composed of soldiers from southern
Germany near the river Danube. 4. *The words of the centurion,
"The Son of God"* (margin "a son of God") must be understood
as uttered by a heathen. He evidently thought of Jesus as a sort
of a demi-god. 5. Jno. 19:31 *recalls the law,* Deut. 21:25, that
one "hung upon a tree" should be taken down before night-fall,
lest his corpse should bring pollution to the land. 6. *The Romans*
left the bodies to moulder under the sun and rain, or to be de-
voured by wild beasts (as was done in the middle ages). The Jews
demanded more humane treatment. 7. Jno. 19:34 *establishes beyond* a doubt the reality of Christ's death, which is a condition
of a real resurrection. 8. Jno. 19:35 shows that we have no *hear-
say evidence,* but eye witness. 9. Jno. 19:35 makes it probable that
John was the only one of the twelve who had witnessed the entire
tragedy. 10. What was the *physical cause* of Christ's death? (a)
It was due to a rupture of the heart; or (b) to the struggles and
agonies through which Jesus had passed; (c) his physical nature had
not exhausted itself and the Lord laid down his life by an act of
his own will (Jno. 10:18.) In support of this last opinion it is
cited that even Pilate was surprised that Jesus had died so soon,
and that the evangelists report that Jesus died as a strong man
with a loud shout. 11. The *beginning of the Sabbath* (called high,
i. e. double sacred, because in the passover week, Jno. 19:31) made it
necessary to postpone any special preparation of the body to Sunday.
12. *Pilate was surprised* that Jesus had died so soon, because death
seldom supervened before three days, and was the result of gradual
benumbing and slow starvation. Sometimes a fire was kindled
below them, or lions and bears came to devour them. The Jews did
not allow such barbarities, and substituted breaking of the bones
and the *coup de grace* with a view of hastening death and mitigating
the suffering. 13. *The traditional site* of Christ's tomb is under
the church of the Holy Sepulchre within the present walls of Jerusalem. It has lately been thought that it may have been one of
the tombs discovered near the "New Calvary," not far from Jeremiah's grotto. 14. *While Christ's body* lay in the tomb, his soul
descended into hades (the O. T. sheol) to proclaim his victory
(Acts 2:29-32; 13:35-37); or to preach (1 Peter 3:19, 20; 4:6).
15. As *this watch* had been placed there on the Sabbath and by
the enemies of Christ his friends seemed to have known nothing
about it at the time, for the women on Easter morning are not troubled about a Roman guard but only about the stone. 16. *The stone*
was sealed probably by passing a cord round the stone to the two

sides of the entrance. This was sealed with wax of prepared clay in the centre and at the ends, so that the stone could not be removed without breaking the seals on the cord.

450. **Practical Lessons.** 1. The cross a revelation, 1, of the enormity of sin, 2, of God's vicarious love, 3, of Christ's kingdom in its conquering march through the world. 2. "In hoc signo vinces," was the inscription on Constantine's standard. 3. In the cross of Christ I glory. 4. Sin killed Christ in a double sense; the sin of the world and the sinful behaviour of Judas, Caiaphas, Pilate. But Christ kills sin by crushing the serpent's head. (See symbol of serpent at the foot of crucifixes.) 5. This enforced service brought upon Simon the blessing that he and his sons become prominent members of the church. 6. Like other weak men, Pilate was stubborn in little things and weak in great crises. His refusal to change the inscription did not show courage but childish stubbornness. 7. The famous old cathedral at Treves, Germany, claims to possess the Holy Coat and exhibits the same every 25 years to millions of pilgrims. 8. The object of each of the 7 words: 1, intercession for foes; 2, pardon for penitents; 3, tender regard for the bereaved; 4, expression of mental anguish; 5, physical suffering; 6, shout of triumph at the completion of his mission; 7, laying down his life. 9. All three died because of sin. Their attitude to sin is as follows: the impenitent robber died *in* sin; the penitent, *to* sin; Christ *for* sin. 10. Christ's promise to the thief contradicts the doctrines of purgatory and of the "sleep of the soul." 11. That there is one case of deathbed repentance recorded in Scripture encourages hope to the last, that there is but one discourages presumptuous delay. 12. Analyse the characters of the church at the cross. 13. The rending of the veil symbolized that by the death of Christ the Jewish ceremonial system was brought to an end, that the darkness of the Jewish dispensation had given way to the clear revelation of the Gospel; that the way to the mercy seat was free to all without a priest (Heb. 9:8; 10:19-22). 14. The memory of the enemies was better than that of the disciples. (Matt. 27:63; Jno. 20:9.)

451. **Reference Literature.** Farrar, Ch. 61; Andrews, p. 544; Stalker, §§ 190-198; Stalker's Trial and Death, Ch. 11-23; on Calvary, see Davis, D. B., Barton, Week of Passion, p. 188; Thirty Years' Work in the Holy Land by the Pal. Explor. Fund, p. 228; on crucifixion, Davis, D. B.; on the various patterns of crosses, see Barton, Week of Passion, p. 190; Davis; Encycl. Biblica, I; Maclair, N. T. Hist. p. 311; Smith's N. T. Hist. 330 and 344; for the fulfillment of Lu. 23:28 see Jos. Bell, Jud. 6:8, 5; 9:4; on the superscription, McConaugh, Life of Christ, p. 161; Aldrich, J. K.—

"Critical Examination of the Time of Our Saviour's Crucifixion;" Der Heilige Rock za Trier, Herzog Encl.; on the seven words, Hast. D. of C. II, 616; Piery's D. B. 811. Sieghardus, oder der Hauptmann, der beim Kreuze stand. (a story); Oberammergau Passion Play, see Sanford's Herzog and Schaff—Herzog Encl. Stroud, W.—"The Physical Cause of the Death of Christ;" also in Hanna's Life of Christ; Denny, Death of Christ; Hoellenfahrt, see Herzog and Schaff-Herzog; Barton's Week of Passion, 188-200, on Via Dolorosa, stations of the cross, the superscription, scala santa, the sigmata, physical cause of Christ's death, the darkness, the finding of the true cross, legends of the tree of the cross, Church of the Holy Sepulchre; Paintings by Hofman and others; passion music: Stabat Mater, by Rossini; Bach's on St. Matthew; Stainer's Crucifixion, Schnecker's, etc.

452. **Questions for Discussion.** 1. In what sense was it true that Jesus could not save himself? 2. What did the rending of the veil signify? 3. Why occurred the appearance of the saints after Christ's resurrection (1 Cor. 15:20)? 4. What was the effect of the same occurrences on the centurion, the people, the friends of Jesus (Lu. 23:47-49). 5. What does the expression "body of Jesus," so carefully used by all the evangelists indicate as to the reality of Christ's death? 6. Show how the sealing of the tomb strengthens the evidence for the resurrection?

DIVISION VI.

The Forty Days of Resurrection Life.

From Easter to Ascension, Sunday, April 9, to Thursday,
May 18, A. D. 30.

CHAPTER 48.

The Resurrection and Five Appearances.

Matt. 28: 1-15; Mk. 16: 1-14; Lu. 23: 56-24: 43; Jno. 20:
1-25. Harmony 143-146.

453. **Earthquake and the Women at the Tomb.** (1)
When the Sabbath was passed (on Saturday after sunset),
Mary Magdalene, Mary, the mother of Jesus, Salome and
Joanna bought spices that they might anoint him. (2)
Early on Sunday morning there was a great earthquake;
for an angel of the Lord descended from heaven, and
rolled away the stone, and sat upon it. His appearance was
as lightning, and his raiment white as snow: and for fear
of him the watchers did quake, and became as dead. (3)
About the same time, while it was yet dark, the four women
left the city, and arrived at the tomb when the sun was
risen. They were saying among themselves, Who shall
roll us away the stone from the door of the tomb? and
looking up, they see that the stone is rolled back: for it
was exceeding great.

454. **The Empty Tomb.** (1) These four women entered into the tomb and found not the body of the Lord
Jesus. While they were perplexed behold, two men stood
by them in dazzling apparel: and as they were affrighted
and bowed down their faces to the earth, they said unto

268

them, Why seek ye the living among the dead? He is not here, but is risen. See the place where the Lord lay and remember how he spake unto you when he was yet in Galilee, saying that the Son of man must be delivered into the hands of sinful men, and be crucified, and the third day rise again. Go quickly, and tell his disciples, and Peter, He is risen from the dead; and lo, he goeth before you into Galilee; there shall ye see him: lo, I have told you. And they departed quickly from the tomb with fear and great joy, and ran to bring his disciples word, but said nothing to any one else on the way, for they were afraid. (2) Mary Magdalene separated from the other women and arrived first at the house where the apostles were, and said, They have taken away the Lord out of the tomb and we know not where they have laid him. These words appeared to them as idle talk; and they disbelieved them. But soon afterwards Peter and John went toward the tomb. They run both together; but John outran Peter and came first to the tomb. Stooping and looking in, he seeth the linen cloths lying; yet entered he not in. When Peter arrived he entered into the tomb; and he beholdeth the linen cloths lying, but the napkin, that was upon his head, not lying with the linen cloths, but rolled up in a place by itself. Then John also entered and saw and believed. For as yet they knew not the Scripture that he must rise from the dead. Then the disciples returned to their home.

455. **First Appearance: to Mary Magdalene.** (1) Mary Magdalene had slowly followed Peter and John from the city to the garden and arrived after they had returned. She was standing at the tomb weeping. Looking into it she beholdeth two angels in white sitting, one at the head, and one at the feet, where the body of Jesus had lain. They say, Woman, why weepest thou? She saith, Because they have taken away my Lord, and I know not where they have laid him. (2) When she turned back she beholdeth Jesus standing, and knew not that it was Jesus. Jesus saith, Woman, why weepest thou? whom seekest thou? She, supposing

him to be the gardener, saith, Sir, if thou hast borne him hence, tell me where thou hast laid him, and I will take him away. Jesus saith, Mary. She saith in Hebrew, Rabboni; Jesus saith, Touch me not; for I am not yet ascended unto the Father; but go unto my brethren, and say to them, I ascend unto my Father and your Father, and my God and your God. Mary Magdalene telleth the disciples, I have seen the Lord; and *that* he had said these things unto her.

456. **Second Appearance: to the three Women.** (1) Soon after Peter and John had gone to the tomb the other three women arrived and delivered the message from Jesus. Then they also went back again to the garden. Here Jesus met them, saying, All hail. And they came and took hold of his feet, and worshipped him. Then saith Jesus unto them, Fear not: go tell my brethren that they depart into Galilee, and there shall they see me.

457. **Report of the Watch.** (1) After the earthquake some of the guard came into the city, and told unto the chief priests all the things that were come to pass. And when they were assembled with the elders, and had taken counsel, they gave much money unto the soldiers, saying, Say ye, His disciples came by night, and stole him away while we slept. And if this come to the governor's ears, we will persuade him, and rid you of care. So they took the money, and did as they were taught: and this saying was spread abroad among the Jews, and continueth until this day.

458. **Third Appearance: On the Way to Emmaus.** (1) In the afternoon of the Resurrection Day, Cleopas and another of Christ's followers were going to Emmaus. (2) They communed with each other of all these things which had happened. (3) Jesus drew near, and went with them. But their eyes were holden that they should not know him. He said, What communications are these that ye have? Cleopas said, Dost thou alone sojourn in Jerusalem and not know the things which are come to pass there in these days? He said, What things? They said, The things con-

cerning Jesus the Nazarene, who was a prophet mighty in
deed and word before God and all the people: how our
rulers delivered him up to be crucified. But we hoped that
it was he who should redeem Israel. It is now the third
day since these things came to pass. (4) Moreover women
of our company amazed us, having been early at the tomb;
and when they found not his body, they came, saying, that
they had seen angels, who said that he was alive. And certain of them that were with us went to the tomb, and
found it so: but him they saw not. (5) He said, O foolish
men, and slow of heart to believe in all that the prophets
have spoken! Behooved it not the Christ to suffer these
things and to enter into his glory? (6) And beginning
from Moses and from all the prophets, he interpreted the
scriptures concerning himself. (7) When they drew nigh
unto the village he made as though he would go further.
But they constrained him, saying, Abide with us; for it is
toward evening, and the day is now far spent. And he
went in to abide with them. When he had sat down with
them to meat, he took the bread and blessed; and breaking
it gave to them. (8) Then their eyes were opened, and they
knew him; and he vanished out of their sight. They said,
Was not our heart burning within us, while he spake to us
in the way, while he opened to us the scriptures? They returned to Jerusalem, and found the eleven gathered together, and them that were with them, saying, The Lord is
risen indeed, and hath appeared to Simon. And they re-
hearsed the things that happened in the way.

459. **Fourth Appearance: to Peter.** Of this appearance we have the reports of the Ten (Lu. 24: 34) and of
Paul (1 Cor. 15: 5), but no particulars as to time, place
and attending circumstances.

460. **Fifth Appearance: to the Ten.** As the disciples
from Emmaus yet spoke to the Ten, who met behind closed
doors for fear of the Jews, Jesus stood in the midst of them,
and saith, Peace be unto you. But they were terrified, and
supposed that they beheld a spirit. He said, Why are ye

troubled? and wherefore do questionings arise in your heart? See my hands and my feet, that it is I myself: handle me, and see; for a spirit hath not flesh and bones, as ye behold me having. And when he had said this, he showed them his hands, his side and his feet. And while they still disbelieved for joy, he said, Have ye here anything to eat? And they gave him a piece of a broiled fish. And **he ate before** them. The disciples were glad, when they **saw the Lord.** Jesus said again, Peace be unto you; as the Father hath sent me, even so send I you. When he had said **this, he** breathed on them, and saith, Receive ye the Holy Spirit: whosoever sins ye forgive, they are forgiven, whosoever sins ye retain, they are retained. But Thomas, called Didymus, was not with them. The other disciples said, We have seen the Lord. But he said, Except I shall see in his hands the print of the nails, and put my finger into the print of the nails, and put my hand into his side, I will not believe.

461. **Explanatory Notes.** 1. Name and compare *sources;* locate places; give an accurate outline of the events of the day; memorize Lu. 24:29. 2. The *difficulty of arranging* all the events of the Easter day in such a way as to exhibit a perfect harmony of the four gospels has always been felt by accurate Bible students, and has always been used to discredit the records by negative critics. It arises not from any contradiction between them, but from the fact that none gives a complete report of all the appearances. The order of events as given above may claim probability, if not certainty. 3. *The report* of the earthquake came no doubt from the watchers, some of whom may even have become Christians. 4. *The stone* that closed the tomb's mouth was not a rough boulder, as most people believe, but was formed like a cart-wheel or mill-stone which moved in a track. Many tombs still exist in Palestine that were fitted with such rolling doors. Even so it troubled the women, "for it was very great." 5. The *act of the Lord's* rising, and his coming forth from the tomb was seen by no human eyes. Exactly at what hour, in what manner, in what garment he came forth is not reported. This is significant. If the accounts were the inventions of men we should look for information on these very points, as is seen in the "Gospel of Peter," written at the beginning of the second century which professes to

give information in regard to the very act of resurrection. Having described how two youths descended from the open heaven and entered the tomb in the sight of the soldiers, it continues—"They see three men come forth from the grave and the two support the one and a cross followed them and the heads of the two reach to the heaven, but the head of the one whom they lead rises above the heaven. And they heard a voice out of the heaven which said, Hast thou proclaimed to those who were asleep? and there came from the cross an answer, "Yes." 6. *The minute description* in Jno. 20:6, 7 is intended to show that the body could not have been stolen; for then would the grave-clothes have been carried off with the body. 7. The *soldiers* did not report that Jesus had risen, but only that the tomb had been suddenly and wondrously opened. It is probable that the priests satisfied themselves of the truth of the soldiers' report. 8. It *must be noticed* that Matthew does not imply that the chief priests believed in the resurrection of Jesus on the report of the soldiers. 9. It has been objected that *Roman soldiers* would not have risked their lives by allowing the story to go abroad that they slept at their post. But there was little risk with the Sanhedrin on their side. The high priests had lately given evidence that they knew how to bend Pilate's will, and moreover, there was money to be had. 10. *The location of Emmaus* is in dispute. Perhaps the most probable site was about 8 miles northwest of Jerusalem. 11. *Luke probably* did not know the name of the second disciple. Peter, Luke, James the Less have been guessed at. But Peter and James were in Jerusalem (Lu. 24:33) and Luke was converted many years later. 12. *Cleopas* has been identified with Clopas, the husband of Mary (Jno. 19:25). 13. The *breaking of the bread* refers to a peculiarity which they had often noticed, and not to the Lord's Supper, for these two had not been present at the institution of the sacrament. 14. The *sudden vanishing* of Jesus and his sudden appearance indicate that the Resurrection body of Jesus was no longer subject to the known laws of matter. We have here one hint as to the nature of the glorified resurrection body. It was the *identical* but not the same body. (cf. Prof. Fullerton on "Sameness and Identity.") 15. Lu. 24:33 uses the *term "eleven"* somewhat loosely as the name of a body of men whether every member is present or not. ("The Com. of 100;" "Philad. Presbytery," etc.). Only ten were present (Jno. 20:24). 16. *Keim speaks rashly* by saying that Jno. 20:22 does away with Pentecost. Here they received the earnest of the gift which came in fuller measure "not long after these days." (Lu. 24:49.) 17. The eating in Lu. 24:43 was intended to emphasize the reality of his appearance; that he is the same whom they had known before, not a mere spirit; certainly not a delusion.

462. Practical Lessons. 1. The difference between Christ's resurrection and the raising of Lazarus and others was this: Jesus rose to die no more (Rom. 6:9), but ascended to heaven, while the others died again. 2. Christ forbids Mary Magdalene to touch him, for she was determined to hold him back, while he was to ascend first and then return, "for it is expedient that I go." In the case of Thomas he invited his touch in order to prove to him the reality of his appearance and his identity. 3. The intellectual difficulty springing from the shattering of an erroneous dogma respecting the true nature of Christ's Messiahship did not wreck their faith in him as one sent from God. To the person of Jesus their hearts still cling, Luke 24:19-21. 4. The Jewish rule was that when at least three were eating together they were bound to give thanks aloud. One of their ancient table prayers is as follows: "Blessed be thou O Lord, our God, King of the universe, who bringest forth fruit out of the earth." 5. They recognized Jesus by the tone of his voice, or some well-known gestures, or by the marks in his hands. 6. It is the very doubt of the apostles that make their faith afterwards so valuable to us. They were not too anxious, they were only too unready to believe. The psychological conditions for believing in Christ's resurrection were absent. 7. Christ still enters through the closed doors of his followers and bestows his peace.

463. Reference Literature. 1. Farrar, Ch. 52; Andrews, p. 596; Stalker, §§ 199-205; on the resurrection, see Davis; Hast. D. of C. II; Barton, Week of Passion, pp. 205-214, on Easter, Lent, the fish symbol; famous paintings by Hofman, Mueller and Plockhorst of the various subjects of the resurrection; the famous statue by Thorwaldsen in a church at Copenhagen of Christ in the Act of Blessing.

464. Questions for Discussion. 1. What was the purpose of the earthquake? 2. Show the ridiculousness of the report of the watch (Matt. 26:13). 3. What new titles are given to Jesus in Lu. 24:3, 15. 4. How does the slowness to believe in the resurrection make the subsequent testimony of the apostles all the more conclusive? 5. What are some of the teachings of Moses and the prophets to which Jesus doubtless referred on the way to Emmaus? 6. What is the difference between doubt, scepticism, and despair? 7. Was Thomas altogether absent, or did he come later after Christ's appearance?

CHAPTER 49.

The Last Five Appearances of Christ and His Ascension.

Jno. 20:26-21:25; Matt. 28:16-20; Mk. 16:15-20; Lu. 24:44-53. Harmony 147-151.

465. **Sixth Appearance: to the Eleven.** (1) After eight days again his disciples were within, and Thomas with them. Jesus cometh, the doors being shut, and stood in the midst, and said, Peace be unto you. Then saith he to Thomas, Reach hither thy finger, and see my hands; and reach hither thy hand, and put it into my side: and be not faithless, but believing. Thomas said, My Lord and my God. Jesus saith, Because thou hast seen me, thou hast believed: blessed are they that have not seen, and yet have believed.

466. **Seventh Appearance: to Seven Disciples.** (1) At the sea of Tiberias there were together Simon Peter, Thomas called Didymus, Nathaniel of Cana in Galilee, the sons of Zebedee, and two other of his disciples. Peter saith I go a fishing. They say, We also come with thee. They entered into the boat; and that night they took nothing. (2) When the day was breaking, Jesus stood on the beach: yet the disciples knew not that it was Jesus. Jesus saith, Children, have ye aught to eat? They answered him, No. And he said, Cast the net on the right side of the boat, and ye shall find. They did so and were not able to draw it for the multitude of fishes. (3) John said to Peter, It is the Lord. When Peter heard that it was the Lord, he girt his coat about him, and cast himself into the sea. But the other disciples came in the little boat (for they were not far from the land), dragging the net full of fishes. So when they got out upon the land, they see a fire of coals there, and fish laid thereon, and bread. Jesus saith, Bring of the fish which ye have now taken. Peter drew the net to land, full of great fishes, a hundred and fifty and three.

Jesus saith, Break your fast. None of the disciples durst
inquire of him, Who art thou? knowing that it was the
Lord. Jesus taketh the bread, and giveth them, and the
fish likewise.

467. **Restoration of Peter.** (1) When they had broken
their fast, Jesus saith to Peter, Simon, son of John, lovest
thou me more than these? He saith, Yea, Lord; thou
knowest that I love thee. He saith, Feed my lambs. He
saith a second time, Simon, son of John, lovest thou me?
He saith, Yea, Lord; thou knowest that I love thee. He
saith, Tend my sheep. He saith the third time, Simon, son
of John, lovest thou me? Peter was grieved because he
said unto him the third time, and said, Lord, thou knowest
all things; thou knowest that I love thee. Jesus saith, Feed
my sheep. (2) When thou wast young, thou girdest thyself, and walkedst whither thou wouldest: but when thou
shalt be old, thou shalt stretch forth thy hands, and another
shall gird thee, and carry thee whither thou wouldest not.
This he spake, signifying by what manner of death he
should glorify God. Then he saith, Follow me. (3) Peter,
turning about, seeth John following. Peter saith to Jesus,
Lord, what shall this man do? Jesus saith, If I will that
he tarry till I come, what is that to thee? follow thou me.
This saying went forth among the brethren, that that disciple should not die: yet Jesus said not that he should not
die, but, If I will that he tarry till I come, what is that to
thee?

468. **Eighth Appearance: to the Apostles and the 500
Brethren.** (1) The eleven disciples went into Galilee, unto
the mountain where Jesus had appointed them. Probably
on this occasion came together more than 500 brethren.
(2) When they saw him, they worshipped him; but some
(of the 500) doubted the reality of the appearance. (3)
Jesus said, All authority hath been given unto me in heaven
and on earth. Go ye therefore, and make disciples of all
the nations, baptizing them into the name of the Father and
of the Son and of the Holy Spirit: teaching them to ob-

serve all things whatsoever I commanded you: and lo, I am with you always, even unto the end of the world. And these signs shall accompany them that believe: in my name shall they cast out demons; they shall speak with new tongues; they shall take up serpents, and if they drink any deadly thing, it shall in no wise hurt them; they shall lay hands on the sick, and they shall recover.

469. **Ninth Appearance: to James, the Lord's Brother.** Only the fact is reported by Paul (1 Cor. 15:7). In his list of appearances, which is the oldest extant, he places it after the appearance to the "five hundred brethren."

470. **The Tenth Appearance: to the Eleven.** (1) For the last time Jesus appeared to the eleven apostles somewhere in Jerusalem, on Thursday, May 18, A. D. 30, forty days after Easter. (2) He said to them: These are my words which I spake unto you, while I was yet with you, that all things must needs be fulfilled, which are written in the law of Moses, and the prophets, and the psalms, concerning me. (3) Then opened he their mind, that they might understand the scriptures; and said, Thus it is written, that the Christ should suffer, and rise again from the dead the third day; and that repentance and remission of sins should be preached in his name unto all the nations, beginning from Jerusalem.

471. **To Wait for the Power from on High.** (1) At this last meeeting, the disciples asked, Lord dost thou at this time restore the kingdom to Israel? He said, It is not for you to know times or seasons, which the Father hath set within his own authority. But ye shall receive power, when the Holy Spirit is come upon you: and ye shall be my witnesses both in Jerusalem, and in all Judæa and Samaria, and unto the uttermost part of the earth. (2) But tarry ye in the city until ye be clothed with the power from on high.

472. **The Ascension.** (1) When he had said these things, he led the apostles out of Jerusalem until they were over against Bethany; and he lifted up his hands and blessed

them. While he blessed them, and as they were looking he was taken up; and a cloud received him out of their sight and they worshipped him. (2) And while they were looking stedfastly into heaven as he went, behold two men stood by them in white apparel; who also said, Ye men of Galilee, why stand ye looking into heaven? this Jesus, who was received up from you into heaven, shall so come in like manner as ye beheld him going into heaven. (3) Then returned they with great joy unto Jerusalem from the mount called Olivet, which is nigh unto Jerusalem, a sabbath day's journey off. And when they were come in, they went up into the upper chamber, where they were abiding; and the eleven disciples with one accord continued stedfastly in prayer, with the women, and Mary the mother of Jesus, and with his brethren.

473. **The Conclusion.** (1) Many other signs did Jesus in the presence of the disciples, which are not written in this book: but these are written, that ye may believe that Jesus is the Christ, the Son of God; and that believing ye may have life in his name. (2) If all the other things which Jesus did should be written every one, I suppose that even the world itself would not contain the books that should be written.

474. **Explanatory Notes.** 1. Name and compare *sources;* locate places; memorize Matt. 28:18-20. 2. *There is no record* that Christ appeared during the week after his resurrection. The phraseology of Jno. 20:26 seems to preclude it. This, as well as the fact that the Holy Spirit descended on a "first day" together with the fundamental importance of Christ's resurrection, and possibly also unrecorded considerations led the disciples very early to believe that a transfer of the weekly rest-day from the last to the first day of the week would be according to the mind of Christ. 3. *At any rate,* whatever may have been the reason, the fact of its early observance is clear from Acts 20:7; 1 Cor. 16:2; Rev. 1:10, and from early extra-biblical testimony, such as the famous letter of Pliny and the writings of the apostolic fathers. 4. *The two N. T. names* for the weekly Easter day are (a) "The Lord's Day" (Rev. 1:10) because it commemorated the fact that the Father through the resurrection declared Christ to be "Lord"; (b) "The

First Day of the Week" (1 Cor. 16:2; Acts 20:7). 5. *Jesus always refused* to manufacture evidence to convince those who did not wish to believe. But he is most considerate of the weakness and doubt, even the blameworthy doubt of those who are willing to believe. There are honest and dishonest doubters and we must always make a distinction between doubt and skepticism. 6. Jno. 20:29 means: He who will learn *by experience* does well, but he does better who is willing also to accept the testimony of good, reliable witnesses. 7. *The seventh appearance* is the first recorded as occurring in Galilee at a time not definitely stated ("after these things"). No doubt soon after the passover which in that year ended on Thursday, April 13, Nisan 21, the disciples left for their homes in Galilee. 8. Jno. 21:14 *"the third time"* may mean the third time to the *circle* of disciples or the third of which John was a witness, or the third recorded in the gospel before the company of the apostles. 9. Jno. 21:1-24 *constitutes an appendix* to the gospel of John which had already been brought to a conclusion in chapter 20:30, 31. It seems to be from the same hand as the rest of the gospel, but has been added after the gospel was regarded as complete. The motive of its addition is probably to be found in Jno. 21:23. John's survival to extreme old age had given rise to the mistaken interpretation of Jesus' words to him that he should leave the world without tasting death or that he should live until the second coming of Christ. Hence John deemed it advisable to point out exactly what Jesus had said and what he really meant. 10. In the first and second question, *Lovest thou me,* Christ uses the Greek word "agapao," which means "respectful regard." Peter answers both times with the stronger word, "phileo,"— expressing warm affection. The third time Jesus uses Peter's word. (Trench, Synonyms, I, 48; Maclear, N. T. Hist. p. 334.) 11. *According to Origen* (Euseb. III, 1) Peter was crucified in the Neronian persecution, 67 A. D., in Rome, with his head downward, and was buried on the spot where St. Peter's Church now stands. For the legend found in St. Ambrose touching his death, see article "Peter" in Smith's B. D. and "Quo Vadis." 12. The *mount* in *Galilee* on which the eighth appearance occurred cannot be identified. It may have been the mount of the Beatitudes. 13. This appearance is *probably identical* with the one to more than 500 believers reported in 1 Cor. 15:6. For the statement Matt. 28:17 that some doubted, implies the presence of others besides the eleven, because any hesitation on the part of the apostles as to Christ's resurrection had by this time been completely removed by repeated interviews. Moreover, only in Galilee could so large a number of disciples be found. On this supposition the eighth appearance is the most important. (a) Because, while the seven preceding appearances were to individuals, this one was to the entire then existing church. (b) Because the great commission was then addressed not to the eleven alone but to them and the entire membership of the church. 14. *From a very early date* it became customary to employ the words in Matt. 28:19 "Father, Son and Holy Ghost," as a solemn formula accompanying baptism. See, for instance, in the "Didache" (Teaching of the Twelve) which is a church manual written not far from 100 A. D. But the apostles either used also a shorter formula, "in the name of Christ" (Acts 2:38; 8:16; 19:5; Rom. 6:3), or these passages do not intend to quote the exact words of the baptismal formula, but only mean to express the relationship into which the baptized person entered.

475. 1. If *the words in Luke* 24:51 "And was carried up into heaven" are to be omitted, as some ancient manuscripts do, then Luke simply says that Jesus was separated from his disciples—vanished from them. In this case we have no report of the ascension in the four gospels as originally written since the paragraph Mark 16: 9-20 is almost universally admitted to be a later addition. Our only historical source would then be Acts 1:6-11. This however would in no way weaken the evidence in favor of Christ's ascension, for: (a) Even if this event had not been recorded, it might easily have been inferred as a normal conclusion to Christ's earthly ministry. (b) The appendix in Mark rests undoubtedly on an ancient trustworthy tradition; (c) The phrase in Luke 24:51 "And was carried up into heaven" is omitted only by some authorities and, if not in the originals, certainly rests also on an ancient tradition; (d) In Jno. 20:17 we have in plain words of Jesus himself a distinct reference to his ascension; (e) The ascension is directly affirmed in Rom. 8:34; Col. 3:1; Rev. 3:21; 22:1. 2. *The purpose of* the ten appearances which were all to his friends and none of which were to his enemies (Acts 10:41), was to prove the reality of his bodily resurrection, to show himself alive, a fact which neither friend nor foe would have believed if he had never appeared in his identical body to any one. 3. But *the great evidence* for the resurrection is the existence of the church. Historic Christianity itself is an effect which demands a cause, and to no cause can it be so rationally referred as that which the early church accepted as an unquestionable fact that Christ who lived in Galilee and died on Calvary still lives. 4. *For a fuller* discussion of the resurrection see the chapter on the "Problems of the Life of Christ."

476. **Practical Lessons.** 1. The doubt of Thomas had its seat in the mind. not in the heart. Many great men have followed him

in this. But Jesus said, it is better to trust to reliable testimony than fight one's way to true faith in Christ through all the labyrinths of negative criticism. 2. The great commission, (a) comes from an Almighty King; (b) requires an aggressive ministry; (c) defines Christianity as a universal religion adapted to all nations; (d) describes the duty of the church to disciple all nations; (e) appoints baptism as the initiation; (f) promises the perpetual presence of its Lord. 3. *At Christ's final appearance* (Luke 24: 44-49) he defines the preacher's subject, field, mission and power. 4. Evangelistic appeals, which do not contain or are not followed by sober instruction must vanish in the smoke of shapeless emotions. 5. *The ministry* is not an order of sacrificing and mediating priests, but men called by Christ and set apart by lawful authority to preach Christ's gospel, and to be teachers and leaders of Christ's people in all good works. 6. The ninth appearance, not recorded in the gospels, but by Paul (1 Cor. 15:7), was that to James, the Lord's brother, and the author of the epistle, by which he was evidently led to believe in the Lord. For while Jno. 7:5 states that he and his brother did not believe on Jesus, in Acts 1:14 we find them all as believers. The Apocryphal Gospel of the Hebrews tells the legend that James had made a vow not to eat or drink till he had seen Jesus. Soon Jesus appeared to him and said: "My brother, eat thy bread, for the Son of man is risen from the dead."

477. **Reference Literature.** Farrar, Ch. 52; Andrews, p. 623; Stalker, § 199; Davis, D. B. on baptism; resurrection; on the activity of the Exalted One, see Drummond's Apost. Teaching and Christ's Teaching, p. 305; Hast. D. B., II, 640, on the resurrection; Paintings by Schoenherr, Dorè and Hofman.

478. **Questions for Discussion.** 1. What was the mode of life of the risen Christ during the forty days? 2. What is the difference between doubt, scepticism and despair? 3. What trait of Peter's weakness is recalled by the form of the Lord's first question? 4. Did the Apostolic church transfer the day of rest from the last to the first day of the week? 5. By what authority? 6. What did the outstretched hands at Christ's ascension symbolize regarding his future relation to his followers?

479. Review Questions.

1. Name the first four chief divisions of the Life of Christ; also the subdivisions of each, and give the dates of the four chief, and of their subdivisions. 2. Enumerate the events of each subdivision in the order of time. 3. Of the *Week of Passion*, (a) explain the name; (b) state the events and dates of

its beginning and end; (c) trace the movements of Jesus on the map from place to place; (d) enumerate the events of each day; (e) the source of information by gospels and chapters, and what amount of the gospel narrative refers to this week.   4. Give a very accurate outline of the six parts of the Lord's trial, inserting Peter's denials and Judas' suicide in their right places.   5. State the ten appearances of the risen Christ in exact chronological order. 6. Give a detailed account of the day of the Resurrection.   7. What do you know of Caiaphas, Annas, Pilate, Herod Antipas?

PART III.

General Aspects of the Life of Christ.

480. The foregoing *analytical* study of our Lord's life has sufficiently acquainted us with his character and work. But in order to gain a still deeper impression of his holy personality we will in these closing chapters construct from the fragmentary statements scattered over his entire life a more compact, connected and *synthetic* portrait of some of the general aspects of his career, such as (1) his character; (2) his mission and work; (3) the chief problems of his life; (4) his influence on the world; closing (5) with a refutation of the chief non-biblical views of the Life of Christ.

CHAPTER 50.

The Character of Jesus.

481. Character is the sum total of the qualities by which a person is distinguished from others. It is the result of three determinants: 1. A man's *individuality,* that is, his original constitution, and inherited tendencies; 2. His *environment,* that is, the external circumstances which influence life; 3. His *free will,* that is, his own modification of the possible effects on himself of Nos. 1 and 2. Character expresses itself in a man's *body,* the instrument of action; his *mind,* the light or guide to action; his *emotions,* the heat, or spur of action; his *will,* the control of action. In analyzing our Lord's character we will make use of these four time-honored psychological categories.

I. The Lord's Physical Characteristics.

482. Information from the Scriptures. (1) Nothing definite is recorded in the New Testament as to Christ's outward appearance. (2) But inferences have been drawn from various passages. For example, from Isa. 53:2, that he lacked beauty (so Justin Martyr, Clement of Alexandria and Tertullian); from Psalm 45:2, that he was "fairer than the children of men" (so Jerome, Augustine, Ambrose, Chrysostom); from John 8:57, that he looked older than he was; from John 18:6, that there was an overawing dignity in his appearance; from John 19:23, that he was well dressed; from several passages that he had a strong voice. It is certain that Christ had not a repulsive face. For if the face of man, as a rule, reflects his soul, the features of Jesus must have, in a high degree, expressed the majesty and greatness of his spirit.

483. Descriptions of Jesus. (1) The earliest extant actual description of Jesus is very late. It dates from John of Damascus in the eighth century, and may rest on some faint but true tradition, handed down from the Apostle John through Polycarp, Papias and Irenæus. He says that Jesus resembled his mother, had a very beautiful face, curling locks, an olive complexion and a look expressive of nobility and wisdom. (2) In a spurious letter, manufactured in the twelfth century, and addressed "to the Roman Senate," a fictitious "Lentulus, president of the people of Jerusalem," gives the following description of Jesus: "A man of tall stature, beautiful, with venerable countenance, which they who look on it can both love and fear. His hair is waving, somewhat wine-colored; his brow is smooth and most serene; his face is without any spot or wrinkle, and glows with a delicate flush; his nose and mouth are faultless; the beard is abundant and his eyes prominent and brilliant; in speech he is grave, reserved and modest."

484. Pictures of Jesus. (1) *Legendary Portraits.* According to unreliable legends, Jesus sent by the hand of the

Apostle Thaddaeus his portrait to *Abgarus,* king of Edessa, who had sent the Greeks to him with an invitation to teach his people (John 12:20), and on his way to Golgotha he is said to have impressed his true picture on the napkin of *Veronica,* who handed it to him to wipe away his sweat and blood. 2. *Real Pictures.* From the above follows that all portraits of Christ are the work of imagination. The earliest of them are in the *catacombs* of Rome, and show us how he appealed to the artistic minds of the primitive Church. They knew him as Friend, Helper, and Comforter, and painted him turning the water into wine (a favourite subject in the catacombs), talking tenderly to the Samaritan woman, raising his friend Lazarus, or carrying a lamb in his bosom. Later, when persecution pressed harder still, and it was death to show the Nazarene in any shape or form, they took to symbolic painting, Greek and Roman youths, anagrams, eagles, the fish, the lamb. The Roman Emperor *Alexander Severus* (222) is said to have placed in his temple the image of Jesus, but no one knows how it looked. Eusebius (325) saw at *Caesarea Philippi* a bronze statue of Christ, with the inscription "To the Saviour, the Benefactor," which Julian the Apostate (361) destroyed. But Gibbon, in his "Decline and Fall of the Roman Empire" believes that it was the statue of an emperor, and that the inscription misled the people. In the *middle ages,* when altars came with the crucifix, the demand arose, "Paint us the Son of God dying on the tree." The thing was impossible, and, in the attempt the painter's art became degraded, and religion too. Hence we have "Crucifixions" and other paintings of Christ, a few beautiful, but for the most part gross in thought and treatment—Christ emaciated, worn, weary, an appalling figure, the dark phantom of a thousand years. With the *Renascence* came expression, and power to paint the whole story of the Son of Man as he appealed to the greatest artists of time. This was the time of the Masters, including the great quintet, Leonardo da Vinci, Michael Angelo, Titian, Raphael, and Correggio. In the

Reformation period and later we have Cranach, the friend of Luther, Duerer, Van Dyck. Modern masters are Ruben, Von Uhde, Hofman, Doré.

485. **Criticism of the Conventional Type of the Christ Portraits.** (1) *Archaeologists* object to the conventional pictures of Christ because they are not true to history. A German painter, L. Fahrenkrog, says: "Christ certainly never wore a beard and his hair was beyond a doubt closely cut. For this we have historical proofs. The oldest representations, going back to the first Christian centuries, and found chiefly in the catacombs of Rome, all picture him without a beard. All the Christ pictures down to the beginning of the fourth century at least, and even later, are of this kind. The further fact that Christ must in his day have worn short hair can be proved from the Scriptures. Among the Jews none but the Nazirites wore long hair. Christ was indeed a Nazarene. but not a Nazirite, the facts of his life supporting this view. If he was not a Nazirite, then like the rest of the Jews he wore his hair short. Further evidence is furnished by Paul in 1 Cor. 11:14, where it is expressly declared that it is a dishonor for a man to wear his hair long, something that the apostle would not have said had his Master worn it thus." Even from Leonardo da Vinci and Michael Angelo we have pictures of Christ in the Final Judgment according to this older type. (2) *Modern exegetes* object to the conventional face of Jesus, as untrue to the New Testament outlines of Christ's personality, because (a) it is not a very intellectual face except in Hofman's pictures; (b) it is not a happy, but a very sad face; (c) it is not a strong face, such as a man of our Lord's force and determination must have had.

486. **Modern Conceptions of a Portrait of Christ.** (1) Taking into account our Lord's nationality and age, the customs of the times and the fact that the incarnation was the taking on of perfect humanity, we will not be very far out of the way when we picture Jesus as of medium height, olive complexion, closely cut hair, no beard, bright

eyes, Jewish facial lines, gracious expression, of perfect health, of dignified appearance. His apparel consisted of a tunic (a closely fitting shirt), a mantle (a square of cloth draped over the shoulders and kept in place by a girdle), a turban, for protection against heat and cold, and sandals of wood, leather or felt, protecting merely the soles of the feet. (2) *Friedrich von Uhde's* very remarkable pictures of scenes in the life of Christ, in which he portrays the Lord amid perfectly modern surroundings, have aroused warm discussions in church circles for years. He believes that not historical but ideal reasons should decide how Jesus should be painted. On the whole he adheres to the traditional type. (3) Recently Prof. Burnant, at the request of the church authorities of Germany, laid down seven principles according to which Christ-pictures should be drawn. He says, Christ must be pictured as a superior and superhuman being; he must at the same time appear as a true man; his human characteristics must be perfectly free from all evidences of sin or its results; the leading characteristics of love, poverty, and patience must be in evidence; the perfect union between the spiritually perfect holiness and the special human conditions of his life must appear; a proper moderation in portraying these seemingly contradictory characteristics must be observed; and, finally, the beauty of Jesus must be found chiefly in his expression.

II. The Lord's Intellectual Powers.

487. **Four Mental Qualities.** Our Lord's education was limited (see Chapter 14). Very conspicuous, however, in his mental life are the four qualities of penetration, keenness, breadth, and originality. (1) By *penetration* is meant his full and accurate knowledge of men. He knew by a glance what was in man. He called Peter a rock, Nathanael an Israelite without guile, Herod Antipas a fox, the Pharisees hypocrites and the Samaritan woman, by implication, an outcast. His knowledge of character is il-

lustrated by the treatment accorded by him to each of the three would-be disciples (Luke 9: 57-62). Neither did his insight fail him when he called Judas, for that disciple's moral descent was gradual. (2) The *keenness* of Christ's mind is amply illustrated by his frequent encounters with the wise men of his nation in debate. He worsted them on their own proper field (cf. Mark 12: 28-34; Math. 22: 41-46). Read also in John 7 and 10 the rapid-fire criticism and Christ's quick and telling replies. The people marvelled, saying: "How hath this man learning, though he hath not studied?" Jesus' answer is his claim of divine revelation (John 5: 20). (3) By the *breadth* of Christ's intellect we mean his far-seeing, liberal tendency. All other great men represent sectional, not universal humanity. Socrates, e. g., was never anything else than a great Greek; Luther, a German; Calvin, a Frenchman; Washington, an American. But Christ was free from limitations. He was a patriot, but no nativist (John 4); he selected his disciples from all classes, and of various temperaments, and sent them to all nations. He embraces publicans and other outcasts. Over against narrow ultra-conservatism, he was liberal in his views on religious, moral and ceremonial questions, such as the traditions of the elders and unscriptural views of the Sabbath. This brought him into constant conflict with his countrymen and eventually to the cross.

488. **Christ was Original.** (1) In his *person;* he was not a copy of great predecessors (Abraham, Moses); nor of famous contemporaries (Hillel); nor a mere embodiment of the "Zeitgeist" (the Age-Spirit) i. e. the mere result of race, heredity, training and environment. (2) In his *life-plan.* A man who had never seen a map of the world proposes to establish a universal kingdom of God. Dr. Reinhard has shown with great erudition that such a plan had never entered into the calculations of the greatest kings, statesmen and philosophers. Hence this idea was not borrowed by him from predecessors. (See testimony of Napoleon I.) To-day we can easily see that his was not an

unsubstantial dream.   (3) In his *teaching;* (a) as to its matter, the distinctive thoughts being new, and not derived from the Essenes, Judaism, the Persians or the Buddhists, but brought from heaven.   His teaching grew out of the Old Testament, and while it contained not many new words or startling phrases, yet the impression upon the people was, "A New Teaching! We have never seen it after this fashion!"   Stalker says: "The more we study the literature of his times the more is the originality of Jesus enhanced, for nothing else in the whole range of human records is more utterly wearisome and worthless. (See Carlisle on "Originals" in Stalker's Christology, p. 67.)   (b) As to his leading conceptions expressed by the terms Gospel, kingdom of God, Son of man, eternal life, ransom, the cross which were entirely new.   (c) As to his claim that he is not only the preacher, but the object of the faith which he proclaimed; that the faith, love and worship of believers should be concentrated upon him because he is God manifested in the flesh; that he is the giver of eternal life and the pardoner of sin,—all this was certainly original and startling.   None of the great teachers ever made such a claim and made good.   (d) As to his eclecticism. He altered the proportion of truth as taught in the O. T., and changed the point of emphasis, exalting or expanding what had been previously in the background (as the fatherhood and the immanence of God) and taking for granted doctrines like the unity and holiness of God; (e) as to *new interpretations* of well-known truths, as the spiritual interpretation of the law and Isaiah 61:1, at Nazareth. "He rarely quotes a text without revealing in it some hidden meaning which no one had suspected before, but which shines clearly to all eyes as soon as it has been pointed out." (Stalker, Imago Christi, p. 162); (f) as to its new *claim of authority,* and of a unique knowledge of God. He sets his authority against that of Moses, saying repeatedly, "but I say unto you." The people noticed this and exclaimed after the Sermon on the Mount: "With authority he teaches

and not like the scribes," "no man ever spoke like this man."
(g) As to *his method,* which was picturesque, clear and decisive.   He possessed the two prime requisites of a great
orator: information and sincerity; (h) as to the *vitalizing
power* of his words giving operative force to ideas which
had already floated before the minds of men in a dormant
state. (See Watson, Mind of the Master, p. 38.); (i) as to
its outward *results;* no man's teaching before or after him
was accepted so generally; (j) as to its *potency;* he breathed
into mankind a life and worked out a code of ethics that
will bring about the real millennium in proportion as it is
put into practice.

III.   The Emotional Life of Jesus.

489.   **The Love of Christ to God.**   The deepest feeling
in Christ's soul was *Love*—(1) to the Father, (2) to all
men, (3) for nature.   Jesus' love to the Father expressed
itself in his complete trust, his constant communion, his
reverence, his submission.   (a) *"He trusted God,"* said even
his enemies (Matt. 27:43).   His first and last words were
expressions of faith.   In the Sermon on the Mount, when
he spoke of the lilies and the birds, and also in Gethsemane,
he emphasized his confidence in the Father.   (b) Christ's
uninterrupted *communion* with the Father is expressed in
his *habit of prayer.*   (Luke 3:21, 22; Mark 1:35; Luke 5:
16; 6:12; Matt. 14:23; Lk. 9:18-28; Matt. 26:36; Lk.
23:46.)   We all know his longest, his most submissive and
his last prayer.   He prayed in public, in solitary places
(mountains and in Gethsemane), for long periods (temptation), before important events (the choosing of the
Twelve), and on the cross, three of his seven last words
being prayers.   He exhorted others to pray and taught his
disciples a form of prayer.   (c) An atmosphere of *reverence* surrounds the entire life of Christ.   In prayer, his
language was not familiar but reverent, his posture showed
respect.   He cultivated habits of reverence; he prayed
before meals, he was regular in attendance at the temple

and synagogue services; he observed the passover meal, going through the usual ritual. (d) By *submission* we do not mean any doubt of his own powers, or inferiority of essence, but a deep consciousness that, as he and the Father are one, all credit for his deeds, his words and his mission should be given to the Father. (Jno. 5:19; 7:17, 28). Not my, but thy will be done.

490. **Christ's Love to Men.** Christ's love for men manifested itself in his high appreciation of man, his sympathy, his generosity, his accessibility, his longing for intimate friendship, his humility, simplicity, self-surrender, his obedience, his candor and sincerity, his graciousness. (1) No one ever emphasized the *value of man* as he did (Mark 8:36; Matt. 16:26). He interested himself in the children, watching them at play (Matt. 11:16), rebuking his disciples for keeping them from him (Matt. 19:13), and declared the child an example for his disciples (Matt. 18:2). He protected woman and therefore severely censured the lax interpretation of the divorce laws by the liberal school of Hillel. Socrates, Plato and Aristotle slurred woman. (Speer, the Man Jesus, p. 136). (2) Christ's great *sympathy* is exhibited on every page of the Gospel. With the exception of about eight, all his miracles are works of mercy. His throbbing heart is shown in phrases constantly recurring: "He was *moved with compassion*," (Matt. 20:34; 9:36; Luke 7:13; Matt. 14:14; 15:32). Twice it is reported that Christ wept. His pity went out to all sorts and conditions of men: to the poor, the hungry, the bereaved (the three raisings of the dead), the sick in body and mind, the erring (publicans, fallen women), his enemies (people of Jerusalem), on the cross (Jno. 22:50; 23:34). (3) Christ was a *generous* soul. When he said, "It is more blessed to give than to receive," He spoke of his personal experience. He had no money, but he gave his time, strength, ideas, heart and life. Sympathy consumed his life blood. He pleased not himself (Rom. 15:3). His death was a free surrender, a self-sacrifice (John

10: **17, 18**). While severe towards himself, he was **very** *considerate* for others. He remembers the frailty of human nature and offers the disciples a vacation (Mark 6:31). (4) Christ was also very *accessible* to all kinds of people: to simple fishermen (John 1:37; Mark 1:16), to anxious parents (Mark 5:22; 7:25; 10:13), to publicans (Matt. 9:10; 10:3; 11:9; Luke 19:2); to sinful women (Luke 7:37; Matt. 21:31). (5) But while embracing all men, he was *eager for more intimate friendship;* he was individualizing in his love (Young Ruler, John, Martha, Mary, Lazarus.) Even before the beginning of his public ministry, he surrounded himself with special friends (Jno. 1:39). In the course of time, wider and closer circles of friends gathered around him (the Seventy, the Twelve, the Three, the beloved Disciple). His friendship was unselfish (John 18:8; his prayer in John 17 was mostly for them), and loyal (John 13:1: "Once a friend, always a friend"), and without showing favoritism. He loved each one to the measure of his receptivity. He gave all of them his love (John 13:34), his knowledge (John 15:15), his example (John 13:15). (6) The Lord's *humility,* which, according to Ruskin, is the first test of truly great men, was emphasized in all he said and did. The incident in John 13 was characteristic of his whole life. He said, "I am meek and lowly in heart," and Paul emphasized that he "emptied himself" (Phil. 2:5-11). He was free of that restless desire for distinction which is so common in great men; he hated disputes as to who should be the greatest, and often enjoined silence on the beneficiaries of his miracles. His great popularity did not make him vain, as is the case with most great men. He refused even a king's crown, the hardest thing among men. (7) He possessed *simplicity of heart,* which Fenelon defined as that grace which frees the soul from all unnecessary reflection upon itself. (8) His *self-surrender.* He surrendered all, even his home, and became a wanderer (John 9:58). (9) One of the oldest

daughters of love is *obedience*. This he had to learn (Heb.
5:8). To his Father's business he was faithfully devoted
(John 4:34; 6:38; 8:29). In his family, he was a dutiful
son and brother, probably the bread-winner after Joseph's
death; on the Cross he makes provision for his mother.
The address "woman" in John 2:4 is not disrespectful according to custom and the idiom of the language. (10)
But love is not genuine if it is not *candid* (from candidus—
white) and *sincere* (from the Latin "sine cera," without
wax), that is, outspoken, open, frank, without guile and
craft, not tricky. He hated hypocrisy. (a) Jesus was candid in his teaching. He said what he believed and believed
what he said. (b) He never held back the truth from
his friends. He told his disciples, "behold, I send you forth
as sheep in the midst of wolves" (Matt. 10). Thrice he announced his death, when all expected a great triumph. His
candor at Capernaum reduced the number of his followers
materially (Jno. 7:66). He candidly speaks of limitations
to his knowledge and authority, during his lifetime on earth
(Mark 13:32; 10:40). In John 14:1 he assures his disciples that they always may expect candor from him. He
urges men to count the cost (Luke 14:25), instead of winning them by promises; (c) towards his foes, he used plain
words, calling the rulers liars, Herod a fox and the Pharisees, hypocrites. (11) *Graciousness* is also very conspicuous in Jesus' character. Even saints are at times bad
neighbors whom we like at a distance. But Christ had that
amiable unconstrained expression of a self-forgetting
mind. He had the happy faculty of doing the right thing
in the right way at the right time.

491. **Christ's Aesthetic Emotions and Humor.** (1)
As far as our sources inform us, Christ was no artist, nor
a poet. But his aesthetic emotions came into play mostly
in his loving appreciation of nature. He watched the
weather, the lightning, sunrise and sunset, and knew the
weather signs of his day (Jno. 12:54). He used the lilies.

the raven, the fig tree as illustrations. (2) Did Christ have a *humorous vein?* Certainly not, if we understand by that term levity and mere fun. But in the higher sense of that term he possessed this great gift of God. Being a normal man it is reasonable to suppose that Christ could not help smiling when little Zacchaeus climbed down from his odd perch, or when he saw the Pharisees who had so confidently attacked him, completely cornered, so that they quietly retired. Many of our Lord's sayings are so evidently surcharged with true humor and witticism that the reading of them would at once cause a broad smile or a hearty laugh, if they were not so familiar and if we did not think it irreverent to give such expressions of approval. We quote from D. G. P. Eckman (Meth. Review) as follows: "Observe his quaint characterizations of those who carefully cleanse the outside of the cup and platter, forgetting that they drink and feed from the inside of these vessels; of men who carefully strain out a gnat but incontinently swallow a camel. Notice how he hits off the absurdity of trying to serve two masters, of feeding pearls to swine, of putting a light under a bushel, of proffering a stone instead of bread, or a serpent instead of a fish, or a scorpion instead of an egg, of pitting Beelzebub against himself. What a grotesque thing it is for a camel to attempt to squeeze through the eye of a needle, or for a blind man to try to lead another sightless mortal, with the result that both pitch into the gutter. How preposterous it is for a man with a beam in his eye to offer to remove a mote from his brother's eye. Consider the ludicrous plight of the architect who places a house on the shifting sands, of the general who goes to war without thinking it worth while to estimate the possible resources of his enemy, of the man who makes himself the laughing-stock of the town by commencing to build a tower which he has no means to finish. These are delicious bits of our Lord's humor with a high moral purpose. Remember the pathetic humor of his response when the Pharisees warned him that Herod was on his track: 'Go ye, and tell that fox, Behold, I cast out devils, and I do cures to-day and to-morrow, and the third day I shall be perfected, ... for it can not be that a prophet perish out of Jerusalem.' Recall his quiet remarks, probably accompanied by a tremulous smile, when the disciples brought out two old swords with which to confront the world, 'It is enough!' Run through his parables, and observe how a rich vein of humor pervades nearly all of the more important ones. What further need is there of illustrations?—though the number of those not mentioned here is very considerable."

492. **The Effect of these Emotions on Jesus.** (1) As to his personal life a large measure of *joy* and *gladness* was poured out over his entire personality. The painters represent him as sad and melancholy, but on friend and foe he made the opposite impression. The latter called him a glutton and winebibber, a boon companion of sinners, i. e., a light-hearted man. These charges were slanders, but as slanders are usually based on, and simply exaggerate, a man's general habits, these very slanders show that he did not impress his contemporaries as morose. His friends tell us he attended a wedding and various social occasions, that he discouraged fasting, compared himself to a bridegroom, declared that the child is the pattern for a true disciple, compared his kingdom to a marriage feast, and bade them even to express their joy outwardly: "Rejoice and leap for joy." True, the sources do not record that he ever laughed, but this may be due to their brevity; moreover, they mention only twice that he wept because it was so exceptional. Also considered on general principles, Jesus' life must have been happy and cheerful, because he was active, loving, hopeful, godly. (2) In reference to his *great work* in the future, these emotions made Jesus hopeful and spread over the entire life of the Saviour the spirit of optimism; not that brainless feeling which is often called by this name, but that strong conviction that the good will finally triumph,

a feeling born of faith in God and belief in the possibilities of human nature. He saw the rocky element in Peter, he knew that publicans can repent, and that the crown follows the cross (John 12:32). "Be of good cheer, I have overcome the world," was one of his last words. He was "an incorrigible optimist." (Farewell addresses—"Gospel.") (3) In the *discharge of his duties,* these hopeful feelings surcharged everything with a glowing *enthusiasm,* which may be defined as the condition of one being possessed of God (Luke 2:41; Matt. 4:1). He was so wrapped up in his work that his friends considered him on the verge of nervous prostration and insanity and his enemies said he was possessed of a demon (Mark 3:21-31). This quality of optimism drew like-minded men to him.

IV.   The Will-Power of Jesus.

493.   **Outgoing Manifestations of Christ's Will-Power.** Modern psychology divides the manifestations of the will into two classes: 1. The *outgoing* manifestations, by which is meant the capacity of man to assert himself in life and to change the existing state of things. 2. The *inholding* manifestations, that is, the ability to subject one's self to divine and human laws and customs. Prominent among the outgoing manifestations of Christ's will are his self-assertion, courage, energy, self-limitation and indignation. 1. Christ's *self-assertion* expressed itself in words and actions, against friends and foes. (a) In His teaching: he firmly insisted on his deity and the attending prerogatives. He was little affected by the spirit of the times, because he was a universal genius. He opposed false traditions and standards. He was absolutely certain of what is the truth. He affirmed that God had a great plan and that he knew what it was. Though the political confusion of his times made it dangerous to speak of a "kingdom of God," he freely used that term, even before Pilate. (b) He cleansed the temple, raised Lazarus and entered Jerusalem as the Messiah. (c) Neither friend nor foe could bend or manipu-

late him. He overrode family influences, opposing his
mother at Cana and Capernaum (John 2:1; Matt. 12:46-
50), and his brethren (John 7:31). His will clashed with
that of the Baptist. He repulsed Peter when he tried to
dissuade him from going to Jerusalem, and with manly
firmness and prophetic clearness he approaches his passion.
That neither the prince of darkness nor his helpers could
frighten or bend Jesus needs no illustration. (d) Self-
assertion in itself is not a vice. All depends upon its motive. It was Christ's vocation to assert the truth, and
weakness here would have been wickedness. 2. Side by
side with firmness in Jesus' character goes undaunted *courage,* physical, moral and intellectual. (a) He faced the mob,
his traitor, the desecrators of the temple, the rulers. Notice his calmness in the tempest, before his judges and at
the crucifixion. (b) He remained firm when many left him
at the crisis in Capernaum, and dares to offend good society by disregarding conventionalities. He preached good
sermons to small audiences (Nicodemus, Samaritan woman). (c) He preached unpopular truths and traced them
out in all their consequences. 3. He was a man of intense
energy. The people agreed that he even surpassed the
Baptist, that great man of action (Matt. 14:2), and they
expressed the conviction that if he was not the Christ, the
real Christ could not surpass him (John 7:31). 4. But
hand in hand with this energy goes what we might call his
self-limitation, both in extent and scope. To know how far
to go also requires will power. His personal work, and also
that of his disciples during his lifetime was to be restricted
to the Jews only, and when he was asked to interfere in
questions of inheritance, taxation, etc., he refused. "In
der Beschraenkung zeigt sich der Meister" (Goethe). 5.
Another manly virtue in the Lord's character is his *indignation.* He repelled temptation (Mark 8:33); hypocrisy
roused him to a flame of judgment (Mark 3:5, 11, 15-17;
Matt. 23:1-36); treachery shook him to the centre of his
being (John 13:21); desecration of the temple angered

him; perversion of the true idea of death aroused him at the grave of Lazarus (John 11:38). He was indignant at the treatment the rulers accorded to the people. Indifference toward wrong is an unerring sign of moral deterioration and of a weak will. In Jesus, indignation never passed the limit, when it becomes sin; it was one manifestation of his love.

494. **The Inholding Manifestations of Christ's Will-Power.** These are seen in his patience and caution. 1. Patience is *self-restraint,* an active virtue, and may be defined as a calm waiting for something hoped for. He waited for many years till the Baptist arose. When urged to hurry on, he replies: "Are there not twelve hours in a day; my hour has not come" (see also John 7). Instead of setting Palestine on fire with a Messianic declaration, before the people were prepared, he says, "tell no man," and after the transfiguration he says: "keep still." The slowness of his disciples tried his patience, but he never lost it (Matt. 15:16; 16:5-12). How patiently did he treat Judas, warning him again and again of the lurking danger. The cursing of the fig tree was not a lack of patience, but an acted parable. He never lost his temper, or the ability to reply wisely, and was never disconcerted by interruptions. Notice his calm during his enemies' plotting, at his trial and on the cross. Socrates and the Stoics came nearest to him in this respect. 2. The Lord's courage never degenerated into foolhardiness. Jesus was *cautious* and circumspect. Several times he fled from danger, for eighteen months he stayed away from Jerusalem, after the rulers had taken official action to kill him (John 5:18). After the meeting of the Sanhedrin on the Hill of Evil Council he withdrew to Ephraim (John 11:47-54).

495. **The Unity of Christ's Character.** (1) The total impression ("der Gesammteindruck") of Christ's personality is, first, that his was a *perfectly harmonious* character. In him all virtues were finely balanced and the three manifestations of personality, intellect, feeling and will, were

perfectly correlated. He was love, but also truth; merciful, but just; firm, but not obstinate; strong, but gentle; tender, but not effeminate; courageous, but never rash. Ordinary men are in constant *danger of extremes.* From enthusiasm they run into fanaticism and intolerance, from firmness into harshness, from mildness into weakness. On account of the even balance of his faculties we cannot attribute to Jesus any one of the *four temperaments.* "He was neither sanguine, like Peter; nor choleric, like Paul; nor melancholic, like John; nor phlegmatic, like James. He combined the vivacity without the levity of the sanguine, the vigor without the violence of the choleric, the seriousness without the austerity of the melancholic, the calmness without the apathy of the phlegmatic temperament." (Schaff, Person of Christ.) (2) The gospels portray him, negatively, as a *sinless* and positively as a perfect man. This was his own conviction and the testimony of friends and foes: the Baptist, Peter, Judas, Pilate and his wife, the malefactor and centurion, the false witnesses (1 Peter 2:22; 2 Cor. 5:21; 1 John 3:5; Heb. 4:15; 7:26). He is intolerant of evil. He never prayed for, but bestows, pardon. More than this: it is moral *perfection,* absolute goodness that he possesses according to the gospel story. "One there is who is good." "None is good save one, even God" (Mk. 10:18), does not contradict this. Here Jesus refused the attribute, because the speaker regarded him as a mere man. Both these qualities constituted his *spiritualmindedness,* by which we mean the general bend of thought and motive toward divine things. He moves habitually in the realm of heavenly realities. Proofs of this are too abundant to be specified in detail. (3) Jesus was a *strong man* of commanding personality. As such he produced in others admiration (Luke 23:40, 47); astonishment (Matt. 7:28; Mark 7:37; 9:15); shame (Luke 13:7; John 8:9); confidence (Luke 18:37); fear and hatred (Luke 8:37; John 11:53). By his power of personality he drew the good and repulsed bad men. "Follow me," he said to the disciples, and they felt a strange fascination which drew them towards him. The paintings which make him appear subdued and effeminate are not true to the colors furnished by those who saw him every day. (4) As a result of all these perfections even the world has considered him a truly *great man* in the most comprehensive sense of the term. The better he was known the readier was his superiority acknowledged. Notice the testimonials by the Baptist, ("He is greater than I"), by his mother, brothers, Peter, the other disciples, popular opinion. In his enemies the growing respect expressed itself in growing hatred. Finally it must not be overlooked that Jesus was great in all things that pertain to perfect manliness, while others are often only great artists, great conquerors, great statesmen, but small men. In contrast with the jealousy, pettiness and malice of his friends and foes, Christ's greatness shines forth gloriously. "Behold the Man!"

496. **How to Account for Christ's Character.** How do the writers of the New Testament account for this unique personality? Simply by accepting Christ's own testimony concerning his superhuman and divine origin and character—his coequality and coeternity with the Father, as explained in the first chapters of Matthew, Luke and John, and in many other passages. On any other theory the appearance of absolutely perfect and sinless manhood makes a much larger draft on reason and faith than the Biblical accounts do.

497. **Reference Literature.** Barrows, Personality of Jesus, Ch. I; Jefferson, Character of Jesus; A. W. Hitchcock, The Psychology of Jesus; A. E. Garvie, Studies in the Inner Life of Jesus; Maclaren, The Mind of the Master; Schaff, The Person of Christ; Davis, D. B. on "Jesus"; also Hast. D. C. and others; Godet, Stud. in N. T. p. 84; Bushnell, Char. of Jesus; Speer, Personality of Christ; Farrar, Christ in Art; also Hast. D. C., I, 308; on dress, I, 498; looks of C. Hast., D. C. 2; Gestures, I, 645; Catacombs, in Sanford's Encl.; "Haar," and Veronica, see Herzog; Emerson, Uses of Great Men; Jewitt, W. H., "The Nativity in Art and Song";

Johnson, Franklin, "Have We the Likeness of Christ?" Bailey, H. T., "The Great Painter's Gospel"; Mental Char., in Hast. D. C., II, 161; Bernard, H. N., "The Mental Characteristics of Christ"; Swayne, W. S., "Our Lord's Knowledge as Man"; on his originality see Hast. D. C. II, 285; Pfleiderer, Origins, p. 31 and 83; Christ and Science, in Hast. D. C., II, 577; Hast. D. C., on "Man of Sorrows," II, 665; Obedience, II, 256; self-control, II, 546; sinlessness, II, 636; Ullman, Sinlessness of Jesus.

CHAPTER 51.

The Work of Jesus.

I. The Life-Plan of Jesus.

498. (1) Our Lord not only was good, but he did good. His motto was: "My Father worketh hitherto, and I work." (Jno. 5:17; 9:4.) (2) This fact raises the important question, *Did Jesus have a definite plan of work,* or was he the unconscious instrument working out God's purposes, without seeing the end from the beginning, like many great men (Paul, Luther). The gospels show plainly that the life of Jesus was but the gradual unfolding of a vast design, of which not only the Father was conscious, but also the Son. A strong and clear consciousness of his mission is expressed in Matt. 5:17; 9:13; 20:28; Mk. 1:17; 2:17; 8:45; Lu. 12:50; 19:10; Jno. 5:30; 6:38; 7:16; 8:18; 18:37.

499. **What was Christ's Plan?** (1) This may be inferred from his work. It was, negatively, expressed at his temptation when he rejected the plan of worldly and devilish wisdom, and, positively, by his constant declaration that he came to establish the Kingdom of God, or of heaven. That this was the keynote of Christ's teaching is clear from the fact that the first phrase occurs five times in Matt., fifteen times in Mk., thirty-three times in Lu.; twice in Jno., and seven times in Acts; and the latter expression is found one hundred and two times in Matt., but not in the other gospels. (2) The term has *various meanings* in the N. T.; but in most of the passages it denotes the reign of God in

302 *The Modern Student's Life of Christ.*

the heart of man, being made effective among men by the operation of the two great laws of love to God and men. The operation of this law in the soul of the individual is to work itself out in the gradual change of existing social and political conditions. (3) Hence, in one sense this kingdom has already come (Mk. 1:15; Lu. 10:9; 11:20; 16: 16; 17:21), namely, in Christ's person and in those who have begun practicing its principles. In another sense it is yet to come, extensively and intensively, i. e., more men must be brought under the benign rule of God's spirit, and those who profess to be subjects of this kingdom must be more thoroughly sanctified. (4) *At what period* of Christ's life did he become conscious of God's plan? Either when he became a "Son of the Law," a full member of the Jewish Church, or at his baptism through the voice from above, or at his temptation, or on Palm Sunday, when he decided to enter into Jerusalem as the Messianic king. (5) Did his plan undergo any *material change* during his lifetime? Some affirm it, but the details of the realization of his program show that the great end in view remained unchanged, while he adapted his method to the varying circumstances brought about by clearer revelations from the Father and by the exercise of man's personal freedom. (6) The *general outline* of his plan may be found in his life as described in the gospels. (7) What were the *means* by which Christ executed his great plan? By preaching, teaching, example, miracles and death. Thus he became the world's greatest prophet, eternal king and only High Priest.

II. Christ as a Preacher.

500. **A Preacher of Marked Ability.** (1) He spake as never man spake. He was preaching continuously: in the synagogues, the temple, the streets, the squares, the hillsides, and at the sea shore. (2) In his *audiences,* all classes were represented: Pharisees, politicians, doctors, common people. (3) The *magnet* which drew most of them was his doctrine and his method and spirit. (4) The *substance* of

his teaching was, "what man is to believe concerning God, and what duty God requires of men." In pregnant language he told Pilate that his life-work was to declare the truth (the reality of things). Christ knew that for all the ills of life, political, social and personal, there is but one remedy —Divine truth; and that all real reformation begins in the mind and soul of the individual. The centre of his teaching was Christ himself (against Harnack: "Jesus is not a part of his gospel"). The ethics of Jesus embrace individual, social, political and business morality. The predictive element is found in Matt. 25. Of scientific subjects he spoke in the language of the day, for it was not his province to reveal the principles of science, for which work God has given man the light of reason. (5) The *chief subjects* of his preaching were the kingdom of God, the nature of God, Christ's own personality and work, the condition of salvation, man's eternal destiny. (6) We have only a *few fragments* of his three years' teaching. His recorded words number about 38,422, or the equivalent of ten short sermons. (7) *The source* of Christ's preaching was neither Buddhism nor Phariseeism, nor Rabbinism (Jno. 7: 15), nor Essenism, but the O. T. on which he had a firm and unique grasp, and the manifestation and unfolding of his Divine mind. (8) The *aim* of his preaching was to give right conceptions, to move to right actions, to change dispositions, to reveal new truth which unaided human reason could not reach, to thrill souls by a Divine impulse.

501. **Christ's Qualification as a Preacher.** (1) His preaching gifts were of the highest order. He had knowledge of his *subject;* he knew the truth, the Father, the Scriptures, he also knew his hearers (Pharisees, Peter, Judas, Thomas), and could therefore adapt his teaching to their needs. (2) The general *characteristics* of his preaching were authority, plainness, directness, earnestness, compassion, love and tact. (3) Jesus considered also the *form of preaching* of importance. His sayings present illustrious examples of most of the means known to rhetoric by which

speech is made effective. And even to-day Christ's sermons owe their attractiveness, in no small degree, to their exquisite form. No preacher ever made a profound impression on the average mind who has not studied the form in which to put his thoughts. (4) His rhetoric consisted in (a) plain didactic teaching; (b) a wealth of illustrations, because they attract attention, quickens apprehension and aids memory; (c) the question; John alone records 157 questions of moment: 51 asked by Jesus, 45 asked of him and 62 provoked by him, many of the latter being interruptions. The question method tests the hearer's knowledge, arouses his attention and awakens his thought; (d) reiteration (Jno. 3); (e) the use of Scripture for explanation and confirmation; (f) sententious sayings, often arranged in the parallelism of Hebrew poetry—crisp, pointed, easily remembered and hence effective (Matt. 23:12; Mk. 2:17; 4:22; Lu. 13:30; Jno. 4:24).

502. **Christ's Parables.** (1) A very effective method of the Lord's preaching was his use of parables (paraballo to throw side by side, that is an incident and a spiritual truth, for the purpose of comparison). (2) There are *two classes*—(a) parabolic sayings, figurative forms, involving mental but not expressed comparisons. (Mk. 2:17, 21; Matt. 7:16; Jno. 3:8; 13:16.) (b) developed parables, comparisons drawn from real life. (3) The *number* of parables recorded depends on the range given to the term. Trench reckons 30, others as high as 50. All are in the Synoptists, none in John. (4) They may be divided into *three groups*—(a) drawn from nature and having for their subject the laws of the kingdom of God—the eight in Mt. 13 and Mk. 4; (b) after an interval of several months we find 16 parables drawn from the life of men—Two Debtors (Lu. 7); Merciless Servant (Mt. 18); Good Samaritan (Lu. 10); Friend at Midnight (Lu. 11); Rich Fool (Lu. 12); Wedding Feast (Lu. 12); Fig Tree (Lu. 13); Great Supper (Lu. 14); the three of the Lost Found (Lu. 15); Unjust Steward (Lu. 16); Rich Man and Lazarus {Lu.

26) ; Unjust Judge (Lu. 18) ; Pharisee and Publican (Lu. 18) ; Laborer in the Vineyard (Mt. 20).—(c) The last group contains seven which were spoken toward the end of Christ's ministry. They have for their general subject the final consummation of the kingdom—The Pounds (Minae) (Lu. 19) ; Two Sons (Matt. 21) ; Wicked Husbandmen (Matt. 21) ; Marriage Feast (Matt. 22) ; Ten Virgins (Matt. 25) ; Talents (Matt. 25) ; Sheep and the Goats (Matt. 25). (5) The *law for interpreting* parables : (a) do not press the parable and deduce from it meanings not intended, and (b) do not empty it of its evidently intended meaning. Find the intended point, the real purpose of the parable, and regard all other features as drapery and coloring. The standard by which all interpretations must be measured is the direct teaching of Christ in plain language. (6) The parabolic teaching is not *original* with Jesus. Hillel, Schamai and other rabbis used parables to convey to their pupils the treasures of wisdom of which the people were ignorant. Yet his are the choicest specimens in the world's literature. At the beginning of Christ's ministry, he used the direct method of teaching. When this was met with scorn and unbelief, he adopted the Rabbinical method. When his disciples expressed astonishment the Lord assigns two reasons for his use of parables : (a) they withdraw the light from them who love darkness, as a punishment (Matt. 13:13) ; (b) they protect the truth which they enshrine from the mockery of the scoffer, but reveal it to the thoughtful.

III. Christ as a Teacher.

503. (1) As a preacher Christ addressed the multitude, but as a teacher he concentrated his attention on the Twelve. The greatest intellects have devoted their best powers to a few (Socrates, Plato, Aristotle, Hillel, Philo). (2) While his work as a preacher was more fascinating, Christ devoted most of his time to the training of the Twelve, especially during his last year. (3) In most respects Christ's *methods*

of teaching the Twelve were similar to those which he pursued with the multitude. The distinctive features were the permission to ask questions (he even provoked them to do so, like Socrates) and his endeavor to teach them the deeper principles of the truth. (4) His *chief aim* was to train men to become his accredited successors.

IV. Christ as a Controversialist.

504. (1) A very large part of Christ's recorded sayings are controversies. Religious controversies are unpleasant but often necessary. Because Christ knew the truth, he was prompted to combat error. (2) His *method* was an appeal to Scripture, to his own consciousness, and to common sense and reason (e. g. the Tribute Money). (3) Especially towards the *end of his life,* Jesus poured on the rulers a torrent of scorn never equalled in its withering annihilating vehemence (Matt. 23). (See Stalker, Jesus as a Controversialist, ch. 15 in his "Imago Christi.")

V. Christ Our Example.

505. Jesus was not a mere theorizing Socrates or Seneca, but interwoven with his teaching was his conduct, the influence of his holy personality, his ordinary good deeds, and his great miracles. The Lord's mere presence had a sanctifying influence upon the people, which is true of all good people. It is helpful to study his dealings with various classes of men: (1) *those outside of the kingdom;* (a) the openly lost (publicans, Samaritans, the great sinner, the adulteress, the malefactor); (b) the self-righteous; (c) the cavillers who watch and tempt him; (d) those that remained impenitent (Jerusalem, Bethsaida); (2) *those on the border of the kingdom* (the 5,000; 4,000; blind men at Jericho, Zachaeus, Nicodemus); (3) *those inside the* kingdom (the Baptist, the Twelve, Peter, Thomas).

506. Also in the *various relations* of life Jesus set us an example by his conduct. (1) He honored the family, and therefore severely denounced the Pharisees for allowing

divorces on frivolous grounds, and for teaching the children
to break the fifth commandment by their shameful "corban"
scheme. He often relieved domestic trouble (Cana, Nain,
Lazarus) (2) He respected the *Church,* though it was by
no means ideal. He attended the services regularly, observed its institutions, partook of its sacraments, but also
tried to reform its abuses. (3) He *enjoyed society,* attended feasts, noticed the courtesies of life when shown
him (Mary) and when neglected (Simon the Pharisee).
He was himself an entertainer, feeding 5,000, and 4,000, and
presiding at the paschal meal. (4) He had the *habit of
prayer.* He went to quiet places, at quiet hours; often he
takes disciples with him; he prayed before important
events, and after them (Matt. 14:23); he died praying.
(5) Jesus was an assiduous *Bible student.* While he did
not own a Bible owing to the great expense for a man of
our Lord's poverty, yet he found means to study the
word, as his sayings show. He knew all parts of it, as his
quotations prove; though he had his favorites (e. g. Deut.,
Psalms, Isa.). He memorized much of the O. T., and this
enabled him to use it more effectively for defence (Matt.
4 and 22), for inspiration, for guidance in his work. (6)
He was *industrious,* almost strenuous, as a worker, considering that he was an Oriental. The Jews expected a Prince,
but God decreed that the Messiah should be a workingman
—a "tecton" (a house-builder, not a carpenter). He knew,
also, how to *rest.* He often withdrew to calm his soul and
urged his disciples after their strenuous missionary tour
to "rest a while." He made good use of the Sabbaths. (7)
Jesus *suffered* the pain of anticipating coming evil (Gethsemane), and his sensitive mind felt the deep shame of being
mocked, spit in the face and of having a Barabbas preferred
to himself. He was surely cast down when the charge of
blasphemy and high treason was made against him. In all
this Jesus acquired the art of the comforter. (8) The Lord
was also a *philanthropist.* He gave alms, and almost all his
miracles were works of mercy. What a shining example is
our Lord!

VI. The Miracles of Christ.

507. Most conspicuous among the works of Christ are
his miracles. (1) *Definition.* A miracle is a personal inter-
vention of God in the chain of cause and effect. It is not
the breaking of the laws of nature from without, but the
working out in nature of higher and permanent laws of reason and the moral order. Hume, the English Deist, says:
"A miracle is no contradiction of the laws of cause and
effect; it is a new effect supposed to be produced by the
introduction of a new cause." (2) *Names:* works (Greek,
erga), in the special sense of the word, i. e., immediate acts
of God; signs (semeia), because they indicate the real character of Jesus; wonders (terata), because they inspired men
with amazement; wonderful things (thaumasia); mighty
works (dynameis), because divine powers were displayed
in them. (3) *Number.* About 36, of which only eight are
not miracles of healing. (4) *Classification:*   Miracles
wrought upon nature, and those on men. (a) The nature-
miracles were few (about 9), and are peculiar to Jesus,
proving him to be more than a divine messenger in a dele-
gated sense. They are as follows: Change of Water into
Wine, Draught of Fishes (Lu. 4), Tempest, Feeding of the
5,000, Walking on the Water, Feeding of the 4,000, Coin in
Fish's Mouth, Withering of Fig Tree, Draught of Fishes
(Jno. 21). (b) The *healing miracles* indicate that Jesus
came to redeem. But they are more than symbols of redemption, they are in themselves part of his redemptive
work. (c) Another classification divides them into miracles
of healing; of mercy (Wine, Tempest, Feedings), and of
instruction (Withered Fig Tree, Draught of Fishes). (d)
A third classification is: Miracles of nature, of healing, of
casting out demons, of raising the dead. (5) *Distribution*
in the several gospels. (a) Eleven are recorded in all
Synoptists, including at least one specimen of each of the
first-named classes. The rest are peculiar to one or more of
the Synoptists. (b) John records fewer miracles. The

Feeding of the 5,000 he has in common with the Synoptists; while those of Changing Water into Wine, the Healing of the Nobleman's Son, the Infirm Man, the Man Born Blind, the Raising of Lazarus, the Draught of Fishes, are peculiar to him. He introduces most of them for didactic purposes, as they are generally followed by discourses. (6) *Purpose:* to relieve suffering, to furnish evidence of Christ's Deity (especially the nature miracles), to produce credentials of his mission (demand of "signs"), to seal the truth of his revelation. (7) *Tests.* The rabbis distinguished true from false miracles by six chief tests: the object must be worthy of the Divine author, (excludes those silly miracles of the apocryphal gospels); the performance must be public and submitted to the senses for judgment (excludes sorcery, etc.); the mode of working must be independent of second causes (excludes God's providential dealings); they must be attested by contemporaneous evidence; they must be recorded in some permanent form.

508. **Defense of Christ's Miracles.** (1) Their *possibility:* "Given the person of Jesus and it is more natural that he should than that he should not work miracles." (Fairbairn). (2) *Credibility.* The modern scientific conception of the universe has made the appeal to miracles rather a hindrance than a help to faith. But this is rapidly changing, and the "ages of true faith" are yet to come. Modern conceptions of the order of nature, of human personality and of the Divine Being are becoming decidedly friendly toward the Biblical world-view. (a) A clear distinction is insisted on between the unity and the uniformity of nature. The miracles are not regarded as an interruption of the order of nature, but as a revelation of the infinite extent of that order. Ancient and modern philosophy has always sought in the universe an ultimate unity. Recent discoveries in physical science suggest that matter and force in their infinite forms are merely different manifestations of one single force. The Bible teaches that the universe is a manifestation of that Living Will from which all things

proceed (Gen. 1), and in which we live and move and have our being (Acts 17:28). If then all events proceed from one central intelligent force, miracles are not violations of natural laws, but merely unusual manifestations of that Divine will. Unprejudiced scientists are becoming more and more averse to the dogmatizing about the impossibility and incredibility of the miracles of Jesus. (b) Modern psychology is showing that beneath and above the ordinary consciousness and powers of men are larger powers at present uncontrolled but manifested in exceptional phases of human life, such as dreams, hypnosis, clairvoyance, clairaudience, somnambulism. If ordinary men can perform wonderful feats, what then may be expected from the perfect personality of a God-man! (c) While firmly retaining the belief in the personality and transcendence of God, the thinkers of the day conceive of him more and more as Infinite Will and Intelligence that animates the whole creation, ever seeking self-realization and self-revelation in his creation. This makes it believable that this Divine power dwelt in its fulness in Jesus and expressed itself in the miracles (Condensed from Hastings D. of C. II, 186). (3) The *reality* of miracles may be proved (a) from the trustworthiness and intelligence of the eye-witnesses. (b) The evidential value of the miraculous element is not as strong to-day as formerly. Once men believed in Christ because they believed in miracles. Now they believe in miracles because they believe in Christ. They find miracles the natural expression of an extraordinary person. (c) To-day the most convincing proof for Christ and his miracles is the great and beneficial influence of Jesus on the world. (See Ch. 53.)

VII. Christ Casting out Demons.

509. This class of miracles deserves detailed statement. (1) *Record of the N. T.* Connected with the ministry of Jesus there are recorded ten references to cases of demoniac possession; six are described in detail (Mark 1:23;

5:2; 7:25; 9:25; Matt. 9:32; 12:22); in one case the name is given—Mary Magdalene (Lu. 8:2), and three general references (Mark 1:34; 1:39, and 3:11). It is also recorded that the Twelve cast out many demons (Mark 6:13), and of the seventy it is reported that the demons had been subject to them (Luke 10:17). Mark 9:38 speaks of an unknown man whom the disciples found casting out demons. (2) *The terms used* for the evil power which was said to possess the man are: demon (Mark 1:34; Matt. 8:31); spirit (Mark 9:20); unclean spirit (Mark 1:23), and evil spirit (Luke 7:21). A man is never said to have the devil or a devil or Satan. Also Jesus is charged with having a demon (Jno. 7:20; 8:48; 8:52; and 10:20).

510. **Gospel Demonology.** This may be briefly summed up thus: (1) Demons are under a head, Satan; they form a kingdom. (2) They are incorporeal, and generally, though not necessarily, invisible. (3) They inhabit certain places which they prefer to others. (4) They tend to live in groups. (5) They have names, and are sometimes identified with their victims, at other times differentiated from them. (6) They are the cause of mental and physical disease to men, women, and children. (7) They can pass in and out of men, and even animals. (8) More than one can take possession of a man at the same time. (9) Christ made it one of his chief aims to overthrow this kingdom, and set up his own in its place. (10) He cast out demons through his own name, or by his word. (11) He could delegate this power, which was regarded as something new. (12) He never treats the possessed as wilful sinners, which is in strong contrast to his words to the scribes and Pharisees, yet they may have belonged to the world rather than to God. (13) Only on the rarest occasions does he come into direct contact with the possessed. (14) At his second coming the members of this kingdom are to be condemned to eternal fire (Hastings: Dict. of Christ, vol. I, p. 442). (15) It was characteristic of the demoniacs that they recog-

nized Jesus as a divine being and supreme power. They call him "The Holy One of God" (Mark 1:24), "The Son of God" (Mark 3:11), "The Son of the Most High God" (Mark 5:7). They ask whether he had come to torment or destroy them, thus recognizing his supreme power (Mark 1:24; 5:7). Weiss says: "The recognition of Jesus by the possessed is explicable only on the supposition that the possessed ones were really under the influence of a superhuman spiritual power, which was conscious not only of its absolute opposition to the Holy One of God, but also of his supremacy over the kingdom of evil which Christ had come to destroy." For, surely disease and sin do not clarify the vision for the recognition of the divine and give a clearer insight into the character of Jesus than the disciples had.

511. **Interpretation of the Phenomena:** Arguments against the reality of demoniacal possession (1) all the New Testament cases were due to natural causes; (2) the New Testament writers shared the common belief of their age; (3) this belief, like that in witchcraft, disappears before the growth of better knowledge; (4) the symptoms mentioned in the New Testament can be paralleled in the insanity and epilepsy of the present day; (5) insanity constantly tends to take forms suggested by popular beliefs; and (6) either Jesus shared the superstition of his time, or as to-day skilful physicians for the insane, humor their fancies, so Christ by addressing these unfortunates from their point of view adopted the most effective way of stimulating their faith in his own power to heal.

Arguments in favor of their reality: (1) The words and deeds of Christ in connection with miracles of this class clearly imply the real existence of the demons whom he claimed to cast out; in many cases, indeed, they would otherwise be meaningless (see Mk. 3:23-27; 5:8-13); (2) an actual demoniacal possession in these instances cannot be denied without assuming that Christ either shared the ignorance of his time or accommodated himself to it, either of which supposition is held to be inconsistent with his divine character. If Jesus knew better, why did he not tell the disciples the truth in private. (3) The words of the demoniacs indicate a knowledge of Jesus as the Son of God, and a moral recoil from him, that cannot be explained on the theory of mere disease; (4) the Gospels clearly distinguish between diseases which were demoniacal and those which were not, showing that the writers did not blindly attribute all kinds of evil to demons (Matt. 4:23, 24; Mk. 1:34, etc.). (5) It is no more difficult to understand how an evil spirit can enter into a man and control him than to understand how the Holy Spirit can enter into a man, though both are not exactly the same. (6) It is probable that some extraordinary manifestation of Satan should accompany the extraordinary manifestation of God in Christ. Jesus came to destroy the works of Satan and it was natural that Satan should make special efforts to counteract the influence of Jesus. (7) To ignore the difference between Gospel demonology and popular superstition in spite of similarity, is most unscientific. There is the contrast between folly and seriousness; the Gospel demonology is in close connection with the subject of sin. The Gospels ascribe the cause to sin, and we to "natural causes." But may not the principle of evil be the deeper cause and explain both theories. Much that was formerly ascribed to the first cause (good or evil) is now ascribed to second causes, the forces in nature. No one may positively and safely assert what even now is, or is not, the connection of supernatural beings with those mental and physical diseases, whose seat is in moral obliquity of will (Robinson, Christian Theology, p. 115). (8) Modern psychology has revealed to us how extremely little we know "of secondary personality," the "subliminal self," "change of control," etc.—in a word, how hidden still are the secrets of the region of the supersensuous, and how careful science should be in dogmatizing (Hastings D. of C. II, p. 443).

For these reasons, many of recent interpreters feel constrained to admit the reality of demoniac possession in

the time of Christ, although denying that such possessions
in that age necessarily involves the reality of similar possessions in other ages. Yet from missionaries in China and
other lands it is learned that diseases closely resembling
the cases of possession recorded in the New Testament are
frequently met with, and are often cured by native Christian ministers. And Dr. Strong (Syst. Theol. p. 229) writes:
The network of influences which support the papacy, spir-
itualism, modern unbelief, is difficult of explanation, unless
we believe in a superhuman intelligence which organizes
these forces against God. In these, as well as in heathen
religions, there are facts inexplicable upon merely natural
principles of disease or delusion.

VIII. Jesus Our King.

512. A description of Christ's work without mentioning
his Kingship would be incomplete. But the truth that Jesus
is King has been so plainly and extensively emphasized in
the preceding pages that a brief reference on this great subject will suffice. The Messiah was to be a king, and the
Lord claimed the royal title and function, even before Pilate. The superscription over his cross was prophetic. His
miracles prove his kingly power; in his teaching he re-
peals worn out laws, interprets old laws and enacts new
ones. As a reformer, he cleansed the temple. Modern
Christians cannot emphasize too much the Kingship of
Jesus. The welfare of our nation depends on our submission to his rule. The laws of Christ, little by little, must be
made the laws of business and politics and pleasure; of
the city, the state, the nation, the world.

IX. The Death of Christ.

513. The death of Jesus is viewed in the New Testament as the culmination of his redemptive *work*. He is
active in it. He laid down his life by an act of his own
will, and on Easter he took it again. For these reasons,
some hold that Christ's death was not due to any physical

cause, but was a voluntary act. Hence Christ on the cross was not a mere martyr suffering what others had inflicted on him, but he was paying, as he himself said, a ransom, the price due for the release of mankind from bondage, and to alter the relation of God to sinners. He did not make God love men, for this God had always done, but the ransom removed an obstacle to the free outflow of the Divine love. With the fragments of the paschal lamb before him, he speaks of his death as a substitute for others. In Jno. 12: 24 he speaks of the motive that actuated him, and the result he will gain by his death. One entire book, the epistle to the Hebrews has been written to exalt the death of Jesus as his greatest redemptive act. The Lord's death belongs therefore to his works.

514. **Reference Literature.** On the Plan of Jesus: Liddon, Divinity of our L. p. 100; Newman, Church H. I., 72; Zoeckler, Theol. Wissenschaften, I, 497; Lange, Life of C., I, 364; Neander, p. 73; Edersheim, I, 291; Ullman, Sinlessness of C., p. 264; Dawson, L. of C. p. 70; Speer, The Man Christ Jesus, p. 28; Bishop, Jes. the Worker, p. 225; Schmid, Theol. Classiker, Vol. 42, p. 84; Stalker, L. of C. p. 25; Barth, Hauptprobleme, p. 32; Hast. D. of C. on Plan, II, 369; on offices of C., II, 263; Mission of C., II, 191; Godet, Work of C. (in N. T. Studies).

Christ as a Teacher. Burrell, Wonderful Teacher; Dalman, Worte Jesu; Briggs, Eth., Teaching of Jesus; Mathews, Soc. Teaching of J.; Spurgeon, Pred. ueber die Gleichnisse; Wendt, Teach. of J.; Gilbert, Revel. of J.; Trumbull, on Jewish Teaching in his Yale Lect. on S. Sch.; J. the Supreme Tea. in Maclaren's Mind of the Master; Smith, N. T. Hist. on Parab. p. 283; origin of parables in Juelisher, Gleichnisse, p. 149; Stoecker, Leben Jes; Hast. D. of C. on Parables, II, 312; O. T. Quotat., II, 464; Teach. of Jes., II, 699; Popularity II, 381; Jes. and Hillel, Excur. III, in Farrar's Life of C.; N. T. Theol. by Sheldon, Oosterzee, Stevens, Beyschlag, Weidner, Weiss, Gould; Charles, Jes. Eschatol; Heuver, Teach. of Jes. Concerning Wealth; Newman, Ch. Hist. I, 74; Paromia, Hist. D. C., II, 521; on Phar. quibbles as to the Sabbath, see Dawson, Life of C., p. 75; Hitchcock, Psych. of J. on the World View of Jesus; Feine, Theol. des N. T.

Jesus Our Example. Stalker, Imago Christi; Clarke, Ideal of Jes.; Blakie, Publ. Min. p. 256; Hast. D. of C., on example I, 155;

on Ideal, I, 767; on C. Ministry, II, 184; on Jes. C. Davis, D. B. p. 364; Walker, Jes. and His Surroundings.

On the Miracles. Bruce, Mir. Element in the Gos. Steinmeyer, Mir. of our Lord; W. M. Taylor, Mir. of J.; Modern Negat. of Mir. in Christlieb, Mod. Doubt, p. 285; Barth, Hauptprobleme, p. 106; Beth. Das Wunder; Spurg. Pred. ueber die Wunder; Trench, Notes on the Mir.; Jefferson, in "Things Fundamental," p. 191; Smith, N. T. Hist., p. 211; Davis, D. B., p. 481; Herzog, Realencycl. Hast. D. C., II, 186, on Accommodation, I, 15; and Sanford's Encl.; Hast. D. B., II, 624; III,, 379.

On the Demons. Alexander, Demoniac Poss.; Nevin's Dem. Poss. and Allied Themes; Encyc. Brit.; Hast. D. C., I, 438; and Sanford, Encyc.

On Christ's Death. Mabie, Divine Reason of the Cross; Stevens, Doctr. of Salv. p. 53; Med. Work of C., in Chas. Hodge, Syst. Theol., II, 455; Denney, Death of C.; Crawford, Atonement; A. A. Hodge, Atonement; Bushnell, Vicarious Sacrif.; Steinmeyer, Passion of C.; Hast. D. of C., II, 793; and On Atonement, I, 132; Physical Cause of Christ's Death by Dr. Stroudt (in Hanna, Last Days, p. 323); Bibl. Ideas of Atonement, by Burton and Smith.

CHAPTER 52.

Chief Problems in the Life of Christ.

515. The scientific study of the life, the character and the work of Christ has given rise to a number of problems, that is, to questions proposed for solution (pro-ballo, to throw before). Some of them are of minor importance, as, for example, the chronology of the life of Christ, his true relation to the men called his "brethren," the right place of certain events in his life, etc. But there are three problems which involve the very essence of Christianity and of which a text-book of this character should therefore take cognizance. These are the problems of the incarnation, of Christ's self-consciousness, and of his resurrection.

I. The Incarnation of Christ.

516. Its true meaning. (a) It does not mean that an entirely new being, which had not existed before, was

created nineteen hundred years ago, a person of which the Holy Spirit was the father and Mary the mother. It does mean that a divine person who had existed from all eternity, assumed a human body and a reasonable soul. "The Word became flesh," Jno. 1:14 (Latin: in-caro, enters into the flesh). The first supposition could be called a true incarnation, but Christ's incarnation is not thus taught in the New Testament. (b) It does not mean that Jesus was born like any other man of the union of Joseph and Mary, but with such unusually large capacity for divine things that he developed into a marvel of history, soaring far above every other man ever born. Those who hold to this view never tire of speaking of Christ's general "divinity," but they deny his essential Deity. (c) It does not mean a generic or universal or ideal incarnation as over against personal, individual incarnation. The advocates of this theory say, God is in the world and comes to consciousness and expression in every great moral character who has helped to develop the idea of human perfection and introduced new powers. Jesus was one of the greatest. It does mean that Christ was conceived of the very essence of God, "very God of very God." (Nicene Creed.)

517. **Mode of the Incarnation.** (1) There are two passages, Matt. 1:18-25 and Lk. 1:26-37, which are very explicit and clear as to its mode (see Ch. 11). The announcement to Mary was necessary to relieve her of any perplexity when her physical condition appeared, and that to Joseph, in order to confirm the astounding account given him by Mary. (2) The other New Testament writers assume these narratives. John says, "The word became flesh," and Paul in Phil. 2:6 teaches Christ's pre-existence, in Gal. 4:4, his human birth, and in 1 Cor. 15:47 he means to say that as God was in a special manner active in the birth of the first Adam, so also in that of the second. (3) Because Paul does not explicitly repeat the narrative of the supernatural conception it has been argued that he did not know anything about it, and that consequently, it was not a part

of the faith of primitive Christianity; or, he did know of it, but did not accept it, and therefore did not teach it. Answer: It it a rule of the law of argumentation that the argument from silence must not be pressed too far. This is essentially true in Paul's case because (a) his epistles are silent on almost all the facts of Christ's life, as he assumed their knowledge from the constant oral teaching; (b) we have after all very little literature from Paul; (c) the evangelist who stood nearest to Paul, Luke, contains the fullest account of the mode of Christ's incarnation. (4) This method of the incarnation was essential (a) because the Saviour of mankind was to be the embodiment of God's eternal nature, while the ordinary process of generation is the beginning of a new personality, (b) because only a real incarnation guarantees the sinless perfection of Christ. Gabriel brings these two ideas into their logical relation by saying: "The Holy Ghost shall come upon thee—*therefore* also that which is to be born shall be called holy." What is born of the flesh is flesh. Anyone born into the full solidarity of the human race shares the taint of sin; (c) only a physical incarnation makes the moral miracle of a sinless man on earth believable; (d) Christ was destined to mark a new departure in human life and history—he was the new Adam giving a new starting point; (e) this mode of the incarnation makes faith in the real Deity of Christ easier, because it makes the two natures in Christ's personality plainer than the idea of the deification of a mere man; (f) how, when, where and in what sense the divine element was joined with the human is as yet a mystery.

518. **Purpose of the Incarnation.** On this there are two views both appealing to the Scripture for confirmation: (a) it was necessary to secure a complete communion with God. The incarnation was no afterthought, conditioned by man's fall. Man could not have realized the full possibilities of his nature, and no development could have brought a true knowledge of God without God coming personally among us, for not only man's sinfulness, but also his lim-

itations stand in his way, (b) it was necessary for the redemption of the human race. When man fell the incarnation became inevitable. The first view is speculative and based on inferences, while the latter view is clearly expressed in the Bible (Jno. 3: 16).

519. **Objections to the Incarnation Answered.** (1) The New Testament reports embody a myth, i. e. in a poetical form they express the great truth that the divine has come in closest contact with man (Strauss and many others). Answer: (a) Myths take a long time to form, while our documents are very near as to date to the fact recorded. (b) No such myth could have originated among the Jews, because the very idea of a supernatural conception is entirely foreign to the prevailing Jewish modes of thought. Wherefore the Jewish-Christian sect, the Ebionites, went so far even as to omit the section which contained the record from the Ebionitish copy of the Gospel to the Hebrews. Obj. (2): The birth story of Jesus has arisen like similar stories of the birth of heroes, such as those of Buddha and Zoroaster. Answer: (a) it is asserted by some that the stories about Buddha and Zoroaster are post-Christian imitations, (b) at any rate the pagan myths of Divine incarnations are not the source of the New Testament record, but a providential though unconscious preparation for the real incarnation, a prophetic instinct molding the forms of thought in which it was to find expression. Obj. (3): If such events had really preceded the birth of Christ, his own relatives would have been better disposed to recognize him as the Messiah. *Answer.* It is very probable that these facts were kept from his relatives. This, together with the thirty years of obscure life in Nazareth, in which Jesus made no claims to be the Messiah, was sufficient to account for his brothers' unbelief. As for Mary, she never lost the memory of her experiences, and at the marriage in Cana she confidently expected a miracle immediately after the proclamation of her son's Messiahship by John the Baptist. Obj. (4); Jesus is repeatedly called the "Son of Joseph." *An-*

swer. (1) Reserve kept Mary from making public the details of her son's birth during his life on earth. Jesus also kept silence as it would have invited calumny, which it did later, as seen in the Talmud. Hence even the apostles may not have known the facts until later. The obvious meaning is that Joseph was Jesus' foster father. The same Gospel which speaks of his miraculous conception, calls Joseph Christ's reputed father (Lu. 3:23). Obj. (5): These stories are the outgrowth of the belief in Christ's Deity and a conclusion drawn from the doctrine of the sinlessness of Jesus. Answer: Both Paul and John teach emphatically the sinlessness of Jesus, and yet are silent on this mode of the incarnation. This proves that the primitive church did not believe in the miraculous conception simply because it considered it an absolute condition to the belief in a divine and sinless being, but because the doctrine was true. Obj. (6). Science maintains that conception without a human father is a physiological impossibility. *Answer.* This is one of the assertions based on the belief in the infallibility and omniscience of "science." Huxley, in his famous letter on parthenogenesis, and Prof. Romanes, both liberals, concede the possibility of a virgin birth on scientific grounds.

II.　The Self-Consciousness of Christ.

The problem is, whom did Jesus consider himself to be? Our sources answer clearly and distinctly: he was conscious of being (a) the Messiah, (b) the Son of Man, (c) the Son of God.

520.　**Jesus the Messiah.** (1) This was the official title by which the Jews designated the promised deliverer. The name means "the Anointed," and was applied to the "coming one" (Matt. 11:2) because he was believed to be a great king, and as the king was anointed with oil, so the Messiah would be anointed by the Spirit. Jesus declared himself to be the Messiah, to the Samaritan woman (Jno. 4:25, 26); at Nazareth (Lu. 4:8); in his answer to the Baptist (Matt. 11:5); to the rulers (Jno. 10:24, 25); at Cesarea

Philippi (Matt. 16), on Palm Sunday (Matt. 21), before the Jewish and Roman courts (Matt. 26:64; Jno. 18:37). The Lord's self-designation, "Son of Man" is also an allusion to his Messiahship. (2) He openly or tacitly accepted the title when suggested by others (Lu. 19), and whenever he was tentatively or directly addressed as "Son of David," which was one of the Messianic titles. (3) The Greek translation of Messiah, "Christ," is therefore the name which, with the exception of his birth-name, "Jesus" (Saviour), has clung most firmly in the memory of the world. (4) It was originally a title, "the Christ," but already in the N. T. it became a proper name without the article.

521. **The Son of Man.** (1) But Messiah being a title of office, the next question arises, what did Jesus think concerning his real nature? This is shown by his self-designations: Son of Man and Son of God or merely, the Son. (2) The phrase "Son of Man" was never applied to Jesus by the evangelists or other persons, but is the Lord's favorite self-designation (Matt. 8:20; 11:19; Mk. 13:26; Lu. 5:24). (3) It occurs in Matt. 32 times, in Mk. 15, in Luke 25, in John 12 times. (4) *Origin:* Jesus did not invent the term but took it from Dan. 7:13. It is used in the O. T. (a) to express in poetical form a person's connection with humanity and simply means, "a man"; (b) to contrast human weakness and dependence with divine independence and power (Ps. 8:4; Ezek. 2:1; 3:1). (5) Why did Jesus choose it as his favorite from many other names offered in the O. T.? (a) It intimated his pre-existence since the figure in Daniel was in fellowship with the Ancient of days before descending to earth; (b) as it became gradually a designation for the Messiah (Book of Enoch, 37-71), it suited his purpose of concealing his Messianic claims, while it expressed them to himself and hinted at them to others. (c) But while it implies his humanity, it implies also his consciousness of a unique, a representative relation to the entire human race. In him the race, alike in its actual lowliness and weakness and in

its sublime dignity and destiny, finds its supreme manifestation "He was the ideal man who made real the ideal of humanity." (Neander.)

522. Christ the Son of God. (1) This is a designation of Jesus used more frequently by others than by himself, and oftener in the fourth gospel than in the synoptics. (2) Jesus did not invent the phrase but either received it from the Father at his baptism and transfiguration, or adopted it from the Old Testament where it occurs frequently. (3) It has a wide range of application in both Testaments. In the Old Testament the phrase was variously applied to angels (Job 1:6), to men (Ps. 82:6; Hos. 1:10), and to Israel (Ex. 4:22; Jer. 31:9). The theocratic king as representing the Messianic idea (see "Messiah") was also called the "Son" of God (Ps. 2:7). In all these cases those upon whom the title was bestowed were regarded as in some degree representatives of the majesty and authority of Jehovah. In this sense the term "Son of God" came into common use before our Lord's time as an equivalent for "Messiah" or "Christ," he being looked upon as the supreme representative of God. (4) Four times Jesus explicitly proclaims himself the "Son of God"; to the man born blind (John 9:37), to the Jews at the feast of the dedication (John 10:37), and at the night and morning trials before the Sanhedrin he did so under oath. (5) He called himself "the Son," especially in the famous passage Matthew 11:25-27, and in many other places, as John 5:25; 10:36; 11:4. (6) *Jesus accepted* the title "Son of God" when applied to him by others; twice by Peter who called him "the Christ, the Son of God" (John 6:69, and Matt. 16:16); by Nathaniel, by the apostles and Martha (John 1:49; Matthew 14:33; John 11:37; even by demons (Matt. 8:29; Mark 3:11). Jesus is addressed "Son" by the Father at his baptism and transfiguration. (7) Jesus indirectly claims Sonship by calling God "Father," in Matthew and its parallels twenty-one times and more than one hundred times in John. In Lu. 23:46 Jesus quotes from the O. T., but adds very significantly the address, "Father." (8) In all the gospels Jesus carefully distinguishes his own *unique Sonship* from that of his disciples. He speaks constantly of "my Father" and "your Father," but never of "our Father." (9) That Jesus was known to claim divine Sonship is indirectly shown by the fact that Satan (Matthew 4:3); the centurion (Mark 15:39); the malefactor and the evangelists (Mark 1:1; John 3:18; 20:31) apply that title to him. (Lu. 2:49; Matt. 7:21; 10:32; 15:13; 16:17). The most intense consciousness of this unique relationship to God is expressed in Matt. 11:25; Luke 10:21.

523. **Definition of the title "Son of God."** (1) In which sense did Jesus apply the name "Son of God" to himself? No doubt in the literal sense. That Jesus was conscious of being the "Son of God" as to his very essence is clear from the following passages: he claims personal pre-existence (John 8:56-58), sinless perfection (John 8:29-46), he makes attachment to his person the imperative condition of salvation (Matt. 28:19), he required of men a faith he never exercised; he forgives sin and offers rest for the soul (Matt. 11:28), he frequently claims to be the supreme and final revealer of truth sweeping away whole pages of the Mosaic legislation, his last claim is "All power is given unto me," co-ordinating himself with the Father (Matt 28). There are also remarkable utterances in connection with his miracles, such as "be thou clean" and "peace be still," modeled after the words of Divine command at the creation "Let there be light." These and many other considerations show that Jesus' Sonship was more than ethical; i. e. being in harmony in mind and will with the purposes of God; it was also metaphysical (supernatural, one in essence). It was indeed profoundly ethical just because it was metaphysical. For ethical unity becomes less possible the farther any two beings are metaphysically separated from each other (as e. g. man and beast), while coequality of nature makes ethical harmony less difficult (husband and wife). Even Mark 13:32, which is often

quoted to refute Christ's metaphysical Sonship, clearly specifies four classes of being:—that of men, of angels, of the Son, of God—evidently emphasizing that the Son is above angels and men and nearest to God. The not-knowing is limited to his incarnate life when the son "emptied" himself of some of his divine attributes—a great mystery (Phil. 2:7). All this is confirmed by the message of the Father through Gabriel who calls the child the Son of God, not because he is to be the Messiah, but because of the derivation of his human nature from the special creative act of God. Jesus is to be the Son of God in such a sense as to be without an earthly father. (Lu. 1:35). (2) How did others apply the term "Son of God" to Jesus? (a) At Cesarea Philippi Peter proclaimed his faith in the Lord's Messiahship and his Deity (Matt. 16:16); for the second phrase is not simply a variation of the first, without the addition of anything new. Here Peter places Jesus above the Baptist, Elijah and the prophets who were all sons by adoption. (b) The Sanhedrin understood Jesus to claim deity at his night and morning trials. For if his claim to be the "Son of God" implied nothing more than a human messiahship wherein consisted the blasphemy? (Matt. 26:63; Lu. 22:66); the high priest would not and could not have condemned him for claiming a prerogative common to all pious Israelites. (c) John 5:18 and 10:33 says that the Jews understood Jesus to claim equality with God. (d) The church at the earliest date fixed upon the name "Son of God" or even "God" to express its sense of the uniqueness of her Lord's nature (Acts 9:20; Rom. 1:4; 9:15; Gal. 2:20; Eph. 4:13; Heb. 4:14; 1 Jno. 4:15; Rev. 2:18). (e) The conclusion is inevitable: Christ was not a man aspiring to be a God, but God, condescending to be a man. The world admires Christ's singular perfection which arises, by almost universal consent even of unbelievers, so far above every human greatness ever known, that it can only be rationally explained on the ground of such an essential union with the Godhead as he claimed himself and his apostles ascribed to him. (f) At what time Christ's self-consciousness of being the Son of God broke through, and how rapidly it developed we do not know. Time and circumstances acted on Christ as they do on all men, widening the horizon of knowledge and making clear the path of duty. (See § 499.)

III. The Resurrection of Christ.

524. (1) The problem is, in what sense did Christ rise from the dead? (2) The N. T. sources are unanimous in recording the fact that on the third day after the Lord's death his friends found the tomb empty; that Christ appeared to them ten times during a period of forty days, and that thus was created in their hearts the firm faith in their Lord's bodily resurrection and ascension. (3) This conviction among Christians was not a slow growth spread over a long period, but dates from the very morning of the resurrection itself. And no difficulty of weaving the separate incidents into an orderly narrative and of other minor details has ever succeeded in impugning the unanimous belief of the Church which lies behind the reports, that Christ rose and appeared to the disciples.

525. **Evidential Value of Christ's Resurrection.** (1) It establishes the Divine character of Jesus; (2) it sets God's seal to Christ's teaching; (3) it proves the possibility and actuality of life beyond the grave; (4) it certifies our own immortality and resurrection; (5) it shows that "truth crushed to earth will rise again."

526. **Credibility and Possibility.** As to the possibility of a real bodily resurrection most Christians hold that we are confronted by a genuine *miracle* which man will never be able to explain. An increasing number of scholars, however, believe that Christ's body was raised through the operation of laws as yet unknown to us, and that the spiritual body in which he appeared, was, as Paul declared, as real as any earthly body (1 Cor. 15). In these days of discovery of new laws and the scientific demonstration of

truth which hitherto had rested merely on faith, scientific men are becoming very slow in denying the basic facts of the Christian faith merely on the plea of being "impossible" or "contrary to the natural laws." Such assumptions are philosophical and materialistic prepossessions but are very far from being scientific.

527. **Non-Miraculous Interpretations of the Records.** Christ's real resurrection being the pivotal point of Christianity, as Paul already declares (1 Cor. 15), it has always been the center of attack, beginning with the lying reports of the rulers and the Roman soldiers (Matt. 28). Modern attempts to explain away the real sense of the Gospel story may be classified as follows: (1) *The Swoon Theory* (Scheintod). Jesus had not really died on the cross, but had fallen into a death-like stupor. In the coolness of the tomb he revived and his friends nursed him back to life. Answer: (*a*) the spear-thrust had certainly killed Jesus, even if he had not been dead before; (b) how could the pitiable appearance of one just recovering from wounds have given rise to such a sudden and enthusiastic belief that he was the conqueror of death? Even Strauss cast ridicule and biting scarcasm on this hypothesis. (2) *The Theory of Fraud.* His friends (especially Joseph and Nicodemus) removed his body and the rumor was allowed to spread among his other disciples that he had risen. This explanation is as old as the resurrection itself (Matt. 28). Another version of this theory is that Joseph, or his family, were afraid that a crucified body might defile their tomb, and so he removed it quietly. And according to a third version the Jewish rulers themselves removed the body to deceive the disciples. Answer: Why did the rulers not say so, or show the place and remnants of the body when they made such strenuous efforts to stop Peter and Stephen from preaching the resurrection (Acts, Ch. 3-7). These theories have now been almost entirely abandoned because they are so unspeakably ridiculous, and create much greater difficulties than they propose to allay. . (3) *The Spiritual Resurrec-*

tion. Christ remained dead in the tomb but his spirit arose in his disciples and kindled a new hope and faith. When Jesus foretold his resurrection he meant it in a figurative sense, as if he were to say: I shall die, but my cause will revive in a short time. And so it proved. After the first stupefaction was over the disciples realized that their Master, though his body was in the tomb, still existed in another state of being, and so by degrees they resumed the work which he had dropped. And this was his resurrection. Answer: This is twisting the text, a procedure which is unworthy of serious and sincere men. Let the text speak for itself, whether you believe it or not. (4) *Legendary Theory*. This theory holds that the belief in the resurrection grew up during the first century, and gradually came to be accepted by a credulous and uncritical age. Answer: Legends require long time for development. On the contrary, the synoptic Gospels written within forty years of the event, and Paul's first epistle to the Corinthians (ch. 15) written within thirty years, revealed not only the universal conviction of the Church, but a conviction not a whit stronger than that of the disciples on the day of Pentecost, six weeks after the crucifixion. (5) *Subjective Vision Theory*. After their return to the familiar places in Galilee they lived over their former life with Jesus. This led to mental hallucinations, which excitable natures like Peter and Mary Magdalene objectified and materialized to such an extent that they believed they had seen him bodily stand on the Sea of Galilee. Answer: "The critics would have us believe that the witnesses began this dreaming simultaneously, and kept at it off and on for about six weeks, the dreaming fit embracing no less than 500 persons on one of these occasions, and then suddenly ceasing so as to admit of the resurrection idea getting launched as history." (6) *An Objective, Divinely Given, Real Vision of Jesus,* such as Paul had, caused by Jesus himself for the express purpose of creating the very belief in which it issued, namely, that Jesus was the Son of God the Messiah and spiritually alive, sitting at the right hand of God. (7) *The chief objections* to all these theories are (1) the empty tomb, (2) their violent contradiction to the reports in the Gospels, (3) their failure to account for the change in the disciples; for the psychological conditions were entirely absent. The disciples did not only not expect a resurrection but regarded the reports as "idle tales" and some of the 500 "doubted" (Lu. 24:21; Matt. 28:17). It is a gratuitous assumption to suppose that these hard-headed men could not distinguish between subjective experience and objective fact. (4) Their failure to give an adequate explanation of the origin and power of Christianity. (5) The moral objection to these and all similar theories is, if possible, still stronger. They make not only the faith of the early Church, but the entire subsequent development and influence of the most potent and beneficent moral force the world has ever known, rest on self-deceptions, hallucinations, actual falsehoods. (6) The strong, joyful, living faith of the early Church cannot be satisfactorily accounted for except on the ground of an actual resurrection. Christ's enemies would have left no stone unturned to prevent such a report gaining ground if it had not rested on irrefutable proofs. The concensus of opinion among evangelical critics is that no past event stands on firmer historical grounds than that Jesus being dead arose again, and that his appearance to the disciples begot their faith anew, and filled them with enthusiasm for their future work. Those who cannot personally investigate the evidence may confidently join in this conclusion.

528. This is a sketch of Christ's Christology. However, there are others. But all the hundreds of conceptions of Christ's person can be reduced to two: (a) Jesus is a man— a great man, the greatest, but only a man; and (b) Jesus is the only Son of God, unparalleled, unlike any other person. From the beginning the Christian Church took the higher of these two conceptions. The lower conception is easier to grasp; but we are not after easy conceptions, we are after the truth. The Ptolemaic theory is far simpler

than the Copernican, and yet we hold the latter. We must assume the higher conception of Jesus in order to explain the phenomenon which must be accounted for, e. g. the existence of the church. The lower conception requires less time for its mastery and is more congenial to the unspiritual heart than the higher view. But why has the Church accepted the higher view? (1) Because of the testimony of the N. T.; (2) because of the powerful influence of the Biblical Christ in history; (3) because of individual Christian experience, the great test of truth ("Things Fundamental," by Jefferson). The essence of Christianity is no mere message of love to God and man, delivered by a human teacher, but a drama of redemption. Thus liberal Christianity is a radical departure from the teaching of Christ; tame, bleached, bloodless, void of all mysteries which make religion attractive. Christ's christology has ever been the christology of the Church Universal, taught in all her official creeds, defended by her greatest teachers, proclaimed by her soul-stirring preachers, contained in all her liturgies and underlying all her immortal hymns. The reason for this strong hold is not far to seek. It lies in the fact that this Christology is contained in the N. Test., that it answers more questions, explains more difficulties, satisfies more wants, agrees better with sound philosophical principles, is truer to the facts of history and human convictions, and responds more readily to the religious need of man than any other system. Untold millions have traced the principle of a new life in their souls to the faith in Christ as taught by the Church in her catechisms, hymns and prayers. If therefore we repudiate the Christology of the N. T. we should be clearly conscious of what we do. We are making a choice between Christ and the modern, negative critical school. We reduce the N. T. to a piece of tradition.

529. **Reference Literature.** Koegel, Problem der Geschichte J.; Or the Incarnation, Sheldon, N. T. Theol. p. 56; Purpose of J. by C. C. Morgan (in "Fundamentals, I, p. 29); Bosworth, Tea. of J., p. 23; Orr, Virgin Birth (in "Fundamentals, I); Cook, Incarn.

and Recent Crit.; Sweet, Birth and Inf.; Gruetzemacher, Jung‑
fraeuliche Geburt; Hast. D. C. I, 796.

On Christ's Self-Consciousness. Kaftan, Menschheit Jesu; Jef‑
ferson, Deity of J. (in "Things Fundamental," Ch. 6 and 7); Ull‑
man, Sinlessness of C.; Adeney, N. T. Theol., p. 26, 59; Sheldon, N.
T. Theol., p. 59; Mathews, Mess. Hope in N. T.; Hitchcock, Psych.
of J., p. 89; Warfield, in Fundamentals, I, 21; Denny, J. and the
Gos., Consciousness, pp. 177-324; on the resurr., pp. 99-138; Warfield
Lord of Glory; Garvie, Inner Life of J.; Luthard, Apol. Vortraege,
II; Barrows, Personality of J; Ihmels Wer war Jesus? Barth,
Hauptprobleme; Bettex, Was duenket dich um Christo? Hale, Who
Then Is This? Godet, N. T. Studies; Forsyth, Person and Place
of J.; Moorehead, Moral Glory of J. (in Fundamentals, III, 42);
Speer, God in Christ (in Fund., III, 61); Kuehl, Selbstbewusstsein
J.; Mueller, Unser Herr; Baldensperger, Self-Consciousness of J.;
Lemme, Jesu Wissen und Weisheit; Jesu Irrthumslosigkeit; Dor‑
ner, Person Christi; Liddon, Deity of Our L., p. 154; Hast. D.
of C., on Metaphys, II, 179; pre-existence, II, 407; Son of Man, II,
659; Son of God, II, 654; humanity of C., I, 753; Consciousness, I,
361; divinity, I, 467; Kenosis, I, 929.

On the Resurrection. Christlieb, Mod. Denial, in Mod. Doubt,
448; Torrey (in Fundamentals, V, p. 81); Royce, Immort.; Charles,
Hebr. Eschat; see D. B. by Davis, Hast., Smith and Piercy,

CHAPTER 53.

Christ's Influence in the World.

530. The influence of Christ and his gospel has come
down through the centuries like a gulf-stream of love, pow‑
erful, continuous, far-reaching. He impressed his image
on (1) his disciples during his life-time; (2) on the be‑
lievers in him after his ascension (Paul); (3) on the
Church, which at the first council at Nicaea (325) rendered
her testimony to him as the "very God of very God"; (4)
on the martyrs who gave their lives for their faith in him
(Ignatius, Polycarp). (5) The Lord's influence was never
greater than to-day, over the greatest intellects (philoso‑
phers, scientists, poets and painters), as well as over the
common people who liked him and whom he liked so much
during his life on earth.

531. Christ has radically influenced the individual, the social and moral life of man, and all signs indicate that the world stands on the threshold of a more powerful realization of Christ's teaching, extensively by the conversion of the whole world, and intensively by impressing our statesmen and the business world that the Golden Rule, surcharged with his spirit, is the most practicable rule of life for individuals and society. Bismarck was right when he answered an attack of free thinkers in the German Diet by saying: "All your conceptions of right and wrong, of honor and fidelity, of purity and virtue, are simply the petrified remnants of your Christian training." Christ has infused so much of his spirit of love and righteousness into the world that even those who disregard him would not care to live in it if his influence were withdrawn. Besides the Bible, Christianity can point to other credentials of the most convincing kind. For the space of two thousand years it has proved itself to be the chief source of moral illumination, of comfort for the sorrowing, of strength for the weak, of deliverance for the oppressed, of hope for the dying. It is the spring of modern philanthropy, the basis of modern civilization, the fountain-head of those ideas of human brotherhood that permeate and modify social life at every point. Wherever it touches humanity it purifies, lifts, inspires, re-creates. Its power in transforming a single human life is a promise and pledge of its power over all life.

532. We will close this book by giving a careful selection of testimonies to Christ. For obvious reasons we exclude theologians and other very pronounced Christians: (1) because even a selection of testimonies from them would fill a volume, and (2) because eulogies to Christ may be taken for granted from such sources. We have admitted the testimonies of a few sceptics, for the reason that the estimates of unbelievers have in some respects greater evidential value than those from Christians though their consistency cannot be defended.

533. The object of giving these testimonies is: (a) to answer the question which is always being raised since the Pharisees sneeringly asked it, "Do the rulers believe on him?"—the rulers in government, science and art. The impression is sometimes studiously created as if only a few really great men believed in the Jesus of the Gospels. Truth remains truth, even though the great and learned should reject it, but it is a source of joy to Christians, especially the educated part of the rising generation, to know that they will be in excellent company when following Jesus. (b) It will also be helpful to learn what impression Jesus made on the choicest spirits and the finest intellects the world has seen. (c) Finally, these testimonies will especially serve young Christians as authorities at a time of their lives when in the nature of the case they lack the deeper experiences of life, until the time shall come for them when they can say with the Samaritans, "Now we believe, not because of thy speaking; for we have heard for ourselves, and know that this is indeed the Saviour of the world." (Jno 4:42.)

I. Testimonies of Kings.

534. 1. **Alfred, the Great,** king of England, (died 907). Whether poor or rich, fear and love the Lord Jesus Christ. He is the Lord of life, our great teacher, our kind Father.

2. **Napoleon I** (Life, Vol. II, p. 612). I know men, and I tell you Jesus Christ was not a man. Superficial minds see a resemblance between Christ and the founders of empires and the gods of other religions. That resemblance does not exist. There is between Christianity and other religions the distance of infinity. Everything in Christ astonishes me. Here I see nothing human. The nearer I approach, everything is above me. Alexander, Cæsar, Charlemagne and myself founded empires. But on what did we rest the creations of our genius? Upon force. Jesus Christ alone founded his empire upon love, and at this hour millions of men would die for him. Christ proved that he was the Son of the Eternal.

3. **William I,** German Emperor (died 1888). Faith in the Lord Jesus Christ is the only firm foundation on which we may stand in the storm of life. At the very moment when I took the crown from the altar to put it on my head, there overcame me a deep sense of responsibility and fear. I instinctively withdrew my hand. In so doing my eyes caught sight of the crucifix and this aspect gave me comfort and strength. I thought, Christ, who wore the crown of thorns for me, will help me to wear the royal crown.

4. **William II,** German Emperor (since 1888). Christ was the most personal of all personalities that ever lived. The words of no other man have had the effect of his, and this can only be explained by the fact that his words are the very words of the living God. The attitude of a man toward his Saviour is decisive for him. Christ cannot be ignored. Our only help and refuge is and remains the Saviour. The world-renewing power of the gospel teaches us that the gates of hell shall not overcome our Evangelical Church. What the German nation is to-day is due to the cross on Calvary.

2. Testimonies of Statesmen.

535. 1. **Admiral Coligny** (murdered 1572). In Christ and in him alone I seek salvation and pardon of sin.

2. **Thomas Jefferson** (Works, Vol. IV, p. 479). I am a Christian, sincerely attracted to his doctrines, in preference to all others. His moral doctrines were more pure and perfect than those of the most correct of the philosophers.

3. **Benjamin Franklin** (To President Stiles of Yale College). I think Jesus Christ's system of **morals** and religion, as he left them to us, the best the world ever saw, or is likely to see.

4. **Daniel Webster** (Argument in the Girard Will Case). I believe Jesus Christ to be the Son of God. The miracles which he wrought establish in my mind his personal authority and render it proper for me to believe what he asserts. When little children were brought into the

presence of the Son of God, his disciples proposed to send them away; but he said: "Suffer little children to come unto me."

5. **Gladstone** (Review of Ecce Homo). Through the fair gloss of his manhood we perceive the rich bloom of his divinity. If he is not now without an assailant, at least he is without a rival. If he be not the Son of righteousness, the Friend that gives his life for his friends and that sticketh closer than a brother, the unfailing Consoler, the constant Guide, the everlasting Priest and King, at least, as all must confess, there is no other to come into his room.

6. **President Paul Krueger** of the Transvaal. I hope all the teachers before me know by experience the faith in the Lord Jesus Christ, and that you are anxious to lead your pupils to the Lord.

7. **Prince Bismarck,** Imperial Chancellor of Germany (died 1898). Let me remind those of you who do not believe in the Word of God, that the best you still possess, all your conceptions of morality, honor and duty, are simply the remnants of your Christian training. I confess openly that my faith in our revealed religion, determines my work as a servant of the state. I, the Chancellor of the German Empire, am a Christian, and I am fully determined to act as such, according to the light which God will give me. ... After a few years it will be immaterial to us how Prussia will be ruled, if only the mercy of God and Christ's redemption remain with us. Last night, in order to banish the tormenting worries about the political situation I opened the Bible at random and read Ps. 110:5: "Oh! how little is all that men have created! The wind bloweth over it and it is gone."

3.   Testimonies of Philosophers.

536.   1. **Spinoza** (Life and Philosophy, Secs. 22, 24). No man ever came to that singular height of perfection but Christ, to whom the ordinances of God that lead man to salvation, were revealed, not in words or in visions, but im-

mediately: so that God manifested himself to the apostles by the mind of Christ. Therefore, the voice of Christ may be called the voice of God. Christ is the way of salvation.

2. **John Locke** (Works, Vol. II, p. 582). Before our Saviour's time, the doctrine of a future state, though it were not wholly hid, yet it was not clearly known in the world. He brought life and immortality to light. And that not only in the clear revelation of it and in instances shown of men raised from the dead; but he has given an unquestionable assurance and pledge of it, in his own resurrection and ascension into heaven. How hath this one truth changed the nature of things. The philosophers, indeed show the beauty of nature, but leaving her unendowed, very few are willing to espouse her. It has another relish and efficiency to persuade men that if they live well here, they shall be happy hereafter. Upon this foundation, and upon this only, morality stands firm; and this is the gospel Jesus Christ has delivered to us.

3. **Voltaire** (Toleration, p. 95). If we may compare God with man, his death greatly resembled that of Socrates.

4. **Rousseau** (Works, Vol. II, p. 215). Is it possible that the sacred personage should be a mere man? If the life and death of Socrates were those of a sage, the life and death of Jesus Christ are those of a God.

5. **Kant** (The Existence of God, p. 249). In the life and the divine doctrine of Christ, example and precept conspire to call men to the regular discharge of every moral duty for its own sake. Christ is the founder of the first true Church; that is, that Church which exhibits the moral kingdom of God upon earth.

6. **Fichte** (Religion, p. 483). He was the Absolute Reason clothed in immediate self-consciousness. or what is the same thing,—Religion.

7. **Hegel** (Philosophy of History, p. 337). If Christ is to be looked upon only as an excellent, even impeccable individual, and nothing more, the conception of the speculative idea of Absolute Truth, is ignored. The real attestation

of the divinity of Christ is the witness of one's own spirit, not miracles; for only spirit recognizes Spirit.

8. **Emerson** (Prose Works, Vol. I, p. 69). Jesus is the most perfect of all men that have yet appeared. The unique impressions of Jesus upon mankind are not so much written as ploughed into the history of this world. He saw with open eye the mystery of the soul. Alone in all history, he estimated the greatness of man.

9. **Thomas Carlyle** (Sartor Resartus, p. 155). All men can recognize a present God, and worship the same. Look on our divinest symbol, Jesus of Nazareth, and his life and his biography. Higher has the human thought not yet reached.

4. Testimonies of Poets and Others.

537. **Shakespeare** (Last Will, 1616). I commend my soul into the hands of God, my Creator, hoping and assuredly believing, through the only merits of Jesus Christ, my Saviour, to be made partaker of life everlasting.

9. **Goethe** (Conversations with Eckermann). I look upon all the four Gospels as thoroughly genuine; for there is in them the reflection of a greatness which emanated from the person of Jesus, and which was as divine a kind as ever was seen upon earth. If I am asked whether it is in my nature to pay him devout reverence, I say, Certainly; I bow before him as the divine manifestation of the highest principle of morality. Let mental culture go on advancing, let the natural sciences go on gaining in depth and breadth, and the human mind expand as it may, it will never go beyond the elevation and moral culture of Christianity, as it glistens and shines forth in the Gospel.

3. **Charles Dickens** (Last Will). I commit my soul to the mercy of God, through our Lord and Saviour Jesus Christ, and I exhort my dear children humbly to try to guide themselves by the teachings of the New Testament.

4. **Tolstoi** (My Religion, pp. 46). If the progress is slow, it is because the doctrine of Jesus (which, through its

clearness, simplicity, and wisdom, appeals so inevitably to human nature), has been cunningly concealed from the majority of mankind, under an entirely different doctrine falsely called by his name. Our existence is now so entirely in contradiction with the doctrine of Jesus, that only with the greatest difficulty can we understand its meaning. Why is it, that men have not done as Jesus commanded them, and thus secured the greatest happiness within their reach, the happiness they have always longed for and still desire? The reply is: The doctrine of Jesus is admirable; and it is true that if we practiced it, we should see the kingdom of God established upon the earth; but to practice it is difficult and consequently this doctrine is impracticable. We repeat this and hear it repeated so many, many, times, that we do not observe the contradiction contained in these words.

5. **Lord Byron.** If ever man was God or God man, Jesus Christ was both.

6. **Richard Wagner** (died 1883). The founder of Christianity was not wise, but divine. Happy is the man who has from childhood been trained in our religion. To know that we have a Redeemer, remains the greatest treasure of man. To throw away this precious faith shows our dependence on wild demagogs.

7. **Tennyson** ("In Memoriam")—
    "Strong Son of God, immortal Love,
        Whom we, that have not seen thy face,
        By faith, and faith alone, embrace,
    Believing where we cannot prove."

    "Thou seemest human and divine
        The highest, holiest manhood, thou:
        Our wills are ours, we know not how;
    Our wills are ours, to make them thine."

    "Our little systems have their day;
        They have their day and cease to be:

They are but broken lights of thee,
And thou, O Lord, art more than they."

538. **Reference Literature.** Farrar, Witness of Hist. to C.; Young,
The C. of Hist.; Uhlhorn, Conflict of Christianity with Heathenism;
Pfannmueller, Jesus im Urteil der Jahrhunderte; Zoeckler, Gottes-
zeugen im Reiche der Natur.; Jefferson, in Things Fund., p. 174;
Pfennigdorf, Christus in Mod. Geistesleben; "Jesus Christ and the
Christian Character," F. G. Peabody; Speer, The Principles of
Jesus applied to the present life; Forrest, The C. of Hist. and Ex-
perience; Bonwetsch, J. im Bewusstsein der Kirche; "Christian
Belief Interpreted by Christian Experience," Charles Cuthbert Hall,
D.D.; Mathews, W. A., "Witness of the World to Christ"; Hillis,
N. D., "The Influence of Christ in Modern Life"; Hinsdale, B. A.,
"Jesus as a Teacher"; "The Gospel for an Age of Doubt," Henry
van Dyke; Leighton, J. and the Civilization of To-day; Brooks,
Infl. of J.; Carpenter, Witness to the Infl. of C.; Newman, Ch.
Hist., I, 78; Knowling, Test. of Paul to C.; Henning, Was be-
ruehmte Maenner ueber Christus sagen; Hast. D. C., C. in Jewish,
Mohamed, Lit. and in Paul, II, 876-886; C. in the Church, II, 849;
Infl. of C., II, 824.

CHAPTER 54.

Non-Biblical Portraits of Jesus.

539.   Side by side with the N. T. portrait of Jesus as de-
lineated in the previous chapters there have always been a
great variety of non-Biblical pictures of him. They vary
very much in detail, from the liberal view to the total denial of the historicity of the N. T. Jesus. But they have
certain features in common, such as the denial of his true
Godhead, his personal pre-existence, his personal incarnation, and his resurrection. As the N. T. portrait, so has
this non-miraculous picture of Christ become traditional
in its main outlines, tracing its principal features from the
errorists at Colossæ and in John's time, who denied Christ's
incarnation and true Deity, through the Ebionites, Gnostics
and the Arians in the first four centuries and the Socinians
of the Reformation period, to the Unitarians, radicals and
liberals of our own time.   Hence if "traditional" is a term

of reproach, both, evangelical and liberal Christians, will have to share it. While it is not pleasant to exhibit some of these caricatures of Christ, it is, however, necessary to forewarn Bible students and acquaint them with the evangelical estimate of the radical views of Christ which on the platform, in some pulpits and in the press are constantly presented with such great plausibility as the real scientific portraits of Jesus.

540. The ancient sketches painted by the Ebionites, Gnostics and other sects, as well as that by the Wolfenbüttel fragments, which made Christ or his apostles, or both, common frauds and imposters are entirely faded and have to-day only antiquarian interest. The principal types of modern portraits of Christ are those of the rationalistic, the liberal, the mythical, the antiquated, the diseased, the Buddhistic, the socialistic and the non-historical Christ.

I. The Christ of Rationalism.

541. The German rationalists of the old school (Gabler, Teller, Loeffler, Kant), the English Deists (Hobbes, Shaftesbury), and the American Unitarians (Emerson, Parker, Channing) conceded, in the main, the historicity of the Life of Christ as recorded in the Gospels; but by a very arbitrary method of exegesis they explained away all that is miraculous in the records. They considered Jesus to be merely a Jewish rabbi who endeavored to purify the Jewish religion, and to instil into his people the three great truths, God, Virtue, Immortality (Fr. Schiller, "Drei Worte des Glaubens"). They held that most of what is reported as going beyond human powers and comprehension did indeed happen, but in an entirely natural way. Jesus was in possession of occult powers, such as magnetism, mesmerism, suggestion, hypnotism, etc., but his simple-minded disciples misunderstood his cures and attributed them to miraculous causes. They said, we must decide between the husk and the kernel, and the standard by which to do that is human reason. Hence they were called "Rationalists," not be-

cause they employed reason, but because they made unaided reason the absolute standard of deciding what is truth. Their exegesis is in many cases preposterous. While denying Christ's miracles they performed veritable miracles of exegesis. Some of their feats in this direction still serve as amusement for the students at German universities. (For examples of Rationalistic exegesis see Christlieb, Modern Doubt and Christian Belief, p. 346.) This portrait of Christ has been almost entirely erased from the minds of our generation, and to-day has only antiquarian interest. We have given this sketch, however, because modern liberalism has appropriated some of the Rationalist's colors for painting its own portrait of Jesus.

II. The Christ-Portrait of Modern Liberalism.

542. More plausible and therefore more dangerous is the Christ of modern liberalism, which varies much, from the mild liberalism of Beyschlag, to the more pronounced type of Harnack and the radicalism of Pfleiderer. Its main positions are these: (1) As documents most N. T. writings are beyond a doubt authentic, i. e. they were written by their traditional authors, with perhaps the exception of the fourth gospel. This is a gain over Baur, and the Tuebingen school which accepted only Rom., I and II Cor., Gal. and Rev. as genuine. (2) But these gospels do not report pure history. Much of it never happened. As old paintings are often retouched by admiring artists, so the real life of Christ suffered much from the retouching by the faith and enthusiasm of his first followers. Speculation about Jesus arose very early, even before Paul, among his adherents, and hid the simple features of the Nazarene beneath heavy coats of lurid colors. Especially Paul covered the picture of the man Jesus with such a halo of supernaturalism, calling him not only the "Son of God" but unqualifiedly "God" (Rom 9:4), that the man of Tarsus must really be considered the founder of Christianity. If asked, were the N. T. writers, then, common frauds? the answer is, By no means. This

was all done unconsciously; it was an outflow of their love
and faith, and of speculations natural to a man like Paul,
and to the magnifying and transfiguring influence of death,
especially of such a death as Christ's. (De mortuis nil nisi
bene—we must speak only good of the dead.) So when
our oldest life of Christ, the original Mark, was written,
the real picture of Jesus was already painted over with the
glowing colors of the faith of the Christians. (3) The
sacred duty of modern scientific research is to do what
artists do with old paintings, which Puritan fanaticism or
misguided taste and enthusiasm have covered over with
whitewash or retouched with more glaring than the natural
colors were—we must carefully, patiently, sympathetically
peel off those later additions, and present to the gaze of
modern men the simple features of the Man of Nazareth.
This is what they call, "back to Christ"!—the restoration
of the real Christ from beneath the varnish! (4) The
sharp instrument by which the peeling off is done, is higher
criticism and the guiding principle is the preconception of
liberalism that miracles are impossible. This leads to a
purely non-miraculous interpretation of our N. T. sources.
(Bousset, What is Religion, p. 234.) (5) How does the restored, the supposed real Jesus look? Here are his outlines: He was a great man, a profound teacher, a splendid
example, a heroic martyr, but merely a product of his times,
a mere man with all the limitations of his period. He had
sin in his nature, but he conquered this defect. He was
born like any other man; his body never rose from the
grave, though his spirit and memory induced his followers to believe he did rise. The great influence of his name
is due to Paul's Christological speculations, to Greek philosophy and to Teutonic virility, and these are really the
three ingredients of our present day Christianity.

543. **Serious Objections to the Liberal Portrait of
Jesus.** (1) Its advocates use the sources in an entirely subjective and arbitrary manner. They read their philosophical
ideas into the Gospels, exactly as the old rationalists did.

and as they charge orthodoxy with doing. The ordinary, the common, that which every man can do, is made the standard by which Jesus is measured, and whatever goes beyond his merely human proportions is arbitrarily eliminated as a reflection of the exalted Christ upon the Jesus of history. We have to trust to the "clear eye" of Harnack, and "the intuition" of Pfleiderer. They make gods in their own image, and their evolutionary, non-miraculous dogma is employed to correct history. (Cardinal Manning at the Vatican Council, 1870.) This makes the liberal Jesus a fiction. Renan went farthest in reading his ideal of humanity into the person of Christ, making the life of Christ a regular French novel. (2) Even those fragments of history which liberalism accepts as true sources (as found in their purest form in Mark's Gospel) present to us, not the human Jesus of liberalism, but the divine Christ of the Church. (Denny, Jesus and the Gospels.) (3) Liberalism encourages idolatry, by first degrading Jesus to the measure of a mere man, and then by presenting this emasculated figure to the people as the God of Christianity. This the Germans dubbed "Jesuanismus," and "Jesus-Cultus." Using the phraseology of the church, but infusing radical ideas into them, borders on immorality because it undermines the people's sense of truthfulness. (4) The attenuated bloodless Jesus of liberalism will never succeed in conquering the modern world. The N. T. Christ overcame the old world, and the measure of Christian influence in modern times is due to the power of the Christ whom the Church proclaims. Nowhere does liberalism by trimming down the Christian religion succeed in drawing the people. (5) The most withering criticism against the Jesus of liberalism comes from the radicals (Kalthoff, Jensen, Pfleiderer, Strauss). While they reject both portraits of Jesus, that of the New Testament as well as that of liberalism as unscientific, they consider the portrait painted by the church as more scientific. In their view the liberal Jesus is not the product of pure historical criticism and

hence is not modern at all. The liberal portrait is as antiquated as that of old rationalism. The modern man will
feel a much stronger affinity for the "massive Christ of the
Church" than for the liberal picture of the dreamer of
Nazareth.

III. The Mythical Jesus.

544. Strauss, Renan and Wellhausen are the chief representatives of the view that the Gospels in the main consist of myths, fiction and legends. (2) There is only a
difference of degree between the liberal and the mythical
Jesus. Liberalism accepts a considerable part of the Gospels as historical, but the mythical theory reduces this to a
minimum. It does not labor to give a natural explanation
of the miracles, but relegates all of them to the realm of
legend. As miracles are impossible, the fact that the Gospels contain so many is proof enough of their fictitious
character. (3) *Objections.* (1) This portrait of Jesus is
the result of philosophical preconceptions. It was Hegel-
ian Pantheism which dictated to Strauss his famous dogma:
"The idea is averse to manifesting itself fully in one personality," ("Die Idee liebt es nicht, ihre ganze Fuelle in ein
einziges Exemplar auszugiessen") and his other dictum,
Miracles are impossible; (2) Myths are of slow growth.
A great amount of reflection lies back of the origin of each
individual myth, as seen in the history of all nations. Hence
the time between Christ's death and the writing of the
oldest Gospels was too short for the development of myths.
(3) The Gospels do not only report incidents which glorify
Christ, but also attribute to him ignorance as to the time of
his second coming, and the saying that he could not do
miracles at certain places. Legends would not have reported such a saying of their hero. The apocryphal Gospels show what legends really are. (4) Strauss' method
is dishonest, as he exaggerates the most trivial variations
in the Gospels into proofs of their mythical character.
(Christlieb, Modern Doubt, 404.) (5) The persecutions

would have sobered the enthusiasm of the apostles, for no one cares to die for his imaginations and dreams. (Christlieb. Modern Doubt, pp. 380, 383; Ebrard, Gosp. Hist., p. 473.)

IV. The Diseased Jesus.

545. **Was Jesus Mentally Sound?** (1) Modern research in general psychology has given an impetus to the psychological study of Jesus. The question is being widely discussed by friend and foe, what was it, precisely, that took place in the soul of Jesus. (2) Very soon a number of physicians and others shifted the question to one side of psychology, to the side of pathology, and raised the question, *Was Jesus mentally sound* or *not*. Representatives of negative criticism have taken advantage of the situation and are ascribing all manner of mental defects and diseases to Jesus, such as general insanity, epilepsy, ecstasy (concentration of attention on one point), visionary enthusiasm, etc. (3) *Alleged Evidence:* (a) inherited tendencies. The Baptist, a relative of Jesus (Lu. 1:36) was supposed to be possessed by a demon (Matt. 11:18; Lu. 9:33); (b) Jesus' friends said of him, "he is insane" (Mk. 3); (c) his enemies charged him with having the devil, not only a demon, within him. In their language this meant that he was mad; (d) he lived in the atmosphere of Messianic hopes and insurrections, and by way of suggestion his mind became unbalanced; (e) his highly exaggerated self-consciousness, bordering on mania, his frenzy (cleansing of the temple), his unreasonable fear (Jno. 7:16-20; Gethsemane) his quarrelsomeness (in his controversies with the rulers) —all point to mental derangement.

546. **Refutation.** (1) These defamers of Jesus lack the means of personal observation and diagnosis which are absolutely essential to decide such a momentous question as the Lord's sanity. We know only the Lord's soul-life, but knowledge of his bodily life would be essential to prove their slanders. (2) All his assertions, fears and

promises were fulfilled, and this shows that they were not hallucinations. (Jno. 5:16, 18; 7:25). (3) The Lord's self-possession, his mental clear-sightedness, his sharp dialectics prove conclusively his mental health. (4) If health is the harmonious co-operation of all the functions of body, mind, soul and will, then Jesus was the healthiest person that ever trod the earth (see "The Character of Jesus"). (5) The strongest proof of Jesus' health, is, however, the Lord's great work and his enduring influence. His is not the work of a mentally diseased man! (6) The opponents of great men were always ready to consider them insane because they could not or would not understand them. Goethe, in his "Faust" says, "We are accustomed to make light of what we do not understand." Socrates was considered half insane. In 1640, the Jesuits wrote a book proving to their own satisfaction that Luther was insane. Goethe in his younger years was considered mentally unsound. Bismarck was commonly called "der tolle B." (the mad B.), and on June 11, 1866, the Vienna Medical Journal tried to prove that a man with such gigantic plans as Bismarck could not be mentally sound. When Ex-President Roosevelt, in 1908, sent one message after the other to the U. S. Congress urging reforms, several physicians, in all seriousness, diagnosed his malady as "paranoia reformatoria" (reformatory insanity).

V. The Antiquated Jesus.

547. (1) Many socialists, Haeckel in his "World Riddles," Pfleiderer, Ed. von Hartmann, the philosopher, Fred Nietzsche (the "superman" with the burning hate of Christ bordering on insanity and blasphemy) maintain that the message of Jesus may have contained some useful elements for his own times, but that the culture, civilization, science and art of the modern world have superseded it completely. Christianity is not the last word on religion, it is only one step toward a higher religion. A person of the

past cannot be the absolute guide for the present or the future. (2) Answer: (a) If the supreme law of action is arrogant self-assertion and not love, then Christian ethics may be considered antiquated and the morality of the "superman," which in its essence is rude or refined self-ishness, may be preferable. But who, knowing history, present condition, and the lives of the representatives of this idea, grants the premise? (b) Present conditions in the world do not exhibit all the great possibilities latent in Christ's teaching and example. The kingdom of God has indeed come with power, but by no means with all its powers. Attacks like these, however, should arouse the church to insist on the realization of the entire Gospel in individual life, in society, in church and state.

VI.   The Buddhistic Jesus.

548. (1) The religio-historical method has raised the question whether some of the essential features of Christianity had not been derived from Buddhism. (2) Proofs. The miraculous conception of Jesus resembles the story of Buddha's birth; modern theosophy and Schopenhauer's pessimistic philosophy see in Jesus not a personality but a personification of the negation of the will to live; Richard Wagner, in his "Parsifal," sees the essence of Christ's teaching as a longing for salvation from suffering by means of sympathy and love. A certain Notovitsch declared a few years ago that he had found in a Buddhist monastery a history of Jesus which showed that Jesus had spent several years in that place during the "18 years of silence." This report was, however, proved to be a falsification. (3) Answer: (a) Whatever in Christ's teaching resembles Buddhism has not been derived from it, but is a common possession of all wise men; (b) Karl von Hase, in his book "N. T. Parallels to Buddhistic Sources," comes to this conclusion: "It is incredible that the Christianity of the first century admitted Buddhistic legends into the Gospel." (c)

There is a great difference between the pessimism of Jesus and that of Buddha. Jesus considered sin the deepest misfortune, but with Buddha it is suffering. Even death brings no rest, for new suffering may follow it; only nirvana (extinction of desire by returning into the all-pantheism) secures happiness. Jesus destroys sin and grants eternal life. (d) Asceticism is found in both; but Buddhism insists on the extinction of the desire for pleasure, because this would remove the opportunity for disappointment; while Jesus encourages the desire for true pleasure (friendship, nature, sociability). Jesus suffered and died, not because he considered it a good thing in itself, but because it was an essential part of his mission of redeeming the world.

VII. The Jesus of the Socialists.

549. (1) The Socialists number about ten million voters in Europe and America. In all their platforms religion is declared to be a "private affair of the individual," but in practice almost all of them are outside of the church. (2) Attitude toward Jesus. The obvious fact that love was the ruling motive of Christ's life, has led many Socialists to the conclusion that Jesus' life-work was simply social regeneration. This one-sided view has induced most of the leaders of socialism to denounce the church as the great falsifier of the true Gospel, while expressing deep reverence for Jesus. (3) A few years ago, Dr. Rade sent a circular letter to thousands of Socialists asking their opinion of Jesus. The answers are highly interesting and instructive to Christian workers. Here are a few samples: (a) Jesus was the great tribune who fought the people's battles; he was himself a laborer (Mk. 6:31). (b) The Christ of the Church is not the Jesus of history; (c) Jesus was a social revolutionist. If he were teaching to-day, the plutocrats would never allow him to be outside of prison; (d) Jesus was a very good and noble man, the greatest social reformer; (e) Jesus was a righteous man. Conditions which to-

day Christians can contemplate, without being moved to protest and action—abject poverty and great wealth on the same street—aroused Jesus to most vehement denunciations; (f) Kautsky, one of the scientific writers on socialism, says: The history of apostolic Christianity is the history of ancient socialism. It is plain that the first Christians were communists (Acts 2). When the church became united with the state, she suppressed the principles of the Gospel. (4) *Answer:* (a) The socialistic portrait of Christ is not wrong but one-sided. The kingdom was Christ's ideal and this includes the spiritual salvation of the individual and through it the regeneration of society. (b) Socialism overlooks the great work of charity and the indirect but powerful influence exerted by the Church through her members on every phase of public and private life; (c) more and more prophets are heard in the pulpits of the church and her councils, pleading for the larger righteousness of economic justice and social equity, while not overlooking the minor moralities of individual life.

VIII. Jesus Only a Myth.

550. The height of absurdity! The height of absurdity is reached in the form of doctrine which holds that not only are there mythical elements in the Gospels, but the whole Jesus is an entirely mythical figure. But how? (1) Bruno Bauer (not to be confused with F. C. Baur, the founder of the Tuebingen School), believes that the unknown man who wrote the original Gospel of Mark, about 120 A. D., a highly educated man, gathered together and summed up all the elements of religion, education and culture of his time, and constructed a fictitious hero whom he named Jesus; (2) Dr. Anderson, in his "The Collapse of Liberal Christianity" (Hibbard Journal, Jan. 1910), offers this version: Among the Greeks were various cults and clubs, each of which had a patron-god. One of these clubs selected a god

named "Christos," long before our era. This club greatly increased in numbers and influence. In some unexplained way the religious belief of this "Christos Club" was loosely attached to a man named Jesus, living in the first century. But he and the god "Christos" were surely not identical. Gradually attributes of the god "Christos" were attached to this Jesus, who probably was a beloved member of the club. This was done perhaps long after his death. Hence Christianity was not founded by a single historical person, but by many persons and causes. It was the synthesis of the factors that controlled the historical development of the time; the issue of the advance of the world, especially in Judea, Greece and Rome, for many centuries before the Christian era. The story of the Gospel is a nature-myth. The dying and rising of God expresses a deep truth, namely, the implanting, the suffering and the rising of the truth in man's soul. (3) Jensen holds that the "Jesus-legend" is simply the old Babylonian Xisuthros myth contained in the Gilgalmesh epic, in a Semitic garb. (4) Kalthoff believes that Jesus was not an individual but the personification of the social-religious movement among the masses of the first and second centuries. If there was such a Jesus, he was merely a leader of the masses. (5) As evidence for these preposterous notions the following is adduced: (a) We have no contemporaneous, disinterested and impartial records concerning the historical Jesus. Only worshippers of him wrote books, but centuries afterward; (b) Josephus' words about Jesus are a falsification; and Tacitus, Suetonius and Pliny had no first-hand sources; (c) for the N. T. teaching we find ample parallels in Greek and Roman philosophy and religion of the 2nd century (Seneca, Epictetus; Stoicism).

551. Answer: (1) The whole hypothesis is what it asserts Jesus to be—a myth; a preposterous, fanciful, ridiculous idea without a scintilla of real evidence. Well-deserved satire has been heaped upon it by humorists who have "proved" that Napoleon, Bismarck and Roosevelt were

purely mythical figures. (2) It was natural that his contemporaries did not write much about Jesus. It is fundamentally wrong to judge a matter from the back, and suppose that the great power of Christianity must have been noticed in Roman literature. The Jews were only one of the many little subjected nations; many messiahs arose at that period, and the world saw many new religious cults arise. Only later history saw in the birth of Jesus a world-historical act. (3) Many of the best biographies were written by the friends of the men described (Socrates by Plato and Xenophon).

552. **Reference Literature.** Jordan, Jesus und die Mod. Jesusbilder; Weinel, Jesus im 19. Jahrh; Schaff, Person of C., p. 131; "Back to C," in Hast. D. C., I, 164; Harnack, Wesen des Christentums; (Egl.) Gruetzenmacher, Ist das liberale Christusbild modern? Schnehen, Der Mod, Jesuscultus; Arnold, Was uns Jesus heute ist; Bousset, "Jesus" (English); Myth, in Hast. D. C., II, 214; Eysinger, Indische Einfluesse auf evang. Erzaehlungen; Seydel, Evang. und Buddhasage; New Testament Parallels in Buddhistic Literature, Prof. Karl Von Hase; Notovitch, N., "Unknown Life of Jesus Christ from Buddhistic Records"; Dods, "Mohammed, Buddha, and Christ"; Christ and Evol. in Hast. D. C., I, 552; Bierbrower, Socialism of Christ; C. and Soc. in Enc. of Soc. Reform, p. 196; "Jesus Christ and the Social Question," F. G. Peabody; Rauschenbusch, Christianity and Social Crisis; Mathews, Soc. Tea. of Jes.; Stoecker, Christlich-Social; Rade, Gedankenwelt unserer Arbeiter; Nauman, Jesus als Volksmann; Losinsky, Waren die ersten Christen wirklich Socialisten? and, War Jesus Gott, Mensch oder Uebermensch; Classen, Christus heute als unser Zeitgenosse; Tolstoi, Leo, Count, "Christ's Christianity"; Werner, Psych. Gesundheit J.; Jordan, J. im Kampf der Parteien der Gegenwart; Holtzman, War Jesus Ekstatiker? W. James, Rel. Experience; De Loosten, J. vom Standpunkt des Psychiaters.—Gunkel, Zum religionsgeschichtlichen Verstaendniss des N. T. Jeremias, Babylonisches im N. T., Loof's Anti-Haeckel (against Haeckel's World Riddies); Nietzsche, Der Anti-Christ; Ed. von Hartman, Das Christenthum des N. T.— Robertson, Pagan Christs, Kalthoff, Entstehung des Christentums; and Das Christusproblem; Drews, Die Christus-Mythe; Smith, The Pre-Christian Jesus; Jensen, Das Gilgamesch Epos in der Weltliteratur.

553. **Review Questions.** *The Character of Jesus.* (1) State what character is, how it manifests itself; the conjectures as to our

Lord's outward *appearance;* some old descriptions of him; the four principal mental qualities. (2) Which were the *deepest feelings* in Christ's soul, and how did each one express itself? Show that Christ had humor. (3) Enumerate and explain the outgoing and inholding manifestations of Christ's *will power.* (4) Describe the unity of his character. Which of the four temperaments did he have? *The Work of Jesus.* (1) Did Jesus have a definite plan? What was it? When did he become conscious of it? (2) Describe Jesus the *preacher,* his subjects, method, aim, audience. In what sense was he a teacher and a controversialist? (3) In what respects is Jesus our example? (4) State definition, name, number, classification of Christ's miracles. Give the number and nature of the demoniac possessions. In what sense may Christ's death be classified under his works? *The Three Problems.* (1) Which are the three chief problems in our Lord's life? State (a) the meaning, (b) the mode, and (c) the purpose of the incarnation and answer the objections raised. (2) Whom did Jesus believe himself to be? In what sense was he the Son of man, and the Son of God? (3) In what manner did Christ rise from the dead? State and refute some of the non-miraculous conceptions of the resurrection. *Christ's Influence.* In what ways did Christ influence the world? Non-Biblical Portraits of Jesus. State and refute each of those discussed in chapter 54.

CHAPTER 55.

General Review of the Entire Life of Christ.

Prepare, mentally or in writing, brief but very accurate answers to the following questions:

I. *The World in Which Jesus Lived.* (1) Explain *name* of Palestine, state dimensions, describe important waters and mountains, give physical and political divisions. (2) Give an outline of Jewish history from the Babylonian captivity to Christ, including the genealogy of the Herodian house; explain what is meant by "the dispersion." (3) State names and time of reign of the two Roman emperors during the period of Christ's life. (4) Describe the 3 parties among the Jews; also explain the names, Herodians, Zealots, Scribes, Sanhedrin. (5) State origin, arrangement of building and officers of the synagogue. (6) Describe the Jewish church year; the seven feasts; time and meaning of each, and method of celebration. (7) Give the names of the leading Jewish teachers of this period, and the three groups of Jewish literature. (8) Give a sketch of the schools of Greek philosophy in this period.

(9) What was the social and moral condition of the world in this period; cite facts and writers to confirm your statements. (10) What are the pagan, Jewish and Christian sources of information for the life of Christ? (11) When was Christ born? When baptized? When did he die, rise and ascend to heaven? How do we arrive at these dates?

II. General Outlines of the Life of Christ. (1) State the three great periods of Christ's existence; (2) the length of his life upon earth; (3) the principal divisions and subdivisions of his life, with dates; (4) the events of each day from Friday before Palm Sunday to Easter Day; (5) give an accurate analysis of the six trials of Jesus, and (6) of the ten appearances of the Risen Christ.

III. The Home Towns and Home Life of Jesus. (1) Name and locate the home towns of Christ and other places where he spent considerable time; (2) locate on the map the places in and around Jerusalem which our Lord visited during the passion week; (3) what foreign countries did Christ visit, and when? (8) How did Jesus make his living, before and during his ministry? (5) Name the brothers of Jesus and state the three theories as to their relation to Jesus.

IV. The Lord's Friends and Co-workers. (1) What figures are found in the N. T. giving the number of Jesus' followers during his life-time? (Jno. 1; Lu. 6:13; Lu. 10:1; Acts 1:15; 1 Cor. 15:6.) (2) Give the names of the Twelve; time and place of their appointment; blood relationship of some to Christ and among themselves. (3) Give name, relationship, and social station of some of his female disciples. (4) Point out the three stages of the fellowship of the apostles with Christ. (5) Trace the development of the apostles' conception of the person of Christ.

V. The Thirteen Principal Journeys. (1) From Nazareth to his baptism and return to Capernaum. Jan.-March, A. D. 27. (2) From Capernaum to first passover (Cleansing of temple), Samaria, Nazareth, Capernaum, April-Dec. A. D. 27. (3) First Preaching Tour in Galilee, Spring, A. D. 28. (4) From Capernaum to the Unnamed Feast and return, March-May, A. D. 28. (5) Second Preaching Tour, Summer, A. D. 28. (6) Capernaum-Gadara and return, Autumn, A. D. 28. (7) Third Preaching Tour, Nazareth, Crisis at Capernaum. Spring, A. D. 29. (8) First Northern Journey to Tyre, Summer, A. D. 29. (9) Second Northern Journey to Cæsarea Philippi. (11) To the Feast of Dedication, Dec., A. D. 29. (12) To the Raising of Lazarus, Feb., A. D. 30. (13) From Ephraim to the Triumphal Entry, April, A. D. 30.

VI. Important Questions. Why was Jesus, (1) sent into the world, (2) born of a virgin, (3) circumcised, (4) presented in the temple, (5) taken to the passover when just 12 years of age, (6) baptized, (7) tempted?

VII. Locate by periods or context the following events: (1) the three adorations; (2) the five hymns recorded by Luke; (3) the best known prayers of Jesus; (4) the three raisings of dead persons in chronological order; (5) some of the longest discourses; (6) the two cleansings of the temple; (7) the two rejections at Nazareth; (8) the two anointings; (9) the two miraculous feedings; (10) some of the figurative allusions to his death; (11) the three chief plain foretellings of his death and resurrection; (12) the different visits to the family at Bethany; (13) the two miracles at Cana.

VIII. Name events which occurred (1) at Bethlehem; (2) Nazareth; (3) Aenon near Salim; (4) Bethsaida; (5) Machaerus; (6) near the treasury in the temple; (7) at Ephraim; (8) at Jericho.

Printed in the United States of America.